PATRIOTISM IS

A CATHOLIC VIRTUE

PATRIOTISM IS A CATHOLIC VIRTUE

IRISH AMERICAN CATHOLICS AND THE CHURCH IN THE ERA OF THE GREAT WAR, 1900–1918

THOMAS J. ROWLAND

The Catholic University of America Press
Washington, D.C.

Copyright © 2023
The Catholic University of America Press
All rights reserved

ANSI Z39.48-1992.
ISBN 978-0-8132-3771-8 (paperback) |
ISBN 978-0-8132-3772-5 (ebook)
∞
Cataloging-in-Publication Data is
available from the Library of Congress

To my grandparents
Patrick and Ellen Rowland &
Thomas and Alice Cassidy
I can only hope to have recaptured
the times in which you lived

CONTENTS

Acknowledgments ix

Introduction 1

ONE STAKING THE AMERICAN CLAIM:
Aspects of the Irish American
Experience on the Eve
of the Great War 14

TWO OF MATTERS AMERICAN:
The American Catholic Church
& Irish American Catholics
on the Eve of the Great War 74

THREE THE OUTBREAK OF THE
GREAT WAR & THE CRISIS
OF NEUTRALITY 125

FOUR NEUTRALITY UNDER
STRAIN IN 1915 169

FIVE IRISH AMERICAN CATHOLICS
& THE 1916 EASTER REBELLION 211

CONTENTS

SIX   1917:
      Toward a Declaration of War   250

SEVEN   ONWARD CATHOLIC SOLDIERS:
      The Church & the War, 1917–1918   293

Bibliography   331

Index   343

ACKNOWLEDGMENTS

Among my thoughts while I was considering a workable dissertation topic was the fact that both of my grandfathers (Patrick Rowland and Thomas Cassidy) had been born in Ireland. Grandpa Rowland hailed from County Mayo, while Grandpa Cassidy was born in County Wexford. By coincidence, both were born in the year 1883, and both emigrated from Ireland in the first decade of the twentieth century. Once here, they met my grandmothers (Ellen Hayes and Alice Delehanty), both of whom were the daughters of Irish immigrant parents. Both married their respective spouses in the years shortly before the outbreak of the Great War in 1914, and did so as American citizens and fervent Catholics. I never had the opportunity to sound the grandparents out on their opinions about either the American entry into the war in 1917 or the matter of Irish nationalism. Grandpa Rowland died in 1941, well before my birth in 1952. Grandpa Cassidy died six months after my birth, and although I have been assured that I bobbed on his knee a few times, I am equally convinced we held no coherent conversations. Grandma Hayes died in 1955, but I cannot say that I have any recollections of her. My grandmother Delehanty lived until 1966 and, as my own family lived with her for eight years, I have distinct memories of her, not necessarily all fond. She was militantly Catholic, with a profound distrust of anything Protestant, and she would occasionally rant about the historical abuse the British had heaped upon their Catholic subjects in Ireland, as well as the bigotry that American Protestants exhibited toward the Catholic Church in America. As one of her sons, Thomas, was killed by a mine near the Ardennes Forest in November 1944, she imposed a taboo on any discussion about war, whether it be World War II or the earlier one, the Great War. All four of my grandparents were young adults when the Great War erupted in 1914. I have often wondered where they might have stood on the matters explored in this study. But the sands of time

ACKNOWLEDGMENTS

will never allow for the uncovering of their thoughts and feelings, such as they may have been.

It has become almost cliché for an author to concede that, whereas writing a book is a solitary journey, it can only find its way into publication with the assistance of an army of colleagues, archival and library staff, editors, and friends. As this book's origins date back nearly four decades, several of my assistants have passed away and several more have escaped my memory. In paraphrasing Lincoln's Gettysburg Address, "[T]he world will little note nor long remember what we say here," but I will try to note and remember all those who helped me in producing this work.

I extend my heartfelt thanks to Dr. Trevor Lipscombe, Director of The Catholic University of America Press, for his help in facilitating the advancement of this book into publication. The process went smoothly and professionally. I came to thoroughly enjoy his humor, wit, and wisdom throughout our many interactions. By extension, I thank the members of his staff, and the editorial board that saw the possibility of publishing this work in such a respected press. I particularly thank the two anonymous peer reviewers for their expert analysis of my first draft of the manuscript. Their keen insights, endorsements, and critical suggestions for revision surely made this a better book.

This book has its genesis in a predicament about my dissertation proposal, and who among the history faculty at The George Washington University might direct it. In 1987, I was "stoked" about the announcement that the department would be appointing a prominent military historian to the faculty in the fall of the following year, and I was advised to wait for his arrival to determine how I would proceed with my dissertation. My original concept was to write a revisionist study of a Union general during the US Civil War. However, weeks before the fall semester was to begin, the newly appointed military historian withdrew from his contract for personal reasons. It appeared that my doctoral degree was in jeopardy. That was when Professor Leo P. Ribuffo stepped in and saved the day. While he had little interest in military history, he did have research interests in American religious history. As my new topic placed war within a religious context, he was willing to work with me. This book is a major revision and expansion

ACKNOWLEDGMENTS

of that dissertation, revisited many years later. I am also grateful to Leo for his conviction that a dissertation should not be the culmination of a budding historian's professional work, a *magnum opus*, as it were. Rather, he viewed a dissertation as a hurdle to be respectfully overcome. While he certainly challenged some of my interpretations and encouraged some revision, he allowed me to carry onward with minimal obstruction. Consequently, I was not subjected to the endless rejection or countless revisions that many other doctoral candidates have had to endure from their directors. Finally, he was tremendously supportive during the somewhat intimidating dissertation defense, deflecting questions from some faculty members that bore no relevance to the dissertation whatsoever. I know that I profusely thanked him after all was done, and only wish he were still alive to read this acknowledgement today.

Writing a book is a somewhat individual undertaking, but many persons and institutions assisted my research in dusty archives. There are institutions that offered financial support, colleagues who both lent encouragement and provided feedback on manuscript drafts, and family and friends who sacrificed personal engagement to provide time and space for my research and writing. I can only hope to acknowledge as many as possible here, and apologize in advance for any I might overlook:

I did much of my archival research while I was a doctoral candidate at George Washington University in the District of Columbia. As I was working full time and had limited financial resources, that research was limited to the Washington-to-New York corridor. This was the pre-internet era, which meant that digitalized versions of material were nonexistent. Be that as it may, I was able to spend considerable time in the repositories at hand.

As much of my archival research was conducted between the years 1988 and 1990, and as I never had any notion this research would result in published form thirty-five years later, I cannot recall the names of staff who helped me in manuscript collections. Staff in the Manuscript Division of the Library of Congress were tremendously adept at finding the requested collection boxes in the bowels of the building and bringing them to the reading room with celerity. Several days were spent at the archives of the Archdiocese of Baltimore, where the letters and papers of James Cardinal Gibbons are stored. It also

ACKNOWLEDGMENTS

provided microfilm copies of the Baltimore *Catholic Review*. Staff at The Catholic University of America's main library granted me private access to the room that stored microfilm of many of the Catholic newspapers featured in this study. I spent many hours in this room, within the labyrinthine corridors of the library. Many years later, when I needed to expand my research of Catholic newspapers, I was greatly aided by Lin Schrottky of the Inter-Library Loan Division of Polk Library at the University of Wisconsin Oshkosh. She must have spent hours tracking down microfilm from libraries around the country. The Polk Library was also able to retrieve secondary sources when it became necessary to expand my research into works published after my dissertation. I enjoyed access to the many university libraries surrounding the District of Columbia, including those at Georgetown, American University, The George Washington University, Catholic University, and the University of Maryland at College Park. If a hard-to-find secondary source was not available at any one of these institutions, it invariably could be found at another.

I would also like to thank the staff at the New York Public Library for their assistance in retrieving several manuscript collections for my perusal during my week-long visit to New York. Much of that research has found its way into this book. That week's stay was made possible by the hospitality of my late aunt, Sister Alice Cassidy, then stationed in Bloomfield, New Jersey, who provided room and board with easy access to Manhattan.

I would like to extend my thanks to Tim Meagher, a much-respected Irish American historian, who engaged me in many a conversation about the Irish nationalist era, and offered suggestions about two chapters of this work. As my academic and research interests were of a more eclectic nature, I found myself frequently tapping into his expertise in the Irish American experience. Kindly, Tim put me in touch with Miriam Nyhan Grey, who graciously included my discussion of the Irish-American Church's reaction to the Easter Rising and its aftermath in the well-acclaimed edited essays, *Ireland's Allies: America and the 1916 Easter Rising* (2016). I would also like to acknowledge the publishers of three journals—*The Catholic Historical Review, The Journal of American Ethnic History,* and *Eire-Ireland*—for permission to use parts of articles published in their journals.

ACKNOWLEDGMENTS

A special thanks is extended to the University of Wisconsin Oshkosh Faculty Development Program for providing me with substantial research grants that not only helped me to survive summer salary droughts, but allowed for additional research, writing, and revision of several chapters in this book.

There are a host of family and friends who have provided assistance and moral support during the time I was working on the dissertation, and on its revision. During the dissertation period my late sister, Virginia Anne May, and Michael Nagy, provided proofreading that undoubtedly spared me great embarrassment. Later, colleagues in the History Department of the University of Wisconsin Oshkosh were always there to discuss and give reflection upon various parts of my thesis. My nephew, Michael P. Rowland, was kind enough to proofread sections of the revised narrative and weed out grammatical errors and stylistic debris. Any remaining errors are entirely my responsibility. Others must have helped along the way, and the fact that I cannot recall their names should not be construed as ingratitude. I am forever grateful to all those who helped see this work to completion.

I have secretly thought that I was not designed for the twenty-first century, especially with respect to technology. Two friends assisted me tremendously with the vagaries of word processing. Matt Lynch consistently aided me with the intricacies of Microsoft Word, and with a change of computers in the later stages of writing. I am particularly grateful to Joshua Sukkert for his timely intervention at the end-stage of manuscript revision. At this critical moment, my laptop froze, and I feared that I had lost my entire manuscript. Very calmly and expertly, he restored my system and all its documents. Weeks later, my laptop's hard drive went kaput. Josh was ever so helpful in setting up an entirely new laptop and restoring all files and programs. Mine is a debt of gratitude that I doubt I will ever be able to repay. Thank you.

Slainte to all.

Thomas J. Rowland
January 1, 2023
Milwaukee, Wisconsin

INTRODUCTION

This is a history of the American Catholic Church and Irish Americans during America's Progressive Era, a time of remarkable domestic political and social change, culminating in the entry of the United States into the Great War. It is also a parallel study of the challenges facing the American Catholic Church and its paramount role in guiding Irish Americans along paths that aided both their inclusion into mainstream American society and the emergence of a triumphant Catholic America. Whether it was, as Jay P. Dolan claims, "Catholic triumphalism, Catholic Big at its best," or, as Mary Oates asserted, that as a result of Catholic contributions to the common good, "[this] outsider church became more confident of their place in American society," it would appear that the Catholic Church in America had not only "arrived" by the dawn of the twenties but was on the cusp of entering a golden age.[1] This phenomenal turnaround of Catholic fortunes did not come easily. The Church had to endure the crucible of rapid and turbulent social change in the first two decades of the twentieth century, as well as contention among Catholic ethnic groups about the belligerents in the Great War. Also, this very Irish American church would be sorely pressed to navigate between the political shoals of the Great War and Irish America's interest in the cause of Ireland's freedom.

Catholic hopes for inclusion in American society were forwarded by skillful hierarchical leadership, a proactive press, the engagement of a responsive laity, and the patriotic enthusiasm of the Irish

---

1. Both Dolan's and Oates's assertions can be found in Justin Nordstrom, *Danger on the Doorstep: Anti-Catholicism and American Print Culture in the Progressive Era* (Notre Dame, IN: University of Notre Dame Press, 2006), 119. See also Leslie Woodcock Tentler, *American Catholics: A History* (New Haven, CT: Yale University Press, 2020), 204–6.

INTRODUCTION

American-dominated Catholic organization, the Knights of Columbus. In the period immediately prior, 1880 to 1900, little progress toward Catholic acceptance in American society had been made by Catholic leadership, constrained as it was by subservience to Rome and several Romanist prelates within the American hierarchy. Even though Pope Leo XIII's encyclical *Rerum Novarum* (1891) had jarred open the door for American prelates to support labor and the poor who had been left in the dust by the barons of capital in the Gilded Age, the American Catholic Church's support for reforms had been tepid at best. This was particularly unfortunate because many of the Church's faithful were among those working poor.[2]

The complexion of the Catholic Church in America and its relationship to American society and its political institutions underwent a substantial makeover in the early years of the twentieth century. Chief among these changes was the end of the American Church's status as a mission church of Rome in 1908. This allowed the American church, over Rome's tenuous objections, to attempt reconciling Catholicism with American society and politics. This decade was also pivotal in the progressive Americanization of the Church in the United States. Despite the rising star of the conservative William H. O'Connell, archbishop of Boston (appointed 1907), the principal opponents of Americanism, such as Michael Corrigan, archbishop of New York, and Bernard McQuaid, bishop of Syracuse, had passed from this earthly

---

2. Peter R. D'Agostino makes the case that the Church in America was still dominated by Roman directives. This was certainly true in matters of faith and doctrine, and in the pastoral care of Italian immigrants—subjects that dominate his study but don't reflect the general direction that the American Church was heading. See Peter R. D'Agostino, *Rome in America: Transnational Catholic Ideology from Risorgimento to Fascism* (Chapel Hill: University of North Carolina Press, 2004), 84–131. Joseph M. McShane's *"Sufficiently Radical": Catholicism, Progressivism, and the Bishops' Program of 1919* (Washington, DC: The Catholic University of America Press, 1986) suggests that Pius X's encyclical *Pascendi Dominici Gregis* (1907) appeared to slam the door on ideas spawned by Modernism, but I prefer the assessment of a renowned Catholic historian that "[a] compassionate pastor, a reverent liturgy, a sense of communal rootedness—such things nearly always mattered more than pronouncements from Rome." Tentler, *American Catholics: A History*, 205.

INTRODUCTION

life by 1909. The vacuum of influence was filled by Cardinal James Gibbons (Baltimore) and Archbishop John Ireland (St. Paul), and their numerous allies throughout the United States. Both prelates had been longstanding advocates for American Catholicism to accommodate itself to America's dominant political, social, and cultural strains; this accommodation would combat deep-seated anti-Catholic sentiment and diffuse the widespread conviction that Rome was intent on destroying the American democracy.

Gibbons and Ireland proved to be a capable team. Both had gone through the Americanist crisis of the late nineteenth century and had shared the disappointment of several setbacks to their strategy. Maligned by some of his detractors as "Slippery Jim," Gibbons emerged in the early twentieth century as the "de facto American primate." Consummate politician that he was, he threaded the needle adroitly in his shuttle diplomacy with his Roman superiors, earning him the enmity of conservative prelates like Corrigan, McQuaid, and, later, O'Connell. Simultaneously, Gibbons aroused the suspicion of liberals within the hierarchy who wondered exactly how much the silver-tongued leader was committed to the cause. If Gibbons was the diplomat, John Ireland was the proselytizer of Americanism. Eloquently feisty, Ireland was an unabashed disciple of Americanism in both word and deed, and served as a willing lightning rod for the strikes of criticism that might otherwise have been hurled at his comrade Gibbons. Within the hierarchy, Gibbons and Ireland are of paramount interest and will figure prominently in this work.[3]

---

3. Charles R. Morris, *American Catholic: The Saints and Sinners Who Built America's Most Powerful Church* (New York: Times Books, 1997), 14–15; Scholar Jay P. Dolan describes Gibbons as the "quintessential American who wanted all Catholics to become more American and less ethnic." Dolan also identifies three other Irish American prelates, John Ireland, Denis O'Connell, and John Keane, as committed "to push for a more modern, American expression of Catholicism." See Jay P. Dolan, *The Irish-Americans: A History* (New York: Bloomsbury Press, 2008), 133. The American Church paid lip service to Rome's greatest complaint over the loss of the temporal power of the papacy to Liberal Italy, but it never pressed the American government to address the matter. It should be noted, however, that with the deaths of John Ireland (1918) and James Gibbons (1921), the Church returned to its more Romanist inclinations.

INTRODUCTION

As the American Church was institutional, the leadership's instruction was disseminated through the hierarchy. The ranks of the clergy, usually in step with their local ordinaries, served as the foot soldiers within their all-important local parishes. They exercised extraordinary influence among the faithful around the turn of the century. Most were either foreign-born or second-generation Irish. The faithful were either fearful or reverently and lovingly in awe of them. Most clerics were, like their leadership, dedicated to the task of cultivating good American Catholics and subordinating their ethnic attachments. By 1900, newer European Catholic immigrants flooding America's shores came with very different understandings of what it meant to be both Catholic and American. Frequently, the Irish-dominated clergy grew frustrated with their attachments to unusual devotions and their ignorance of the basic tenets of the faith. Both the hierarchy and the clergy would turn to Irish American Catholics as role models for what it meant to be both exemplary Catholics and Americans. The looming crisis of the Great War, wherein many ethnic Catholics held opposing views of the European belligerents, would merely accelerate the process of making Catholics outstanding Americans.[4]

Within the institutional arsenal of the American Church, no agency exercised greater influence upon Irish Americans than Catholic journalism, particularly in cases involving Catholic relations to the state. By the twentieth century, the Catholic press was on the threshold of enjoying its own golden age. Print was virtually the sole popular medium of the era, and Catholic newspapers enjoyed wide circulation and popularity among Catholic audiences. Funded by advertisers, these papers were distributed at a meager subscription rate, even *gratis* in some dioceses. The breadth of their coverage was such that they

---

4. Throughout his tenure as Archbishop of New York, Michael Corrigan and his Irish priests were continually dispirited by the lack of favorable responses from their Italian constituents, leading to Corrigan's throwing up his hands in frustration. In New York, matters between Irish and Italian Catholics became so quarrelsome that, for a while, services for Italian parishioners were held in church basements, much to their resentment. See Stephen Michael DiGiovanni, *Archbishop Corrigan and the Italian Immigrants* (Huntington, IN: Our Sunday Visitor, Inc., 1994), 195–207. Ethnic tensions among fellow Catholics were commonplace, from the nation's coal fields to the industrial cities.

INTRODUCTION

appealed to a wide readership, from the family patriarch to the spouse, to the mother, all the way down to the domestic and scullery maid.

While there did exist a handful of non-English Catholic newspapers, mainly in German, diocesan papers were generally printed in English, and they slanted their coverage to appeal to Irish and American readers. This proclivity was enhanced by the fact that virtually all the editors, clerical or laity, were themselves Irish American. Moreover, these papers were either sanctioned by or granted the *imprimatur* of the local ordinary, himself most likely of Irish extraction. Whereas the hierarchy was frequently constrained from opining on matters political and social in nature, Catholic editors were free to articulate observations and positions that the hierarchy were hesitant to articulate. In myriad ways, Catholic newspapers reflected and influenced the positions that the diverse Irish American community would take during America's Progressive Era, positions which were frequently at odds with those of secular Irish American organizations. Much of this study explores the role that the Catholic press played among the faithful from 1900 to 1918.[5]

The remaining weapon in the American Church's arsenal was the role played by a variety of Catholic societies, several of which were geared to promoting Catholics as respectable Americans. For instance, The Holy Name Society, with roots in the late European Middle Ages, encouraged Catholic men to adopt model Christian behavior by eschewing profane and vulgar language, moderating alcohol consumption, and engaging in charitable causes. Yet, standing head and shoulders above all other organizations was the Knights of Columbus. Founded in 1882 by a young priest, Father Michael McGivney in New Haven, Connecticut, its initial purpose was to provide young men with an alternative to secret societies antithetical to Church doctrine, and to provide financial security for the families of

---

5. In his work *War against War*, Michael Kazin, preeminent scholar of both the Populist and Progressive eras, cites my original dissertation several times, concluding that it provides a "sophisticated analysis of the views of Irish-Catholics who essentially ran the American Church...." See Michael Kazin, *War against War: The American Fight for Peace, 1914–1918* (New York: Simon & Schuster, 2017), 31 n.21.

INTRODUCTION

departed members. In 1900, fraternal charity and American patriotism were added to its mission, by which time Irish American Catholics were overrepresented in both its leadership and ranks. Throughout America's Progressive Era, the Knights were stalwart in the Church's campaign against anti-Catholicism and religious bigotry. Both before and during America's involvement in the Great War, the Knights turned their attention to the promotion of American Catholics as sterling examples of citizenship and patriotism.[6]

The rate of political and social change during America's Progressive Era was not only a "many-splendored thing" for the nation; it also presented a host of challenges and opportunities for the American Catholic Church. Exactly how would the Church balance genuine labor reforms, aimed at improving the quality of life for the working class, with traditional Catholic respect for capital and private property? More pointedly, how would the Church address Catholics' possible attraction to the substantial temptations of socialism? Likewise, how would the Church contend with the momentum of the suffrage movement, after it had spent decades crafting a message that the proper roles for Catholic women are obedient spouse and mother? Finally, for a Church desperately seeking a respectable place in mainstream American society, how would it address the lamentable condition of Black America at the zenith of the Jim Crow era? These issues will be examined in this study, and while certainly germane to the status of the American Catholic Church of the time, they are peripheral to the fundamental focus of this work.

Three assertions form the thesis of this book. All concern the influential role that the American Catholic Church played among Irish American Catholics during the Progressive Era and the Great War. The first claim is that, throughout the first two decades of the twentieth century, the American Catholic Church, marked by its indelible Irish imprint, waged a tireless, vigorous, and largely successful campaign against the forces of nativist anti-Catholic bigotry. The second claim

---

6. The best study of the Knights' commitment to citizenship and patriotism is Christopher J. Kauffman, *Patriotism and Fraternalism in the Knights of Columbus: A History of the Fourth Degree* (New York: Crossroad Publishing Co., 2001).

INTRODUCTION

is that the American Church, more than any secular Irish American organization, political faction, or Irish nationalist movement, was the most consistently moderate and influential agent of Ireland's ultimate freedom. Finally, the Church was the principal actor in promoting Catholics and Irish Americans as not only loyal Americans but exemplary patriots. Each of these assertions have been addressed by existing historical literature but, surprisingly, in only marginal and limited ways. Anti-Catholic assaults during the Progressive Era are ably addressed in Justin Nordstrom's *Danger on the Doorstep*, but it is sketchy in tracking Catholic print reaction. The cause of Irish nationalism in this era is a well-plowed field in the literature but is generally tilted toward the role played by Irish American societies, such as The Hibernians or the United Irish League of America, and most demonstrably favorable to more radical ones, such as the Clan na Gael and the Friends of Irish Freedom. Catholic opinion on the matter is little addressed. Lastly, the part the Church took in elevating Irish American Catholics as loyal and patriotic citizens is a more cultivated field of inquiry, but only in specialized studies that focus on the irregular announcements of the hierarchy and the achievements of the Knights of Columbus. Little mention is made of the significant role played by diocesan newspapers in this effort.[7]

---

7. On the matter of venomous anti-Catholic print media, see Nordstrom, *Danger on the Doorstep*. Irish American nationalism has been broadly covered in the literature, too many times to cite specifically here, but in most sources I have reviewed, the more radical nationalist cause is elevated at the expense of American Catholic sentiment. For instance, one of the more recent works on Irish American nationalism, admittedly extending its scope beyond 1918, does allude to the importance of Irish American identification with Catholicism but then hardly mentions Catholic opinion thereafter. See Michael Doorley, *Irish-American Nationalism: The Friends of Irish Freedom, 1916–1935* (Dublin: Four Courts Press, 2011 [paperback ed.]), 21–23. While not as scarce, commentary on the Church's strident efforts to present Catholics as model citizens and patriotic Americans is limited to Kauffman's *Patriotism and Fraternalism*. One can find passing reference to the Church's rallying Catholics to the flag in several generalized works, including J. P. Dolan, *The Irish-Americans: A History*, 212–19; and James R. Barrett, *The Irish Way: Becoming American in the Multiethnic City* (New York: The Penguin Press, 2012), 259–60.

INTRODUCTION

The composite of these assertions on my part serves as the thesis of this book. Exploring a little further, the case for the herculean task undertaken by the Catholic Church, especially its press, needs some grounding in the historical past. Anti-Catholicism was a perennial reality dating back to America's colonial era, and only intensified after the nation became a Republic. Throughout the nineteenth century, anti-Catholicism experienced ebbs and flows in intensity yet it remained persistent enough to compel the American Church to retreat into a fortress-like defiant isolation, best illustrated in the feisty image of New York's Archbishop John Hughes. The swell of Catholic immigrants arriving in the last two decades of the nineteenth century compelled nativists to reenergize and organize their attack upon Catholicism in their midst, leading to the creation of the American Protective Association (APA) in 1887. Their venom was sufficient to draw American Catholics, mostly Irish Americans, from the shadows to defend themselves. The most effective defense would be articulated in the Catholic press; the surging increase in diocesan newspapers was not merely coincidental. The meteoric rise of the APA's popularity was followed by a precipitous fall in the first decade of the twentieth century, although it resurfaced briefly in a celebrated court case regarding the APA's circulation of a bogus oath, alleging nefarious pledges taken by members of the Knights of Columbus to destroy American Protestantism. With the demise of the APA, the cudgel of anti-Catholicism was taken up by a host of nativist newspapers and magazines. Most of these were both insignificant and short-lived. Two of them, however, enjoyed a degree of sustained popularity. One was *Watson's Magazine*, created in 1905 by Tom Watson, an acclaimed populist, occasional politician, and inveterate anti-Catholic. The other was a Kansas-based newspaper *The Menace* (founded in 1911). Its very name indicates the tone of its message, suggesting in lurid description that Catholicism was the single greatest peril facing American Protestantism and the American Republic. Needless to say, the Catholic press would be actively engaged with these radical antagonists, and it proved equal to the task.[8]

8. An excellent analysis of the aims and effectiveness of the APA, *Watson's Magazine,* and *The Menace* can be seen in Nordstrom's *Danger on the Doorstep.*

INTRODUCTION

The American Church adroitly guided Irish Americans along moderate paths when it came to the tempestuous matter of Irish nationalism, during the years leading up to the Great War and through America's entry into the war itself, much to the frustration of ardent Irish American nationalists. In part, John Redmond's moderate trajectory toward Home Rule for Ireland within the British Empire proved popular among the Irish themselves and was greeted with approbation by America's Irish American community. More significant was the inexorable progress of Irish Americans toward assimilation and their increasing focus on their fortunes as Americans, which blunted their engagement with purely Irish affairs. Nonetheless, once the guns of August 1914 were unleashed, Redmond proved willing to suspend Home Rule's enactment and direct Irish support to the British, the reverberations of which were felt both in Ireland and Irish America. In America, Redmond's choice rekindled tensions within the Irish American community that had been dormant for years. Fervent nationalists were nearly ecstatic, as prior to the outbreak of the Great War, their calls for a "physical force" path to Irish freedom had largely been ignored by the greater Irish American community. All the same, New World concerns collided with Old World memories as Irish Americans had to reconcile their animosity toward British supremacy in Ireland with the possibility that the United States might join Britain in the war against Germany. For a brief spell, all factions within Irish-America's ranks, including the Catholic Church, could link arms with the nation as a whole and demand a stance of neutrality by the Wilson administration. They found in Wilson a president who was thinking the same way.[9]

This harmony among Irish Americans would not last long. Strains to the maintenance of American neutrality between 1914 and 1917, including Wilson's preferential absolution of Britain for violating US maritime neutrality and America's brisk munitions trade with the Allies, fueled the fires of debate within the Irish American

---

9. The argument that Irish Americans linked their inclusion in American society along respectable lines with the establishment of an autonomous Ireland has become an article of faith among historians. It was first articulated by Thomas N. Brown, *Irish-American Nationalism, 1870–1890* (Philadelphia: J. B. Lippincott, 1955).

INTRODUCTION

community. Then, the cold-blooded executions of Irish rebels in the Easter rising sent nationalists in America into paroxysms of rage against British butchery and the Wilson administration's failure to condemn them. These incidents did inspire greater sympathy for the nationalist cause but, perhaps, not as much as conventionally thought. Just as there was a transnational dimension to Roman Catholicism that the American hierarchy had to tactfully manage during this era, so, too, was there an international dynamic to Irish nationalism that had its roots in the Famine era, in which Irish nationalists and their counterparts in America negotiated the course of Irish freedom, forging a transatlantic identity.[10]

In the matter of Irish freedom, three factions vied for influence among Irish Americans: radicalized and ardent "physical force" Irish American nationalists; moderate and constitutional Home Rule advocates; and the American Catholic Church whose views tended to the moderate, even conservative side. All three factions had their own agenda, goals, and strategies for influencing Irish American Catholics throughout the course of the Great War, although the moderates' interests frequently dovetailed with the Church's. More significantly, both nationalists and moderates sought validation from the Church, as they instinctively understood the influence it had among Irish Americans. Much to the dismay of the physical force nationalists, they were never able to enlist the support of the Church during the war. John Devoy, the fiery chief nationalist spokesman, admitted as much three months after the end of the war, at an Irish Race Convention held in February 1919 in Philadelphia. He conceded that the cause of Irish freedom had languished up to that moment until Cardinal Gibbons and several members of the American hierarchy attending that convention gave tacit support to the cause. But this support, as Devoy knew at the time, was quite vague and would not proceed along the path that the old Fenian preferred. The reality was that Gibbons and the Church he represented were more interested in making Catholics good Americans. Devoy was absorbed only with Ireland's affairs. Few works in this field of inquiry pay anything more than lip service to the part the Irish-led

---

10. Mary C. Kelly, *The Shamrock and the Lily: The New York Irish and the Creation of a Transatlantic Identity, 1845–1921* (New York: Peter Lang, 2007), 1–12.

INTRODUCTION

American Catholic Church played in shaping Catholic positions; fewer still appear willing to accord it any significant role.[11]

American Catholicism, then, emerged in the Progressive Era as the most effective vehicle for Irish Americans to clarify their allegiances as Catholics and Americans. If, in the nineteenth century, Catholicism had proven to be the outstanding obstacle to acceptance in American society, it had by 1914 become the most dynamic and useful agent in promoting integration and paving the way toward eventual inclusion.[12] By the early twentieth century, Irish American Catholics were determined to confront the remaining vestiges of nativist bigotry. First generation Irish immigrants had been too absorbed with carving out a meager existence to effectively counteract Protestant discrimination. What little political energy they did possess was directed towards influencing foreign policies adversarial to British interests. By the turn of the century, the pursuit of Irish freedom assumed a poignant second meaning that was distinctly American in context. The cause of Irish nationalism became more a product of Irish American struggles with a dominant Protestant society than a sentimental expression of support for their ancestral home. The poverty and repression of Ireland imposed by the British enraged Irish Americans and reminded them of the bigotry, prejudice, and oppression they were experiencing in America at the hands of Anglo-Saxon Protestants. Supporting liberation movements in Ireland, no matter how conservatively, would usher in a day when their own status in America would be elevated to a parity with their Protestant antagonists. No one, certainly not John Devoy and his ilk, was better armed to achieve this goal than the American Catholic Church. The route towards Irish liberation was circuitous, however, as the American Church was more interested in promoting Catholic respectability. Most Irish Americans incrementally

---

11. Terry Golway, *Irish Rebel: John Devoy and America's Fight for Ireland's Freedom* (New York: St. Martin's Press, 1998), 254.

12. This inclusion needs qualification. Inspired in part by the movie *Birth of A Nation* (1915), the rebirth of the Ku Klux Klan was delivered in that same year, reaching its height in the mid-twenties. Added to their traditional hatred of black Americans were immigrants and Catholics, something Al Smith, the first Catholic presidential candidate, discovered in the campaign and election of 1928.

INTRODUCTION

took the position that the Irish would need to determine their own destiny; they themselves, on the other hand, were about securing their own fortunes in America The outbreak of war in 1914, the years of American neutrality, and the American entry into the war itself in 1917 provided the Church with an unequalled opportunity to showcase American Catholics, particularly the Irish ones, as intensely loyal and patriotic to the American Republic This is a book that tells the story in a way that has not been told before.[13]

A few clarifications might help the reader to navigate this book. Except when mentioning them specifically, this work does not address the role, if in fact, there was one, for America's Irish Protestants within the scope of this study. The first chapter explains the reasons for this exclusion; for now, let it suffice to say that, well before the dawn of the twentieth century, the designations of "Irish" and "Catholic" were virtually synonymous in America. Another point of order is to clarify terms related to the process of Americanization that Irish American Catholics underwent during the Progressive Era. The terms that many writers use are "assimilation" or "acculturation," and at times, these terms are appropriate. I prefer the term "inclusion," as it more aptly describes both the process and experience Irish American Catholics underwent at the time. The other two terms might imply that Irish Americans somehow bowed low, even in craven submission, to the dominant culture in America. As will be explored in the final chapter, Irish Americans inserted themselves into American society yet retained strong attachments to both their religion and ethnic culture.

This study specifically targets the American Catholic Church and the diverse Irish American Catholic community from the beginning of the twentieth century to the end of the Great War in 1918. The story

13. An important caveat is required here. Neither Irish American Catholics nor Irish American nationalists should be viewed as monolithically homogenous on all matters related to the pursuit of Irish freedom during this era. Some were ardent in their support of violent means to advance Ireland's freedom. Others sought moderate and constitutional redress, while still others believed up until late in the Great War that Home Rule was the ultimate solution. Moreover, there were considerable shifts and fluidity in opinion in response to events in Europe and Ireland during the war that confound any attempts to place categorically and irrevocably Irish Americans and Catholics in any inflexible positions.

INTRODUCTION

continues through the period of the Irish War of Independence and Ireland's Civil War, but the extent of detail would be such as to require an entirely different study. The paradigms shifted dramatically for all parties after the war. The progress made by the American Catholic Church was abated or stalled by the resurgence of nativism in the twenties in the form of the KKK, requiring it to go back into a defensive posture. Moreover, the changing of the guard within the hierarchy with the deaths of James Gibbons and John Ireland placed the Church back into the Romanist fold. Similarly, the end of the war dramatically altered the strategies and tactics that Irish American nationalists would need to employ to advance the cause of Irish freedom, considering the new geopolitical realities.

The book is organized largely along chronological lines, from 1900 to 1918. If we can subscribe to Shakespeare's dictum in *The Tempest* that "what's past is prologue," and that history establishes a context for understanding the present, then the first two chapters of this book acquire real importance. Both chapters are period snapshots of the status arrived at by the Irish American community and the American Catholic Church in turn-of-the-century America. As both chapters are synthetic and historiographic by nature, there is a considerable reliance on secondary sources. The remainder of the book relies on primary source material.

CHAPTER 1

STAKING THE AMERICAN CLAIM:
Aspects of the Irish American Experience on the Eve of the Great War

> They have Irish on the screen. Even the money here is green. Cardinal Gibbons he runs the show and George Meany helps him to get all the dough. John McCormack is an Irish star. Henry Ford makes all the cars. Dempsey and O'Sullivan are the thing for they are the champions of the ring. There's Scott Fitzgerald and Flan O'Connor and New York's Alfred E.... there's Curley and Mayor Daly, Joe McCarthy and Eugene O'Neill. There's Keaton and Kelly and Kelly and Hart and Mother Jones aboo ... and George M. Cohan and there's Spencer Tracey too. There's Cagney and Bing Crosby and the Kennedys too. And they're all Irish through and through....[1]

---

1. Lyrics can be found in Mick Moloney, "There's a Typical Tipperary Over Here" (Apple, Inc., 2023). It is an unvarnished yet entirely incomplete tip of the hat to the impact made by the inclusion of Irish Americans into the mainstream social, cultural, economic, and political life of the United States. Except for Flannery O'Connor (b. 1924) and Robert F. Kennedy (b. 1925), all had been born before 1920. Excluding Henry Ford, all were at least nominally Roman Catholic. It celebrates the Irish arrival in America.

STAKING THE AMERICAN CLAIM

Of Emigres and Immigrants

Any attempt to limn a categorically homogeneous portrait of Irish American Catholics in the early twentieth century is so beset by uncertainties, fraught with difficulties, and conditioned by variables as to lead to imprecise, even misleading conclusions and claims. On the eve of the Great War, Irish American Catholics both constituted and represented such an array of diversity along practically every measurement of the socio-economic and political line as to defy simple categorization. More than anything else, this was an ethnic constituency that was no longer a generation of emigrants exiled from their native land. Nor did post-Famine immigrants constitute the solidifying mass of Irish American Catholics in the United States. By the first decade of the twentieth-century, second- and third-generation Irish Americans had reached the age of maturity and outnumbered first generation immigrants by a resounding ratio of three to one. Census data at the turn of the century bears clear evidence that a multi-generational Irish America had fully flowered. It is estimated that nearly 3.37 million American Irish were recorded as native-born, a number that would only continue to grow as third generation Irish Americans continued to swell their ranks. By contrast, the numbers of Irish-born had declined from its peak in 1890 of 1.87 million to 1.6 million by 1910.[2]

The demographic profile of Irish America in the early twentieth century is not only significant to the focus of this study. It suggests that Irish Americans on the eve of the Great War harbored interests, concerns, anxieties, and perspectives that would be both reflective of, and textured by, multi-generational layers of nuanced positions on Ireland, America, and Catholicism. The emergence of the European

---

2. Kevin Kenny, *The American Irish: A History* (New York: Longman, 2000), 131; and Alan O'Day, "Imagined Irish Communities: Networks of Social Communication of the Irish Diaspora in the Late Nineteenth and Early Twentieth Centuries," *Immigrants and Minorities* 23 (July–November 2005): 403–6. For an interesting analysis of data from the censuses of 1900 and 1910, see *IPUMS*, http://ipums.org/. See also David Noel Doyle, "Catholicism, Politics and Irish America; Some Critical Considerations," in P. J. Drudy, ed., *The Irish in America: Emigration, Assimilation and Impact* (Cambridge: Cambridge University Press, 1985), 191.

CHAPTER 1

war in 1914 only exacerbated these palpable tensions. With the obvious exception of German Americans, no other European ethnic immigrants would find themselves as distressed by the guns of August 1914 as did Irish Americans, as they were now compelled to assess their stake in the United States, clarify their allegiances, and suppress (or at least moderate) their innate disdain for the British government. When it came to vested interests in this country, two matters—political and economic—would have a direct bearing on positions taken by Irish Americans in the crucible created by the Great War. This chapter will examine a handful of socio-economic, political, and cultural phenomena that beckoned inclusion or assimilation into mainstream American society. Irish American dedication to Roman Catholicism and its sympathy for Irish nationalism—two issues that thwarted inclusion—will be also discussed in the first two chapters of this study.

In one form or another, the Irish had been arriving on American soil since the English colonial era. The first waves were comprised largely of Scots Irish of the Presbyterian stripe, beginning in the early eighteenth century, and they arrived as exiles as much as immigrants. Earlier, they had been cajoled by the Tudors to settle in Ireland as a means of subduing Irish Catholicism and to establish English and Protestant hegemony over the land. Lowland Scots flooded the northern reaches of the island. In one regard, the English appreciated these Presbyterians, as they could always be counted on as a bastion of anti-Catholicism. They had, after all, performed a yeoman's service during the great Jacobite uprising of 1689–1690, most notably in their enthusiastic resistance during the siege of Londonderry by the armies of James II. In the wake of the failed uprising, the English decided to reinvigorate the Penal Laws to thoroughly emasculate the Catholic population. Initially, the Presbyterian Scots Irish were granted a reprieve from inclusion in these strictures, but this was not to last for long. The English were determined to establish a general unity and conformity in all matters and would use religion as the bludgeoning club to effect.

In truth, the English had always been wary of the Scots-Irish Presbyterians, considering them dissenters who placed themselves outside the established Protestant Church of Ireland. Through the Anglo-Irish Parliament, the English enacted a series of local ordinances during the first half of the eighteenth century. In 1700, Presbyterians had a stronghold in northeastern Ulster. They had constructed and populated many relatively wealthy towns and, as they excelled in commerce, they had emerged as a formidable mercantile class as early as 1690. This alone was galling to the Anglo-Irish Parliament in Dublin, but the Presbyterian adherence to an independent creed, and their refusal to follow the instruction of the established Church, was deemed treacherous. With Catholic Ireland momentarily cowered by its defeat in the Jacobite uprising, the confident Anglo-Irish Parliament found it a convenient time to divert its attention to the suppression of the Presbyterian Irish. They were to be marginalized within Irish society.

The emasculation of the Presbyterians began with the Irish Parliament extending application of the Penal Laws to the Scots Irish. Fully understanding the relationship between land ownership and political power, the Anglo-Irish Parliament used allegiance to the established church and adherence to its creed as the yardstick for land ownership. The aim, as with the Catholics, was complete domination of any competing religion or ideology. Laws disallowing the bequeathing of land ownership to any single male son meant the land was parceled out so thinly that it was both hardly sustainable and bereft of any local power and influence. Presbyterians were excluded from public office and from sitting on the boards of municipal corporations. Their ministers saw that any elements of legal force that lay behind their services were removed from them: they could not celebrate the Lord's Supper, they could not marry couples, nor could they conduct funeral services. By the second decade of the eighteenth century, the Irish Parliament was firmly ensconced in a power that brooked no competition and was buttressed by the ascendancy of the Protestant Church of Ireland. All the same, much like Irish Catholics, there were few converts to the established Church from the Presbyterian ranks. Stripped of their land, suppressed in their faith, and economically disenfranchised, the Scots Irish looked about for pastures greener than their own green shores. Many looked westward, far across the Atlantic, and decided to uproot themselves and leave for North America.[3]

---

3. Mike Cronin, *A History of Ireland* (New York: Palgrave, 2001), 63–86.

CHAPTER 1

Emigrants from the Ulster province had been flooding America's shores from the late seventeenth century through the establishment of the American republic. Disillusioned with their lot in Northern Ireland, these Scots Irish, mainly Calvinist Presbyterians, arrived in America with an assertive, defiant, and feisty attitude towards the established government that they encountered already cemented in the thirteen original English colonies. With few opportunities available in the coastal regions of colonial America, compounded by pronounced English discomfiture with their presence, the Scots Irish wended their way to the western frontier along the line of the Appalachian Mountains. Major Scots Irish settlements stretched from New Hampshire in the North to South Carolina in the South. By the eve of the American Revolution, in places like western Pennsylvania, Virginia, and North and South Carolina, the Scots Irish had cultivated a culture and a political independence that stood in stark contrast to the entrenched centers of colonial government existing along the Atlantic coast. In matters of land grants, expansion, Native American affairs, and a host of other political issues, the Scots Irish found themselves frequently at odds with policies adopted by eastern authorities. On the eve of the Imperial Crisis with Great Britain, they were in open defiance of colonial governments over land acquisition and the policies towards Native Americans on the frontier, leading to the dismantling of Quaker proprietary control in the colony of Pennsylvania and the rise of the Regulator movement in North Carolina.[4]

The Scots Irish who played prominent roles in the Revolutionary War era are legion and, from that point onward to the ascendancy of Andrew Jackson in 1828, both their numbers and their influence increased. Irish immigration remained predominantly Ulster in

---

4. On the suppression of Scots Irish Presbyterians see Mike Cronin, *A History of Ireland.* (New York: Palgrave, 2001), 80–85. Scots Irish immigration can be traced in innumerable studies. Perhaps three of them are most insightful. See James G. Leyburn, *The Scotch-Irish: A Social History* (Chapel Hill: University of North Carolina Press, 1989), 184–256; Kerby A. Miller, *Emigrants and Exiles: Ireland and the Irish Exodus to North America* (New York: Oxford University Press, 1985), 132–79; and Patrick Griffin, *The People with No Name: Ireland's Ulster Scots and the Creation of a British Atlantic World, 1609–1764* (Princeton, NJ: Princeton University Press, 2001), 65–156.

character, but Irish Catholics from the other three provinces became increasingly numerous as the nineteenth century advanced. Between 1828 and 1912, eleven presidents of the United States had some Scots Irish ancestry. Andrew Jackson and James K. Polk courted the Irish vote by trumpeting their Irish roots. James Buchanan cherished his origins by declaring that his "Ulster blood is a priceless heritage." Woodrow Wilson, the last of these presidents under review, was the grandson of a printer from a small village in County Tyrone. Sandwiched between Jackson and Wilson, presidents Andrew Johnson, Ulysses S. Grant, Chester A. Arthur, Grover Cleveland, Benjamin Harrison, William McKinley and, somewhat remotely, Theodore Roosevelt, had Scots Irish blood coursing through their veins, courtesy of either their paternal or maternal lineage. All the same, whatever political leverage might have been accrued by referencing their Irish heritage largely became a moot point by the mid-nineteenth century. Their common Protestant grounding had morphed or translated into a British heritage and their assimilation into American society was easily confirmed. So conspicuous was their identification as Americans by the mid-nineteenth century that these Scots Irish descendants counted themselves among the nativist surge that swelled during the remainder of the late antebellum period and beyond. To be clear, Irish Americans of the Protestant stripe continued to pay lip service to their Irish roots in their various organizations and Orange Lodges, but the emphasis in these organizations was their Protestantism and Americanism. The infamous Orange Riots of 1870 and 1871 in New York City pitted Protestant Irish against Catholic Irish. All told, more than sixty died in the mayhem.[5]

Notwithstanding the predominant Scots Irish immigrant strain in the late colonial and early republican eras, Irish Catholics nonetheless

---

5. The reasons why Scots Irish Presbyterians left Ulster are succinctly discussed in Cronin, *A History of Ireland*, 83–86. On the Orange Riots, see Michael A. Gordon, *The Orange Riots: Irish Political Violence in New York City, 1870 and 1871* (Ithaca, NY: Cornell University Press, 1993). By 1900, the Orange Order had shed its ethnic Irish identity and became more of a Protestant fraternal organization. See Sean Connolly, *On Every Tide: The Making and Remaking of the Irish World* (New York: Basic Books, 2022), 13.

CHAPTER 1

filtered into America at the same time. Catholics had as much reason to emigrate as their Presbyterian counterparts, if not more. By 1715, Catholic land ownership throughout the isle had diminished to but 5%, whereas in 1703 it had been 14%. And as great as religious oppression was in persuading Irish Catholics to depart Ireland, the most compelling reason was economic and general impoverishment. Cyclical crop failures between 1717 and 1729, and a later one in 1740–1741, were especially acute and during this period it is estimated that nearly 480,000 Irish died, which as a percentage of the population was greater than that a century later during the Great Famine. Compounding these agricultural catastrophes, Irish tenants faced ever-increasing rents. Absentee Anglo-Irish landowners were indifferent to the hard times facing their tenants, and strove for maximum profit off their lands. This invariably led to evictions and further displacement of the haggard peasant. Moreover, a decline in the linen industry created even more hardship. In 1720, linen had made up nearly half of Irish exports to England and cottage industries where tenants produced it were humming. Decreased English demand and European competition collapsed the industry by mid-century, sparking an ever-greater exodus from Ireland. Wooed by colonial agents with the lure of free land, boundless opportunities, and the promise of freedom from religious harassment, many thousands chose to emigrate to North America. The bulk of these emigres were from Presbyterian Ulster. Still, adventurous Catholics who could scrape enough money for passage or signed on as indentured servants made their way to America as well.[6]

By the Jacksonian Era, Irish Catholics had become a recognizable presence, settling mostly in the cities along the east coast, such as New York, Boston, Providence, Philadelphia and, to a lesser extent, Charleston and Savannah. Most Famine immigrants and later ones replicated this pattern, as they had either family or former neighbors now anchored in these cities. Among several reasons causing this demographic feature was the stark realization that most of the Irish brought with them only bitter memories of a vicious and exploitative system that dispossessed them of their land. Moreover, they had

---

6. See Dolan, *The Irish Americans: A History,* 5–7.

virtually no capital and few of the skills necessary to succeed in the highly individualistic and competitive agriculture practiced in America. Whatever treasury of adventurism they might have left Ireland with had been exhausted during the harrowing Atlantic crossing, and the availability of menial jobs, at wages undreamt of at home, plus the comfort of their fellow exiles, gave them reason enough to stay where they landed. By 1850, this tendency to cluster in the seaboard cities, such as in the Five Points neighborhood of lower Manhattan, had become firmly entrenched. To be sure, many single Irishmen grasped the shovel and the pick to labor on the Erie Canal, and the railroads thereafter transporting them, in effect, to the Great Lakes communities of Buffalo, Detroit, Cleveland, and even Chicago, St. Louis and Milwaukee by the 1840s.[7] Initially, they possessed but little political clout, but their social, cultural, and religious proclivities aroused both the attention and fear of native-born American Protestants. In Charlestown, just outside of Boston, long a bastion of Calvinism with a history of anti-Catholicism, working class Protestants, goaded by scurrilous and unsubstantiated rumors of indiscretions being committed at the Ursuline Convent there, moved upon the nunnery and burned it to the ground. Two years later, Maria Monk, a purported postulant in a Montreal convent, regaled readers with tales of submissive nuns who were raped by predatory priests, followed by agonizing tales of infanticide, fanning the flames of anti-Catholicism within the United States. In 1844, full-scale riots erupted in Philadelphia's neighborhoods of Kensington and Southwark, ostensibly involving a dispute over which version of the Bible would be read in public schools, resulting in the burning of two Catholic churches, scores killed, and the calling out of the Pennsylvania militia. So ominous was this episode that Archbishop John Hughes guaranteed municipal officials in New York that, should one Catholic Church in his diocese be attacked, he would make the city a "second Moscow."[8]

7. See Marvin R. O'Connell, *John Ireland and the American Catholic Church* (St. Paul: Minnesota Historical Society Press, 1988), 16.

8. On the Ursuline Convent riot see Jack Tager, *Boston Riots: Three Centuries of Social Violence* (Boston: Northeastern University Press, 2000), 104–12. For Maria Monk's inflammatory "revelations," see the reprint version

CHAPTER 1

The Dynamics of Inclusion: The Political Irish

In the first half of the nineteenth century, there is but little evidence to suggest that Irish Catholics played any significant role in national elections. In the presidential election of 1824, Andrew Jackson failed to carry the lion's share of electoral votes in the state of New York, leading in part to his loss that year. Four years later, leaving no stone unturned, Democratic Party organizers created a concerted strategy to undermine the reelection hopes of John Quincy Adams. During the campaign—one that would set the bar high for all subsequent negative campaigning—Jackson surrogates in the western regions baselessly accused Adams of routinely conversing with Catholic priests in Latin, while in eastern cities such as Boston, Philadelphia, and New York, they planted rumors that the virtually atheist Adams reviled Catholics and immigrants. Democratic smears directed at the sitting president were buttressed with paeans glorifying Jackson's unadulterated animus toward the British, and charges that Adams—like his father—was an inveterate Anglophile. Jackson carried the city of New York, winning the majority of electoral votes in the Empire State, and capturing the election of 1828. Following his reelection in 1832, Jackson expressed his gratitude to the Irish for their support of his candidacy at a rally of the Charitable Irish Society of New York, acknowledging the respect they had shown him and touting the role that Irishmen had played in the creation of the American Republic.[9]

Twelve years later, James K. Polk, another Ulster descendant, made similar overtures to the Irish and Catholic constituency in New York during his presidential campaign, as did his opponent, Henry Clay.

Awful Disclosures of the Hotel Dieu Nunnery of Montreal (New York: Arno Press, 1977). The Philadelphia nativist riots can be most easily traced in Kenneth W. Milano, *Philadelphia Nativist Riots: Irish Kensington Erupts* (Charleston, SC: The History Press, 2013). Archbishop Hughes's remarks can be found in Richard Shaw, *Dagger John: The Unquiet Life and Times of Archbishop John Hughes of New York* (New York: The Paulist Press, 1877), 197; and Tyler Anbinder, *Five Points* (New York: Free Press, 2001), 256.

9. Robert V. Remini, *John Quincy Adams* (New York: Times Books, 2002), 121–22, 145; and Edward O'Meagher Condon, *The Irish Race in America* (New York: Ford's National Library, 1887), 294.

Clay's fortunes, however, were considerably dampened in New York, the richest electoral treasure in the country, when Democrats insinuated that the Whigs were consummate nativists. Polk won a razor-thin victory in the Empire State, with votes cast in New York City decisive in the outcome. In a postmortem election analysis, Millard Fillmore informed Henry Clay that the principal reason for losing New York had been the ability of the opposition to tar the Whigs—particularly "Mr. Freylinghuysen," Clay's running mate—with animus to the "foreign Catholics." The nativist Fillmore's own gubernatorial bid, he conjectured, was also undermined by the "foreign Catholic vote," as he not only lost the vote in New York City but nearly failed in capturing his own ward in Buffalo.[10]

The mid-century mark proved to be a signal and signature moment in Irish America. Approximately a million Irish emigrated and landed as immigrants in the United States in the first decade of this era, owing to the Great Famine raging throughout Ireland. The earlier dominance of Protestant Irish immigration was but a prelude to that of the Catholic Irish. In 1860, it is estimated that nearly 1.6 million Irish-born people lived in the United States, and that a significant majority of them were Catholic. Subsequent decades leading up to the eve of the Great War would see, on average, another half-million flooding American shores. According to the census of 1910, 4.5 million Americans identified themselves as Irish-born or had at least one Irish-born parent. These statistics do not account for the millions of grandparents and great-grandparents who identified themselves as Irish. From the very start, this acceleration in immigration caused serious alarm among the native-born American population. As Irish Catholic immigrants arrived, the relatively mild variety of Whig nativism gave way, briefly, to the rise of the aggressively anti-immigrant and anti-Catholic Know-Nothing movement, which, in turn, was subsumed by the anti-slavery Republican Party of the North. The political dynamism of the 1850s increased Irish American attachment to the Democratic

---

10. Theodore Frelinghuysen was Clay's running mate in 1844, and was an outspoken adversary of the Catholic immigrant. See Thomas J. Rowland, *Millard Fillmore: The Limits of Compromise* (New York: Nova Science Publishers, 2013), 32.

CHAPTER 1

Party. Irish Americans voted for the Democratic presidential standard bearer in virtually all elections up to Wilson's in 1912.[11]

The devotion of Irish Americans to the Democratic Party, however, was not without condition, as Grover Cleveland discovered in the three elections of 1884, 1888, and 1892. As a reform-minded governor of New York, Cleveland had successfully confronted and temporarily diminished the political clout of the Irish-led Tammany Hall organization of New York City. The Republican candidate in 1884, James G. Blaine, whose own mother was Irish Catholic, was viewed as a viable alternative to Cleveland up to the moment he failed to repudiate the remarks of a Protestant minister made in a New York meeting with the candidate in attendance shortly before the election. When the Reverend Samuel A. Burchard proclaimed the Democrats as the party of "Rum, Romanism, and Rebellion," without Blaine's immediate repudiation, the Democrats seized upon the moment to paint the Republican candidate as an anti-Catholic bigot. Churchgoers exiting Mass on Sundays were greeted with pamphlets excoriating Blaine's candidacy, and when combined with the crossover votes of disaffected Stalwart Republicans, Cleveland captured New York and the election. In the latter two elections, Cleveland's perceived truckling to British interests elicited howls of protest from the ranks of more ardent Irish nationalists. In 1888, Cleveland would lose New York's rich electoral treasure and go down in defeat to Benjamin Harrison. Four years later Cleveland recaptured New York and, with it, the presidency. An analysis of election results in all three elections revealed that in Irish districts within New York City, Brooklyn, and Boston the voters continued to support the Democrat Cleveland, the difference being that they did not support him in the same percentage as they had previous Democratic candidates, such as George B. McClellan (1864), Horatio Seymour

---

11. The demographics of Irish immigration to the United States can be found in a report by the Commission on Emigration and Other Population Problems (Dublin: Ministry of Social Welfare, 1954), 309–11, based on Reports of the Colonial Land and Emigration Commissioners, 1851–1872, and on Board of Trade Returns, 1873–1921. See also Maldyn A. Jones, *American Immigration* (Chicago: University of Chicago Press, 1960); and Alan J. Ward, *Ireland and Anglo-American Relations, 1899–1921* (Toronto: University of Toronto Press), 2–3.

(1868) and Winfield Scott Hancock (1880). Throughout the nineteenth century, the Irish Catholic remained important in both national and state elections, but only in those places where Irish voters were concentrated. Office seekers were at least sensitive to the Irish vote, even though it might not determine the ultimate result of a general election.[12]

While it is arguable that Irish American political influence over national affairs was minimal at the turn of the century, it flourished on the local, urban level, and given the needs of the American Irish at this time, this sphere of influence was of greater pertinence and value. Moreover, it could well have been one of the first ways in which the Irish gained entrance into American society without groveling to White Anglo-Saxon Protestant (WASP) convention. It is hardly surprising that Irish Americans became fascinated with the access to power and its uses. To acquire a political voice was something well-ingrained in the Irish psyche, as it was something long denied to their ancestors. Moreover, it would become the first step and the most tangible expression of membership and inclusion, real or imagined, in the country of their adoption. In the America of 1870, Irish Americans harbored no illusions they could wrest control from WASPs over the political levers throughout the nation, but they were aware that in their concentrated numbers in urban centers they could express that political voice. Thus, the story of the Irish and the emergence of urban political machinery merits consideration.

For centuries, their Irish ancestors had been denied political expression in British-ruled Ireland, and nativists in America had long been successful in curbing Irish political empowerment. But the Irish knew how democratic government was supposed to work. Almost instinctively, Irish Americans knew that the franchise was the vehicle by which they could advance their own interests and defend them against attacks by others. By 1914, Irish Americans had gained political control, for the better part, in many cities and in certain regions where their numbers were strong. In most places, the instrument with which they gained control of local politics was the

---

12. Thomas N. Brown, *Irish-American Nationalism, 1870–1890,* 187, n. 4, 5, 6. As will be demonstrated later in this study, there were a significant number of Irish American senators and congressmen by the early decades of the twentieth century.

CHAPTER 1

urban machine. In some locations, such as Kansas City, Jersey City, and Albany, control rested with the cult of personality in the form of Irish bosses. In Philadelphia and Pittsburgh, where no organized Irish Democratic machine flourished, Irish Americans played a role disproportionate to their numbers—they simply accomplished it through Republican machinery. A growing phenomenon in the later nineteenth century, Irish-dominated machines reached their apex in the years just before the Great War. Although they occasionally secured the mayoralty position itself, it was largely insignificant, as mayors found themselves, with few exceptions, beholden to the greater organization. Irish American machines quickly consolidated their power through an efficient and judicious implementation of the patronage system. Through patronage, the machine addressed the urban voter's needs and established a bond of loyalty based on economic realities and material gain. So complete was Irish American hegemony in the cities by 1914 that the vulgar Victorian image of a cigar-smoking, frequently corpulent, ruddy-faced political boss was less a coarse caricature than a rueful acknowledgement by nativists that the reins of power had shifted to his kind.[13]

On the eve of the outbreak of the Great War Irish American political machines dominated many of the nation's major cities and underscored the fact that native control of power was retreating in the face of the Irish ability to manipulate the electorate. Viewing the political

---

13. Edward Levine, *The Irish and Irish Politicians* (South Bend, IN: Notre Dame University Press, 1966), 7–8; Niles Carpenter, *Immigrants and Their Children* (Washington, DC: U. S. Government Printing Office, 1927), 137; John Allswang, *A House of All Peoples* (Lexington: University of Kentucky Press, 1971), 66–90; and Thomas N. Brown, "The Political Irish: Politicians and Rebels," in David Noel Doyle and Owen Dudley Edwards, eds., *America and Ireland, 1776–1976: The American Identity and the Irish Connection* (Westport, CT: Greenwood Press, 1976), 37. Although he eventually had somewhat of a falling out with the Tammany boss Charles Murphy, George B. McClellan, Jr., son of the celebrated Civil War general and 1864 Democratic presidential candidate, served as a hugely successful mayor of New York between 1904 and 1909. See *The Gentleman and the Tiger: The Autobiography of George B. McClellan, Jr.*, edited from the original manuscript in the possession of the New York Historical Society by Harold C. Syrett (Philadelphia: J. B. Lippincott Co., 1956).

realm as a way of securing economic benefit and influence, Irish Americans worked at discrediting the legitimacy of WASP institutions, substituting Irish ones in their place. When unable to grasp power with overwhelming numbers, they mobilized other immigrant groups to their advantage. The native was simply outvoted. According to one observer, it was the nativists' steadfastness to the constitutional guarantee of the franchise that sealed their own fate.[14]

Once in power, Irish Americans were equally successful in holding off newer immigrants from usurping their power. One of the earliest of the ethnic European groups, the Irish held not only the advantage of longevity here in America but the benefit of the English language, an understanding of American culture, control of incipient labor organizations, and a monopoly of the patronage system. When necessary, the machine was not loathe to elevate a prominent outsider; such a move frequently diffused organized opposition and normally secured the allegiance of still more voters. In the process, Irish American politicians evolved into excellent managers and brokers of municipal patronage in many of the major American cities. They employed whatever means were available to produce rich dividends of power and influence.

Wherever and whenever conditions permitted, Irish Americans bullied their way into political power. Whereas Boston never produced a machine along the lines of New York and other cities, emergent Irish leadership was generally able to marshal the large Irish American electorate in the very restricted environs of that municipality. In New York, Tammany Hall demonstrated it was flexible enough to share limited power with the ever-increasing number of Jewish immigrants without surrendering ultimate control. In other cases, particularly

---

14. Richard Krickus, *Pursuing the American Dream: White Ethnics and the New Populism* (Bloomington: Indiana University Press, 1976), 161–62. Various theories of the origin and fundamental operating mechanisms of the Irish American political machine and the parsimony with which they handed out patronage to non-Irish immigrants can be found in Steven P. Erie, *Rainbow's End: Irish-Americans and the Dilemmas of Urban Machine Politics, 1840–1985* (Berkeley: University of California Press, 1988), 196–220, 244–45. Thomas N. Brown asserts that by the 1880s politics was their dominant passion. See Brown, *Irish-American Nationalism,* 179.

CHAPTER 1

around the turn of the century, Tammany Hall warded off serious challenges to its power by exploiting inter-ethnic feuding among newer immigrant groups. In Chicago, Irish-Americans were able to minimize challenges from the numerous Poles, Lithuanians, and Germans by playing one group off against the other, effectively dividing and conquering the opposition. Over the long run, Irish Americans proved "skilled in the trading of votes ... and in the accumulation of bits and pieces of power."[15]

In Boston, where the Irish had for some time controlled the "political world," they emerged to wrest outright control from Yankee Democrats. The narrow defeat of popular reformist James Jackson Storrow by John "Honey Fitz" Fitzgerald in the 1909 mayoral race marked the definitive end of Yankee dominance and the triumph of Irish ward politics. This Irish American triumph served as a clarion signal that the Irish could coordinate city-wide efforts and deliver crucial votes when needed. Fitzgerald's successor, James Michael Curley, won the 1913 election, and despite his public disparagement of bossism, it was the last-minute timely support of Martin Lomasney, the powerful boss of the West End, that propelled Curley to a six thousand vote plurality.[16]

---

15. Richard Krickus, *Pursuing the American Dream*, 163–64; Steven P. Erie, *Rainbow's End*, 210–19; Martin Meyerson and Edward C. Bonfield, "A Machine at Work," in Edward C. Bonfield, ed., *Urban Government* (New York: Free Press, 1967), 169–70; Brown, "The Political Irish: Politicians and Rebels," 140.

16. Geoffrey Blodgett, *The Gentle Reformers: Massachusetts Democrats in the Cleveland Era* (Cambridge, MA: Harvard University Press, 1966), 261, 278–80; Oscar Handlin, *Boston's Immigrants: A Study in Acculturation* (Boston: Belknap Press, 1959), 227; Constance K. Burns, "The Irony of Progressive Reform: Boston, 1898–1910," in Ronald Formisano and Constance K. Burns, *Boston, 1700–1980: The Evolution of Urban Politics* (Westport, CT: Greenwood Press, 1984), 133–64; James Michael Curley, *I'd Do It Again: A Record of All My Uproarious Years* (New York: Arno Press, 1957), 113–20; Peter K. Fisinger, "Ethnic Political Transition, 1884–1933," *Political Science Quarterly* 93 (Summer 1978): 219–26. Worcester, Massachusetts was another Massachusetts city that witnessed the rise of Irish American political power, though less militantly than Boston, at the turn of the century. See Timothy J. Meagher, *Inventing Irish America: Generation, Class, and Ethnic Identity in a New England City, 1880–1920* (Notre Dame, IN: University of Notre Dame Press, 2000).

STAKING THE AMERICAN CLAIM

Descending south of Boston, the remaining New England cities of Providence, Rhode Island and Hartford and New Haven, Connecticut fell under the spell of Hibernian magic by the turn of the century, although, like Boston, no organized Irish American machinery took root. In Providence, the first Irish American mayor, Edwin D. McGuiness took office in 1896. He was born in Providence, and although he ran on the Democratic ticket, McGuiness was known for running a non-partisan campaign. In 1907 Patrick J. McCarthy, born in County Sligo, Ireland, was elected the city's mayor. Four years after McCarthy's term expired, Joseph H. Gainer, the son of Irish immigrants, captured the mayoralty and served seven consecutive terms until his retirement in 1927. All these mayors were Catholics. The experience in Providence was largely replicated in New Haven and Hartford. By 1899, in New Haven, Irish Americans had secured the mayoralty and quickly expanded control over the municipal government.[17] Further south, Irish American power was brandished more brazenly than in New England. In Jersey City, for instance, the elevation of Frank Hague as mayor in 1913 signaled the inception of nearly four decades of total personal control. Satellite cities, such as Newark, Patterson, and Passaic were also swallowed up by Irish American machines.[18]

In upstate New York, the Irish established virtual machines in places, such as Buffalo and Syracuse. In Albany, an entrenched Republican machine was on the brink of being upstaged by a Democratic insurgency at the close of the Great War in 1918 in the person of Daniel O'Connell. He would run Albany for nearly forty

---

17. For Providence, see Scott Malloy, "The Irish in Rhode Island: A Long Struggle to Enter the Mainstream," March 17, 1887, Rhode Island Irish Famine Memorial, https://www.rifaminememorial.com/articles/The_Irish_in_Rhode_Island.html. For Connecticut, see Robert Dahl, *Who Governed?* (New Haven, CT: Yale University Press, 1961), 32–51.

18. Richard J. Connors, *A Cycle of Power: The Career of Jersey City Mayor Frank Hague* (Metuchen, NJ: Scarecrow Press, 1971), 10–17; Dennis Clark, *Hibernia America* (Philadelphia: Temple University Press, 1973), 63. Additional information on Frank Hague can be found in Leonard F. Vernon, *The Life and Times of Jersey City Major Frank Hague: I Am the Law* (Charleston, SC: The History Press, 2011).

CHAPTER 1

years. But it was in the City of New York itself where Irish American domination of the political process became enshrined, in the reign of Tammany Hall. Three political bosses—"Honest John" Kelly, Richard Croker, and Charles Francis "Silent Charlie" Murphy—held sway between 1874 and 1924. Kelly, the son of Irish immigrants, had made his mark as early as 1855 when he was elected as the first Irish American Catholic to the House of Representatives, accomplishing this feat during the halcyon days of the Know-Nothing movement. His moniker, "Honest" was more ironic than truthful, as he amassed a relative fortune in his position as sheriff and his role as Tammany's chief sachem. Croker, a Protestant who had been born in Ireland but raised in the slums of New York, emerged as Kelly's successor. His rise up the political ladder had its origins in his muscular, street-savvy youth. But his control of Tammany Hall was indisputable. Of Croker it has been remarked that "he understood completely the worthlessness of the superior American in politics ... gentlemanly subscribers of the *Century, the Nation,* and the *Arena* would never persist, in effecting any permanent organized force." Yet, facing charges of corruption, Croker decided in 1902 to retire to a lavish estate in Ireland, opening the door to his successor, Charles F. Murphy. "Silent Charlie" ruled Tammany as its chief sachem until his abrupt death in 1924. Murphy was in many ways an atypical city boss. Not only was he shy and a taciturn in conversation, but he totally abstained from the consumption of alcohol. Yet Murphy was responsible for transforming Tammany's image from one of corruption to respectability and launched the city's Democratic Party onto the national stage. His domination was without parallel, leading one biographer to conclude that "he maintained the most powerful and smoothest running machine in the United States ... [and] his were the golden years of Tammany." While Murphy was attending to the political business of Manhattan, John McGooey controlled Brooklyn and Ed Flynn was already beginning to emerge in the Bronx.[19]

19. Terry Golway, *Machine Made: Tammany Hall and the Creation of Modern American Politics* (New York: Liveright Publishing Co., 2015), 70–73, 105–22, 144–50, 170–79; Alfred Connable and Edward Silberfarb, *Tigers of Tammany* (New York: Holt, Rinehart & Winston, 1967), 234; Thomas Beer, *The Mauve Decade*

STAKING THE AMERICAN CLAIM

Although not as remarkably formidable as they were in the coastal cities of the East, Irish Americans wielded significant political clout in the cities dotting the Midwest. Most Midwestern cities did not feature the classic version of Irish American machinery. In Chicago, Irish control of several city wards did not necessarily translate into any monopoly in the mayoralty until well after the Great War. Chicago's first Irish American Catholic mayor, John Patrick Hopkins, served a rather undistinguished term in that office (1893–1895). Yet the conveniently corrupt, native-born Carter-Harrison family (which largely controlled the office of mayor between 1879 and 1911) and the spectacularly corrupt administrations of William "Big Bill" Thompson, the last Republican mayor of Chicago (who entered office in 1915) were quite responsive to Irish American pressure and demands.

Irish American political domination in Chicago at the turn of the century was limited, in part, by the fact that the city, and the State of Illinois, the "Land of Lincoln," had longstanding attachments to the Republican Party. Moreover, as the twentieth century dawned, Chicago was inundated by widely diverse immigrant arrivals, most notably Germans, Scandinavians, and Poles, who did not necessarily gravitate to the Democratic Party. Nevertheless, two Irish politicians—Roger Charles Sullivan, a second-generation immigrant, and Edward Fitzsimmons Dunne, son of ardent Irish nationalist Patrick William Dunne—rose to prominence in turn-of-the-century Chicago. For over two decades, beginning in 1895, the extraordinarily wealthy Sullivan bossed both the Chicago and the state Democratic Party, although in the Windy City he was frequently challenged for control by the Carter-Harrisons. Elected to the Democratic National Committee in 1906, Sullivan elevated an already existing feud with William Jennings Bryan and is generally credited as having played an integral role in handing the 1912 nomination to Woodrow Wilson. Dunne, born in Watertown, Connecticut, moved with his parents to Illinois as a two-year-old in 1855. His father, Patrick, became a prosperous businessman who raised funds for the Fenian movement and frequently

---

(New York: Carroll and Graf, 1997 [reprint]), 142; and Nathan Glazer and Daniel P. Moynihan, *Beyond the Melting Pot: The Negroes, Puerto Ricans, Jews, Italians, and Irish of New York City* (Cambridge, MA: MIT Press, 1970), 226.

CHAPTER 1

hosted traveling Irish politicians, political exiles, and Fenian rebels in his home. Edward spent several years studying at Dublin's Trinity College and completed his law degree at Union College in Chicago. His years as a practicing attorney came to an end when he was elevated to a judgeship in 1892, a position he maintained until he ran for Chicago mayor in 1905 as a Democrat and won by a comfortable margin. Both a reelection bid in 1907 and a comeback attempt in 1911 met with failure. Undeterred, Dunne ran for governor of Illinois in 1912, and with the Republicans woefully divided in that presidential election year, Dunne captured the office. He served one term as governor, from 1913 to 1917. Dunne's political inclinations were progressive, and he championed causes, such as women's suffrage, that did not always resonate with his constituents, which may have resulted in the failure of his reelection bid in 1916. One constant through his adulthood was his activism in the cause of Irish liberation, most likely a legacy from his Fenian father. Once the Great War ended, Dunne was selected by the Irish Race Convention to serve on the American Commission on Irish Independence, to influence Woodrow Wilson to advocate for an independent Ireland at the Treaty of Versailles.

But it was in the wards of Chicago that Irish Americans held sway. Legendary names, such as Johnny "De Pow" Powers, John "Bathhouse" Coughlin, and Michael "Hinky Dink" Kenna, pulled the levers of power in Chicago's seamy underside. Alternately known as the "Lords of the Levee" or the "Gray Wolves," they were able to maintain power by the art of patronage, and by employing the personal touch of distributing free turkeys, ducks, and geese to voters at Christmas. Powers' inability to keep his 19th Ward clear of garbage, or to maintain good schools, led the famous Protestant social reformer Jane Addams to challenge his reelection bid in 1904. Addams attacked Powers for his cronyism and corruption, accurately deploring his ownership of three saloons and a gambling house. Powers countered with charges of anti-Catholicism on Addams' part and promptly won the election. For the constituents of the 19th Ward, jobs and gifts proved more endearing than clean streets.[20]

20. James W. Sanders, *The Education of an Urban Minority* (New York: Oxford University Press, 1976), 122–23. The first of nine Irish American Catholic

STAKING THE AMERICAN CLAIM

In St. Louis, Irish Americans on the eve of the Great War acquitted themselves quite well in the political world. The two political parties vied for control of the city during the second half of the nineteenth century, limiting the ability of either one to establish a monolithic political machine. This changed around 1880, when "Colonel" Edward Butler, a native of County Wicklow, emerged as the leader of the Democratic Party. While he enjoyed neither the power nor influence of his cross-state rival, Big Jim Pendergast of Kansas City, Butler managed to dominate municipal St. Louis by the practice of "boodling," essentially raking in monetary contributions from St. Louis' business elite. His was a physical regime. His minions, notably the notorious street thugs called the "Bottoms Gang," practiced the muscular art of electoral bad behavior: they clobbered politically incorrect voters, intimidated election judges, stuffed ballot boxes, repetitively voted, and frequently battled with the police should they dare to interfere. Butler's corruption was so rampant that he became a poster boy for Lincoln Steffen's excoriations in *McClure's Magazine*. Butler's reign lasted until 1904, when an enterprising new governor was gutsy enough to prepare indictments against him. Once eviscerated, Butler blithely admitted to a *New York Times* reporter that St. Louis Democrats won every election dishonestly.[21]

---

mayors, John Patrick Hopkins, was elected mayor in 1893. Nonetheless, his election is viewed as somewhat anomalous. See also Richard Allen Morton, "'A Man of Belial': Roger C. Sullivan, the Progressive Democracy, and Senatorial Elections of 1914," *Journal of the Illinois State Historical Society* 91, no. 3 (Autumn 1998): 133–59. Dunne's biography & political career is ably written by Richard Allen Morton, *Justice and Humanity: Edward F. Dunne, Illinois Progressive* (Carbondale: Southern Illinois University Press, 1997). Dunne's interest in Irish affairs can be found in Francis M. Carroll, *American Opinion and the Irish Question* (New York: Palgrave Macmillan, 1978), 133, 198. An excellent examination of Irish American power in ward politics on the eve of the Great War can be found in Dick Simpson, *Rogues, Rebels, and Rubber Stamps: The Politics of the Chicago City Council, 1863 to the Present* (Boulder, CO: Westview Press, 2001). See also Douglas Bukowski, *Big Bill Thompson, Chicago, and the Politics of Image* (Urbana: University of Illinois Press, 1998), 95–96, 159, 190.

21. Martin G. Towey, "Kerry Patch Revisited: Irish-American in St. Louis in the Turn of the Century Era," in Timothy J. Meagher, ed., *From Paddy to*

CHAPTER 1

At the same time, across the state in Kansas City, a city that did not feature a significant Irish population, the largest and most powerful Midwestern political machine was developed at the turn of the century by Big Jim Pendergast. A second-generation Irishman, he arrived in Kansas City with his family and siblings in 1876. He opened a hotel and saloon hotel in the West Bottoms neighborhood along the Missouri River. His engaging personality, coupled with the ability to tender sound political advice, made him somewhat of a kingmaker for aspiring politicos. He began his aldermanic career in 1892, and in short order emerged as the city and county boss. Big Jim's style was prototypical of the Irish American boss of the era. He acquired his money through moderate graft and contractual kickbacks, but otherwise remained out of the spotlight. He maintained his power base by "doing favors." He padded Kansas City's operational budget so that he personally was perceived as the one dispensing municipal employment. And his patronage extended to feeding and housing his constituents when they were down on their luck. Promoting himself as advocate of the common working man, he actually cared for the city he called home. He embraced the era's "City Beautiful" movement (the introduction of green space within industrialized and commercial metropolitan areas) that led to the formation of a celebrated county parks system. One year before his death in 1911, he had tired of both politics and business and handed over the reins of power to his youngest brother, Thomas. Whereas Big Jim had tread lightly, believing infinitely more in friendly persuasion, Tom Pendergast, Chair of the Jackson County Democratic organization, adopted a more belligerent and forceful *modus operandi.* Although it was during Tom Pendergast's reign that an irritating rival machine headed by Joseph B. Shannon was finally crushed, his tactics became increasingly odious and controversial. His open alliance with organized crime, his election manipulations, his high style of living, his promotion of the city as a wide-open vice den, and his insatiable

---

Studs: Irish-American Communities in the Turn of the Century Era, 1880 to 1920 (Westport, CT: Greenwood Press, 1986), 151–53The extent of Butler's corruption and his downfall are explored in brief articles in the *New York Times* (November 20, 1904) and the *Chicago Tribune* (July 2, 1904).

gambling habits eventually caught up with him. Abandoned by the Roosevelt administration, Tom Pendergast was convicted of income tax evasion in 1939 and was sentenced to a brief prison term. His career abruptly ended. Well before Pendergast spiraled out of control, a young haberdasher from Independence, Missouri, Harry S. Truman, launched his political career by attaching himself to the machine, a decision he spent years trying to downplay.[22]

Other than St. Paul, Minnesota, Irish American influence in the municipal politics of the four remaining Midwestern cities of prominence—Cleveland, Cincinnati, Indianapolis, Milwaukee—was largely anemic. The two Ohio cities were simply not places to which large numbers of Irish gravitated, or proved to be mere springboards for subsequent migration. Throughout most of the period leading up to the outbreak of the Great War, these cities were remarkably Republican and dominated by longstanding Yankee political establishments. While Cincinnati was a beacon for German settlers in the second half of the nineteenth century, their influence was largely relegated to the wards and the neighborhoods they settled. Milwaukee, like Chicago, had a sizeable Irish influx in its early years, courtesy of being one of the destination points on the Eire Canal-Great Lakes waterway. Midway through the nineteenth century, its celebrated Third Ward was an Irish stronghold, and in the era of the American Civil War, the Irish were a force with which to be reckoned. The combination of the growing opportunities afforded by Chicago, and a disastrous fire that swept the Third Ward in 1892 and scattered the survivors to other parts of the city, greatly diminished the influence of the Irish in Milwaukee. German immigration had been so staggeringly enormous throughout the second half of the nineteenth century that it, too, reduced Irish influence. Milwaukee may well have been the most immigrant city in the country, registering nearly eighty-six percent of the city's population as foreign

---

22. Lyle Dorsett, *The Pendergast Machine* (New York: Oxford University Press, 1968), 3–5; Lawrence Larson and Nancy J. Hulston, *Pendergast!* (Columbia: University of Missouri Press, 1997), ix. See also William M. Reddig, *Tom's Town: Kansas City and the Pendergast Legend* (Columbia: University of Missouri Press, 1986).

CHAPTER 1

born in 1890. Poles, Italians, Balkan peoples, and a host of others swamped the city at the turn of the century, rendering the Irish, but not the Catholic, imprint nearly indistinguishable by 1914.[23]

Unlike most Midwestern cities that were characterized by strong German immigration, or swamped some other single immigrant ethnicity, St. Paul was ethnically diverse, and the early Irish immigrants sank a deep anchor in this city, unlike its twin municipality of Minneapolis. In a decidedly working class and rough-and-tumble town, St. Paul's Irish seized the opportunity afforded them to play an instrumental role in the city's politics, and they had vigorous voice in the sphere of labor politics. As early as 1885, the citizens of St. Paul elected Christopher D. O'Brien, a native of Roscommon, Ireland, as mayor. O'Brien's pledge to support temperance measures in the city met fierce resistance from all ethnics, as well as from the flourishing brewing industry that had cropped up in the latter years of the nineteenth century. The mayor wisely declined to seek re-election. Democratic power in St. Paul "derived from a complex web of ethnic and working-class alliances," enhanced by a very large Catholic population and accelerated by the Republicans' reputation as nativists. As early as the 1890s, cries of Irish corruption in the political life of St. Paul began ringing from the elites and presses of neighboring Minneapolis. They bewailed the baleful influence that the "Irish Ring" of Patrick Kelly and Michael Doran played in the Democrats' lavish patronage system, promoting a scurrilous image that St. Paul was no

---

23. John Myers and Judith G. Cetina, *Irish Cleveland* (Charleston, SC: Arcadia Publishing, 2015), 39; Kevin Grace, *Irish Cincinnati,* (Charleston, SC: Arcadia Publishing, 2012), 41–60; Martin Hintz, *Irish Milwaukee* (Charleston, SC: Arcadia Publishing, 2003), 62–63; John Gurda, *The Making of Milwaukee* (Milwaukee: Milwaukee County Historical Society, 1999); and John Gurda, *Milwaukee: City of Neighborhoods* (Milwaukee: Historic Milwaukee, Inc., 2015). Indianapolis became home to a number of early Irish immigrants in the 1840s. But with the demise of canal building and the general lack of opportunity, many of the Irish left the city. A relatively small community of Irish formed in a neighborhood on the near south side of downtown. Interestingly, a Scots Irish immigrant, Thomas Taggart, emerged as both the city's and state's political kingpin at the turn of the century. See James P. Fadley, *Thomas Taggart: Public Servant, Political Boss, 1856–1929* (Indianapolis: Indiana Historical Society, 2007).

more than a corrupt Irish ghetto. As one astute observer of St. Paul at the turn of the century has observed, "these jeremiads against Irish American Catholics served as an affront to civic and ethnic pride and compelled St. Paul citizens of every sort to rally in defense of the city's Irish." By 1900, many of St. Paul's Irish were entering into the upper echelons of the city's society, "which smoothed their integration into the fabric of the city at the same time that it enormously enhanced the range and value of Irish ethnic networks."[24]

In the Mountain West, and along the Pacific coast, Irish political influence was less intensely organized than it was elsewhere on the eve of the Great War. An Irish and Catholic presence had been established in Denver, Colorado, but it was more associated with local labor politics than broad-based civic control. In the various mine fields surrounding Denver, the Irish were conspicuous leaders of the Western Federation of Miners, a group characterized by one critic as made up of "Austrians, Slavs, [and] Italians ... with enough hot-headed Irish to lead these foreigners into devilry." Notwithstanding his disparaging testimony, there is some truth embedded in this characterization, as a report in 1899 indicated that over half of the membership of one local union were first- or second-generation Irish immigrants, and that "they contributed much to its militant style."[25]

In what might appear to be an unlikely place, Butte, Montana, became an Irish American stronghold in the late nineteenth century. Irish-born businessman Marcus Daly had arrived in New York City as a young boy. As a young man, Daly apprenticed himself to one of the companies that exploited the Comstock silver mines in Virginia City, Nevada, and in 1872, he hooked up with a syndicate that produced enormous profits from the mines near Park City, Utah. In 1876, the enterprising Daly arrived in Butte as an agent for the Walker Brothers of Salt Lake City. The Walkers purchased mining rights and installed Daly as the mine superintendent. Soon after

24. Mary Lethert Wingerd, *Claiming the City: Politics, Faith, and the Power of Place in St. Paul* (Ithaca, NY: Cornell University Press, 2001), 50–51.
25. David Brundage, "After the Land League: The Persistence of Irish-American Radicalism in Denver, 1897–1905," *Journal of American Ethnic History* 11, no. 3 (Spring 1992): 3–26.

CHAPTER 1

operations commenced, Daly discovered that his miners were coming across significant deposits of copper ore. When he was unable to convince the Walkers to purchase a particular mine named Anaconda, Daly bought it himself and very quickly entered the ranks of the multi-millionaire club. Daly's initial success attracted large numbers of itinerant Irish miners to the area, well in advance of any other ethnics. Many of these miners decided to settle in Butte and put an end to their migratory ways.

Daly's preference for Irish miners translated into a community that enabled Irish Americans to thoroughly dominate the municipal rhythms of life. Catholic churches sprang up, as did Irish benevolent organizations and societies. Until his death in 1900, Daly catered to his Irish workers in a paternalistic style and avoided much of the labor agitation that soon followed his passing. In 1894, Daly spearheaded a vigorous campaign to have Anaconda, a town adjacent to Butte, designated as Montana's state capital but was compelled in the end to bow to Helena's candidacy. As in many other regions throughout the country, Montana's Irish miners formed labor organizations and agitated for the eight-hour workday and greater influence in hiring procedures, forming the Butte Miners Union (BMU), even before Daly's demise. And although Irish miners in Butte flirted with radical socialism, and supported Irish nationalist aspirations, the community that had sunk roots in the region became increasingly comfortable and more American in their outlook.

The best evidence for this newfound complacency was provided by two radical socialists and Irish nationalists, James Larkin and James Connolly, both of whom believed that Butte was fertile ground for both ideologies but found their efforts disappointing. In the fall of 1915, with the Great War already over a year in progress, Connolly had abandoned his efforts in Butte, as well as elsewhere in the States, and returned to Ireland, where he would ultimately play the martyr's role in the Easter rising of 1916. Larkin, however, continued his agitation for socialism and Irish nationalism in Butte, but discovered an ingrained timidity there that thwarted any progress. He even found it difficult to find a venue to deliver his parting shot against the city's Irish American community, eventually renting space at Finlander Hall, considered somewhat ironic since conservative Irish Americans had driven the Finns out of the BMU in the summer of 1914. In his speech, Larkin spared no venom at what he perceived as the intransigence of Irish Catholic conservatives to adopt a true working-class ethos and a full-throated support of Irish nationalism. His vitriol was largely reserved for those Irish politicians and comfortable union leaders who had betrayed the Irish ideal of combating oppression wherever they might discover it. After declaring his love for his native land, Larkin hammered away at those "Irish politicians and place hunters" that lived in Butte. He had come to Montana at the behest of "sooted-faced miners who worked down in these hells under the city," but found that traitorous labor leaders had demonstrated that they were no better than the "dirty instruments of oppression." In a blistering crescendo, Larkin invoked the names of legendary Irish patriots, such as Emmet, Mitchell, and Tone, noting that all of them would "spit in the faces of these renegade shoneen Irish of Butte."[26]

While Butte may have proven disappointing to the likes of Connolly and Larkin, the door had been opened for mainstream politicians to exploit the Irish presence in Montana. An Irish American Catholic, Thomas J. Walsh, born in Two Rivers, Wisconsin, had moved to Helena in 1890, armed with a law degree which he put to gainful use in mining litigation. Elected to the US Senate in 1912, Walsh became the leader of the Democratic Party of Montana, and quickly became one of the most important supporters of the Wilson administration, often placing himself as a broker between Irish American interests and the president's as the Great War emerged.[27]

26. David M. Emmons, *The Butte Irish: Class and Ethnicity in an American Mining Town, 1875–1925* (Urbana: University of Illinois Press, 1989), 351–53. The term "shoneen" had been coined by D. P. Moran, an Irish cultural nationalist, referring to Irish Catholics who aped English values and mannerisms. Both Connolly and Larkin attempted to link this term to Irish Americans who rejected appeals to Irish nationalism and radical socialism.

27. For Walsh's Irish American Catholic upbringing, see J. Leonard Bates, *Senator Thomas J. Walsh of Montana: Law and Political Affairs from TR to FDR* (Chicago: University of Illinois Press, 1999), 1–7.

CHAPTER 1

Irish immigrants and their sons and daughters wended their way as far as the Pacific coast in the second half of the nineteenth century. But nowhere in these far western states did the Irish settle as prolifically as in the city by the Bay of San Francisco. Early Irish immigrants made their way to Northern California even before the Mexican War, receiving land grants from Mexican landholders in the vicinity of Marin County. The Gold Rush of 1849 brought thousands to the San Francisco area, including many Irish prospectors, miners, and entrepreneurs eager to cash in on the prospective bounty there for the grasping. On the eve of the U.S. Civil War, the Irish were numerous enough to establish their own neighborhoods in the city of San Francisco and across the bay at Oakland. Irish laborers were on hand when the Central Pacific began its arduous task of chiseling a route through the Sierra Nevada Mountains in the late 1860s, and became greatly resentful when the railroad investors hired many Chinese as part of the labor force.[28] By 1870, Irish immigrants and their children were well ensconced in working class neighborhoods such as Irish Hill, located nearby an industrial sector known as Dogpatch. Unlike the Irish in the cities of the Eastern Seaboard, many Irish immigrants and their children in San Francisco enjoyed a high degree of socio-economic mobility, largely owing to a reduced level of social and religious intolerance and unobstructed access to promising opportunities. The relative balance between American-born and ethnics from the very beginning of the city's growth meant that the Catholic Church found fertile soil in which to flourish. The Archdiocese of San Francisco was canonically erected

---

28. An Irish immigrant from County Cork, Denis Kearney, settled in San Francisco in 1871. In 1877, he was responsible for bringing about the Workingmen's Party. He acquired a radical reputation for his demagoguery directed against the railroads, banks, greedy businesses, and the ethnic Chinese. An enthralling speaker, Kearney ended (in a manner like the Roman senator Cato the Elder on Carthage) every speech with the sentence, "And whatever happens, the Chinese must go." His popularity faded in the middle 1880s, leaving behind, as a questionable legacy, the passage of the Chinese Exclusion Act (1882). See Charles J. McClain, *In Search of Equality: The Chinese Struggle Against Discrimination in Nineteenth-Century America* (Berkeley: University of California Press, 1994), 79; and Andrew Gyory, *Closing the Gate: Race, Politics and the Chinese Exclusion Act* (Chapel Hill: University of North Carolina Press, 1998), 11.

in 1853 and was first appointed a Spanish bishop in the person of Joseph S. Alemany. The Church thrived under his tutelage, sprouting dozens of new parishes, many of which were served by Irish priests, until his death in 1884. He was replaced by Patrick William Riordan, who presided over even greater strides in the Church's growth until his passing shortly after the outbreak of the Great War in 1914.[29]

The ambient tolerance presiding over San Francisco meant that Irish Americans and Catholics were actively included in the political life of the city. San Franciscans chose their first Irish mayor years before New York's William R. Grace was elected in 1880. Several aldermen from the city's dozen wards were Irish, and the Democratic Party became the principal vehicle for both local and regional advancement. And it would be from the stronghold of San Francisco that Irish politicians would emerge and attain significant positions on a state and national level. Son of an Irish immigrant stonecutter, David C. Broderick arrived in San Francisco during the Gold Rush of 1849, where he flourished as an assayer of minted gold coins. The following year he vaulted into the office of state senator for the Bay Area district. From that point forward, Broderick virtually ruled San Francisco with a ruthless iron fist that would have made Tammany's Boss Croker blush with envy, and he became the veritable incarnation of municipal corruption. Selected as one of California's U.S. senators in 1857, he entered a frivolous duel with a political rival and was mortally wounded near the end of his second year in office. John Conness, a native of County Galway, came to the United States in 1836 as a fifteen-year-old boy. Like Broderick, he made his way to San Francisco during the Gold Rush of 1849. Despite two failed gubernatorial bids, his political rise in California was otherwise meteoric, and he was selected as a U.S. senator for California in 1863. A Democrat turned Union Republican during the Civil War, Conness worked closely with Abraham Lincoln in keeping California loyal to the war effort. Unlike many of his compatriots, Conness remained conscious of the native hostility toward immigrants,

29. Riordan's long career as archbishop and his somewhat permissive oversight of organized labor and Irish nationalists can be traced in James P. Gaffey, *Citizen of no mean city: Archbishop Patrick Riordan of San Francisco, 1841–1914* (Minneapolis: Consortium Books, 1976).

CHAPTER 1

advocating support for Chinese immigration and civil rights at a time when anti-Chinese bigotry was cresting towards high tide in California. When his term ended in 1869, Conness moved to Boston, dying in an insane asylum there in 1909. Succeeding Conness in office was Eugene Casserly, an Irish American journalist and lawyer who, like Broderick and Conness, moved to San Francisco during the Gold Rush. Upon his resignation from office in 1873, Casserly resumed practicing law in San Francisco, ever remaining active in the political life of the city until his death in 1883.[30]

Even with the retirement from the scene of politicos such as Broderick, Conness, and Casserly, Irish interests were carried by others in San Francisco's Irish community well into the twentieth century. Of note is the celebrated "Blind Boss," Christopher Augustine Buckley, very much in the mold of a boss in the heyday of political bosses. Son of an Irish stonemason, Buckley moved to San Francisco with his family in 1862 at the age of seventeen. As a young man, he acquired a position as a conductor on one of the city's Omnibus Railway Company's lines. By 1880, Buckley had transitioned to bartending at McGuire's Snug Saloon, a celebrated den owned by the impresario Thomas McGuire, builder of the Jenny Lind theaters. A "saloon boss," Buckley emerged in the last decade of the nineteenth century as the major force in the Democratic Party in San Francisco, influencing state affairs and even counseling President Grover Cleveland on federal patronage distribution throughout California.

San Francisco's Irish American political tradition reached its crowning height with the emergence of James D. Phelan on the political scene. His Irish immigrant father had arrived during the California Gold Rush and soon became wealthy as a trader, merchant, and banker. Phelan was born in San Francisco in 1861. Afforded all the

---

30. Melvin G. Holli and Peter d'A. Jones, eds., *Biographical Dictionary of American Mayors, 1820–1980: Big City Mayors* (Westport, CT: Greenwood Press, 1981), 106, 168. A somewhat caustic view of the political career of David C. Broderick can be found in Jeremiah Lynch, *A Senator of the Fifties: David C. Broderick, of California* (Seattle: Createspace Independent Publishing Platform, 2016 [reprint of 1911 edition]), 68–69; and R. A. Burchell, *The San Francisco Irish, 1848–1880* (Berkeley: University of California Press, 1980), 132–38.

benefits that wealth could bestow, Phelan graduated from St. Ignatius College in 1881 and studied law at the University of California at Berkeley. His first career foray was in banking, in which he greatly expanded the business that his father had established. He parlayed his position in the business community of San Francisco into election as the twenty-fifth Mayor of San Francisco, serving from 1897 to 1902. His early political career in San Francisco was marked by his attraction to the movement to exclude Japanese immigrants, securing presidential candidate's Woodrow Wilson's support for restricting Japanese immigration in 1912. Between stepping down as mayor in 1902 and his senatorial candidacy in 1914, Phelan resumed his business activities but remained politically active, always looking for ways to benefit his native community. He spearheaded the drive to expand the territorial limits of San Francisco by buying up land and water acreage, and led the acquisition of water rights from the Tuolumne River in Hetch Hetchy Valley. Ethan A. Hitchcock, Secretary of the Interior, attempted to block Phelan's designs, and John Muir, the great conservationist, proved a worthy adversary, but both their voices were eventually muted by President Theodore Roosevelt, who endorsed the permanent material development of the region. In the first popularly elected Senate race in 1914, Phelan was elected as one of California's senators, serving one term that ended in 1921. Along with Senator Thomas J. Walsh of Montana, Phelan became a stalwart in his support of the Wilson administration and played an instrumental role in the president's reelection bid in 1916. Both Walsh and Phelan would play intermediary roles in brokering Irish American interests during Wilson's presidency, as well as counseling the president on the progress of Irish nationalism from 1915 to 1920.[31]

31. Burchell, *The San Francisco Irish,* 153. Buckley became blind shortly after entering the Democratic Party. He compensated for this affliction by memorizing city ordinances, contracts, and other documents after having them read to him. See William A. Bullough, *The Blind Boss and His City: Christopher Augustine Buckley and Nineteenth-Century San Francisco* (Berkeley: University of California Press, 1979). For Phelan's obsessive anti-Japanese stance, see Roger Daniels, *The Politics of Prejudice: The Anti-Japanese Movement in California and the Struggle for Japanese Exclusion* (Berkeley: University of California Press, 1991).

CHAPTER 1

In and of itself, this catalogue of accrued political power is neither edifying nor useful in understanding the degree to which Irish American investment in America existed by the second decade of the twentieth century. But access to power and influence was one of the first building blocks in Irish American inclusion into the nation at large. All other matters, such as upward mobility and working-class organizational leadership, flowed from it, and without it, they would have been hard commodities to come by. As the fundamental constituency on which they maintained and expanded their own power, Irish Americans had their interests adeptly handled by these politicians,. who also brokered the transition of other ethnic minorities into the American fabric until such time as their own political cohesion and consciousness was established. Not only did political clout enable Irish Americans to advance their own agenda; it also served as a counterpoint in fending off the antagonism and opposition of nativist America. Most importantly, the exercise of political influence conferred a sense of American entitlement to the second and third generations of Irish Americans at the beginning of the twentieth century. Political voice, understood as long denied to the Irish in their historical consciousness, scarring their psyche, was the most tangible expression of membership and inclusion. There might well be remaining hurdles to overcome in the years ahead, but on the eve of the outbreak of the Great War, Irish Americans had indisputably staked their claims as Americans.

Toward Inclusion:
Irish Americans and Socio-Economic Mobility

Paradoxically, increased Irish American political power, especially as it correlated to the community's upward economic mobility, did not necessarily translate to conspicuous communal success in the latter part of the nineteenth century. Arguably, this economic languor may have been perpetrated and perpetuated by the stunting effect of the patronage system practiced by Irish American political machines during this period. Even as late as 1900, the majority of the Irish, particularly in the more concentrated enclaves of East Coast cities, did not figure prominently in the ranks of the professional classes, such as lawyers, physicians, brokers, and bankers. If, in the last two decades of the nineteenth century, the persistent image of the Irish as stalwarts in the police and fire departments, the postal system, and as general municipal workers—the spoils of patronage—proved satisfying and secure, they were not harbingers of upward mobility.

This economic portrait began changing somewhat after 1900. Second- and third-generation Irish Americans increasingly entered the ranks of the skilled worker and the middle class, yet another indication of their increased investment as Americans. Whereas scant few had soared to the top of the economic hierarchy, many could be found in middle-class positions, including shopkeepers, clerks, bookkeepers, and salesmen. Moreover, many sons whose fathers had been at the lowest rungs of the laboring class as day laborers, draymen, longshoremen, or stevedores were entering the ranks of skilled laborers and tradesmen, such as printers, machinists, steamfitters, plumbers, and painters. Even though many continued working as domestics and cooks, young Irish women of these generations were also entering the professional ranks, most conspicuously in the professions of teaching, and to a lesser degree, nursing.[32] One of the best indicators of the improving economic picture of the American Irish is that as they moved up, they began to move out. They were moving out of the old neighborhoods and ghettos of their parents' generation and into better precincts in the city. In New York, for instance, the Irish, despite nativist hopes that Brooklyn would remain a Protestant bastion, had flooded into this borough, tallying 27% of the population compared to 22% for native Protestants by 1890. Similar trends appeared in the

---

32. On Irish immigrant women's economic opportunities, and the corresponding advantages and disadvantages of domestic service, see Hasia R. Diner, *Erin's Daughters in America: Irish Immigrant Women in the Nineteenth Century* (Baltimore: Johns Hopkins University Press, 1983), 70–120. Relying mostly upon Diner's work, Kevin Kenny provides a succinct summary of Irish domestic service in Kevin Kenny, *The American Irish,* 146–50, as does Carol Groneman, "Working Class Immigrant Women in Mid Nineteenth Century New York: The Irish Woman's Experience," in *Journal of Urban History* 4, no. 3 (May 1978): 255–74. See also James R. Barrett, *The Irish Way: Becoming American in the Multiethnic City* (New York: The Penguin Press, 2012), 122–27.

CHAPTER 1

Bronx and in the Jackson Heights neighborhood of Queens. Many more forsook the city altogether and migrated to suburban New York's Long Island, Westchester County, New Jersey, and Connecticut. With each successive American generation becoming "more eager to come to terms with life in the United States ... the lot of the New York Irish improved." These middle-class aspirations, the object of gentle mocking, and perhaps somewhat pretentious badges of honor, were symbols of an emergent "Lace Curtain" Irish American at the dawn of the twentieth century, a conscious effort to shed their "shanty" identification.[33]

The essence of this new-found success and respectability can be seen glowingly in James T. Farrell's fictional characters in *Studs Lonigan: A Trilogy*. The scene opens in June 1916 with Studs's father, Patrick, sitting on the back porch, puffing contentedly on a stogy, a few moments before he would trundle off to his son's and daughter's graduation from St. Patrick's grammar school on Chicago's South Side. He reminisces about his own upbringing, the son of an Irish immigrant greenhorn, growing up in the shadows of the Union Stockyards, living in a veritable shack where the winter drafts were so cold, they often went to bed fully dressed. Now a painting contractor, Patrick could take pride in the fact that he had arrived at a "station where there weren't no real serious problems like poverty." He had recently moved his family into a comfortable home further south of the old neighborhood, which was being passed on to newer immigrants such as Poles, Lithuanians, Italians, and Blacks. On a lark, he mused about taking a trip to the old country, but harbored no doubts as to his true allegiance. He was "a good Catholic and a good American." If there was any identity crisis for Patrick Lonigan, as to whether

---

33. Timothy J. Meagher, *The Columbia Guide to Irish American History* (New York: Columbia University Press, 2005), 103–4. The phenomenon of moving up and out of old Irish strongholds in the inner city was occurring in places like Philadelphia, Boston, and Chicago as well. Kevin Kenny, *The American Irish: A History* (New York: Pearson Education, 2000), 213–15. See also Terry N. Clark, "The Irish Ethnic Identity and the Spirit of Patronage," *Ethnicity* 2 (1978): 305–59; and David C. Hammack, *Power and Society: Greater New York at the Turn of the Century* (New York: Russell Sage Foundation, 1982), 325.

STAKING THE AMERICAN CLAIM

he was Irish or American, it was but whimsical. He, as many of his generation, was first and foremost American.[34]

The one urban exception to this general trend of upward mobility would be found in Boston. On the eve of the Great War, Irish Americans there had made but desultory socio-economic progress. In 1900, the Boston Irish ranked the lowest among native and other immigrant groups in professional occupations, second lowest in general white-collar positions, and lowest in skilled labor employment. While a strong native bigotry played a part in stunting Irish economic growth, limiting economic opportunities in Boston well into the early twentieth century, it was not the only factor. The relative dearth of industrial or occupational skills among the earlier immigrant arrivals impeded progress even more. Handicapped by unusable skills and confronted by nativist obstruction, the Boston Irish tended to close ranks and withdraw into isolation, developing what Oscar Handlin described as a "full, independent institutional life ... a society within a society." Whereas American Catholic leaders in cities throughout the rest of the country were willing to embrace change and reform aimed at elevating the temporal lives of their faithful, it was Boston's misfortune to be saddled with a prelate who almost reveled in his laity's backwardness. Under the tutelage of William Cardinal O'Connell, installed in the Boston Archdiocese in 1911, Boston's Irish Catholics were exhorted by His Eminence to embrace their poverty in much the same manner as did Jesus Christ. O'Connell actively encouraged his faithful to view their assigned lot in life as an enabling vehicle on their path towards eternal rewards in heaven. Despite some tangible progress in their lives as World War I approached, the Boston Irish would continue to struggle upwards and would be obliged to assuage their wounded pride by embracing the comforting, if not self-degrading, platitudes of their local ordinary.[35]

---

34. James T. Farrell, *Studs Lonigan: A Trilogy* (New York: Vanguard Press, 1935), 12–20. Timothy J. Meagher skillfully weaves this same image in the introduction to *From Paddy to Studs*, 1–2.

35. Stephan Thernstrom, *The Other Bostonians: Poverty and Progress in the American Metropolis, 1860–1970* (Cambridge, MA: Harvard University Press, 1973), 131, 191; Oscar Handlin, *Boston's Immigrants: A Study in Acculturation*

47

CHAPTER 1

Irish Americans in Labor Organizations

Not all Irish Americans had deserted the ranks of the laboring classes, particularly in heavy industry and the coal mines. Still, the general sense of Irish American empowerment in the last two decades of the nineteenth century drew many of them into the nascent labor organizations as leaders and activists. The list of labor leadership at the turn of the century reads not unlike the names in a Dublin phone directory, which was noticeable enough to attract the ire and scorn of the WASP establishment. In the anthracite-rich coals fields of Appalachian West Virginia and Pennsylvania, Irish immigrant miners had a long history of labor agitation. In the 1870s, some Irish miners bonded together in a clandestine vigilante organization, dubbed the Molly Maguires, inspired somewhat loosely by agrarian agitation in rural Ireland and among workers in the Irish sections of Liverpool. Irish miners throughout the abundant fields of northeastern Pennsylvania violently struck out against the rapacious practices of mine operators. In 1876, authorities rounded up the principal activists, held show trials, and promptly executed them by hanging.[36]

The working environment for the Irish in the coal fields only continued to deteriorate in the years after the collapse of the Molly Maguires. Mine operators began importing a virtual cornucopia of Eastern and Southern European immigrants. Slavs, Hungarians, Italians, and Balkan and Baltic ethnics, flooded the coal regions. Desperate for jobs, they were willing to work for little money and under ever more dangerous conditions. In 1890, the United Mine Workers of America (UMWA) was formed and elected John B. Rae, a native Scot, their first president. John McBride, who had co-founded the union with Rae, succeeded him as president two years later. McBride, a native of

---

(Cambridge, MA: Belknap Press of Harvard University, 1959), 215–16, 228–29; William Cardinal O'Connell, *Recollections of Seventy Years* (Boston: Houghton Mifflin, 1934), 33; and Donna Merwick, *Boston's Priests, 1848–1910* (Cambridge, MA: Harvard University Press, 1973), 182–83.

36. A completely coherent understanding of the Molly Maguires is somewhat challenging to find. The best understanding may well be found in Kevin Kenny, *Making Sense of the Molly Maguires* (New York: Oxford University Press, 1998).

Ohio, vacated his post in 1894 when he unseated labor icon Samuel Gompers, briefly, as president of the American Federation of Labor. During his tenure as advocate for the Bituminous Coal Miners, he presided over an unsuccessful eight-week strike, one that encouraged hundreds of non-union miners to descend upon the coal fields and replace strikers to extract the black nuggets from the earth. McBride's UMWA position was filled by Phil Penna, a native of Cornwall, who inherited the fallout from the failed strike of 1894. During Penna's two- year term, membership in the UMWA plummeted, as did its treasury, forcing Penna to suspend most union operations and to cease publishing the union newsletter. Declining to run for reelection in 1896, Penna was followed by Michael Ratchford. Born in County Clare in 1860, his family left Ireland and settled in Massillon, Ohio in 1872, where young Michael began working in the coal mines. When the UMWA was formed in 1890, Ratchford led a local union in Ohio and in 1897 became president of the parent organization. Although he would serve but a single term, ending in 1898, Ratchford reenergized the union. He organized a successful national coal miners' strike in 1897, lasting nearly three months, which resulted in mine owners agreeing to sign a national master contract, although it did not extend to miners in West Virginia. The agreement established the eight-hour workday and increased pay based on tonnage mined. More than anything, the largely unheralded Ratchford had re-invigorated the membership of the UMWA, and when he bowed out of the presidency in 1898, the ranks of union members had increased threefold.[37]

Ratchford's foundational efforts were greatly magnified by his successor as president, the legendary John Mitchell, who in addition to holding other labor-related posts, served as head of the UMWA for ten years and clearly guided it on the path to success. He was born the son of Irish immigrants in Braidwood, Illinois in 1870. Orphaned at age six, he began working in the coal mines to support the remaining family. He joined the ill-fated Knights of Labor in 1885 and at the

---

37. Biographical summaries of these first four UMWA presidents can be found in Gary M. Fink, ed., *Biographical Dictionary of American Labor* (Westport, CT: Greenwood Press, 1984).

CHAPTER 1

age of twenty became one of the charter members of the UMWA. In the two years preceding his rise to the presidency, Mitchell had observed two incidents that made it patently clear to him that there was still much more to be done on behalf of miners. On June 28, 1896, a poorly propped pillar (one that had been known for weeks to be dangerous) collapsed with a roar at the Twin Shaft Mine of the Newton Coal Company in Pittston, Pennsylvania. Ninety miners were reported to be in the mine at the time. Fifty-eight of them, men, and boys, were killed, their bodies never recovered. Most of the dead were Irish and Lithuanian miners. An official inquiry into the disaster merely produced a few safety recommendations and absolved the Newton Coal Company of any culpability. Then, on September 10, 1897, an unarmed band of strikers, mostly Slavic miners, highly resented by established English-speaking miners, marched on a mine site near Hazleton. They were confronted by a sheriff's posse on the Luzerne County line near Lattimer. After a brief scuffle, the posse poured volleys into the ranks of the strikers, killing nineteen and wounding scores. Nearly every one of the dead and wounded were shot with their backs to the posse. Again, inquiries and trials were held but the posse members were completely exonerated.[38]

What Mitchell will always be remembered for was his management and direction of the Great Anthracite Coal Strike of 1902, a strike that was not only hugely successful but one that required the intervention of both President Theodore Roosevelt and capitalist magnate J. P. Morgan. There had been a great deal of change in the five years since mine owners had agreed to the terms of the 1897 contract, particularly in the fields of northeast Pennsylvania. Many independent companies had flooded the region and, to remain competitive, owners cut wages, refused to recognize unions, and paid but scant attention to mine safety. Mitchell's genius lay in his ability to communicate to a

---

38. John Mitchell was apparently of Irish-Protestant stock, as he converted to Catholicism around 1907. For Mitchell's early years leading up to his selection as president of the UMWA, see Craig Phelan, *Divided Loyalties: The Public and Private Life of Labor Leader John Mitchell* (New York: State University of New York Press, 1994), 1–92. See also Michael Novak, *The Guns of Lattimer* (New York: Transaction Publishers, 1996, reprint).

complex mosaic of ethnic miners, many of whom were as disdainful of each other as they were of the owners, that they needed to look past their own differences and unite in common interest. He was also able to secure enough pledges from miners to stage a wildcat strike wherein miners walked out of the various mines simultaneously and stayed out until their demands were addressed. And he was judicious in choosing October as the time to strike, the time when demand for heating would rise. Mine owners remained intransigent until Roosevelt prevailed upon Morgan to talk sense to them. The strike ended with most of the goals attained.

Mitchell was greatly aided in his efforts by a firebrand champion of labor in the person of Mary Harris "Mother" Jones, a native of County Cork, Ireland, born in 1837. She and her husband emigrated from Ireland and moved to Chicago, where she was employed as a schoolteacher and dressmaker. Tragedy struck in 1867, when yellow fever swept away her husband and all four of her children, and was compounded four years later when the Great Chicago Fire destroyed her dress shop. On the heels of these misfortunes, Jones turned to labor organizing, beginning with the emergent Knights of Labor, and upon its decline following the Haymarket Square Riot of 1886, she joined the ranks of the UMWA. She had already become radicalized to a degree through her relationship with her brother, Father William R. Harris, a priest, teacher, and writer working in St. Catherines, Ontario. But the more she became embroiled in the great labor struggles of the last two decades of the nineteenth century, the more she was estranged from both her brother and the Church, believing the latter was more likely to come down on the side of capital than on that of the average working man. She referred to priests and ministers as "sky pilots" for their emphasis on the afterlife to the detriment of this side of the soil. In her early activism, Jones ignored many of the issues, such as temperance, that middle class social reformers of the late nineteenth century espoused, yet her aversion to embracing some of the emerging progressive reforms, such as female suffrage, distanced her from a new generation of reformers. Described by one detractor as the "most dangerous woman in America," Jones was tireless in her attacks on capital and her vigorous pursuit of labor reform. She was a riveting

CHAPTER 1

speaker and a charismatic union organizer, and spent her final years as a clarion crusader against child labor. Although the Catholic hierarchy kept a respectful distance from Mother Jones, Irish American workers practically worshipped her.[39]

Toward Cultural Inclusion in America

Again, when it came to staking their claim as Americans, Irish Americans were in the vanguard of immigrant groups at the turn of the century. The percentage of the Irish population that emigrated to America between 1850 and 1914 was more than double that of any other nation—and they were among the highest percentage of those who sunk roots and stayed. During this period, less than 5% of Irish immigrants chose to return to Ireland. Along with the Swedes, the Irish were foremost among European ethnicities not to consider such a course of action. Only Jewish refugees from Eastern Europe, for whom there was little option afforded, topped the Irish for permanent settlement in the United States during this period. By contrast, other Southern and Eastern European immigrants viewed immigration to the United States as a temporary arrangement to secure enough money to permit them to return to their native lands. Though many Italians, for instance, settled permanently in America, as many as 49% between 1905 and 1920 elected to return to their native soil.[40]

    39. Leon Fink, *Workingmen's Democracy: The Knights of Labor and American Politics* (Urbana: University of Illinois Press, 1985), 6–16; Robert E. Weir, *Beyond Labor's Veil: The Culture of the Knights of Labor* (State College, PA: Penn State University Press, 2006), 94; Phelan, *Divided Loyalties*, 1–92; Elliott J. Gorn, *Mother Jones: The Most Dangerous Woman in America* (New York: Hill & Wang, 2002), 33, 45, 74, 81–87, 280–94. Both Mitchell and Jones had cut their activist teeth in the Knights of Labor, which reached its pinnacle in the mid-1880s. The head of the Knights at that time was Terence Powderly, an Irish American Catholic. It is estimated that, at its height in early 1886, there were 800,000 member Knights, the vast majority of whom were Catholics and, among them, many were Irish Americans.
    40. Timothy J. Hatton and Jeffrey G. Williamson, *The Age of Mass Migration: Causes and Economic Impact* (New York: Oxford University Press, 1998), 9; Miller, *Emigrants and Exiles*, 302; and Donna Gabaccia, *Italy's Many Diasporas* (Seattle: University of Washington Press, 2000), 141.

STAKING THE AMERICAN CLAIM

Permanent residency, political empowerment, and economic investment had become the foundational blocks of Irish American claims for inclusion in the American Republic at the turn of the century. And it was being accomplished without a craven submission to WASP culture. Rather than acquiescing to a "melting pot" style of assimilation, the Irish forged their way into American culture, massaging it, and adding to it in such a way as to inaugurate a much broader and more diversified understanding of American society. At the turn of the century, Irish Americans were, as celebrated by Daniel Patrick Moynihan, "everywhere" in the heartbeat of American life, making the Irish increasingly American in the process. Irish American cultural expression, derided in the middle years of the nineteenth century, steadily became respectable, even trendy, by the century's close.

Perhaps the most prolific cultural contributions came in the musical and theatrical worlds. At the risk of shortchanging the multitude of Irish American contributors in these fields, it is nonetheless necessary to point out the incredible success of Edward Harrigan and Tony Hart in the waning decades of the nineteenth century. Celebrated theater critic William Dean Howells spent much of his life searching for a genuinely indigenous American dramatist, and in 1886 he announced he had found it in the person of one Edward Harrigan. "Here was a man," Howells declared, "who wrote, directed, acted and managed his works in the manner of a Shakespeare or a Moliere. Here was a social realist on the order of Dickens or Zola." Such accolades must have raised the hackles of Howell's highbrow readership, for Harrigan was not the product of a university or a conservatory, but rather the self-educated son of an immigrant Irish sailor, who ran away from the Irish slums of Manhattan and went to sea for himself. When he eventually teamed up with actor Tony Hart and songwriter David Braham, Harrigan launched an entirely new direction in theater and music—one that would eventually create Broadway Theater, as it would come to be known, as well as the sheet music industry of Tin Pan Alley. The direction was decidedly popular in its orientation and quintessentially Irish American in its character.

While the sheer output and enormous popularity of the Harrigan and Hart partnership commended itself, it was the pertinence of its

CHAPTER 1

themes and the rearticulation of what it meant to be Irish in America that was most salutary. Harrigan detested the coarse and deprecating stage stereotype of Paddy that encouraged native-born Americans to laugh at the Irish; instead, he aimed to induce Americans to laugh *with* them. Harrigan did not abandon all stereotypes, but he did massage and transform them so that supposed defects in character were morphed into virtues. Paddy's slowness to climb the social ladder and his reticence to abandon his lifelong friends became the virtues of unpretentiousness and fraternal loyalty. Harrigan established a means by which vaudeville, already in existence around the end of the U.S. Civil War, flourished and reached its height of popularity in the period just before the Great War began. Again, Irish Americans were at the forefront of the specialty acts, skits, burlesque comedy, singing, and dancing that characterized this form of entertainment, one that attracted crowds across the socio-economic spectrum of American society. Perhaps, in a world that was shaken by great industrial and technological changes and modernity in general, the introduction of bombastic comedy, general levity, and lighthearted sentimentality through performance provided immigrants a vehicle towards assimilation. "Sitting in the audience," William Williams avers, the "assimilating immigrants could see their former greenhorn selves ... lost in a world of strange customs and words, beset by sharp hustlers of their own group but still, somehow, surviving." Who better, it would seem, than the Irish to provide a palliative and restorative tonic for the vagaries and vicissitudes of modern life? Emerging out of the vaudeville tradition was one of the best-known Irish American theatrical songwriters—George M. Cohan—who would, throughout the Great War, be one of the most enthusiastic promoters of American patriotism.[41]

 41. Howells quoted in Samuel G. Freedman, "What Musicals and Comedy Owe to Harrigan and Hart," *New York Times,* February 27, 1985; William H. A. Williams, '*Twas Only an Irishman's Dream: The Image of Ireland and the Irish in American Popular Song Lyrics, 1800–1920* (Urbana: University of Illinois Press, 1996), 128–30, 141–42; Timothy J. Meagher, "The Fireman on the Stairs: Communal Loyalties in the Making of Irish America," in J. J. Lee and Marion R. Casey, eds., *Making the Irish American: History and Heritage of the Irish in the United States* (New York: New York University Press, 2006), 625.

STAKING THE AMERICAN CLAIM

The same ironic wit and hint of social inadequacy that Harrigan revealed in the late nineteenth carried over into the general field of hyphenate literature that Irish Americans produced in the early twentieth century. Once again, there is the potential of damning by faint praise in mentioning but a handful of the many Irish Americans who dipped their quills in the field of fictional writing during the Great War era. Eugene O'Neill, the brilliant, sometimes pessimistic dramatist, started his career in 1917 by writing a series of one-act plays that tapped into the Gaelic Revivalist School of the Abbey Theater in Dublin. Some of his later works provided autobiographical insights—particularly *Long Day's Journey into Night*, in which the disintegration of the fictional Tyrone family mirrored his own. A "damning indictment of family and culture," O'Neill somberly magnifies "Irish-American dysfunction and failure." Posthumously, his wife released for production another of his plays, *A Touch of the Poet*, that portrays the life of a hard-drinking Irish immigrant of the early nineteenth century, Con Melody, who vainly hopes to retain the status he had enjoyed in the Ireland he had left behind. It is a mere phantasm. His feeble attempts to stand above his fellow Irish immigrants by wearing a British military uniform and forbidding his daughter to speak with a brogue comes crashing down at the end with his drunken cavorting and revelry with low-life Irish neighbors. O'Neill was joined by other Irish Americans, such as Betty Smith, James T. Farrell, John O'Hara, and F. Scott Fitzgerald, all of whom tried to come to terms with what it meant to be both Irish and American in the post-World War I era. All of them struggled to reconcile their middle-class status (in Fitzgerald's case, upper-middle class) with their shared Gaelic roots. In the end, both traditions, Irish and American, played substantial roles in their personal catharses.[42]

On the more popular plane, spanning the turn of the century, a couple of literary contributors are worth mentioning. One is the journalist, humorist, and social commentator, Finley Peter Dunne. Of Irish ancestry, Dunne was born in Chicago in 1867, and after completing

---

42. Daniel J. Casey and Robert E. Rhodes, "The Tradition of Irish-American Writers: The Twentieth Century," in Lee and Casey, *Making the Irish American*, 649–54; Ron Ebest, "The Irish Catholic Schooling of James T. Farrell, 1914–1923," *Eire-Ireland* 30, no. 4 (Winter 1996): 18–32.

CHAPTER 1

high school in 1884, he entered the ranks as a reporter and editor with a local Chicago newspaper. He hit his mark in 1893 with the creation of a serialized dialect sketch in which his spokesman was an Irish bartender-philosopher, Mr. Martin Dooley, a resident of Bridgeport, an Irish neighborhood on Chicago's South Side. Mr. Dooley would find his way into the national press, entertaining countless readers until the sketches came to an end in 1919. One of Dunne's greatest fans, Theodore Roosevelt, often the butt end of Mr. Dooley's witty observations, cultivated the artist's friendship and invited Dunne to both the White House and to his home at Oyster Bay, Long Island. In his earliest sketches, Dunne portrays Dooley in desperate straits back in his poverty-stricken native Ireland; he comes to America only to become disillusioned by the hard life here. As Marion Casey and Robert Rhodes astutely observed, Dooley's life, as revealed by Dunne over the course of many years, became a paradigm for all immigrants in its depiction of the squalor and hardship that accompanied the transition from the old to new worlds. Rather than dismiss Dooley as a bitter malcontent, Dunne reveals him as a sensitive, generous, well-informed, and honest man, a humanist of the highest order. Martin Dooley became the quintessential Irishman and the model for Irish characters in Irish American literature to follow. But he is also the model of an Irish immigrant who had transitioned into becoming an American.[43]

Like Dunne, George McManus, a son of Irish immigrants from St. Louis, was interested in examining the comical interaction, the proverbial yin and yang, between Irish Americans grasping for social respectability and the equally strong pull to remain true to their humble and sociable roots. A skilled cartoonist, McManus hit the jackpot with his creation of a comic strip known as *Bringing Up Father*, alternately known as *Jiggs*, or *Maggie and Jiggs*. First released in 1913, his creation became an immediate success and was syndicated with McManus at the creative helm until his death in 1954. The strip was a playful swipe at the travails of a *nouveau-riche* Irish American couple, Maggie and Jiggs. Jiggs, on the one hand, represented Irish Americans

43. Casey and Rhodes, "The Tradition of Irish-American Writers," 650–51; Charles Fanning, *The Irish Voice in America: 250 Years of Irish-American Fiction*, 2nd ed. (Lexington: University of Kentucky Press, 2000), 153–237.

"in their ascendancy into the sweet-smelling region of money." His penchant for associating with his old working-class cronies was offset by his wife Maggie's shock at such recidivism; Maggie, on the other hand, was always attempting to solicit an invitation to the opera from the Van Snoots, or some other feckless members of Manhattan's aristocracy. For forty years, the very popular strip played out this rollicking Irish American success story. It was hardly accidental that this playful, yet respectful, portrayal of Maggie and Jiggs included an English son-in-law, irreverently named Lord Worthnotten.[44]

During this era when Irish Americans were showcasing their respectability and cultural uniqueness, they still maintained a vigilant watch over, and displayed a raw sensitivity about, cultural expressions that dredged up old stereotypes or somehow reflected poorly upon their condition. Whereas most of these assaults were carried out by nativists, venting their spleens over Irish American attachment to the Church of Rome, there were occasions when Irish American Catholics felt compelled to strike back against what they perceived as gratuitous insults hurled towards them. The Ancient Order of Hibernians sallied forth to counter such slights, adding their demands that the pernicious Irish stereotypes come to an end. One such casualty of Irish American disfavor was John Millington Synge's play *The Playboy of the Western World*, which premiered in the Abbey Theater in Dublin to full scale rioting stirred up by Irish nationalists who perceived the play as both an insult to public morals and an affront against Ireland itself. It was hardly surprising, then, that when the play was introduced in the United States in 1911, it was greeted in similar fashion. On opening night in New York, hecklers treated the cast with a chorus of disapproval, throwing rotten vegetables and lobbing stink bombs, while men scuffled in the aisles. John Devoy, the premier American Irish nationalist of the time, stood up at one point and shouted, "Son of a bitch, that's not Irish." In Philadelphia, the theatrical company was arrested and charged with putting on an immoral performance, though the charges were soon dismissed. In truth, there was already an established tradition in Irish cities in the Northeast to disrupt any

44. William Kennedy, introduction to *Jiggs Is Back* by George McManus (Berkeley, CA: Celtic Books, 1986), 7–8.

CHAPTER 1

shows that perpetuated the stereotypes of "Irish men as baboons and Irish women as oafish and unfeminine." In 1903, stink bombs had been lofted on to the stage in Philadelphia for the vaudeville play, *McFadden's Row of Flats*, and in the same year that Synge's *Playboy of the Western World* debuted in Dublin, a crowd of Irish nationalists hounded the duo of cross-dressing Irish impersonators—the Russell Brothers—off the stage in New York City. The Irish American press was joined by the Catholic press, which judged the play as insidious for its churlish treatment of women and the Church. It was regarded by many Irish Americans as a "degrading spectacle which set back the course of Irish nationalism for years to come."[45]

Irish immigrants and their children were able to thread their way deeper into the evolving American cultural fabric of the turn of the century by their involvement in sports, both on the amateur and professional levels. The industrial and technological developments of the Gilded Age, particularly the rise of steel-constructed stadium facilities, and advancements in transportation, permitting attendance at events at greater distances, allowed for a new age of professional sports to develop. Certainly, the Irish brought their physically demanding games of rugby and Gaelic football to the fore, along with numerous other recreational sports, enabling them to retain their uniquely Irish identity. By the early twentieth century, organized Gaelic Leagues were formed and in many urban parks, such as Prospect Park in Brooklyn and Gaelic Park in St. Louis, games were routinely played with the outcomes reported in many of the Catholic newspapers. But it was on the national level that the Irish made their most notable mark, particularly in professional boxing and baseball.

---

45. John J. Appel, "From Shanties to Lace Curtains: The Irish Image in *Puck*, 1877–1910," *Comparative Studies in Society and History* 13 (October 1971): 365–75; William Shannon, *The American Irish: A Political and Social Portrait* (New York: Macmillan, 1963), 263; M. Alison Kibler, *Censoring Racial Ridicule: Irish, Jewish, and African American Struggles over Race and Representation* (Chapel Hill: University of North Carolina Press, 2015), 54–55; Alan Himber, ed., *The Letters of John Quinn to William Butler Yeats* (Ann Arbor, MI: UMI Research Press, 1983), 18; and Terry Golway, *Irish Rebel: John Devoy and America's Fight for Freedom* (New York: St. Martin's Press, 1998), 185–86.

STAKING THE AMERICAN CLAIM

Pugilism was nothing new to the Irish. And it became ever more popular in the United States in the second half of the nineteenth century. But it would not become an accepted professional sport until the close of century, even though it remained banned in many states. The Irish had figured prominently in amateur boxing as early as the antebellum era, and like many ethnic and racial successors, used it as a vehicle to lift themselves out of poverty and obscurity. Among boxers who rose to the top of their careers, none could match John L. Sullivan for sheer notoriety, a second-generation Irish immigrant, born and raised in Boston. Recognized as the first heavyweight champion of the sport, the rough-hewn and fond connoisseur of the "bachelor subculture of the saloon," Sullivan became the first boxing celebrity, possessed of such a flamboyant flair that his fame reached the distant shores of the globe. His title years spanned the transformation of the sport from bare-knuckled to gloved boxing as outlined in the Marquess of Queensbury rules, making the sport less philistine and more acceptable in conventional society's eyes. Interestingly, when he was finally defeated and forced to relinquish the title to another Irish American, James "Gentleman Jim" Corbett, in a bout hosted in New Orleans in 1892, he was said to remark to the crowd that "if I had to be licked I'm glad I was licked by an American." Considered the father of modern-day boxing, Corbett lost an 1897 title bout to Anglo-Irish challenger, Bob Fitzsimmons, who held the title for two years, ultimately losing to a former Corbett protégé and sparring partner, James Jeffries. Both Fitzsimmons and Corbett vainly attempted to wrest the title out of Jeffries' hands during the champ's reign, one that came to an end with his voluntary retirement in 1905. Neither Sullivan nor Corbett ever considered crossing the color line by scheduling a title bout with a black challenger. In 1910, Jeffries was ill-advisedly coaxed out of retirement to fight the black boxer Jack Johnson, who had won the title in a victory over Tommy Burns in 1908. Dubbed the "Fight of the Century," Jeffries became one of several "Great White Hopes" to try and unseat Johnson. In a racially charged promotion to the fight, Jeffries, though contemptuous of black boxers, refused to participate in the unsavory rhetoric, remarking only that the best man would win the fight. A six-year retirement and a bloated 227lb. frame

CHAPTER 1

did not serve Jeffries well. Worn down by the 14th round, Jeffries was knocked to the canvass three times. His handlers threw in the towel and Johnson retained the title he had won in 1908.[46]

The Irish American affinity for pugilism may not have earned them a revered place in the halls of civilization, but it did earn them a niche of respectability in American society that still attached great importance to the rubrics of manly behavior. The bold expression of physicality, courage, and pluck were essential features of the American male ethos. Other immigrant ethnics took their cues from the Irish by dropping their own surnames and adopting Irish-sounding ones. This was conspicuously the case with Jewish and Italian boxers. A 1903 report in the *National Police Gazette* noted that boxing fans invariably gave furious cheers for an Irish boxer, good-humored tolerance for a German one, but distinct hostility to an Italian or black boxer. Promoters felt it necessary for Italian boxers to adopt Irish names to become palatable to the predominantly Irish boxing audience. Tony Caponi, who fought between 1902 and 1917, changed his professional name to T. C. O'Brien. Heavyweight contender Andrew Chiariglione, exasperated over the inability of announcers to pronounce his name correctly, was said to have bellowed at one pre-fight ceremony, "Oh hell, just call me Jim Flynn." From that point onward he became known as "Fireman" Jim Flynn, the only fighter to ever knock out the legendary Jack Dempsey.[47]

---

46. Ralph Wilcox, "Irish-Americans in Sports," in Lee and Casey, *Making the Irish American*, 444–45. Adam Pollack does a remarkably good job in covering the boxing careers of the Irish American giants of the ring, Sullivan and Corbett. See Adam J. Pollack, *John L. Sullivan: The Career of the First Gloved Heavyweight Champion* (Jefferson, NC: McFarland Publishing, 2006) and, *In the Ring with James J. Corbett* (Iowa City, IA: WIN BY KO Publications, 2012).

47. Rolando Vitale, "Italian Boxer, Irish Name: Inside the Ropes of America's Ring," *Italian America* 10 (Spring 2016), 10–13. Heavyweight Champion Tommy Burns was born a German Canadian with the name Noah Brusso. He adopted the Scottish, although, possibly Irish, name of Burns. See Dan McCaffery, *Tommy Burns: Canada's Unknown World Heavyweight Champion* (Toronto: Lorimer Press, 2000), 11–12. See also James Silas Rogers, *Irish-American Autobiography: The Divided Hearts of Athletes, Priests, Pilgrims and More* (Washington, DC: The Catholic University of America Press, 2016), 7–20.

STAKING THE AMERICAN CLAIM

The second sport that attracted large numbers of Irish Americans, and one in which they excelled around the turn of the century, was baseball. By the latter part of the nineteenth century, baseball, on competitive, recreational, and professional levels, had earned the sobriquet, "the national pastime." Although liberal arguments were made that the sport was loosely based upon an ancient Gaelic game of *Iomain*, baseball was quintessentially American. Irish Americans flocked to the diamond, and while other immigrants embraced the sport as well, it was Irish players who garnered the laurels for Irish America. One stroll through the Baseball Hall of Fame in Cooperstown, New York, Ralph Wilcox contends, provides sufficient evidence of the commanding position Irish Americans held around the turn of the century. As in the case of boxing, the reputation of Irish American players was so great that others took to adopting Irish names to promote advancement in their careers. And because baseball was virtually synonymous with being American, it was a sport that enabled the Irish player, spectator, and fan to embrace an American identification.[48]

On the Matter of Ireland's Freedom

And so it was on the eve of the Great War that in the political, socio-economic, and cultural arenas Irish Americans were striding unapologetically into the American mainstream. But they did so without forfeiting their unique characteristics, helping to mold an expanding understanding of what it meant to be American. Two matters, however, remained a troubling source of contention for Irish American Catholics as well as a focus of suspicion about them, at the very moment they

48. Ralph Wilcox, "Irish-Americans and Sports," 447–48. Cornelius McGillicuddy, a.k.a. Connie Mack, was an icon of Irish American respectability. As a player, he was of mediocre ability and was known as a trickster. His real claim to fame was as a manager of the Philadelphia Athletics, a position he held for fifty years. He insisted that his players abide by a set of "Gentlemen's Rules," managed from the dugout in sport coat, tie and bowler hat. A devout Catholic, he would not permit profanity, obscene language or personal insults coming from the bench. See Rogers, *Irish-American Autobiography*, 20–25. Ty Cobb, arguably the dirtiest and most reviled figures in baseball, declared, "I shall never forget Connie Mack's gentleness and gentility." Quoted in *New York Times*, September 19, 1948.

CHAPTER 1

made inroads into the fabric of American society. One of these issues was the long history of Irish nationalist aspirations, dating back to the early decades of the nineteenth century, and the corresponding hatred and distrust of the British who had thralled the Irish for centuries. Although Irish American interest in the cause of Irish nationalism had roots in the early history of the American republic, it came into sharper focus by the mid-nineteenth century. The Famine immigrants and those who followed them brought with them both an inferiority complex as a downtrodden people and an intense hatred of their former British overlords. Interestingly, the fulcrum of Irish American animus towards Great Britain was not centered in Ireland itself but, rather, rested on nativist degradation of the Irish here in America. The disgrace, ridicule, and social ostracism the American Irish experienced at the hands British Protestant stock in the United States was rooted in the fact that they were descendants of a subject people back in Ireland. Many Irish Americans felt that their status in America could only improve when the day dawned that Ireland became a free and independent nation. In this scenario, Irish American nationalism was very much an American phenomenon. The springs of Irish American nationalism "are to be found in the realities of loneliness and alienation, and of poverty and prejudice." In many respects, by the late nineteenth century, it was a yearning for respectability.[49]

All the same, a door was open for Irish Americans in the second half of the nineteenth century to freely vent their vitriol towards the British, as they shared with native-borns an antipathy and distrust of British foreign policy. Ever since the United States won their independence from Great Britain in 1783, and created their own republic in 1789, the British had loomed in the minds of all Americans as the proverbial bogeyman and arch-nemesis of American foreign policy. This disdain for the British continued for the duration of the nineteenth century. Moreover, British imperial designs were fodder for anti-British sentiment in America; hence Irish Americans could gleefully join in denunciation of British policy and participate fully

49. Brown, *Irish-American Nationalism, 1870–1890*, 24; Michael F. Funchion, "Chicago's Irish Nationalists, 1881–1890," (PhD dissertation, Loyola University, Chicago, 1976), 262.

in the popular American sport of "twisting the [British] Lion's tail." In April 1882, *Harper's Weekly* featured a Thomas Nast caricature of Democratic Senator Daniel Vorhees grabbing the British Lion by the tail and whirling him around the Senate chamber while his anti-British "Irish-American Speech" rests on his desk. Similarly, the English magazine Puck limned a portrait of a defiant President Cleveland corkscrewing the Lion's tail over the Venezuelan Boundary dispute in 1895. Invoking the Monroe Doctrine, Cleveland called for a congressional boundary commission, whose findings would be enforced by the U.S. government, to rule in this dispute. On October 3, 1899, the commission found largely in favor of Venezuela. During the intervening years, talk of a war with Great Britain had circulated in the American press.[50]

British acquiescence to the American commission's findings in 1900 marked a signal moment in Anglo-American relations and dictated the way Irish Americans would lobby for Irish freedom here in America. In late 1899, at the same moment Britain meekly conceded to the findings of the Venezuelan Boundary Commission, the British became embroiled in a bitter war with the Boers of South Africa. It was a cathartic moment in the history of the sprawling British Empire. Britannia suddenly realized she was alone and without any friends and allies. Virtually all the European nations had turned their backs on her. The young German Empire, with stakes of her own in Southwest Africa, brazenly declared sympathy with the Boer cause. Additionally, Britain realized that while the "sun never sets on the British Empire," her colonial possessions were so widely scattered throughout the world that she was no longer positioned to safeguard them all. She was now willing to concede whatever minimal imperial interests she

---

50. On the matter of the Venezuelan Boundary Dispute and Britain's tacit acknowledgement of the Monroe Doctrine, see George C. Herring, *From Colony to Superpower: U.S. Foreign Relations since 1776* (New York: Oxford University Press, 2008), 306–8. Earlier, Americans generally had taken solace in the resolution reached in the Washington Treaty of 1871 in which Britain came to terms with American anger over Britain's interference in the American Civil War, particularly the *CSS Alabama* claims. See Thomas J. Rowland, *Ulysses S. Grant: In the Interests of the Whole People* (New York: Nova Science Publishers, 2015), 150–57.

CHAPTER 1

might have had in the Western Hemisphere to the United States and attempt to cultivate American friendship, even to the point of forging an alliance; it is what diplomatic historian Bradford Perkins calls the "*great rapprochement.*" Although Americans were not prepared to make any formal alliances with the British, Anglo-American relations improved considerably in the early twentieth century. This would give pause to those Irish Americans who advocated for a free Ireland, and required new and different tactics.[51]

That a thaw in Anglo American relations had occurred to the detriment of Irish interests was not lost upon the more radical Irish American nationalists. They realized that American influence in Irish affairs was beginning to diminish as the twentieth century began, suggesting that "the gap between the old country and Irish America continued to widen." If mainstream Irish American nationalism lost some of its former luster, the role of unabated agitation on Ireland's part fell to the Clan-na-Gael. There is scarcely any data available to determine the strength of the Clan of that time, its membership, or its financial health. The best estimate of membership was about 40,000 in 1910. When compared to the Hibernians at 180,000 and the Knights of Columbus at 300,000 in 1910, the state of the Clan was "dangerously weak." The Clan found little common cause with the conservative American-focused Knights and only a little bit more with the moderate Hibernians, although under the presidency of Mathew Cummings (1906–1910), the AOH assumed a more militant tone, as was demonstrated in their having cemented an accord with the National German American Alliance in 1907.[52]

---

51. As late as 1899, Irish Americans lustily cheered on the Boers in their struggle against the British in South Africa. It was reported that a contingent of Irish American sharpshooters was sent over disguised as a Red Cross corps. See Maldwyn Jones, *American Immigration* (Chicago: University of Chicago Press, 1960), 235–36; and Ward, *Ireland and Anglo-American Relations, 1899–1921*, 30–69. For the reconciliation of British and American interests, see Bradford Perkins, *The Great Rapprochement: England and the United States, 1895–1914* (Cambridge, MA: Atheneum Press, 1968).

52. John A. Murphy, "The Influence of America on Irish Nationalism," in David N. Doyle and Owen Dudley Edwards, eds. *America and Ireland, 1776–1976: The American Identity and the Irish Connection* (Westport, CT: Greenwood Press,

STAKING THE AMERICAN CLAIM

Irish American agitation for Ireland's independence from the United Kingdom had roots in the era of the Early Republic and Jacksonian Era. The American Irish cheered for the "Great Liberator" Daniel O'Connell, an Irish member of the British Parliament, in his successful campaign that led to the passage of the Catholic Emancipation Act of 1829, effectively abolishing the Penal laws that had long restricted Catholic freedom. Irish America followed with avid interest and lent financial support to O'Connell's efforts to repeal the 1801 Act of Union, which had dissolved the Irish Parliament and brought all governmental matters to London. This campaign failed, but it established the basis for later Home Rule initiatives. But O'Connell's adamant opposition to slavery and his pointed criticism of American slaveholders attracted little support in America outside of the emerging abolitionist movement. By the time of his death in 1847, the cause of Irish liberation in both Ireland and the United States had passed into the hands of more radical and violent revolutionaries, even though they did not gain much traction with America's Irish.[53]

The first organization to take up the mantle of Irish freedom by physical force was the Fenian Brotherhood, a precursor to the Irish Republican Brotherhood (IRB). The Fenians operated on two guiding principles: firstly, that Ireland had a natural right to independence, and secondly, that this right could be won only by armed revolution or physical force. The American branch of the Fenians was formed in the wake of the failed Irish uprising of 1848, and its early years were marked by confusion and leadership squabbling, but it eventually reorganized in 1866. While it raised money for the IRB in Ireland throughout its existence, American Fenians decided to make a bold unilateral strike against British Canada to hold it as hostage until Britain granted Ireland independence. Poorly conceived and dreadfully planned, a motley force approximating 1500 raiders crossed the

---

1976), 113; and Ward, *Ireland and Anglo-American Relations, 1899–1921*, 10, 27–28, 45.

53. On Catholic Emancipation, see Patrick Geoghegan, *Liberator: The Life and Death of Daniel O'Connell, 1830–1847* (London: Gill and Macmillan, 2010). For O'Connell's antipathy towards slavery, which proved his undoing with Irish America, see Christine Kinealy, *Daniel O'Connell and the Anti-Slavery Movement* (London: Pickering and Chatto, 2011).

CHAPTER 1

Niagara River near Buffalo with the plan of seizing Fort Erie. They would then take on any Canadian militia and the small contingent of British regulars coming to the fort's rescue. The attack was launched on June 2, 1866. Failing to take the fort, the Fenian contingent moved out to take on the Canadian militia, and in something resembling a battle, the poorly led Canadians retired from the field. Both sides experienced minimal casualties. The Fenians returned to Fort Erie but during the night decided to break off the siege and retire to New York. There were subsequent planned raids, mostly aborted, and by 1880 the Fenian Brotherhood had effectively dissolved.[54]

As the American Fenian movement began its descent into oblivion, the baton of Irish nationalism was handed off to a newly organized Irish Republican Party approved by the IRB in 1867. In 1870, the inchoate organization adopted the moniker Clan na Gael (Family of the Gaels). And in 1871, John Devoy, a prisoner-exile from a British jail, arrived in New York and assumed de facto leadership of the Clan, and although the hands of leadership shifted from time to time, Devoy remained the consistent voice of influence within the organization. In 1879, Devoy promoted a "New Departure" for the Clan na Gael, linking it with the Irish Parliamentary Party of Charles Stewart Parnell, MP; the political aspirations of the Fenians and Clan were thus coalesced with the agrarian revolution inaugurated by the Irish National Land League. This arrangement was cemented at the first Irish Race Convention held in Chicago in 1881. In addition to his agitation for agrarian reform in Ireland, Parnell secured allies in the form of William Gladstone and the Liberal Party in Britain. However, his involvement in a messy divorce in 1886, which caused him to lose support among Irish Catholics, and his untimely death at the age of forty-six in 1891, stalled the Home Rule movement.[55]

54. Matthew Knight, "The Irish Republic: Reconstructing Liberty, Right Principles and the Fenian Brotherhood," *Eire Ireland* 52, nos. 3 & 4 (2017): 252–71; Peter Ronsky, *Ridgeway: The American Fenian Invasion and the 1866 Battle That Made Canada* (Toronto: Penguin & Allen-Lane, 2011); and Carl Wittke, *The Irish in America* (Baton Rouge: Louisiana State University Press, 1956), 150–71.

55. On the rise and fall of Charles Stewart Parnell and its repercussions for the Home Rule movement, see Alvin Jackson, *Home Rule: An Irish History, 1880–2000* (New York: Oxford University Press, 2003), 38–79; and James J. Green, "American Catholics and the Irish Land League, 1879–1882," *Catholic*

STAKING THE AMERICAN CLAIM

Meanwhile in America, the 1880s witnessed considerable unrest within the Clan na Gael. More aggressive nationalists within the Clan grew disenchanted with the slow pace of Devoy and his close associate Dr. William Carroll. In 1882, two "action men," Alexander Sullivan and Michael Boland, seized the reins of power within the Clan and decided to remain indifferent to the directions of the IRB. They inaugurated the so-called "Dynamite War," wherein London's landmarks were targeted for bombing raids. The IRB was incensed by these reckless plans and formally cut ties with the Irish Americans. Financial scandals plagued the Clan under the leadership of Chicago-based Andrew Sullivan in the late 1880's. The murder of whistleblower Dr. Patrick Cronin, a close Devoy colleague, led to a famous trial that absolved Sullivan of guilt but divided the Clan into two factions, until Devoy managed to reunite the organization around 1900.[56]

John Devoy's realignment of the Clan na Gael with the Irish Parliamentary Party (IPP) and the Home Rule movement was about as disingenuous as John Redmond, MP in his assertion that Home Rule was but the first step in the ultimate Irish detachment from the British Empire. By 1900, circumstances had compelled Devoy to create nuanced strategies to promote the cause of Irish freedom, chief among these circumstances was the evolving Anglo-American reconciliation. Moreover, the violent and erratic behavior of the Clan over the previous two decades had sapped the ardor of most Irish

---

Historical Review 35 (April 1949), 34–38. In the wake of Parnell's demise, another Irish American organization arose—the Irish National Federation of America (INFA)—with the purpose of advancing the cause of Home Rule in Ireland. Briefly popular for a few years, even attracting the support of New York's conservative Archbishop Michael Corrigan, it dissolved in the wake of Gladstone's Home Rule Bill's defeat in 1893. See David Brundage, *Irish Nationalists in America: The Politics of Exile, 1798–1998* (New York: Oxford University Press, 2016), 129–30.

56. Terry Golway, *Irish Rebel: John Devoy and America's Fight for Irish Freedom* (Newbridge, Co. Kildare: Merrion Press, 2015); John Devoy, *Recollections of An Irish Rebel* (New York: Chas. D. Young Company, 1929). One of Devoy's earliest collaborators was O'Donovan Rossa, whom Devoy eulogized as "the very incarnation of its [Fenian] spirit." See Shane Kenna, *Jeremiah O'Donovan Rossa: Unrepentant Fenian* (County Clare: Sallins, 2015), i.

CHAPTER 1

Americans for achieving Irish freedom by physical force. Home Rule and John Redmond's mission became enormously popular in America in the first decade of the twentieth century. Additionally, the Catholic hierarchies, both in Ireland and the United States, much to Devoy's chagrin, fully endorsed Home Rule and heaped scorn upon advocates of revolutionary tactics. Devoy was compelled to lay low for the time being and observe future developments.

This temporary stand-down by Devoy should not imply a dormant phase in his energy in the years leading up to the outbreak of the Great War. He worked tirelessly to build up the Clan's membership and to improve the organization's financial ledger, something approximating a herculean task. In 1903, he launched his own newspaper, the *Gaelic American*, alternately characterized as an Irish Catholic and an Irish American weekly. He paid lip service to the defense of Irish American Catholic virtue in the face of Protestant and nativist indictments, and in the face of popular and secular American culture. Despite his druthers, he tenuously supported the Home Rule movement in Ireland until it became evident that Britain had no interest in installing it in the years leading up to 1914. But his greatest energy was expended in defacing British pretensions of grandeur and altruism, portraying its government as avaricious and oppressive and her Empire as a moral canker upon the civilized world. He proved to be a resolute watchdog, howling against any Anglo-American initiatives towards reconciliation and cooperation with the British. Devoy was given license to write such hyperbolic and dramatic statements until April 1917, when the United States entered the Great War on Britain's side; then, it became too dangerous to do so. In 1914, sensing that the war was an extraordinary opportunity to exploit Britain's predicament, Devoy and other ardent nationalists, such as Philadelphia businessman Joseph McGarrity, and New York's Judge Daniel F. Cohalan, ramped up their rhetoric. McGarrity had left Ireland at the age of seventeen in 1892, whereas Cohalan was a second-generation Irish American who served as Grand Sachem of the Tammany Society between 1908 and 1911, when he was appointed to the New York Supreme Court. The threesome would serve as the effective directors of the Clan na Gael, and by 1914 they formally shed any advocacy for Home Rule and actively directed efforts to physically

STAKING THE AMERICAN CLAIM

force the issue of Irish independence, although they did so as discretely and covertly as possible.[57]

During the same period that Devoy was fulminating over the evils of the British Empire, John Redmond patiently pushed for the Home Rule settlement. The origins of the Home Rule movement coincided with the rise of the Land League—as early as 1868, from which time it was carried forward by Parnell. In 1886, before Parnell's demise, Liberal Prime Minister William E. Gladstone, an admirer and champion of Parnell, introduced the First Home Rule Bill to Parliament. It never made its way to the hostile House of Lords, as it was shot down by a majority of thirty in the Commons. Undaunted, Gladstone, after a ministerial hiatus following his defeat in 1886, returned to power in the general elections of 1892 and quickly had a Second Home Rule Bill introduced in 1893. Even though the Unionist League centered in Ulster opposed the bill, it managed narrowly to pass in the House but was rejected by the Lords. Subsequently, Conservative ministers and their majorities were able to quash any serious introduction of a Home Rule bill. In 1905, however, the Liberals were called to form a majority and selected Sir Henry Campbell-Bannerman as Prime Minister. The government was consumed with enormous budgetary matters and, even if Campbell-Bannerman had been favorably disposed to consideration of Irish affairs, his slim majority could not contend with the Conservatives and Ulster Unionists, let alone the adversarial House of Lords. He did, however, appoint as Chancellor of the Exchequer H. H. Asquith, who understood that Home Rule for Ireland was necessary for the long-term benefit of the British Empire. When Campbell-Bannerman resigned in 1908 due to failing health, Asquith succeeded him as Prime Minister.[58]

---

57. See Terry Golway, *Irish Rebel*, 173–214; Maura Anand, Andrew S. Hicks, and R. Bryan Willits, "The Man in Philadelphia: Joseph McGarrity and 1914," in Miriam Nyhan Grey, ed., *Ireland's Allies: America and the 1916 Rising* (Dublin: University College Dublin Press, 2016), 111. For Cohalan's background, see Michael Doorley, "Judge Cohalan and American Involvement in the Easter Rising" in Grey, ed., *Ireland's Allies*, 151–56. In truth, all three of the revolutionaries had rejected Home Rule well before 1914.

58. Cronin, A *History of Ireland*, 168–77; Cameron Hazlehurst, "Asquith as

CHAPTER 1

Asquith was a highly skilled political tactician who played the game exceptionally well. At first, he dangled limited powers to Ireland in front of John Redmond and the IPP, believing that these could pass muster in Parliament. Ordinarily, the accommodating Redmond might have taken the bait, but he knew they would be unacceptable terms, as they fell far short of even the mildest aspirations that Home Rule would satisfy. Then the elections of 1910, while maintaining a Liberal majority over the Conservatives, did so but with the slimmest of margins. To advance Liberal policies and legislation, it would be necessary to find committed allies in the House of Commons. Compounding this challenge was the question of what could be done with the traditionally ultra-conservative House of Lords, which held the right to veto any bills coming from the House. Later in 1910, Asquith made a more formal overture to Redmond and the IPP, wooing them with assurances that the Liberals would push for a more comprehensive Home Rule Bill. This time, Redmond agreed to an alliance with Asquith's Liberal Party. Asquith quickly moved on the thorny problem of the House of Lords. With considerable aplomb, he threatened to stack the Lords with Liberal peers who would vote along Liberal lines unless they surrendered their veto rights. Asquith's bluff and bluster worked; rather than have their numbers diluted and tainted by Liberals, the Lords reluctantly accepted a curtailment of their traditional right to absolute veto. In the Parliament Act of 1911, this understanding was made law—yet it allowed the Lords up to two years to delay passage. The Third Home Rule Bill was introduced in Parliament in 1912, where it was promptly passed by the House. In practice, it could only be implemented in 1914, after the Lords had mulled it over. In effect, it would give Ireland control over most of its internal affairs while leaving foreign policy and defense matters in the hands of Westminster's Parliament, keeping Ireland within the British Empire. This was the apotheosis of Redmond's life's work, and most of Ireland reveled in this singular triumph. In America, as

---

Prime Minister, 1908–1916," *English Historical Review* 85, no. 336 (July 1970): 502–31. Asquith was also a Peer of the Realm, titled Earl of Oxford and Asquith, but he repeatedly refused a seat in the Lords, preferring a political career in the place where power and influence was wielded.

we shall discover, similar plaudits were heaped upon Redmond and the Home Rule Bill by the vast majority of Irish American Catholics and the American Catholic Church.[59]

What Redmond and Asquith did not envision in 1912 was the fiercely militant opposition to Home Rule that erupted in Ulster. For the Protestant majority in several of Ulster's counties, Home Rule meant they would be linked together with Catholic Ireland and would be compelled to relinquish their economic, social, and religious privileges as a result. Led by the irascible Sir Edward Carson, Ulster condemned the 1912 Home Rule Bill and promptly established any number of leagues, covenants and paramilitary organizations, the principal political unit being the Irish Unionist Party. Starting on September 28, 1912, nearly 450,000 Ulster men and women signed the Solemn League and Covenant before the campaign ended. To demonstrate their resolute opposition to Home Rule, several of the signatories had signed with their own blood. The following year, Unionists formed the Ulster Volunteer Force (UVF) with the express purpose of defending the union with Great Britain. Throughout 1913 and into 1914, nearly 100,000 volunteers regularly drilled, albeit it with broomsticks and anything else resembling rifles. The dearth of arms was partially resolved in April and July of 1914 when arrangements were made to land 20,000 rifles and three million rounds at the port of Larne in County Antrim. They were rapidly distributed to the UVF across Ulster.[60]

Carson's escalated rhetoric and the bellicose measures adopted by Unionists would totally alter stances over Home Rule, both in Ireland and America. The Liberal government of Asquith now sought to have Redmond accept that certain Ulster counties would not be immediately included in the Home Rule provision, something that Redmond was

59. Patrick Maume, *The Long Gestation: Irish Nationalist Life, 1891–1918* (Dublin: Gill & Macmillan, 1999); Dermot Meleady, *John Redmond: The National Leader* (County Kildare: Merrion Press, 2013), 89–243; and Joseph Finnan, *John Redmond and Irish Unity, 1912–1918*, (Syracuse, NY: Syracuse University Press, 2004), 99–101. Redmond's demise is attributed to his 1914 concession that Ulster could be left out of Home Rule and his endorsement that year that Irishmen would serve in the British ranks during the Great War.

60. Carroll, *American Opinion and the Irish Question*, 20–22; and Cronin, *A History of Ireland*, 179–85.

CHAPTER 1

increasingly inclined to consider. The more radical IRB and Sinn Fein Party removed support from Redmond and prepared to counter Ulster's military threats by forming their own unit—the Irish Volunteers. Both the IRB and Sinn Fein began to seriously consider whether armed insurrection might not be the only viable way to secure Irish independence. In the United States, most Americans had applauded the passage of the Home Rule Bill in 1912, if for no other reason than it would both mollify and stabilize Irish American Catholic opinion at home while improving Anglo-American relations. The presidential campaign of 1912 saw former President Theodore Roosevelt, incumbent President Howard Taft, and Democratic candidate Woodrow Wilson vie for Irish American Catholic support. Both Taft and Roosevelt had cultivated good relationships with Catholic prelates, such as Cardinal Gibbons and Bishop Ireland, and the somewhat priggish Presbyterian Wilson made it clear that he supported Home Rule for Ireland, although he would hardly interfere with British policymaking. Moderate Irish Americans and Catholics viewed Ulster's truculence with some consternation, yet still saw Home Rule as the only just settlement for the Irish, although the United Irish League of America (UILA), normally moderate and even conservative in its positions, was unnerved by recent developments regarding Home Rule's implementation by 1914. The Clan na Gael, to no one's surprise, distanced itself from even its pretense of supporting Home Rule, and Redmond and increased its clandestine communications with the IRB in Ireland.[61]

* * * * *

61. On Wilson's disgust with Ulster Unionists' tactics, see Joseph P. Tumulty, *Woodrow Wilson as I Know Him* (Garden City, NY: Doubleday, Page & Company, 1921), 292–97; and *New York Times,* February 28, 1914. A Clan na Gael circular in March of 1913 implied that Redmond had no right to say that Home Rule was the final word on the Irish question. See Carroll, *American Opinion and the Irish Question,* 214, n.30. Both the retreat from Home Rule by New York Democrat Congressman Bourke Cockran and the slide towards radicalism by the UILA can be found in Francis M. Carroll, "The Collapse of Home Rule and the UILA, 1910–1918: The Centre Did Not Hold," in Grey, ed., *Ireland's Allies,* 31–34.

STAKING THE AMERICAN CLAIM

Fervor for Irish freedom among Irish Americans had its ebbs and flows during the turn of the century, but the onset of the Great War in 1914 made agitating for Irish freedom a delicately difficult proposition. The unfolding of the war and the American entrance into that conflict in 1917 required circumspect advancement.

The other matter, and one that serves as the focus for this study, is the Irish American steadfast attachment to Catholicism. The history of the American republic from its earliest years until well into the twentieth century is a narrative of Anglo-Saxon Protestant dominance and its marked disdain for the Church of Rome. Even when the virulence of anti-Irish rhetoric began to abate towards the close of the nineteenth century, strident American anti-Catholicism remained the order of the day. In the main, Irish American Catholics did not buckle under the constant assault of nativist forces. They took both consolation and solace in their faith and looked to the American Catholic Church to wage combat against the forces arrayed against them. The story of how the American Catholic Church, in all its manifestations, guided its faithful through the maelstrom of the turn of the century and into the era of the Great War, boldly asserting that American Catholics were patriots of the highest order, will ensue throughout the remainder of this study.

CHAPTER 2

OF MATTERS AMERICAN:
The American Catholic Church & Irish American Catholics on the Eve of the Great War

The Impact of Nativist Attacks on American Catholics

Rather than their Irish identification, the matter that continued to preclude Irish Americans' inclusion into mainstream American society at the turn of the century was their steadfast attachment to Roman Catholicism. In truth, there was no other time in Irish American history when their interrelationship was as profound as it was in the years leading up to the Great War. The United States had been, since the colonial era and throughout the nineteenth century, a thoroughly Protestant nation in its political, social, and cultural dimensions. The years spanning 1880 and 1914 would witness a veritable avalanche of immigration into the United States. And the pattern of immigration was different than in previous decades, with the numbers shifting from peoples of Northwestern Europe (British, Irish, German, and Scandinavian) towards those from southern and eastern quarters of the continent, including Poles, Italians, Hungarians, Russians, and the numerous ethnicities of both the Balkan and Baltic states. Most of these immigrants were adherents of Roman Catholicism: those not Catholic were not invariably Protestant either. As the twentieth century beckoned, native-born Americans became seriously alarmed by this invasion. As they saw it, the very integrity of Anglo-Saxon Protestant culture was being washed over by foreign peoples who could not conceivably assimilate into American society and institutions. Anti-Catholicism, which had abated somewhat in the early 1880's, was suddenly and vigorously revived by the end of the decade. Once again, American Catholics were forced on the defensive, and the Catholic Church would take the assertive lead in deflecting nativist slings and arrows.

As alluded to earlier, anti-Catholicism was firmly rooted in the American experience. It was present in the early colonial era, throughout the early republic, and it thrived well into the twentieth century. The first truly concerted expression of nativism occurred in the mid-nineteenth century with the emergence of the Know-Nothing movement. Appalled by the escalation in Irish immigration occasioned by the Famine, and by newly arrived immigrants from the troubled German States, Protestant America reacted viscerally to these perceived threats to the prevailing cultural ethos and the maintenance of republican government and institutions. Nativist opposition was most strident in the major cities of the East Coast, and the principal targets were Irish Catholics and their Church. One of the most memorable lithographs of the Know-Nothing era portrayed an Irishman encased in a barrel of whiskey and a German lodged into a barrel of Lager-Bier, hauling a ballot box between them, which they apparently stole. In the background is the polling station, wrapped in absolute pandemonium. Immigrants, it would seem, held no regard for the sacred institutions of the American republic, and celebrated this disregard with apparent relish. While respectable establishment Protestants carried on the ideological war, working class nativists squared off in pitched battles with immigrant Irish in the streets, particularly those in New York City. Anti-immigrant feeling ran high in the first half of the 1850s, cresting to its height in 1856, when the movement went political and created the American Party, coaxing former President Millard Fillmore to head the presidential election ticket. But the sectional conflict intensified that year, and would crowd nativism off the national stage, with Fillmore's candidacy shoved off with it. In the North, disgruntled nativists generally wandered into the new Republican Party, and with the relentless escalation in sectional antagonism, leading to the outbreak of the Civil War, nativist agitation went dormant. Once the

CHAPTER 2

war began, Irish immigrants proved to be an excellent source for filling the Union military ranks.[1]

The relative dormancy of anti-Irish Catholic invective abruptly came to an end in 1870 with the resurrection of nativist attacks. To expand upon events briefly introduced earlier, one of the significant sparks leading to this resurgence was generated by the Orange Riots of 1870–1871 in New York City. On July 12, 1870, Scots Irish Protestants chose to celebrate the legendary victory of William of Orange over the Catholic army of James II at the Battle of the Boyne near Londonderry in 1690. The parade route was purposely designed to march up Eighth Avenue through the Irish Catholic ghetto of Hell's Kitchen and a couple of other similar neighborhoods. As the Orange marchers proceeded along the parade route, they taunted many of the residents of these neighborhoods and received, in turn, considerable vitriol from Irish Catholic residents. When the parade reached its destination at Elm Park and 92nd Street, a couple hundred hecklers were joined by some three hundred Irish laborers working in the neighborhood. A riot ensued. And when police finally quelled it, eight people were reported killed. The following year, Protestant parade organizers attempted to sponsor a second parade but were initially turned down by the police commissioner and the infamous boss of Tammany Hall, William M. Tweed. Pressure exerted by Protestant and nativist forces compelled the revocation of the march's ban. Not only was the ban believed to be a craven submission to the egregiously bad behavior of Catholic mobs, but fears of extensive Irish political influence in the city were

---

1. Nativism in the first half of the nineteenth century is well documented in the classic work by Ray Allen Billington, *The Protestant Crusade, 1800–1860* (New York: Macmillan Co., 1938). Two excellent works, featuring the tensions between Nativists and the Immigrant Irish in New York, are Tyler Anbinder, *Five Points: The 19th Century New York City Neighborhood That Invented Tap Dance, Stole Elections, and Became the World's Most Notorious Slum* (New York: Plume Reprint edition, 2002); and Tyler Anbinder, *Nativism and Slavery: The Northern Know Nothings and the Politics of the 1850s* (New York: Oxford University Press, 1994). A critical deconstruction of the Know-Nothings of the 1850s, published in 1905, can be found in a work by the Catholic editor of Milwaukee's *Catholic Citizen*. See Humphrey J. Desmond, *The Know-Nothing Party: A Sketch* (New York: CreateSpace Independent Publishing Platform, 2012 [reprint]).

rekindled. The march would go on as intended. What ensued on that day (July 12, 1871) was unmitigated chaos and violence. Fifteen hundred policemen had been enlisted to guard the route, joined by five regiments of the National Guard, numbering near five thousand men. From the parade beginning at the corner of Eighth Avenue and 29th Street, the site of the Orangemen's headquarters, Irish Catholic protestors greeted the relatively small number of Orange marchers with stones, bricks, bottles and shoes. The militia fired into the crowd and police managed to get the march moving again by wading into the crowds on horseback, flailing liberally with their clubs. One block later the parade met with even more determined resistance from the mobs. Amid rocks and crockery raining down upon them from rooftops, the police organized mounted charges into the crowd while the militia, sprayed volleys of gunfire among the protestors. Several protestors returned fire. When the march turned east on 23rd Street to Fifth Avenue the Orangemen found respite from the chaos by crowds that were largely supportive. But as they reached 14th Street, they were once again met with Irish Catholic hostility. The toll from the march was staggering. Sixty deaths, mostly Irish laborers, were reported, along with three Guardsmen. Scores of people were wounded, including many Guardsmen and policemen, from the projectiles lobbed at them. In the wake of the riot, Irish Catholics mourned the loss of their kinsmen who had perished when Protestant New York went on the attack.[2]

To appreciate both the nature and tone of nativist assaults between 1860 and 1880 leveled at the Irish and Catholics, one need go little further than to examine the work of the political cartoonist for *Harper's Weekly*, Thomas Nast, appropriately hailed as having "wielded more influence than any other artist of the nineteenth century." Thomas Nast was born in the Landau Barracks in the German state of Rhineland-Palatinate. His father, a trombonist in the Bavarian 9th Regiment band, held political convictions that compromised his

2. Russell S. Gillmore, "Orange Riots," in Kenneth T. Jackson, ed., *The Encyclopedia of New York City* (New Haven, CT: Yale University Press, 1995), 62, 957. The most comprehensive study of the Orange Riots is Michael A. Gordon, *The Orange Riots: Irish Political Violence in New York City, 1870–1871* (Ithaca, NY: Cornell University Press, 2009).

CHAPTER 2

position with the Bavarian government. In 1846, he sent his wife and children to New York City, and at the end of his enlistment in 1850, joined them there. Nast was christened a Catholic at birth and attended parochial schools for a time. While it is difficult to determine the precise date of his conversion to Protestantism, it is speculated that it was formalized by his marriage in 1861. His wife's parents were practicing Episcopalians. He attended school until he was fourteen years old, and while he was a generally bright student, he demonstrated great talent for drawing. Nast made the best of every opportunity that presented itself, and in March 1859 had his first drawing appear in Harper's Weekly, in which he illustrated a report exposing police corruption.

During the Civil War, he became a Republican and a stout defender of the Lincoln administration and the policy of Emancipation. His animus towards the Irish may well have originated in the Draft Riots of July 1863, in which Irish mobs destroyed registration centers and the homes of New York's Republican elite and targeted the black population for violence and execution. In 1864, he skillfully lampooned the Democratic Party's campaign platform, aiding in Lincoln's successful reelection bid. Following the war, he was a stalwart supporter of Radical Republican Reconstruction efforts, mourning its ultimate demise in the 1870s. But his most celebrated success involved his relentless sketching of the corruption attendant to the reign of Tammany Hall's supreme boss, William Marcy Tweed, and the ring that surrounded him, several of whom were Irish politicians. Tweed so feared Nast's campaign that he sent emissaries to offer the artist bribes to study art in Europe. Nast refused the offers and intensified his assaults upon the Tweed Ring, leading to its removal from power in late 1871. Tweed was arrested in 1873 and convicted of fraud. His attempt to escape justice by fleeing to Cuba was thwarted when Spanish officials recognized him there by referring to one of Nast's cartoons.[3]

---

3. Albert Boine, "Thomas Nast and French Art," *American Art Journal* 4, no. 1 (1972): 43–65; Fiona Deans Halloran, *Thomas Nast: The Father of Modern Political Cartoons* (Chapel Hill: University of North Carolina Press, 2012), 33; Albert Bigelow Paine, *Thomas Nast: His Period and His Pictures* (New York: The Macmillan Company, 1904), 181–82, 336–37; and M. Forker, "The Use of

OF MATTERS AMERICAN

Despite being absorbed with exposing the corruption associated with the Tweed Ring, a recurring theme of racism and anti-Catholicism appeared in Nast's sketches in the 1870s. His sketches not only reflected his own views but mirrored those of many native-born Americans, and thusly mirrored the principal fears and concerns of his age. His merciless pillorying of the immigrant Irish, already well-established in earlier sketches, continued to portray them with simian characteristics, as a drunken, combative, and dangerous threat to cherished American institutions. His sketch *The Usual Irish Way of Doing Things* depicted a giddy and rollicking Irishman, sitting atop a powder keg, brandishing an upside-down whiskey bottle in one hand and a cudgel in the other. As he saw it, ignorant Irish Americans, swayed by their equally corrupt political leaders, were a deserving target of his venom. His disgust with the "ignorant Irish" was only surpassed by his utter contempt for the Catholic Church, and his sketches, once again, reflected contemporary nativist themes. Stock imagery of the threat posed by the Roman Catholic Church to American republican institutions was rehashed and trotted out in many of Nast's illustrations. Nast, himself, considered the Catholic Church a formidable threat to American values that required stiff opposition. He was preoccupied by the danger he saw in the encroachment of Catholic ideology into the halls of American education. When Tweed's Tammany Hall proposed a new tax to support parochial Catholic schools, Nast was beside himself with rage. His stark, and arguably most creative cartoon, *The American River Ganges*, portraying mitered Catholic bishops, guided by Rome, as crocodiles moving onshore to attack American school children, protected by a single stout-hearted American school master. The Protestant children are unable to escape the attack by Irish politicians perched on a cliff behind them; this thoroughly encapsulated the nativist argument in absolute detail and bathos. While Nast favored a totally nonsectarian form of public education, minimizing the differences of religion and ethnicity, he nevertheless championed a decision by the Long Island Board of Education requiring all students to hear passages from the

---

the Cartoonists Memory in Manipulating Public Opinion: Anti-Irish Imagery in 19th Century British and American Periodicals," *Journal of Irish Studies* 27, no. 1 (2012): 58–71.

CHAPTER 2

King James Bible. Virtually all his cartoons involving the matter of public education sought to escalate "anti-Catholic and anti-Irish fervor among Republicans and independents."[4]

Nativist sorties against the Irish at the close of the nineteenth century never stopped, but the intensity of them did at least taper off. In part, the meteoric rise in immigration from southern and eastern European quarters deflected nativist attention away from the Irish; moreover, the cultural acceptance of Irish Americans at the turn of the twentieth century softened nativist disparagement of them. As described earlier, these first awkward steps toward assimilation almost made the Irish acceptable—even amusing—if not perplexing at the same time. Things Irish had become virtually chic in the eyes of American society. Undoubtedly, nativist concerns over the truly foreign dimensions of the new immigrants made the Irish appear benign by comparison. For native-born Americans, the new immigrants were so foreign in character, appearance, and culture as to suggest they could not be assimilated. Added to this was the fact that so many of them were Catholic. Consequently, the new nativism of the late nineteenth and early twentieth centuries, while still anti-immigrant in many respects, prompting a major "Americanization" program, veered into an accelerated anti-Catholic campaign, and in the process, Irish Catholics were drawn back into the maelstrom.

In a meeting held in Clinton, Iowa at the law offices of Henry F. Bowers on March 13, 1887, the order of the American Protective Association (APA) was formed. Its six founding members were comprised of various political persuasions and a spectrum of Protestant denominations. Initially, it was designed as a secret society with the expressed purpose of opposing the Catholic Church and the escalation in Catholic immigration to protect the integrity of Anglo-Saxon Protestant America. Its presence and impact were felt most strongly in the Midwest, reflecting its heartland agricultural and populist moorings. After a sluggish start, the APA came into its own in the 1890s.

---

4. "The Usual Irish Way of Doing Things," *Harper's Weekly,* September 2, 1871; "The American River Ganges," *Harper's Weekly,* September 30, 1871; and Benjamin Justice, "Thomas Nast and the Public School of the 1870s," *History of Education Quarterly* 45, no. 2 (2005): 171–206.

OF MATTERS AMERICAN

The heyday of the APA began when W. J. H. Traynor succeeded Bowers as the supreme president in 1893. Traynor, a transplanted Canadian, had become a newspaper proprietor based in Detroit. Long a member of a variety of Protestant fraternities and organizations, Traynor would lead the APA into its most influential period and transformed the organization into a political force of some reckoning in the mid-1890s. Notwithstanding the Association's claim that it did not have an issue with Catholicism or the Irish per se, it would appear as though the Association was thoroughly disingenuous in this regard. In a variety of oaths its members were required to swear, it required its business clients to avoid hiring Catholics whenever possible. The Association bewailed the political infiltration of the corridors of government in the major cities of the country by the Roman Catholic Church, to the exclusion of worthy Protestant candidates. It focused on the Romanization of the American government, public school system, and armed services, and the baleful influence of the Jesuits and other Catholic clerics in the federal government. More than any previous nativist group, the APA stressed the belief that American Catholics were under the Pope's marching orders, and that Catholics were required to obey Church dictates over the laws of the state. Implied in this assertion was that Catholics would compromise their allegiance to the American republic in a contest of wills with Rome.[5]

The APA saw the principal Roman threat coming from Irish American Catholics, and their hierarchy and priests. Hence, at the pinnacle of its popularity in the years 1893–1896, the APA targeted Irish Catholics for specialized character assassination. Particularly venomous and outlandishly hyperbolic was the APA's Secret Oath, which was devised in response to the circulation of "Pope Leo XIII's secret encyclical" instructing Catholics to rise and kill Protestant heretics on the feast of the redoubtable Jesuit Ignatius Loyola, on

---

5. Traynor makes his case for American Catholic fealty to the papacy in W. J. H. Traynor, "The Menace of Romanism," *The North American Review* 161 (August 1, 1895): 13. See also John T. McGreevy, *Catholicism and American Freedom: A History* (New York: W. W. Norton & Co., 2003), 91–165; and Donald L. Kinzer, *An Episode in Anti-Catholicism: The American Protective Association* (Seattle: University of Washington Press, 1964), 213–41.

CHAPTER 2

July 31, 1893. The Secret Oath called upon its swearers to combat the influence of the Catholic Church, to discriminate against Catholics in employment, and to exclude Catholics from political office, among other things. However, the day passed rather uneventfully.[6]

Although the APA did not officially disband until 1911, it was dealt a stinging blow in the 1896 election, when its membership was largely snubbed by both political parties.[7] While anti-Catholicism and its attendant anti-Irish invective remained an impediment to ecumenism, it had largely spent itself by 1914. According to one scholar of the subject, it wore out because "many Catholics had become assimilated into respectable society." Moreover, it was no longer attractive for political candidates to court anti-Catholic votes. It was, in fact, quite harmful to their chances of victory. The APA died somewhat prematurely, as "it suffered from the limitations of anti-Catholic nationalism ... [and] the belief that the papacy lay behind the major national perils was hard to sustain."[8]

---

6. "The Secret Oath of the American Protective Association, October 31, 1893," in John Tracy Ellis, *Documents of American Catholic History* (London: Forgotten Books Publisher, 2012 [reprint]), 499–501. For a clearer understanding of APA activities, see Donald L. Kinzer, *An Episode in Anti-Catholicism: The American Protective Association* (Seattle: University of Washington Press, 1964). Note that the opening of Ellis Island in 1892 and the implementation of the Pledge of Allegiance in American public schools in 1893 were nativist initiatives to "Americanize" newly arrived immigrants.

7. Paul Kleppner, *Cross of Culture: A Social Analysis of Midwestern Politics, 1850–1900* (New York: Arno Press, 1970), 328–51; and Justin Nordstrom, *Danger on the Doorstep: Anti-Catholicism and American Print in the Progressive Era* (Notre Dame, IN: University of Notre Dame Press, 2006), 145–46.

8. John Higham, *Strangers in the Land: Patterns of American Nativism, 1860–1925* (New York: Atheneum Press, 1963), 86–87. The APA attempted to appeal to both political parties until 1896, when parts of its message were absorbed by the Populist Party. The Republican Party rejected nativism outright, as the Catholic vote was too important to alienate, and industrial America held no interest in restricting cheap immigrant labor at this time. One of the last nativists to abandon his scurrilous attacks upon was Tom Watson, a Georgia populist and owner and editor of *Watson's Magazine*. His attacks upon the clergy were truly incredible, and he can be labeled as one who never let the truth stand in the way of a good story. About priests, he employed an inexhaustible number of epithets, such as "chemise-wearing bachelors," "bull-necked convent keepers," "shad bellies,"

OF MATTERS AMERICAN

Earlier nativist movements had sent Irish American Catholics a clear message that they were to be excluded from the mainstream of American society. As 1914 approached, Irish Americans were beginning to surmount the idle rantings of new nativist factions that rose from the ashes of the APA in 1911. However, the memories of the APA's attacks were still too fresh to allow total relaxation, and there were new assaults already on their way. During this entire period, many Irish American Catholics sought and found comfort, solace, and strength in the fold of the Catholic Church. Not only did the Church help ward off the assaults from nativists; more importantly, it helped mold the attitudes of its faithful along lines compatible to American society in 1914.

Irish American Catholics and the American Church

As has been demonstrated earlier, most Irish arrivals in North America throughout the eighteenth century brought with them an indelible Protestant imprint. Those Catholics who did come, finding few churches and even fewer priests, were frequently converted to Protestantism. This demographic characteristic changed enough by the mid-nineteenth century that, by the dawn of the twentieth century, the designations of "Irish" and "Catholic" became virtually synonymous. As Irene Whelan has illuminated, the roots of this phenomenon can be traced to the old country. During a period between 1820 and 1840, evangelical Protestants made great inroads in convincing erstwhile Catholics in Ireland to embrace the Christian merits of turning Protestant. The Catholic Church in Ireland, long downtrodden in its state of submission, stood by lethargically paralyzed during this feverish phase of Protestant zealotry.[9] It did not take long before these anti-Catholic strains reached the United States, in the form of the Second Great Awakening of the 1830s and 1840s. The Philadelphia Kensington

---

and "foot-kissers." Theirs was a "jackassical faith." Quoted in C. Vann Woodward, *Tom Watson: Agrarian Rebel*, 2nd ed. (Milwaukee: Beehive Press, 1973), 420.

9. For an excellent and succinct discussion of Protestant evangelization, see Irene Whelan, "Religious Rivalry and the Making of Irish-American Identity," in Lee and Casey, eds. *Making the Irish American*, 271–74.

CHAPTER 2

Riots of 1844 pitted native-born Protestant against Irish-Catholic immigrants at the very time when concerns about national identity, religious freedom, economic opportunity, and government control were being hotly debated. The largest "race riot" up to that point in U.S. history greatly affected the culture and politics of America, leading to Archbishop Hughes's dire warning of retribution should the assaults be directed at New York churches, and these attacks would be a precursor to the Protestant Know-Nothing movement.[10]

Back in Ireland, after shaking off its passive languor, the Irish Catholic Church inaugurated an impressive revival of its own, reminiscent of the Counter-Reformation of the mid-sixteenth century. Catholic religious belief, particularly in the western reaches of the Isle, had devolved into a cult of near pagan-like practices that embraced the magic of holy springs, wells, and imagined apparitions and specters. Of greater concern to the hierarchy was the people's lack of understanding the basic elements of the faith, such as sacraments, prayers, and devotional rituals. No wonder Protestant evangelical efforts met with some success. The Catholic Church in Ireland instituted a policy of repudiating the Catholic slide into pseudo-paganism, while at the same time thwarting Protestant evangelization. The Irish clergy undertook strenuous efforts to ignite popular religious participation and "encouraged Irish women to mark their homes with more ornate signs of their spiritual lives." The reform became known as the 'Devotional Revolution' wherein Catholics submitted to the discipline of the orthodox moral and theological instruction of the Church under the guidance of its hierarchy and priests. This meant that post-Famine immigrants arriving in the United States were thoroughly indoctrinated in the supreme authority of the Catholic Church and there developed a peculiarly strong relationship between the Irish immigrant and the institutional Church. Prior to 1850, the Catholic parish church was referred to as the "Mass House." It was a plain, even drab structure where the Mass was celebrated on Sunday and the sacraments were administered on an ad hoc basis. Through the remainder of the century,

---

10. For an overview of the Kensington/Southwark Riots and their impact, see Kenneth W. Milano, *Philadelphia Nativist Riots: Irish Kensington Erupts* (Charleston, SC: The History Press, 2013).

the parish church became not only the place of worship, offering myriad devotional services in an increasingly ornate setting, but a comprehensive social facility with a dizzying number of fraternities and sodalities, societies, feasts, and bazaars where parishioners might flock several times a week. By the close of the century, nearly every parish had built parochial schools and convents for nuns who taught in them. As the Church in America grew and established new dioceses throughout the country, the intense relationship between immigrants and the Church grew reciprocally. As James R. Barrett has demonstrated, the Irish in America identified solidly with their local parish and attended Mass at least weekly. Nearly ninety percent of New York City's Irish by the turn of the century claimed they were members of a specific parish. Although the South Side of Chicago had been infiltrated by non-Irish European immigrants by 1900, the Irish who were there were much more likely to identify their residence in Chicago by parish designation rather than by neighborhood.[11]

The American Catholic Church of 1914 was in many respects an Irish American one. The intimate relationship between Irish American Catholics and the American Catholic Church at the outbreak of World War I was so intricately established as to thwart spotting them as separate and distinguishable identities. By the turn of the century, the Irish had come to dominate the Church in staggering ways. Its

11. Irene Whelan, "Religious Rivalry and the Making of Irish-American Identity," 279–81; Kevin Kenny, *The American Irish: A History* (New York: Pearson Educational, Inc., 2000), 163–65; James R. Barrett, *The Irish Way: Becoming American in the Multiethnic City,* 60–62; and Jay P. Dolan, *The Irish Americans: A History,* 115–20. When Farrell's Patrick Lonigan took his "meditative drag" off his stogy on the evening of June 26, 1916, he was taking pleasure in the fact that his son "Studs" and his daughter Frances were graduating from St. Patrick's parochial school the following day. Farrell's family itself moved to the Washington Park neighborhood (roughly centered on East 60th Street and South Michigan Avenue near the Lake) in 1911 where he enrolled as a fifth grader at St. Anselm's Parish School, which appears in his Washington Park canon as St. Patrick's. See Ron Ebest, "The Irish Catholic Schooling of James T. Farrell, 1914–23" in *Eire-Ireland* 30, no. 4 (Winter 1996): 18–19. On a personal note, I, as a seminarian in the 1970s, marveled at how Chicago-area classmates, mostly Irish Americans, identified their location on the South Side by parish rather than by street address or neighborhood designation.

CHAPTER 2

hierarchy was decidedly Irish, and they ruled the Church with iron resolve. Making use of their demographic majority by 1860 and overwhelming other ethnic Catholics, the Irish began to overturn the liberal foundations laid by the early nineteenth century leader Bishop John England; the Irish American Church would embrace conservative views on most matters political and social. In 1886, thirty-five of the sixty-nine bishops in the United States were either of Irish birth or descent; the remainder were scattered among other ethnic entities in minor dioceses as to ensure little chance for challenging the Irish. So complete was Irish domination of the Church's hierarchy by the turn of the century that the institution was derisively referred to by other ethnics as the "hibernarchy."[12]

At the time the Great War broke out, the Irish anchored the episcopal positions in key dioceses, such as Baltimore, New York, Philadelphia, Boston, and San Francisco. The three red hats of the cardinalate in the United States belonged to Irish Americans; there was Gibbons in Baltimore, Farley in New York, and O'Connell in Boston. The real Irish domination of the American Church can be seen in the ranks of the clergy. As a function of their proximate contact with the laity, the clergy staffing Church institutions were arguably more important figures in the life of the Church than the bishop living downtown. Most certainly, Catholics were awed on those rare occasions of a parish visit from the local ordinary, but it was the local priest whom they saw on a regular basis and who played an integral role in their lives. Here, too, the "Irish priest" was disproportionately represented. By 1900, nearly fifty percent of the American clergy were of Irish stock, although in some dioceses, like New York, Brooklyn, Boston, Philadelphia, Baltimore, Albany, Newark, Chicago, Dubuque, and San Francisco, the percentage was higher. Coupled with the gradual diminution of separate, ethnic-national churches in the early twentieth century, Irish American influence spread more evenly and completely throughout

---

12. Robert D. Cross, *The Emergence of Catholic Liberalism in America* (Chicago: Quadrangle Press, 1967), 181; Robert J. Krickus, *Pursuing the American Dream: White Ethnics and the New Populism* (Bloomington: Indiana University Press, 1976), 78; and James Hennessey, SJ, *American Catholics* (New York: Oxford University Press, 1981), 194.

the Church. Their domination was further enhanced by the practice of promoting Irish born curates to pastorships, in some cases vaulting them over the heads of second-generation immigrant priests of other ethnic cultures.[13]

Sometimes overlooked in a review of religious influence among Catholics is the role of nuns. They outnumbered priests by a ratio of nearly four to one. Many religious orders had been invited to come over from Ireland, and to a lesser extent, Germany, by bishops who were feverishly building parochial schools. They served a reputable and indispensable role in schools, hospitals, and charitable institutions. Frequently, as they were the only educated women in working-class neighborhoods, they served as exemplary models for young Irish American women attracted to the convent by their association in the parishes. A variety of religious orders of nuns from Ireland pioneered the creation of Catholic colleges for women, such as Trinity College in the District of Columbia, Notre Dame Academy in Maryland, and St. Catherine College in St. Paul. In 1913, the School Sisters of Notre Dame, a mostly German order, founded Mount St. Mary College in Milwaukee.[14]

The Irish stamped a "national style" upon the American Church. Armed with their disproportionate influence, they largely determined the nature and direction of Church life and structure. Put simply, the Irish seized control of the Church. By 1900, "they ran it; they dominated its organization, its hierarchy, and its point of view; they set the pattern which oriented newcomers first to Americanism, then to American

---

13. By 1926, five additional red hats were handed out to Irish Americans: Dougherty in Philadelphia, Canevin in Pittsburgh, Glennon in St. Louis, Hayes in New York, and Mundelein in Chicago. Mundelein was of mixed German and Irish ancestry. See James J. Walsh, *Our American Cardinals* (New York: D. Appleton, 1926), 1–80; Thomas T. McAvoy, "The Irish Clergyman" in *A History of Irish Catholicism* 6 vols. (Dublin: Gill & Macmillan, 1970), 6:38; and Krickus, *Pursuing the American Dream*, 79.

14. Thomas Shelley, "Twentieth-Century American Catholicism and Irish Americans," in Lee and Casey, *Making the Irish American*, 580. St. Catherine College is mentioned in Hasia R. Diner, *Erin's Daughters in America: Irish Immigrant Women in the Nineteenth Century*. (Baltimore: Johns Hopkins University Press, 1983), 136–37.

CHAPTER 2

Catholicism." Just as astonishing as the dominance of the Irish is the extent to which the Church wielded an influence over its faithful, and the latter's receptivity to the direction that the Church established in the major political, social, and cultural issues around the turn of the century. This will greatly explain many of the attitudes embraced by Irish American communities when the war began in 1914.[15]

Nativism's resurgence in the 1890s only strengthened what was already an intensely intimate relationship between Irish Americans and their Church. The Church provided a bastion of security and comfort for its faithful against the antagonism directed at them by Protestant detractors. It was "loyalty to the Catholic identity [that] superseded the parish, county and province associations that the Irish carried over with them from the old country." Irish adherence to Catholicism became the single factor "most responsible for their sense of ethnic identity and solidarity."[16] In nearly every study of Irish American communities at the turn of the century, the most emergent theme is that of their attachment to the local Catholic Church. While there may have been varying experiences in occupational mobility among Irish Americans,

---

15. Hennessey, *American Catholics,* 4–5; and Edward Levine, *The Irish and Irish Politicians,* 74. To clarify what Catholics should know about their faith, the *Baltimore Catechism* was first published in 1885 and remained firmly in place in every parochial school until the late 1960s. See Father Earl Fernandes' response to a "Letter to the Editor" in the *Catholic Transcript* (Cincinnati), July 31, 2013.

16. Lawrence McCaffrey, *The Irish Diaspora in America* (Bloomington: Indiana University Press, 1976), 82. Irish American loyalty to the Church was not lost upon the hierarchy. Scholar-bishop John Lancaster Spaulding once remarked that he found Irish Americans "more loyal to the Church than any other people on the broad earth ... of all peoples the Irish are the most ready to accept the advice of God's minister." Quoted in Sister Agnes Schroll, "The Social Thought of John Lancaster Spaulding" (PhD dissertation, Catholic University of America, 1994), 193. Levine, *The Irish and Irish Politicians,* 9. Unlike in Italy, France, or Spain, where the Church was associated with the privileged classes, the Irish Church reflected the condition of the "poor, landless, and without power." The clergy in Ireland frequently took part in risings against the English; peasant and priest were partners in the struggle against oppression. The resultant "fusion of religion and nationality" virtually made national traitors out of apostates. The sentiment, if not the details, were transplanted to America in the late nineteenth century. See Harold Abramson, *Ethnic Diversity in America* (New York: Wiley, 1973), 131–32.

and where there may have been some temporizing with respect to social issues like trade unionism or temperance, there were few defections in Irish ranks concerning admiration for and dedication to the Church. Most studies of this phenomenon concur that, among all the facets of acculturation and assimilation facing the Irish in America, they "invested their strongest enthusiasm as well as their best talent in the Catholic Church." And it was in the parish that the integration of both the Irish and other ethnic immigrants, despite their internal conflicts, was accelerated in the late nineteenth century; it was the sustaining force in "forging peasants into devout, disciplined urban dwellers." A study of Worcester's Irish Americans in the years 1880–1920 revealed that no matter how earnestly they attempted to prove their acculturation to American norms during this period, they ultimately saw themselves as "defiantly Catholic" by the time the war erupted in Europe. In eastern Massachusetts at Lowell, a study of Irish Americans there discovered that the "Church had become the dominant institution ... backed by the loyalty of the Irish middle class, it flourished as it shaped Irish community development."[17]

Such Irish and Catholic solidarity was by no means confined to the East Coast, though in Boston, for example, it was manifested in decidedly disadvantageous terms for Irish American Catholics. There, under the direction of Cardinal O'Connell, Boston's Irish were blocked from full participation in mainstream society by his establishing an unwieldy and rigid "cultural strain" for them. In effect, O'Connell both encouraged and enabled the development of an Irish Catholic ghetto.[18] The Boston diocese's regressive policies did not extend much beyond its boundaries. In St. Louis, the Irish community's strong, positive solidarity with the Church was the trademark, as it was in most dioceses.

    17. McCaffrey, *The Irish Diaspora in America*, 83. On Worcester's Irish, see Timothy J. Meagher, *Inventing Irish America: Generation, Class and Ethnic Identity in a New England City, 1880–1928* (Notre Dame, IN: Notre Dame University Press, 2001). Catholic identity in Lowell is explored in Brian C. Mitchell, "'They Do Differ Greatly': The Pattern of Community Development Among the Irish in Late Nineteenth Century Lowell, Massachusetts," in Meagher, *From Paddy to Studs*, 67.
    18. Donna Merwick, *Boston Priests, 1848–1919: A Study of Social and Intellectual Change* (Cambridge, MA: Harvard University Press, 1973), 159–60.

CHAPTER 2

By 1914 Irish Americans, especially second- and third-generation ones, appeared to be shedding more of their ethnic heritage in exchange for identifying themselves as Catholic and American. Evidence of this drift can be detected in the diminishing membership of purely Irish organizations, such as the Ancient Order of Hibernians and the rise of Irish American membership in Church-sponsored groups like the Knights of Columbus and the Knights of St. Matthew. The Hibernians and secular Irish societies would enjoy a resurgence when the Great War started, but they remained largely nostalgic and sentimental in tone and generally remained in step with the Church's direction.[19]

Up the road from St. Louis, Chicago's Irish were undergoing a similar transformation in their self-identity. The development of the parochial school system there reflected an intense devotion to Catholic institutions; indeed, "Irish identity had been transformed into a strictly Catholic identity" as the twentieth century arrived. This transformation was both endorsed and clearly reinforced by the direction of Catholic parishes and schools. Although an Irish imprint could never be totally suppressed, it was clearly submerged in favor of a Catholic one. The same was occurring with the Irish in San Francisco. By the outbreak of the Great War the "Irish community found a group identity in a positive, not defensive, attachment to the Catholic Church." Under the enlightened administration of Archbishop William Riordan, the Church sought to become involved in San Francisco society rather than remain walled off from it. In some ways, the Irish attachment to the Church was a result of social and psychological needs to make sense out of a rapidly changing environment.[20]

---

19. Martin Towey, "Kerry Patch Revisited: Irish-Americans in St. Louis in the Turn of the Century Era," in Meagher, *From Paddy to Studs,* 154–55.

20. Ellen Skerrett, "The Development of Catholic Identity Among Irish Americans in Chicago, 1880–1920," in Meagher, *From Paddy to Studs*, 119. For similar conclusions, see Michael Funchion, "Irish Chicago: Church, Homeland, Politics and Class—The Shaping of an Ethnic Group, 1870–1900," in Melvin G. Holli and Peter d'A. Jones, eds., *Ethnic Chicago* (Grand Rapids, MI: William B. Eerdmans, 1984), 14–45. On San Francisco, see Timothy Sarbaugh, "Exiles of Confidence: The Irish American Community of San Francisco, 1880 to 1920," in Meagher, *From Paddy to Studs,* 161, 166–67. On Riordan, see Gaffey, *Citizen of no mean city*, 254–56. Whereas most histories of American Catholicism take a national

OF MATTERS AMERICAN

By 1900, Irish American clerics had not only reached the apex of their hegemony over Church politics in the United States but were also near the height of their influence over the Catholic faithful. It has been persuasively argued that the clergy and Church institutions of this era commanded an enduring respect and that their opinions and guidance were seriously considered by parishioners. This respect did not translate into absolute obedience in all matters, and the Church itself avoided directing the flock into controversial political and social positions for fear of nativist insinuations that it was meddling in affairs of state.[21]

The Irish American hierarchy were so obsessed with control and conformity within the faithful's ranks that, while they restrained themselves from outright intrusion in political and secular matters, they proved eager to take a firm hand in promoting Catholics as good, conservative, and patriotic citizens. To wit, the Church undertook a rigorous and conscious course of action both to "Americanize" its congregations and to steer them along a safe, acceptable path. Consequently, the Irish American Church first turned its attention to whipping into order the newer immigrants who arrived in great hordes after 1880. With inherent advantages such as language, the Irish "looked, acted and spoke" like Americans. To the newer immigrants, the Irish in America represented power incarnate, as represented in the priests, nuns, prominent parishioners, the bishop downtown, the ward bosses and union leaders.[22]

This ecclesiastical show of force was matched by the vigor exerted in civic affairs by Irish politicians, who relished their role as middlemen to the new, alien-tongued immigrants. By manipulating this brokerage,

---

focus, leading to a homogenization of American Catholicism that overlooks much of the local and regional cultural differences, Michael J. Pfeifer offers a corrective tonic in his work, *The Making of American Catholicism: Regional Culture and the Catholic Experience* (New York: New York University Press, 2021).

21. Andrew Greeley, *That Most Distressful Nation: The Taming of the American Irish* (Chicago: Quadrangle Press, 1972). Thomas T. McAvoy adopts a similar view, asserting that by 1900, "the parish priest generally abstained from discussing politics." See Thomas T. McAvoy, *The Great Crisis in American Catholic History, 1895–1900* (Chicago: Quadrangle Press, 1957), 37.

22. Krickus, *Pursuing the American Dream,* 80–81.

CHAPTER 2

the Irish succeeded in toppling the native elite from control in many urban centers. In a similar vein, the Irish-dominated Church, though initially wary of other immigrant groups, prevailed in their struggle for control after suppressing the German national Church initiative. As to the impact of this achievement, one critical scholar has gone to the point of condemning the Irish Church, accusing it of waging a war of "cultural genocide" in its efforts to mold the immigrants, especially the Italians and Slavs, into useful, loyal urban-dwellers and citizens. Disguised under a veil of altruism, it would seem, was a vulgar desire to "emasculate opposition to Irish rule."[23]

While the degree to which the Church influenced the faithful is questionable, one should not obfuscate the reality that the Irish Church elected to use its power to shape the community's opinion on a wide range of issues. A sociological study has revealed that a close bond existed between the Church and the Irish-American community at the turn of the century, citing that the horizons of most parishioners were their neighborhoods, and, as such, they "remained a people of the parish, where the priest was the authority in most affairs immediately affecting their lives."[24] Other studies have concluded that priests shared leadership in the community with local politicians, and that this guidance was not generally questioned. Indeed, "legitimate authority structures were never questioned; few immigrants ... ever had to choose between loyalty to a parish priest or loyalty to a bishop.... "For the Irish," ... no good Catholic questioned that the priest, and so the Pope, and so the Church, was infallible." Not until 1900 was there any real question that the clergy "were the real leaders of the Irish."[25] Accomplished poet, playwright, and novelist Thomas Beer spun a yarn in one of his novels advising non-Catholics that "... you pagans cannot understand a young Catholic's awe of a priest ... [he] is

---

23. Ibid. Krickus modifies his argument somewhat by admitting that the new immigrant groups lacked the resources, leadership, and thriving middle class to have sustained their cultures in the United States.
24. Levine, *The Irish and Irish Politicians,* 76.
25. McCaffrey, "The Irish Dimension," 12; and Robert D. Cross, *The Emergence of Catholic Liberalism in America* (Chicago: Quadrangle Books, 1967), 182–85.

not just a big man in a black vest speaking, but the Church."[26] And it was not simply by dint of personality or authority that the parish priest or local ordinary exercised such influence over the Irish American community. An entire network of Irish American social organizations was associated with the Church, "under the surveillance of the pastor ... [who] held great sway over the parishioners." The Catholic press augmented Church influence by printing articles or vignettes exhorting the faithful to revere the priesthood.[27]

Perhaps the most intriguing and revealing testimony to the power and influence of the Catholic Church with the Irish comes from two prominent members of the community who resented it. One such figure was the ethically flexible James Michael Curley of Boston. When running for mayor in 1913, he was summoned downtown by Cardinal O'Connell, who asked by him "to withdraw [my] name in favor of an older man [Fitzgerald]." Despite his refusal and the fact that he won the election anyway, Curley was aware that he could not ignore the counsel of the Church because of the influence it yielded with the Catholic Irish. To illustrate the truth of this, Curley was able to cite several occasions in his political career where O'Connell's enmity adversely affected him.[28]

John Quinn was another Irish American Catholic who grew to resent Church interference in affairs outside of religion. A lawyer by profession, Quinn was also a patron and devotee of the arts and conversant with many of Europe's leading literary, artistic, and intellectual giants. The son of Irish immigrants who had settled in Ohio, he attained his law degree from Georgetown University and

---

26. Beer, *The Mauve Decade*, 158. Nearly every recent and contemporary study of Irish American Catholics in the early twentieth century confirms the intensely close relationships Catholics forged with their priests and the Church. For example, see Jay P. Dolan, *The Irish Americans: A History*, 107–34, 229–44; James R. Barrett, *The Irish Way: Becoming American in the Multiethnic City*, 57–104; Thomas J. Shelley, "Twentieth-Century American Catholicism and Irish Americans," in J. J. Lee and Marion R. Casey, *Making the Irish American*, 574–84.

27. Levine, *The Irish and Irish Politicians*, 78–79; *Pittsburgh Catholic*, January 25, 1917.

28. James Michael Curley, *I'd Do It Again: A Record of All My Uproarious Years* (New York: Arno Press, 1957), 113, 249–51, 300–303.

opened his own law firm in 1906 in New York City. He was successful by all standards, and he represented the emergence of the prosperous middle class Irish American of the time.

Quinn's principal difficulty with the Church both in Ireland and the United States was its interference in the intellectual and artistic world. In particular, he frowned upon the censure of the clergy and religious societies of the nascent drama movement in Ireland at the turn of the century. Church censure, accompanied by agitation in both the Catholic and Irish American press, boiled over into riots in Philadelphia when an Irish touring company attempted to present J. M. Synge's play *The Playboy of the Western World. Writing* to the celebrated poet and playwright William Butler Yeats, Quinn opined that the arts would never advance until "the power of the Church was broken." He intimated that Irishmen in Ireland and America suffered from a deplorable lack of education; this, he believed, was the direct result of the Church's myopic domination over intellectual life.[29] Although the particulars of Quinn's remonstrations with the Church were not widely shared by other middle class Irish Americans, they do suggest that as the war approached, there were at least some in the community who were not willing to abide by Church guidelines in all areas of human enterprise.

Lay organizations and societies were also present to lend themselves to the cause of extending Church involvement in the lives of the faithful. And among the myriad organizations that existed at the turn of the twentieth century, the Knights of Columbus stood tallest. Founded by Father Michael McGivney in New Haven, Connecticut, the Knights were formed for several reasons. First and foremost, it was a society representing "the Irish layman's loyalties to Church and country." Secondly, it was designed to provide economic security to Irish American Catholics ostracized from mainstream society; the Knights sponsored a life insurance program for its members.[30] As

---

29. John Quinn to William Butler Yeats, July 13, 1906. Quoted in Alan Himber, ed., *The Letters of John Quinn to William Butler Yeats* (Ann Arbor, MI: UMI Research Press, 1983), 18.

30. Christopher Kaufmann, *Faith and Fraternalism: The History of the Knights of Columbus, 1882–1982* (New York: Scribner's, 1982), 8–9; Maurice F. Egan and John B. Kennedy, *The Knights of Columbus in Peace and War,* 2 vols. (New Haven, CT: Knights of Columbus, 1920), 1:50.

the Order was designed by Irish Americans, and since other ethnic groups had their own societies, the early membership "represented the predominance of Irish-Americans in the Northeast." Of its first 1105 members in 1885, 998 of them were of Irish birth or extraction.[31] As of that date, records suggested that the Knights were "primarily Irish American working class but were already evidencing significant upward mobility ... [and] most of the council officers were drawn from the professional and business groups."[32] These proportions were maintained right up to the close of World War I, when members of other nationalities came flowing in, giving the Knights a slightly more cosmopolitan appearance. Still, membership in 1914 was listed at 326,858, with the greatest numbers found in those states and cities where Irish Americans resided.

As indicated earlier, the growth of the Knights reflected both a rise in the economic standing of Irish Americans and an expanded awareness on their part of their American citizenship. Increased membership in the Knights was quite often, and in many locations, at the expense of more traditional secular Irish organizations like the Hibernians. The Knights drew members because their avowed Catholic identity was in synch with Irish Americans' perception of themselves. Consequently, the Knights vigorously and "explicitly sought to assimilate more recent immigrants into that American Catholic identity."[33]

The Catholic Press

The Irish American and Catholic press, particularly the latter, were the remaining influences upon the Irish American community. In an age without radio and television, Catholic newspapers joined the popular press in serving as windows on the world for the Irish community,

---

31. Kaufmann, *Faith and Fraternalism*, 33–47. The first duly elected officers were all Irish Americans. It took nearly ninety years to elect a Supreme Knight who was not an Irish American. See Egan and Kennedy, 1:53.

32. *The Pilot*, August 8, 1914; Kaufmann, *Faith and Fraternalism*, 47.

33. Towey, "Kerry Patch Revisited: Irish Americans in St. Louis in the Turn of the Century Era," 154; Meagher, "Irish, American, Catholic," 87; Roy Rosenzweig, *Eight Hours for What We Will: Workers and Leisure in an Industrial City, 1870–1920* (New York: Cambridge University Press, 1983), 165.

CHAPTER 2

presenting a glimpse of things beyond the borders of one's own parish. Consequently, these papers expressed attitudes and opinions that went virtually uncontested by any other source readily available to the Irish American community. The ability of the Catholic press to influence and formulate ideas was not lost upon the Church hierarchy. At the 4th Annual Convention of the Catholic Press Association, held in Detroit during September 1914, Bishop James J. Hartley from Columbus, Ohio, paid tribute to the unique opportunity afforded the press by claiming that "90% of the reading public read little else than newspapers."[34] As World War I approached, certain characteristics or traits of the Catholic press had been established. Virtually all papers were either "sanctioned" or "commended" by the local ordinary, making them "semi-official agencies of the bishops ... [which] publicized their attitudes." Any paper that veered too wide of the hierarchical line would be compelled to retract an errant opinion or the editor would come under heavy censure.[35]

The second characteristic of Catholic newspapers was the unmistakably clear Irish American orientation. Given the obvious fact that nearly every Irish American spoke and read English, and that such was not the case with other ethnic immigrants, the readership was more than likely to be Irish American.[36] Even in cities where the Irish were a minority among other ethnics, papers still carried a preeminent tone that was both Catholic and Irish. The distinctive Irish American flavor is due in part to the fact that, as a group, the Irish had developed to a point where they were better suited than any of the other immigrant clusters to articulate Catholic positions on issues of the day. Nearly all editors of prominent Catholic newspapers were Irish Americans, and

---

34. *Michigan Catholic,* September 17, 1914.
35. Patrick J. Buckley, "The New York Irish: Their View of American Foreign Policy, 1914–1921," (PhD dissertation, New York University, 1974), 13; and David N. Doyle, *Irish-Americans, Native Rights and National Empires* (New York: Arno Press, 1976), 343.
36. The *Catholic Sun* of Syracuse is an example of a diocesan paper that was inordinately Irish in character. See John A. Beadles, "The Syracuse Irish, 1812–1928: Immigration, Catholicism, Socioeconomic Status, Politics, and Irish Nationalism," (PhD dissertation, Syracuse University, 1974), 15–16.

many of these were priests.[37]

The third feature of Catholic newspapers of this time was that they were riding the crest of an unprecedented wave of popularity. As Irish American communities moved into the first decade of the twentieth century, there was a corresponding increase in the circulation figures for Catholic newspapers.[38] Part of the reason why circulation figures were on the rise was that, in addition to providing religious news, these papers displayed a secular breadth and truly served as a community organ. Typical of Catholic newspapers of this era, the Brooklyn *Tablet* was published weekly and was roughly fifteen to twenty pages in length. The headlines frequently reflected news of the world, including news from Ireland. The following pages featured editorials as well as more detailed social and religious tidbits in the weekly column titled "In Irish Circles." To satisfy local religious palates, several pages were devoted to local diocesan and parish news. This might include the bishop's upcoming itinerary, announcements of new pastorships and transfers, information on new church construction and the like. News about Irish American and Catholic societies like the Holy Name Society, The Catholic Benevolent Society, the Hibernians, and the Knights of Columbus usually commanded another page. The remainder of the paper was essentially news of a local nature. It featured a multitude of commercial advertisements, recipes, self-help articles, and without a doubt, a feature column or two, espousing some aspect of Irish American Catholic morality.[39] The Catholic press, then, was popular because it appealed on some level to the widest possible Catholic audience. This popularity led one Irish American editor to

37. Doyle, *Irish-Americans*, 343–44.
38. In 1913 Chicago's Catholic weekly, the *New World*, claimed a readership of 400,000 spanning the Midwest. The Boston *Pilot* boasted a circulation of over 200,000 in 1914. *Our Sunday Visitor*, the most popular national Catholic newspaper, declared it had nearly half a million readers. Note that the Boston *Pilot's* circulation was boosted by Cardinal O'Connell's importuning his priests to require every parishioner to have access to it. See Donna Merwick, *Boston Priests: A Study of Social and Intellectual Change* (Cambridge, MA: Harvard University Press, 1973), 189.
39. See the Brooklyn *Tablet*, January 30, 1915. Some newspapers carried descriptions of local Church sporting events, such as Gaelic football.

CHAPTER 2

claim that Catholic papers "were read by all classes of Catholics, from the heads of the hierarchy to the girl in the kitchen, and they really form the basis of Catholic public opinion."[40]

The Church in American Society

As both the American Catholic Church and the Irish American community advanced towards World War I, a harmonious and mutually beneficial relationship had evolved between them. For their part, Irish American Catholics continued to forge their identity in a new and more militant way with their faith, as they strove for social and religious parity with other Americans. The Church. on the other hand. drew enormous financial and personal support from Irish Americans. Throughout the country, Irish Americans sought ways to demonstrate that religious fidelity to the Church did not preclude their fulfilling their civic duties as citizens of the United States. At the same time, they made it clear they were no longer willing to tolerate abuse or rebuke from Protestant nativists. In these matters, as in so many others, the Irish-dominated Catholic Church took the lead.

Just as Irish Americans had to face the challenge of proving their worthiness as American citizens, the American Catholic Church was tasked with the uneasy mission of weaving a course that could come to terms with modern times, American culture, and republican institutions without compromising its obedience to the Church of Rome. Moreover, it was confronted with the formidable and unenviable task of reining in all its disparate elements, exacerbated by the polyglot of languages, traditions and customs introduced by the flood of immigrants since 1880.

The Americanist Controversy

While the American Church had survived many challenges in the past, it now faced a major test of its integrity in the late nineteenth century—the Americanist controversy. This challenge was but one of the many intellectual and social transitions transpiring in the greater

---

40. Quoted in Aaron I. Abell, *American Catholicism and Social Action: A Search for Social Justice, 1865–1950* (Garden City, NY: Doubleday, 1960), 289.

OF MATTERS AMERICAN

Western Catholic world in the late nineteenth century. The Americanist controversy stemmed from Rome's consistent railing against the forces of Modernism plaguing Europe in general.[41] And the controversy vividly exposed the Irish Catholic community's ambivalence about the character of the American Church, casting a long shadow over the tension existing between itself and the greater American society as well as the divisive internal rivalries within the Church at large. The Americanist controversy was the most revealing symbol of the tumultuous change that both Irish Americans and the Catholic Church experienced in the years leading up to the war.

The Americanist controversy is the term given to a series of related incidents spanning the decades immediately before and after the turn of the century. It received the designation "Americanist" because it involved the American Catholic Church's attempt to define its proper relationship to both the U.S. government and American society in general. What ostensibly began as an argument between German American Catholics and the Irish American hierarchy over ethnic national propriety of churches quickly developed into a pitched battle. Within the confines of this conflict, a tension developed in the American Church's hierarchy that became characterized by a considerable degree of petty bickering. From there the controversy was only muddled and protracted by the misinterpretation and inappropriate interference of the Holy See.[42]

---

41. Three consecutive pontiffs (Pius IX, Leo XII, and Pius X), spanning the years 1848–1914, railed against the forces of Modernism in a series of encyclicals. Pius IX, whose pontificate witnessed the loss of the Papal States to the modern forces of revolution and Italian nationalism, set the tone with an addendum to an encyclical (1864) in which he listed a syllabus of eighty errors ("isms") in the modern age. Among them he listed pantheism, naturalism, rationalism, indifferentism, socialism, communism, religious liberalism, and freemasonry. His successor, Leo XIII, sent Cardinal Gibbons a brief (1899) in which he pointed out the dangers of certain doctrines which had been given the name "Americanism." See *Catholic Encyclopedia* for entries on both Pius IX and Leo XIII.

42. On Modernism, see William L. Porter, *Divided Friends: Portraits of the Roman Catholic Modernist Crisis in the United States* (Washington, DC: Catholic University of America Press, 2013), 3–38; Thomas T. McAvoy, *The Americanist Heresy in Roman Catholicism* (Notre Dame, IN: Notre Dame Press, 1963), 30;

CHAPTER 2

The seeds of the controversy were planted at the Third Plenary Council of Baltimore in 1884. Several Irish American prelates under the direction of Cardinal Gibbons of Baltimore had been attempting to steer the American Catholic Church away from a foreign, suspicious image to one that would be in stride with American customs and culture. Theirs was an attempt to restructure the Church along lines that reflected and embraced American culture and institutions. The final document of the Council concluded that a state of harmony "existed between the Catholic Church and the American people," and went on to claim that American Catholics were "acquainted with the laws, institutions and spirit" of the country, and that "there is no antagonism between them." The document concluded with the resounding claim that if the nation were ever in peril, Catholics would respond with fervor equal to that of the founding fathers, by pledging "their lives, their fortunes and their sacred honor."[43]

The opening salvo of the controversy was fired by a German Catholic layman Peter Cahensly, who, in 1883, proposed to Rome that national churches be allowed to flourish in the United States. He continued to hammer on this theme for years afterward and was able to inspire other German nationals to present their cases to the Holy See, such as when Father Peter Abbelen complained that the Irish clergy had made German parishes subordinate to them. Abbelen, a spiritual director for the School Sisters of Notre Dame in Milwaukee, a city abounding with German Catholics. Abbelen wrote in a Memorial (1886) that the absence of German-speaking parishes had caused many otherwise faithful parishioners to leave the Roman fold for Protestant pastures. The Memorial was initially well received in Rome. Both Cahensly and Abbelen were supported by the German hierarchies of Milwaukee and St. Louis, and by a small retinue of conservative Irish bishops. Abbelen expressed concern that the Irish American

---

Lester R. Kurtz, *The Politics of Heresy* (Berkeley: University of California Press, 1986), 46; and Hennessey, *American Catholics*, 198.

43. Quoted in William Shannon, *The American Irish: A Political and Social Portrait* (New York: Macmillan & Co., 1963), 263–64; and Michael Walsh, ed. (2001). *Dictionary of Christian Biography*, Jay P. Dolan, *The American Catholic Experience* (New York: Doubleday Religious Publishing, 2011), 563.

"Americanizers" were systematically dismantling all national customs and traditions. German American Catholics defiantly accused the Americanists of being secularists who were sapping the strength of the immigrant's faith.[44]

While the Irish and Germans squabbled over the issue of national churches, another argument flourished among the hierarchy itself, which transcended simple ethnic differences. The conflict was essentially over the way the American Church would respond to American culture. On one side, the Americanists under Cardinal Gibbons and Bishop John Ireland of St. Paul attempted to have the Church adapt to democratic values and ideals, and in doing so, make the "American Church the paradigm for the [Catholic] Church in the modern world." In addition, this adaptation would smooth the way for assimilation and acculturation and help silence nativist invectives.[45] On the other hand, there were ultra-conservatives such as Michael Corrigan of New York and Bernard McQuaid of Rochester, along with Patrick Ryan of Philadelphia and Patrick Feehan of Chicago, and a handful of German bishops, who, in addition to sharing a sharp personal dislike for Gibbons and Ireland, felt that the American Church should remain

---

44. Colman J. Barry, OSB, *The Catholic Church and German-Americans* (Milwaukee: Bruce Publishing, 1953), vii. Humphrey Desmond, a second-generation Irish immigrant, and an attorney and owner of the Milwaukee Archdiocese newspaper the *Catholic Citizen*, would eventually become a major champion of Americanism. But in 1889, when the Wisconsin Legislature passed the Bennett Law, endorsed by the state's nativist governor William Hoard, a law barring the use of any language other than English in all public and private elementary and secondary schools, Desmond became the principal litigator in a case before Wisconsin's supreme court that saw the law repealed. Irish Catholics joined their German co-religionists in denouncing the Bennett Law, as they saw the black hand of Protestant bigotry behind it. See Steven M. Avella, *In the Richness of the Earth: A History of the Archdiocese of Milwaukee, 1843–1958* (Milwaukee: Marquette University Press, 2000), 185–87.

45. John Keane was a close ally of Gibbons and presented and defended the Americanist case in Rome along with Denis O'Connell, rector of the North American College. In 1912, he was advanced to the position of Bishop of Richmond diocese. See also Robert E. Curran, *Michael Augustine Corrigan and the Shaping of Conservative Catholicism, 1878–1902* (New York: Harper & Row, 1970), iii–iv.

CHAPTER 2

aloof from American society; they tended to cast the Americanist issue in its worst light. After 1907, Cardinal William O'Connell took up the conservative cause and "favored everything which radical and liberal churchmen considered dysfunctional and reactionary."[46]

Liberals and conservatives continued to argue throughout the 1890s. While Gibbons and Ireland should never be construed as liberals on political, economic, or social issues, they were so in the sense that they sought to acculturate the American Church to American society. They earnestly sought to purge American Catholics and the Church of their more foreign practices, such as nationalized churches, foreign tongues, intemperance, political bossism, corruption, patronage, and radical socialism, in order to present themselves as "faultless before secular society," and to participate more fully in the nation's affairs. Only by gaining American approval of the Church, Gibbons reasoned, could Catholics quash the insidious attacks of Protestant bigots. Gibbons was convinced that the Church would remain on the defensive if it could not conform to American society.[47]

Several incidents stemming from the Americanist controversy led to Leo XIII's issuing a letter addressed to Gibbons titled *Testem benevolentiae nostrae* on January 22, 1899. In it, the Pope chided the Cardinal for embracing the heresy of Americanism, expressing his

---

46. John T. Ellis, *The Life of James Cardinal Gibbons*, 2 vols. (Milwaukee: Bruce Publishing, 1952), 2:1–25. One venomous exchange between McQuaid and Corrigan was prompted by an interview that the *New York Times* held with Gibbons. McQuaid wrote Corrigan: "The little man at B. [Baltimore] has simply lost his head ... what will he [Gibbons] not do to keep himself before the public." Quoted in Ferdinand J. Zwierlein, *The Life and Letters of Bishop McQuaid*, 3 vols. (Rochester, NY: The Diocese of Rochester Press, 1925–1927), 3:154–55; Kirby, *Emigrants and Exiles*, 528. Before his elevation to the bishopric of New York, Corrigan had presided over a tempestuous ethnic row between German and Irish Catholics in his diocese of Newark. See Augustine J. Curley, OSB, "The Irish in the Church of Newark," in Maria Dayrup & Maura Grace Harrington, eds., *The Irish-American Experience in New Jersey and Metropolitan New York: Identity, Hybridity, and Commemoration* (Lanham, MD: Lexington Books, 2014), 11–13.

47. Robert D. Cross, *The Emergence of Liberal Catholicism*, 51–70; Ellis, *The Life of James Cardinal Gibbons*, 2:35. For a complete understanding of Gibbons's positions in the Americanist controversy, see Ellis, *The Life of James Cardinal Gibbons* 1:331–88.

concern over the American Church's willingness to embrace American culture. The American Church, Leo advised, should be on guard against the American values of liberalism and pluralism that were undermining the doctrine of the Church. Leo also rejected the theory of particularism and the Americanist view that a particular or a relaxed position should be taken with respect to the American Church. Leo reiterated the idea that Catholic doctrine and teaching was the same throughout the world and was not to be adjusted to suit a particular area.[48] A few years later, in 1893, Catholic participation in the World Parliament of Religions held in Chicago unleashed a flurry of disputes within American Catholic circles as to whether Catholic involvement in such an ecumenical forum was even appropriate. Again, the prelates were split along liberal and conservative lines. Consternation arose over the Catholic position on public schools; the liberals, especially Archbishop Ireland, were willing to concede educational leadership to the state, whereas conservatives argued for parochial control. In 1898, Leo XIII expressed another disappointment when he lamented an America where church and state are "dissevered and divorced," expressing his preference for a closer relationship between the Catholic Church and the State.[49] The influence of Apostolic Delegate Cardinal Francesco Satolli in these affairs proved deleterious to the Americanist cause. Initially favorable to the liberals, he eventually drifted into the conservative camp, and his reports to Rome presented a jaundiced view of Gibbons' efforts as well as the performance of the Irish clergy in the United States.[50]

Of all the episodes involving the Americanist controversy, none had greater impact nor consequences than the poor French translation of *The Life of Father Hecker*. And it was this singular episode that

---

48. Some historians believe that the letter was really directed at liberal and anticlerical currents in France. See John L. Allen, Jr., *The Catholic Church* (New York: Oxford University Press, 2014).

49. "Archbishop Ireland Explains His Stand on Public and Parochial Schools, December 1890," in John T. Ellis, *Documents of American Catholic History* (New York: M. Glazier, 1987), 489–95.

50. "Cardinal Satolli's Visit to New Orleans, February 15–21, 1896," in ibid., 529–45.

brought the weight of the papacy to bear on the Americanists. The English version was written by a Paulist priest by the name of Walter Elliott. Father Hecker had been the founder of the Society of St. Paul and had written extensively on religious and spiritual topics. Some of his positive views on Americanism became popular with many French Catholic leaders. Harassed by a succession of anti-clerical French governments, these leaders hoped that by imitating the Americanists they could arrive at a cordial understanding with the French state.[51]

Inevitably, conservative reaction to the Americanists' endorsement of Hecker, both abroad and at home, led to Leo's issuance of *Testem benevolentiae*. In it he conveyed that, while he was not condemning American Catholics for loyalty to their country, they should not adopt the more radical aspects of Church doctrine as misconstrued by numerous French and Italian clerics.[52] In many ways, Leo condemned a "phantom heresy." It was one that did not exist, as Gibbons was at pains to point out in his response to the pontiff. Most Catholics in the United States had no idea there was even a conflict occurring. After this one general response, Gibbons elected to reduce the tensions by saying no more on the matter, and he accepted what amounted to a minor wrist-slapping from the pope. McQuaid and Corrigan thanked Leo for his intervention; however, their victory was largely hollow, as the effort to forge a closer alignment of the American Church with American political culture moved inexorably forward.[53] There are several reasons why the Americanists eventually eked out a strategic victory in the Americanist struggle. The principal Americanists simply outlived all their significant opponents. Corrigan, the recognized leader of the conservatives, died in 1902, as did Feehan. McQuaid followed in 1909 and Ryan in 1911. The German bishops did not have the wherewithal

---

51. Paul Messbarger, *Fiction with a Parochial Purpose: Social Uses of American Catholic Literature, 1884–1900* (Boston: Boston University Press, 1971), 2–10; Ellis, *The Life of James Cardinal Gibbons*, 2:10–20; and Walter Elliott, *The Life of Father Hecker* (Sydney, Australia: Wentworth Press, 2019 [reprint]).

52. "Testem benevolentiae," in John J. Wynne, ed., *The Great Encyclicals and Letters of Pope Leo XIII* (New York: Benziger Bros., 1903), 441–53.

53. Ellis, *The Life of James Cardinal Gibbons*, 2:66–67; McAvoy, *The Great Crisis,* 353–64.

to carry the struggle further once Corrigan departed from the scene. The Americanists Ireland and Keane lived until 1918. Gibbons passed away in 1921 and the youngest, Denis O'Connell, survived until 1927. Moreover, the Americanists lived during the great crucible of the European war and America's entry into it, a time when Catholics were under great pressure to prove their worth as Americans. Another matter to consider is that Pius X, who succeeded his predecessor to the papacy in 1903 and was every bit as conservative and anti-Modernist as Leo XIII, found the Americanist issue a trifle stale, and was occupied by other concerns. Finally, even Corrigan found it troublesome to cater to some of the newer immigrants who had found their way into his diocese. One case involved the parish of Transfiguration Church in the notorious neighborhood of Five Points. Long an impoverished Irish ghetto, Five Points saw the Irish moving out and the Italians moving in by the 1880s. Italian parishioners began complaining that the Irish pastor and the remaining Irish congregation were treating them as second-class citizens, commanding that they be relegated to the Church's basement for their services held in Italian. Corrigan excoriated the pastor and finally decided that an Italian Church would have to be constructed. That is when his troubles began. It took him a long time to find enough Italian priests who were competent and well trained, eventually settling upon a religious order—the Scalabrinis—to man the parish. He was appalled by the endless festivals that celebrated the somewhat obscure saints, attended by strange rituals. And he became frustrated and dismayed by what he saw as a people, unlike the Irish, who had virtually no knowledge of even the most basic tenets of the faith.[54]

In retrospect, the Americanist controversy revealed several telling characteristics about the American Catholic Church and Irish American Catholics at the turn of the century. It was clear that the Church was

---

54. Curran, *Michael Augustine Corrigan,* iv; Stephen Michael DiGiovanni, *Archbishop Corrigan and the Italian Immigrants* (Huntington, IN: Our Sunday Visitor Press, 1994), 205–7; and Anbinder, *Five Points,* 378–82. In 1907, Pius X issued the encyclical *Pascendi Dominici gregis* that served as a blanket condemnation of modern rational thought over the collective history of Church doctrine.

an inherently conservative institution, despite the apparent liberalism of some clerics regarding a desire that immigrant Catholics accept acculturating within American society. One must not confuse the Americanist struggle with other issues facing the Church. Gibbons and Ireland shared a doctrinal and social conservatism with all other bishops. Both sides understood the need for immigrants to assimilate into American society. The conflict was more a question of timing, with liberals pressing for immediate acculturation and conservatives pushing for a slower, more gradual pace. Neither side argued against the separation of church and state, and whatever disagreements existed between the two sides over Americanism did not imply that McQuaid and Corrigan were any less patriotic than the Americanists. Michael Corrigan may have had his faults, and history has tended to obscure his accomplishments in favor of Gibbons's, but he probably had a greater impact on the way the Catholic Church was internally structured by the outbreak of the Great War than the so-called liberals. The Church of 1914 was "conservative, authoritarian and monolithic" in the way it governed and managed its members.[55]

This marked conservatism was demonstrated in church and state relations. Both Gibbons and Ireland cultivated strong ties with various U.S. presidents. Gibbons was particularly friendly with Presidents Cleveland, Roosevelt, and Taft, while Bishop Ireland, a Republican in sentiment, enjoyed a cordial relationship with McKinley and Roosevelt. Both prelates were occasionally invited to confer with these presidents and were extremely proud of this association.[56] The Americanists carefully nurtured this advisory role with state authorities. During the violent Pullman Strike of 1894, Ireland wrote Gibbons that it was

55. Curran, *Michael Augustine Corrigan*, iv; and DiGiovanni, *Archbishop Corrigan and the Italian Immigrants*, 68–70.
56. Cross, *The Emergence of Liberal Catholicism*, 90. Bishop Spalding had been called by Theodore Roosevelt to serve on the Commission to help relieve the 1902 coal strike. Archbishop Ireland was so enamored of McKinley that he stumped for him during the 1900 campaign. In return, McKinley asked him to be the featured speaker at the presentation of the Lafayette statue donated by France. Gibbons was asked by McKinley, Roosevelt, and Taft for advice on handling the Philippine annexation issue. See John Tracy Ellis, *Perspectives in American Catholicism* (Baltimore: Helicon Press, 1963), 111–12, 116–17, 124.

necessary for the Church to come across "before the American people as the great prop of social order and law." Two years later, Gibbons, in one of his several literary efforts, averred that "the Catholic Church is the great conservative element of society, as all reflecting men are ready to avow ... she pursues a middle course."[57] In pursuing the middle course, the Church was forced to adopt a realistic policy towards many of the heinous social conditions of the day. The policy embarked upon would have to be described as largely passive; it was such, for in confronting injustices, the Church tended to "trust in God and not organized political reform." Rather than confront the systemic source of evil, the Church mobilized its charitable institutions to deal with the casualties of the system.[58]

Whereas the Americanists and conservatives pursued a non-confrontational course towards the sources of social evils in American society, there was another clique, a very distinct minority, largely within the diocese of New York City, who were social activists. For want of another term, they were described as radicals. The most conspicuous of the radical priests in the late nineteenth century was the Reverend Doctor Edward McGlynn (1837–1900). McGlynn was a devotee of Henry George, the author of the bestseller *Progress and Poverty* (1879), which was a penetrating analysis of the disturbing gulf of inequity and poverty amid economic and technological progress, as well as the amassing of wealth by the very few via the monopolization of industrial production during the height of the Gilded Age. He inspired the economic philosophy known as Georgism, the conviction that people should own the value they produce themselves but that the economic value derived from land, including the natural resources within, should belong to all members of society. He argued that a single tax on land would foster a more productive and just society. Many of his ideas would spark more moderate reform movements in the Progressive Era. George's ideas were popular among many Americans,

---

57. Ireland is quoted in Martin Marty, *Modern American Religion: The Irony of It All, 1893–1919*, vol. I (Chicago: University of Chicago Press, 1986), 183. See also James Cardinal Gibbons, *The Ambassador of Christ* (Baltimore: John Murphy, 1896), 262–64.

58. Krickus, *Pursuing the American Dream*, 83.

CHAPTER 2

especially those in the working class and those with lower to middle incomes. But to the capitalists and wealthy Americans, George's ideology smacked of socialism, and to a conservative like Corrigan, George's ideas were anathema. And this is where Edward McGlynn and the radicals enter the picture.[59]

McGlynn received his theological training in Rome, where he obtained a doctoral degree in theology and philosophy and was ordained a priest in 1860. Upon his return to New York, he was assigned to a series of parishes, eventually becoming pastor at St. Stephens Church on East Twenty-eighth Street, where he served until 1887. During his ministry there, he became disheartened by the endless numbers of the poor who rang the rectory bell begging for food and employment, compelling him to wonder if God's order was such that the poor would simply become poorer in the land of endless bounty. It was about this time that McGlynn became deeply impressed by Henry George's *Poverty and Progress*. McGlynn had earlier drawn the ire of Archbishop Corrigan by his enthusiastic endorsement of public schools and his refusal to build a parochial school at St. Stephen's. By 1882, it was clear that McGlynn had embraced many of the teachings of Henry George, especially the communal ownership of property. He met George that year and campaigned for him in his failed bid to be elected mayor of New York City in 1886. Corrigan had seen and heard enough by this time. On September 29, 1886, he suspended McGlynn from exercising his priestly duties for a period of two weeks. Corrigan chastised any cleric who denied the right of an individual to acquire private property. McGlynn publicly criticized the tone and substance of Corrigan's position, which promptly earned him another suspension from His Excellency. When McGlynn learned that Cardinal Gibbons was appealing to Rome to oppose any condemnation of the Knights of Labor, an organization that the priest held dear, McGlynn made public news of Gibbons' intercession, leading to an increased enmity between

---

59. See Henry George, *Progress and Poverty: An Inquiry into the Cause of Industrial Depressions and of Increase of Want with Increase of Wealth, The Remedy* (New York: D. Appleton, 1881 edition). See also Edgar H. Johnson, "The Economics of Henry George's 'Poverty and Progress,'" *Journal of Political Economy* 18, no. 9 (Nov. 1910): 714–35.

Corrigan and Gibbons. At Corrigan's insistence, the case was taken up by Rome, and McGlynn was handed a technical excommunication in 1897, pending a Church hearing on the merits of George's philosophy and the appropriateness of the single tax initiative. In 1892, Pope Leo XIII sent a papal legate to the United States to review McGlynn's case. Finding nothing contrary to Church doctrine in McGlynn's positions on the single tax theory, the delegate lifted the excommunication decree from McGlynn and reinstated him to the ministry. McGlynn served until his death in 1900 and remained unrepentant for his past and his outspoken calls for social justice.[60]

The Church's approach to labor and trade unionism was marked more by moderation than a conservative position. There was a noticeable degree of ambivalence. The uncertainty was caused by the Church's desire to strike a balance between the rights of the laborer and those of employers to generate opportunities and command reasonable profits. Adding to this ambivalence was the large membership of Catholics, most notably Irish Catholics, in labor and trade unions. This situation warranted constant vigilance by the Church, as radical and socialist tendencies had to be curtailed whenever and wherever they emerged.

As early as 1882, Cardinal Gibbons worked with Terence Powderly, the Irish American Catholic leader of the Knights of Labor, to have papal sanctions removed against Catholics who joined unions. The Catholic Church had opposed unions as too influenced by freemasonry rituals. When the Knights removed the words "The Holy and Noble Order of" from their title and promised to abandon any freemasonry rituals, the papacy withheld the sanctions. Consummate diplomat that he was, Gibbons convinced the Holy See that the "oath" taken by the Knights was but a simple pledge and would never have interfered with a Catholic's full confession during the sacrament of penance. In

---

60. Robert E. Curran, "The McGlynn Affair and the Shaping of the New Conservatism in American Catholicism, 1886–1894," *Catholic Historical Review* 66, no. 2 (1980): 184–204. Curran argues that Corrigan's mishandling of the McGlynn matter probably cost him a cardinalate. See Robert E. Curran, *Shaping American Catholicism: Maryland and New York, 1805–1915* (Washington, DC: The Catholic University of America Press, 2012), ch. 8.

CHAPTER 2

fact, Gibbons' pro-labor intervention was so influential that Leo XIII's encyclical *Rerum Novarum*, issued in 1891, was considered not only quite liberal for its time, but it articulated a mandate that some form of "amelioration of the misery and wretchedness pressing so unjustly on the majority of the working class" was necessary. In all, Gibbons and his supporters within the hierarchy and clergy were, in the words of one sympathetic scholar, able to put "the Church and organized labor before the public in a friendly relationship." Candidly, in the forefront of Cardinal Gibbons' motivation and in his stand on such issues as the Knights of Labor and the doctrines of Henry George, was the fear that Vatican condemnation would mean the alienation of Catholicism from American society.[61]

Gibbons' favorable disposition toward the Irish-laden Knights of Labor should not obscure the underlying conservatism of the Church toward labor. After all, with so many Catholics in the Knights, Gibbons could not afford to cavalierly dismiss the organization. In truth, though, Gibbons might have been repelled by the blatant abuses of capitalism, but he never seriously challenged them. Whenever possible, the Church sought to arbitrate labor disputes and to discourage the use of wildcat strikes.[62] Animating this desire for mediation was the Church's abhorrence of anything remotely smacking of socialism, anarchism, and most certainly Marxism in Catholic labor ranks. Given the conspicuously large presence of Irish Americans in the labor movement

---

61. Martin Marty, *Modern American Religion,* 1:179; Robert E. Weir, *Beyond Labor's Veil: The Culture of the Knights of Labor* (Detroit: Wayne State University Press, 1996), 94; Craig Phelan, *Grand Master Workman: Terence Powderly and the Knights of Labor* (Westport CT: Greenwood Press, 2000), 184; and Henry J. Browne, "The Catholic Church and the Knights of Labor," (PhD dissertation, Catholic University of America, 1949), 350.

62. Aaron I. Abell, "American Catholic Reaction to Industrial Conflict: The Arbitral Process, 1885–1900," *Catholic Historical Review* 59 (January 1956), 387, 399. Despite his intervention on behalf of the Knights of Labor, Gibbons was friendly to capital as well. Just after Andrew Carnegie had the Homestead Mill Strike of 1892 ruthlessly suppressed, Gibbons wrote an article praising Carnegie's virtues and called upon the poor "to exercise Christian patience." Quoted in Neil Betten, *Catholic Activism and the Industrial Worker* (Gainesville: University Presses of Florida, 1976), 4.

and a sprinkling of their numbers in the nascent socialist movements, the Church began to mobilize its resources for combat. When Eugene Debs fared well in the election of 1904, the Church rallied labor around more religiously oriented workingmen's organizations. Additionally, the Church undermined attempts by radicals to infiltrate mainstream labor movements by announcing its support for Samuel Gompers's "conservative course and his unionists' rejection of socialism and his defense of private property."[63]

Church aims were enabled by the tendency of mainstream Irish American Catholicism to heed its direction. Priests were actively encouraged by their ordinaries to be knowledgeable and to use the pulpit to preach against social errors. For example, in the Wobblies-inspired strike of 1913 in the mills of Lawrence, Massachusetts, an Irish American priest lambasted the Wobblies for misguiding "ignorant immigrants." His sermon was reputed to be so influential that when the strike committee convened shortly thereafter, no Irish representatives were on hand. This is not meant to imply that all clerics were necessarily heeded, as St. Louis Archbishop John Glennon discovered late in 1909 when he refused to support a garment worker's strike. The editor of the *St. Louis Labor* caustically noted that in a recent sermon of Glennon's he spoke only on the cost of building the new cathedral and the evils of European socialism. "In his sermon" the

---

63. Thomas T. McAvoy, "Bishop John Lancaster Spalding and the Catholic Minority," *Review of Politics* 12 (January 1950): 13–15; Hennessey, *American Catholics*, 213–14; Marc Karson, *American Labor Unions and Politics, 1900–1918* (Carbondale: Southern Illinois University Press, 1958), 225; and Charles Shanabruch, *Chicago's Catholics: The Evolution of an American Identity* (Notre Dame, IN: Notre Dame University Press, 1981), 149. The Catholic Church's resolute position against socialism can be humorously revealed in an exchange between the editor of Chicago's Catholic *New World*, a Mr. O'Malley, and James Connolly, a firebrand socialist and Irish nationalist in the magazine *Harp*, in 1908. O'Malley was accused by Connolly of inciting a riot against a meeting of the Irish Socialist Federation to be held in Chicago, for which O'Malley suggested that attendees "bring rotten eggs." Connolly shot back, labeling O'Malley a "foul-mouthed scribbler and let Mr. O'Malley lay in his supply of rotten eggs—for that meeting will be held." See Carl Reeve & Ann Barton Reeve, *James Connolly and the United States: The Road to the 1916 Irish Rebellion* (Atlantic Highlands, NJ: Humanities Press, 1978), 246.

editor observed, "the archbishop showed what great service he can be to the capitalist class."[64]

Once again, the greatest ally in the Church's struggle against socialism and anarchy within labor's ranks was the receptivity of Irish Americans to Church leadership. When initially thrown on the defensive by socialism's continued popularity, the Church mobilized its vast institutional network of parishes, schools, lay organizations, and the Catholic press to help shape Irish American political thought and doctrine.[65] By the turn of the century, the Church realized it needed to adopt a definitively positive stance regarding labor. Under the watchful eye of the clergy, labor associations sprang up to clearly associate the Church with labor's interests. These unions were able to introduce to their members the virtues of "moderation, sobriety and frugality" to offset whatever radical influences were in circulation.[66] By World War I, the Church had largely succeeded in its efforts to blunt the sharper influences of socialism and to steer Catholic labor along the lines of *Rerum Novarum*. In these efforts, the Church was greatly assisted by both Irish leadership and rank and file membership in the unions.

The Church on American Patriotism and Irish Nationalism

There was one final dimension to the Americanist program that was both central in the drive towards assimilation and that was endorsed by virtually the entire Church. Demonstrating that adherence to the Catholic faith did not preclude Catholics from being loyal and patriotic citizens was of paramount importance to the Americanists.

---

64. Patrick Renshaw, *The Wobblies* (New York: Anchor Books, 1968), 103–4. In San Francisco, labor found an enthusiastic champion in Father Peter Yorke, a native of Galway, who helped the Irish American working man to acquire economic and religious security. Of Father Yorke, it is claimed that "he advanced the unionization of labour [sic] and education under Catholic auspices." See James P. Walsh and Timothy Foley, "Father Peter C. Yorke: Irish-American Leader," *Studia Hibernica* 14 (1974): 90. William B. Flaherty, SJ, *The St. Louis Irish: An Unmatched Celtic Community* (St. Louis: Missouri Historical Press, 2001), 149–50.

65. Karson, *American Labor,* 224.

66. Schroll, "The Social Thought of John Lancaster Spalding," 125–27.

Dating back at least to the Third Plenary Council of Baltimore in 1884, the hierarchy realized that criticism and prejudice against the Catholic Church in America would never cease until Protestant fears of a Catholic insurgency could be quieted. If by 1914 there were doubts entertained about Catholic patriotism, they were not for want of trying on the part of Catholics.

Cardinal Gibbons and Archbishop Ireland led efforts to demonstrate Catholic patriotism. The outbreak of the Spanish-American War in 1898 provided a splendid opportunity, particularly as Spain was such a distinctively Catholic nation and the papacy was concerned about the fate of Catholicism in Spanish colonies. Although Gibbons had hoped that the war could be averted, once it was declared, he enthusiastically endorsed it. Shortly after the war's declaration, he urged Catholics to "loyally and firmly sustain our laws and our governing powers." Once word of the great American naval victories arrived, he led his congregation in the *Te Deum*, the traditional prayer of thanksgiving. As for John Ireland, he required no such change of heart. A former Civil War chaplain with the 1st Minnesota Volunteers, Ireland was one with those who wanted to serve notice to Europe that America was emerging as a world power. He was an imperialist of the highest order.[67]

Although Gibbons was no less an advocate of marketing the notion that Catholics were great patriots, it was Ireland who rushed forward with the greatest conviction, fervor, and eloquence. When the hierarchy of America celebrated the centenary of its establishment in 1905, he presented the faithful to the nation as super-patriots. In his grand opus, *The Church and Modern Society* (1905), Ireland proclaimed that "next to God is country, and next to religion is patriotism ... patriotism is a Catholic virtue ... [and] I would have Catholics be the first patriots

---

67. For representative efforts to track evidence of Catholic patriotism throughout the nation's history, see Gibbons's introduction to John Gilmary Shea, *The Cross and the Flag: Our Church and Country* (New York: The Catholic Historical League of America, 1900). See also Allen Sinclair Will, *The Life of Cardinal Gibbons,* 2 vols. (New York: E. P. Dutton, 1922), 2:595–606; and John T. Farrell, "Archbishop Ireland and Manifest Destiny," *Catholic Historical Review* 33 (October 1947): 300–301.

CHAPTER 2

of the land."[68] When the war with Spain began, he had thrown his entire weight behind the effort, at one point intimating that pacifism was tantamount to treason and cowardice. He had believed prior to the outbreak of the war that an armed conflict might be the ideal tonic to stimulate national pride. In still another patriotic blast, he admonished Catholics about how "America demands that all who live on her soil and are protected by her flag be Americans ... the individual who does not in his own name and from his own heart proclaim this right of liberty for his fellow citizens is no true son of America."[69] Throughout the years leading up to World War I, Ireland constantly defended American Catholics, claiming, at one time, that the Catholic Church was "extra-American," as if to compensate for the derogatory barbs of Protestant critics.[70]

That such emphasis was placed upon the Church's need to demonstrate loyalty to the government has caused some critics to accuse Gibbons and Ireland of succumbing to an intense form of American nationalism. In many ways there is truth to these assertions; Church leadership appeared unconcerned with speaking out against the government concerning the social evils of the day. Instead, they took heart in the increasing acceptance of the Church in America. For them, acceptance was equated with "fulfilling the prophetic mission of the Church."[71] The only notable exceptions to this nationalist perspective were Father William O'Connell in Portland, Maine, who would not vigorously endorse the war with Spain, and Bishop Spalding of Peoria

---

68. Archbishop John Ireland, *The Church and Modern Society*, 2 vols. (New York: Benziger Bros., 1905), 1:163; and Marvin R. O'Connell, *John Ireland and the American Catholic Church* (St. Paul: Minnesota Historical Society Press, 1988), 439–71.

69. Ireland, *Church and Modern Society*, 1:180.

70. Quoted in the *Catholic Bulletin*, August 16, 1913.

71. Dorothy Dohen, *Nationalism and American Catholicism* (New York: Sheed & Ward, 1967), 167–71. It should be noted that it is one thing to say that Gibbons and Ireland willingly subordinated all other interests to that of attaining the nation's acceptance. It is doubtful, however, that they would have realized they were shunning the "prophetic mission" of the Church by not speaking out about the evils of the day as Dohen asserts. "Prophetic mission" is a distinctly Vatican II concept and would have sounded alien to these Vatican I prelates.

who thought patriotism needed to be tempered by a sense of "truth and righteousness." Yet, Spalding's was but the one voice to demur from the paeans to patriotism.[72]

Paralleling the hierarchy's patriotic line were the Knights of Columbus, whose very foundation reflected an ardent desire to "portray Catholic citizenship," by mirroring the "optimism characteristic of several ecclesiastical leaders associated with the Americanist posture in American Catholicism."[73] In 1900, the Knights created a 4th Degree among its membership, honoring those elevated to this distinction for their conspicuous patriotism. According to some of their exuberant participants, banquets held for induction into this elite membership were generally occasions when "the soundest principles of patriotism and morality from the lips of Catholics" were heard to "stimulate patriotism."[74]

As late as 1913, Catholic loyalty to the nation was questioned by the extensive circulation of another "bogus oath" printed in *The Menace*, a vestigial newspaper from the days when the A.P.A. reigned supreme. The oath gained additional credence when it was introduced into the *Congressional Record* via a House Subcommittee. On this occasion, the Knights counterattacked both in print and in the courts with libel suits until nearly every publication either disavowed the oath or paid dearly in fines for having printed it. The Knights were ably assisted in this campaign by the creation of a new weekly national newspaper, *Our Sunday Visitor*, whose express purpose was to "expel religious bigotry" and to undo the efforts of anti-Catholic agitators such as the Guardians, the Patriots, and the Knights of Luther.[75]

---

72. Cardinal O'Connell was still a priest in 1898. Three years later he was consecrated as bishop for the Diocese of Portland, Maine. See Dorothy Wayman, *Cardinal O'Connell of Boston* (New York: Farrar, Straus & Young, 1955), 108; Bishop John Lancaster Spalding, *Opportunity and Other Essays and Addresses* (Chicago: McClurg, 1900), 193–94.

73. Kaufmann, *Faith and Fraternalism*, xiii.

74. Egan and Kennedy, *The Knights of Columbus in Peace and War*, 1:119.

75. 49 Cong. Rec. Part 4, 1st Session (February 15, 1913); Justin Nordstrom, *Danger on the Doorstep: Anti-Catholicism and American Print Culture in the Progressive Era* (Notre Dame, IN: University of Notre Dame Press, 2006), 146–47; and *Our Sunday Visitor*, April 30, 1916.

CHAPTER 2

With organized Protestant bigotry waning by 1914, Catholics—markedly, Irish American ones—began asserting their sense of belonging through the excessive expression of patriotism promoted by their Irish American Church, its lay organizations, and its press. The vertical power structure of Church authority taught Catholics the virtues of obedience and the futility of opposing legitimate authority. In the years leading up to the Great War, Catholics had been trained to be loyal, dutiful, and obedient citizens.

Irish American Catholicism and Cultural Values

Nineteenth-century Irish nationalism tended to be a distinguishing, ever disruptive factor in Irish American assimilation, one that was tolerated because political, economic, and diplomatic considerations permitted it. By 1900, the tone of Irish nationalism among American Catholics was changing. Even though radical agitators continued to engineer the overthrow of British rule in Ireland, mainstream Irish American nationalism reflected increased concern for how Irish Americans were viewed and treated in the United States. Irish American Catholics engaged in a vigorous campaign to impress other Americans with the exalted cultural values of both the Irish and Catholicism. If the course of Irish nationalism between 1880 and 1910 was subjected to the vicissitudes and vagaries of time and circumstance, it increasingly assumed additional meaning for second-generation Irish Americans in the way they viewed themselves within American society. No longer did Irish Americans fret about their political and economic standing. They were now prepared to address the formidable bastion of nativist prejudice-disrespect. Consequently, the pursuit of Irish freedom took on a poignant second meaning that was distinctly American in outlook. Irish nationalism became more a product of Irish American Catholics' struggle with a dominant Anglo-Saxon Protestant society rather than a mere expression of pure sentiment for their homeland. The poverty and oppression of Ireland imposed by the British enraged Irish American Catholics and made them resent the bigotry, prejudice, and oppression that they experienced in America. This resentment led a new generation of Irish Americans to feel a "sense of inferiority" and a marked "sensitivity to criticism in American society." In a phrase from Thomas N. Brown, Irish American Catholics at the turn of the century "yearned for respectability." It was this striving to "achieve and maintain dignity in hostile environments ... [that] cultivated political and cultural nationalism." Supporting liberation movements in Ireland, no matter how conservatively and nonviolently, would bring about the day when their own status in the United States would be elevated to a respectable par with their Protestant antagonists.[76]

"Yearning for respectability" was expressed in nearly all aspects of Irish American and Catholic life. More than anything, the drive for respectability forced a restructuring of Irish American nationalist goals on behalf of Ireland. The triumph of the Home-Rulers over the Clan na Gael in the years leading up to the outbreak of the Great War was due in large part to the former's disassociating themselves from the violent and vulgar image of the latter. The case of Patrick Ford, founder of the newspaper the *Irish World*, underscores this point. Early in his career, he had embraced radical measures. He advocated the physical force solution for Ireland's woes, and at home he supported strikes, labor unrest, and violence. He railed against the Church as "unsympathetic to the needs of poor Irishmen." By the last decade of the nineteenth century, he spurned this course of action and directed his own life and energies in the *Irish World* to generate "a sense of dignity and self-respect ... and encouraged the poor Irishmen's identification with America." For Ford, the editor of the most popular Irish American paper at the time, the ideal Irishman was "respectable, well-to-do, cultured and devoutly religious." The best Irish Americans, according to Ford, "were notably patriotic, democratic, and intensely loyal to American institutions."[77]

The Catholic press also increasingly voiced concern for Irish American respectability. When they were not catechizing on the

---

76. Michael F. Funchion, "Chicago's Irish Nationalists, 1881-1890" (PhD dissertation, Loyola University, 1976), 262; and Thomas N. Brown, "Irish Nationalism and Irish Catholicism: A Study in Cultural Identity," *Church History* 42 (December 1973): 530.

77. Ford's quotes can be found in Paul Rodechko, *Patrick Ford and His Quest for America: A Case Study of Irish-American Journalism, 1870–1913* (New York: Arno Press, 1976), 241–42.

CHAPTER 2

propriety of one action or another, Catholic editors were condemning any slights to Irish virtue from British and American Protestants. They also delighted in claiming how morally superior the Irish and their American cousins were to the Anglo Saxons. A persistent theme in Catholic newspapers was that Ireland was nearly "crimeless," whereas intemperance and lawlessness ran rampant in England.[78]

At the heart of the Church's ingrained conservatism and its "Americanizing" efforts was the quest for respectability. The hierarchy's near obsession with the maintenance of social order and respect for lawful authority was prompted by a desire to make Catholics appear respectable before American society. This yearning carried over into its attitudes toward labor violence and social unrest. Peaceful protest and earnest supplication to legitimate authority could be countenanced by the Church, but violence and radical agitation were viewed as non-American and non-Catholic. This conservative viewpoint apparently struck a chord within Irish American circles, as seen during Chicago's Haymarket Square riot in 1886. When the dust settled, most Irish Americans could not condone the murder of Irish policemen. While large numbers of German American workers rallied to the cause of the rioters, "the more conservative Irish lined up on the side of the policemen."[79] The same disdain for radicalism convinced Gibbons and Ireland to suppress the more blatant strains of radical Irish nationalism. It was no mere coincidence that the relative weakness of the Clan na Gael at the turn of the century was a result of the Church's difficulty with its violent aims.[80]

Intemperance was another target of Irish American Catholics' impulse toward respectability. Among the hierarchy was a genuine concern that Catholics, especially the Irish and Germans, were

---

78. An example of Irish American sensitivity toward British slights was an editorial critical of author Arthur Conan Doyle for his insulting portrayal of the Irish in a serial story. Humphrey Desmond, the editor, was particularly incensed that Doyle had Sherlock Holmes killed in the final episode by a villain named Mulligan. See *Catholic Citizen*, May 22, 1915. Ireland's apparent lack of crime appeared in the *Michigan Catholic*, December 3, 1914.

79. Skerret, "The Development of Catholic Identity in Chicago," in Meagher, *From Paddy to Studs*, 192.

80. Cross, *The Emergence of Liberal Catholicism*, 92.

perceived by American society as immoderate drinkers in a time that frowned upon immoderation. Among the prelates, Bishops Corrigan and Ryan had been early spokesmen for the temperance movement, but it was Archbishop Ireland who led the charge. By 1900, he was the leading crusader, frequently appearing as the featured speaker at the conventions of the Catholic Total Abstinence Union. The obvious appeal of attaining respectability through sobriety was part of the Americanization program; it was a tangible sign of assimilation. The Catholic temperance movement was the "incarnation of Archbishop Ireland's ideal of a prosperous, civic-minded Americanized Catholicism."[81]

The Knights of Columbus had the same zeal for promoting sobriety among its Irish American membership. Irish resistance to collective abstinence was considerable; drinking as a social custom was a deeply nurtured expression of kinship, solidarity, and community. As a result, the appeal of the Father Mathew Society was geared to "self-reform" as opposed to social reform, with sobriety as the personal pledge of a dysfunctional alcoholic individual and not as an assault on drinking as a custom. The temperance crusade attracted a younger, second generation of Irish Americans who sought upward mobility in American society. Membership in the Father Mathew Society and the Knights of Columbus was a statement of achieving stability and respectability. While the Knights eschewed the evils of liquor and even barred saloon keepers from membership, they were not as abstemious as pure temperance societies.[82]

Both the Church and Irish Americans were intensely concerned with their images and took exception to any perceived insults. Both the secular Irish American press and the Catholic press went

81. *The Silver Jubilee Gathering of the Catholic Total Abstinence Union of America* (New York: Columbus Press, 1895), 100; and Sister Joan Bland, *Hibernian Crusade: The Story of the Catholic Total Abstinence Union of America* (Washington, DC: Catholic University of America Press, 1951), 267.

82. Rosenzweig, *Eight Hours for What We Will*, 59, 104–5, 187. Father Theobald Mathew was an Irish Catholic priest who established the Total Abstinence Society in the early nineteenth century. He established a mission in County Cork and is credited with having a salutary impact in reducing the crime rate throughout Ireland.

to great lengths to highlight positive reflections of the Irish. After a Knights of Columbus clambake in Hartford, the *Connecticut Catholic* complimented the Irish American contingent by declaring, "our people are an exceedingly well behaved and orderly class of men." The article proceeded to confound the stereotype of the Irish as "idle, slovenly and often vicious," by noting that they now "compare favorably ... in all that goes to make good citizenship ... [and] the second generation are intensely American in their instincts."[83] There is evidence to suggest that a perceptible shift in the opinion of Irish Americans by outsiders was occurring during the transitional period leading up to World War I. The drunken, simian caricature found in many periodicals of an earlier time was giving way to a gentler mocking of the social-climbing Irish. Thomas Brown even admitted that the "stereotype Paddy was not without its truths"—after all, the Irish "did love a row, were too often found with drink, and did rule over the low life of American cities." Nonetheless, Brown charged that the stereotype failed to reflect the changing realities of Irish American life by the last decade of the nineteenth century. The disheveled and comedic image of the immigrant of the 1880s "was giving way to the solemn, ambitious, second-generation Irish American who was knocking at the gates of the political parties, the professions, and business."[84]

Perhaps the most vivid and appreciable measurement of Irish American anxieties regarding respectability was in the cultural realm. One of the first conventional stereotypes to be assailed by Irish Americans was the stage Irishman. The Hibernians proved equal to the task of eradicating pernicious Irish stereotypes, and by threat of boycott, they succeeded in turning the tide. Disappearing quickly were the ribald and raucous songs of inebriated Irishmen, clad in rags and living in slums. Gone, too, were the insidious references to "shanty Irish," as witticisms and barbs were now hurled at the social pretensions of an emerging "lace curtain" Irish. As previously discussed, J. M. Synge's play *The Playboy of the Western World* incited riots from Irish

---

83. Quoted in Kaufmann, *Faith and Fraternalism,* 57–58.
84. John J. Appel, "From Shanties to Lace Curtains: The Irish Image in *Puck*, 1877–1910," *Comparative Studies in Society and History* 13 (October 1971): 365–75; and Brown, *Irish-American Nationalism,* 45.

American audiences. And in one of those rare incidents, the Catholic Church joined hands with the radicals in denouncing the play as "a degrading spectacle."[85]

Representative of Irish American tastes for more respectable portrayals of their culture was J. Hartley Manners's 1912 play *Peg O' My Heart*, which became an overnight triumph on Broadway. Starring Laurette Taylor, it proved doubly pleasing to Irish Americans, as it not only boasted of the feminine virtues of a simple Irish American maiden, but it contrasted them favorably to the insipid, self-serving vices of her wealthier English relatives. In the following year, Manners expanded somewhat on the play by producing a novel by the same title; however, even Manners was unable to pass Catholic censorship over some ambiguous anti-clerical references that appeared in the book. After promising one week to audiences that the novel would be appearing in serial form in subsequent editions, one Catholic newspaper apologized for canceling it the following week because of Manners' unfortunate choice of words.[86]

The quest for respectability was one of the final stages in the protracted acculturation process for Irish Americans leading up to 1914. However, the transitional process from outcast to insider was not completed in 1914 when the old question of where Irish American and Catholic allegiances lay was resurrected. Too many paradoxes remained within the community to assure an amenable and unanimous response at a moment when such assurances were being sought. In fact, it would take the better part of a worldwide conflagration to draw the saga closer to resolution.

Irish American Catholics were in an ambiguous position in 1914. In the political world, the Irish had secured a way of benefitting themselves, yet the impolitic methods of Irish American urban machines and some Catholic voters tended to prohibit them from inclusion in mainstream Protestant society. Similarly, while it can be asserted that a burgeoning middle class of Irish Americans was emerging around the turn of the century, many others still languished

85. Shannon, *The American Irish*, 263; Himber, *The Letters of John Quinn*, 18.
86. J. Hartley Manners, *Peg O' My Heart* (New York: Gross & Dunlap, 1913); Brooklyn *Tablet*, January 23 & 30, 1913.

in the lower classes. If anything, the path from "Paddy to Studs" was long and arduous, and most Irish Americans appeared to be plodding along rather methodically.[87] Culturally, Irish Americans remained contradictory as well. That the Irish were now supporting temperance movements in unprecedented numbers was, as much as anything else, an admission that there still existed a significant drinking problem in their midst. Likewise, their predilection for demanding respectability betrayed a marked sensitivity to feelings of inferiority and insecurity.

Irish American Catholics stood in a unique position in 1914. Whereas the descendants of earlier Irish or Scots Irish Protestants had become assimilated early in the nineteenth century, "assimilation came more slowly for Irish Catholics." For Irish American Catholics, certain degrees of assimilation had been achieved. But culturally, religious acceptance had not yet been realized. They stood as an "excellent example where a lack of assimilation in some respects to the core culture was not accompanied by complete assimilation."[88] While they defiantly claimed American citizenship and felt second to none in patriotic sentiment, they were not fully accepted by American society. They also declined to "engage in the activities, organizations or mores of American [Protestant] society." While fully acculturated by 1914, Irish American Catholics still had not achieved full assimilation. They maintained a marked degree of distinctiveness, one that was both intrinsically felt and externally perceived by society.[89]

Quite clearly, the greatest factor serving as an impediment to the rapid assimilation of Irish American Catholics in 1914 remained their religion. And their Church leaders were divided over strategies to effect inclusion in the greater American society. On one hand, there was the Americanist Archbishop Ireland, who on many occasions, "warned the

87. Meagher, *From Paddy to Studs*, 181–87.
88. Joe R. Feagin, *Racial and Ethnic Relations* (Englewood Cliffs, NJ: Prentice Hall, 1978), 105–6.
89. Levine, *The Irish and Irish Politicians*, 70–71; John Duffy Ibson, "'Will the World Break Your Heart?': A Historical Analysis of the Dimensions and Consequences of Irish American Assimilation" (PhD dissertation, Brandeis University, 1976); William Leonard Joyce, "Editors and Ethnicity: A History of the Irish-American Press, 1848–1883" (PhD dissertation, University of Michigan, 1974).

Irish that they must not set themselves up as a class apart," chiding them that "it was their duty to become completely identified with the American spirit and institutions."[90] Yet, at the same time, Cardinal O'Connell in Boston was erecting a fortress of isolation, exhorting his faithful to stand aloof and remain uncontaminated by American society. He expressed a deep mistrust for American culture and had nothing but contempt for Boston's Protestants, once quacking that the day of the "Puritan has passed. The Catholic remains." While a patriotic supporter of American institutions, he encouraged the development of an Irish Catholic mental ghetto, isolated and polarized from mainstream Boston society.[91] He once maintained that his Irish Catholics "took joy in their poverty," and when a certain Mr. Murphy of Boston died and gave his estate to Harvard, O'Connell demurred by writing that the "gentleman who died cared little for Catholic institutions ... his money would have done a great deal more for his clan if he had given it to the Catholic colleges where, after all is said, the Murphys belong."[92]

Life in the neighborhood parishes seemed to validate the ambiguous position of Irish Catholics in those cities where their numbers were great in the early twentieth century. In one respect, parish life isolated Irish American Catholic parishioners from other ethnic groups and Protestant America, limiting their horizons to the street grid that defined their own neighborhoods, and as such, "it retarded assimilation." On the other hand, parishes tended to accelerate the integration of immigrants and their children into American life. They also provided a structure for facilitating the emergence of a middle class and a newfound sense of respectability. They aided assimilation by "engendering a respect for private property, family stability, economic mobility, industry, thrift, a work ethic, and progress." Lay

90. James H. Moynihan, *The Life of Archbishop John Ireland* (New York: Macmillan, 1953), 62–63.

91. *Boston Globe,* April 15, 1908. O'Connell once condemned certain young Catholic men for joining the YMCA, admonishing them that, "here is an avowed Protestant society offering them certain material favors while discriminating against them." See Boston *Pilot,* September 3, 1914.

92. O'Connell, William Cardinal, *Recollections of Seventy Years* (Boston: Little, Brown, 1934), 33; Boston *Pilot,* January 22, 1916.

CHAPTER 2

organizations within the parish structure, particularly the Knights of Columbus, inspired patriotism, and an identification with their adopted country, yet did so in a defiantly militant and exclusive way.[93]

This was the state of the Irish American Catholic community in all its complexities and contradictions as it stood on the eve of World War I. The war would serve as a cauldron, boiling all these issues to the surface. By the time the United States was poised to enter the conflict, most of these simmering issues had reached some degree of resolution and the transition period in Irish American Catholic history had ended.

---

93. Skerrett, "The Catholic Dimension," 22–23; Patricia K. Good, "Irish Adjustment to American Society: Integration or Separation? A Portrait of the American Catholic Parish, 1863–1886," *Records of the American Catholic Historical Society of Philadelphia* 86 (March 1975): 19; and Meagher, "Irish, American, Catholic," 87.

CHAPTER 3

THE OUTBREAK OF THE GREAT WAR & THE CRISIS OF NEUTRALITY

It would be quite a stretch to suggest that Americans in the summer of 1914 were completely oblivious to the tumultuous events unfolding in Europe, starting with the assassination of Archduke Franz Ferdinand, presumptive heir to the throne of the Austro-Hungarian Empire, on June 28. Yet most Americans were going about their normal daily routines, engaged in the process of making a living and providing for their burgeoning families. The Fourth of July was but days away and Americans were preparing to revel in whatever way they could afford. Film of the time revealed middle class families crowding the beaches of resort cities like Atlantic City and Coney Island. Elite families were already ensconced in their extravagant summer mansions in exclusive sites like Newport, Rhode Island, or New York's Long Island. Midwesterners and heartland Americans gathered at lakes armed with picnic baskets, anxious to view evening firework displays. In small town America, kids flocked to sandlots to play America's pastime—baseball, while in crowded urban streets they were more likely to be dodging traffic, playing the more primitive game of stickball. On the surface, things looked good in America.

This idyllic portrait of America in the summer of 1914 should not obscure the era's seamy underside. In fact, the comfortable imagery of that year contrasted sharply with a bleaker picture, acutely evident in

CHAPTER 3

America's urban and isolated rural regions. Despite the implementation of some ameliorative measures in the Progressive Era, there remained a plethora of glaring social problems plaguing the country's major cities. Too numerous to catalogue here, the fundamental underlying problem was endemic poverty; most egregious calamities stemmed from this stark reality. Labor unrest, child labor, dreadful working conditions, abandoned wives, orphaned children wandering the streets, and rampant alcoholism were open sores drawing the attention of social reformers and the Progressive Era's "Muckrakers." Coupled with overcrowded tenements, thoroughly inadequate sanitation, and the pestilent spread of disease they sat in hideous counterpoise to the comfortable portraits revealed in the upbeat, ascendant imagery of middle-class America. Whereas Irish Americans were gradually crawling out of these hellish conditions, the American Catholic Church presided over those Catholic immigrants that had not escaped. Not always certain how to address these matters, the Church invested its energies into a vast network of charitable works, preferring to ameliorate the suffering rather than confront the underlying causes.[1]

When German armies rolled into Belgium in August 1914, it gave the American Church cause for concern on multiple levels. Chief among these concerns was, how would it reign over and rein in its polyglot immigrant constituency that could well express sympathies for any number of European belligerents, many of whom were adversaries of each other. Moreover, it must be noted while that the "Americanizing" of the Catholic Church was gaining momentum in 1914, the Church remained an integral part of a broader transnational Church anchored in Rome. Ever since Pope Pius IX had lost his temporal power over the Papal States to the surge of Italian nationalism and revolution, the Roman Church abhorred all modern ideologies and movements. The American Church, in the main, concurred with Rome. It would hardly be surprising, then, that the Church, like the American nation itself, advised Catholics to adopt a policy of strict neutrality with respect

---

1. The deplorable conditions afflicting American cities had been exposed in works such as Jacob Riis's *How the Other Half Lives*, Upton Sinclair's *The Jungle*, and Lincoln Steffens's *The Shame of the Cities*.

to the European war and to refrain from endorsing the revolutionary rhetoric of Irish nationalists. There was, however, one outlet through which American Catholics could demonstrate their solidarity with the transnational Church without seriously compromising their American loyalties, and it lay just south of the border in Mexico.

Mexican Problem

When Europe erupted into war in August 1914, the portent of an era ending was largely lost on the American people. To Irish American Catholics, the convulsions wracking the old order of Europe initially made little impression and did not jar their focus upon narrow and parochial interests. Outside of a small, yet vocal, minority of Irish American nationalists, the inauguration of the Great War was but one issue among several vying for publication headlines and for the attention and resources of the Church.

The matter which commanded the greatest attention among American Catholics in the summer of 1914 was the ever-deteriorating condition of the Mexican Church, snared in the throes of national revolution and anarchy. Since the overthrow of the dictator Porfirio Diaz in 1911, the fortunes of the Catholic Church had faded fast in a wave of resurrected anti-clericalism that swept the impoverished nation. Francisco Madero, a wealthy landowner from northern Mexico, had been the principal opponent of the Diaz regime and, once the long-term dictator had been deposed, Madero was overwhelmingly elected as the next Mexican president in October 1911. Madero genuinely sought to institute democratic reforms, social justice, and the redistribution of landholding in the troubled state. But it was not long before more radical revolutionaries and conservative reactionaries insinuated themselves and destabilized the situation. The first to make a bid for power was strongman General Victoriano Huerta. In 1913, Huerta toppled the Madero government and, after arresting the president, conveniently had him assassinated just outside the prison walls. The emergence of a military figure did not presage peace and stability. The unsettling aspects of the Mexican revolution were much like a minefield where even angels feared to tread.

CHAPTER 3

In a history dating back to the Spanish colonial era, the Church had always propped up the old order and had accordingly benefitted by accruing extensive property and landholdings. The exiled dictator Porfirio Diaz, in addition to inviting considerable American investment and development in Mexico, had maintained an uneasy truce with the Church which Madero's brief tenure did not jeopardize. Huerta's rise to power was hailed by the Mexican Church as a fortuitous signal, as a strongman it seemed, was required to establish as broad a political power base as he could marshal together. In the United States, the American hierarchy sided with the Mexican prelates and business interests and rallied around Huerta so long as he demonstrated that he could maintain power. But the Mexican Church soon became a target for an insurgency of the landless poor. No sooner had Huerta seized power than opposition forces began to contest his control. From the northern regions of Mexico, a large landowner, Venustiano Carranza, leading a faction and heading an army called the Constitutionalists, began moving southwards. Meanwhile, in the southern and coastal areas of Mexico, a popular revolutionary and folk hero, Emilio Zapata, roamed freely, attacking symbols of the privileged landed class, including the Church.[2]

Back in Washington, the Wilson administration watched events unfold in Mexico, alternating between detached aloofness and heightened concern for the safety of both American citizens and business interests. Observing the prevailing chaos, Wilson was not inclined to grant US recognition to any of the contenders, although he favored Carranza, whose promise of a constitutionally based government was more attuned to American sensibilities. Then in March 1914, the lead elements of Carranza's forces approached the outskirts of the port city of Tampico, where they encountered Huerta's army, desperate to hold onto this strategic region. With American citizens in the area, mostly connected to American interests in the regional oil business, the Wilson administration ordered naval warships off the coast as a precautionary measure. Although Tampico was being besieged by Constitutionalist forces, relations between US forces

---

2. Lawrence Lenz, *Power and Policy: America's First Steps to Superpower, 1899–1922* (New York: Algora Publishing, 2008), 186–88.

and Huerta's federal garrison remained amicable. That relationship deteriorated when, on April 2, the gunboat *Dolphin*, the only US vessel able to enter the shallow harbor entrance, glided into port, firing a 21-gun salute in honor of the anniversary of the Mexican expulsion of French forces from Mexico in 1867. Once there, however, an incident broke out between the *Dolphin*'s crew and Huerta's forces, leading to the arrest of several American sailors that generated a diplomatic *contretemps*. Rear Admiral Henry T. Mayo, commander of US naval forces in the area, demanded the immediate return of the incarcerated sailors and a gun salute to an American flag planted on Mexican soil. Huerta complied with most of the demands, including a sincere letter of apology, but was not willing to salute the American flag, as Mexican pride would not permit it. Apprised of the situation, Wilson asked the Congress permission for an armed invasion of the area. On April 22, Wilson received the blessing of Congress. He ordered the occupation of Vera Cruz, south of Tampico along the Gulf Coast, which offered a harbor that permitted the entry of larger warships. American marines and sailors entered the city of Vera Cruz and engaged the federal forces under Huerta. In skirmishes that followed, the Mexicans lost considerably more men and civilians than did the Americans. American forces would occupy Vera Cruz for the next three months, aiding in the downfall of Huerta's regime and earning the enduring enmity of the Mexican people.[3]

When in July 1914 the government and armies of Huerta had been defeated and driven into exile, it appeared that the policies of Wilson had triumphed and that a new era of peace, prosperity and stability would soon be introduced into Mexico. The American Catholic Church's hierarchy did not share Wilson's sanguine view of the Mexican situation. In an interview with the *New York Times*, Cardinal Gibbons, though circumspectly supportive of the president's views, did not express much hope that Carranza and his chief lieutenant,

---

3. Arthur S. Link, *The Struggle for Neutrality, 1914–1917* (Princeton, NJ: Princeton University Press, 1960), 232. An overview of the Tampico incident and the occupation of Vera Cruz can be found in Robert E. Quirk, *An Affair of Honor: Woodrow Wilson and the Occupation of Vera Cruz* (New York: W. W. Norton, 1967), 1–120.

CHAPTER 3

Pancho Villa, would honor agreements to respect the integrity of the Mexican Church.[4] Sadly for the Mexican Church, as well as the general populace, July proved to be only a brief respite in the agonizing pain of anarchy and bloodshed. By July's end, the Constitutionalists were divided and in substantial disarray, with Villa emerging as Carranza's chief challenger and Zapata freelancing as a reckless revolutionary.

By mid-August, it became clear to American Church leadership that the situation in Mexico had deteriorated, and that the depredations against church property and persons had only accelerated. Holding both Carranza and Villa directly responsible, Gibbons encouraged Wilson to intervene on the side of the Constitutionalists, only to learn that the president declined to use his personal influence with the Mexican government, believing that patience was called for until passions died down.[5]

As summer gave way to fall, Church criticism of the Wilson administration increased and began getting a great deal of attention from the Catholic press, easily rivaling news of the war in Europe. Leading the charge was the Reverend Francis C. Kelley, who informed the faithful of the outrages and horrors of the revolution and the administration's indifference to them. Kelley also succeeded in enlisting the support of Richard Tierney, the Jesuit editor of *America,* an immensely popular Catholic journal.[6] Throughout the remainder of 1914, the Wilson administration resolved to allow the Mexicans to settle their own affairs, satisfying itself with admonishing revolutionaries,

---

4. *New York Times,* "Wilson Receives Carranza Leader," July 23, 1914, p. 6.

5. James Cardinal Gibbons to Woodrow Wilson, August 18, 1914, in Link, *The Papers of Woodrow Wilson,* 30:399–400; Woodrow Wilson to James Cardinal Gibbons, August 21, 1914, *The Papers of Woodrow Wilson,* 30:420. Note, however, that Wilson let Villa and Carranza know that "nothing will shock the civilized world more than punitive or vindictive action towards priests and ministers of any Church." On the other hand, Wilson pledged that any clergymen who had committed crimes would eventually be held accountable. See William Jennings Bryan to George C. Carothers and John Reid Silliman, July 23, 1914, in *The Papers of Woodrow Wilson,* 30:297–98.

6. James D. Gaffey, *Francis Clement Kelley and the American Dream,* 2 vols. (Bensenville, IL: Heritage Foundation, 1980), 2:3–15; *America,* August 8, 1914, October 3, 1914, October 23, 1914.

particularly Zapata, for acts of violence against the Mexican Church. The administration's position on the plight of the Mexican Church was conditional, as demonstrated in William Jennings Bryan's missive to Father Kelley noting that Mexican leaders would come to know that should they hope to "gain sympathy and moral support of America, Mexico must have ... just land tenure, free schools, and true freedom of conscience and worship." Meanwhile the American Church continued to inveigh against the administration for failing to take a more action to restore the Mexican Church to her former status.[7]

The Status of Irish Nationalism in 1914

The American Church's preoccupation with the Mexican revolution throughout 1914 obscures the fact that a major worldwide war had been declared, presenting the best opportunity in a long time for the liberation of Ireland. However, when the Irish American community peered outside its parish jurisdictions, Mexico appears to have been their focus, kept there by a clergy seemingly obsessed with righting the wrongs of anti-clericalism. Whatever passion might have been tapped for taking up Ireland's freedom was diminished by the Mexican focus, diverted to the restoration of the pre-revolutionary status of that Church.

Even though Mexico elicited the strongest response from the Church in 1914, Irish affairs grabbed significant attention as well. Irish interests affected the way Irish American Catholics viewed the outbreak of war in 1914. In the years leading up to the Great War, numerous issues involving Irish American interests emerged because of improved

---

7. Memorandum from Paul Fuller to Woodrow Wilson on Mexico Trip, August 20, 1914, in Link, *The Papers of Woodrow Wilson,* 30:417; Paul Fuller to Woodrow Wilson, September 21, 1914 in Link, *The Papers of Woodrow Wilson,* 31:73–74; Remarks at a Press Conference, October 1, 1914, in Link, *The Papers of Woodrow Wilson,* 31:122. Bryan is quoted in Michael Kazin, *A Godly Hero: The Life of William Jennings Bryan* (New York: Alfred A. Knopf, 2006), 231–32. Typical of the Catholic Presses attitude toward Wilson at the end of the year was Dr. Thomas P. Hart's verdict: "We do not hesitate to admit that we have thought and still think—that Mr. Wilson did not use sufficient pressure to protect those in religion, and especially the defenseless Sisters, from the bestial passions of the so-called Constitutionalists." See *Catholic Telegraph,* December 10, 1914.

CHAPTER 3

Anglo-American relations. Some Irish Americans, especially those referred to as "professionals," doubted the Wilson administration's willingness to steer clear of the Anglophile orbit.[8]

One of the more unsettling challenges facing Irish American Anglophobes in their resistance to the growing Anglo-American *rapprochement* of the early twentieth century was the proposed Root-Bryce Arbitration Treaty, first proposed in 1907 and forwarded to the Senate for ratification in 1911 with President Taft's approval. Arbitration treaties had been in vogue throughout the latter half of the nineteenth century, but this one, in the eyes of Irish nationalists, suggested more of an alliance with Great Britain than a mere willingness to submit grievances between the two countries for mediation. Leading the charge against its ratification was John Devoy, the editor of the *Gaelic-American*, who had so often fought uphill, even quixotic, battles against Anglo-American friendship. In arguably his best crusade, Devoy mounted a full-scale assault upon the popular perception that the two English-speaking nations somehow shared a common destiny. In a rally at New York's Cooper Union on February 19, 1911, the aging Fenian harangued the crowd, vowing that those in attendance loved America "more than we hate England." He pleaded that the Senate "stand by George Washington's policy of no entangling alliances" and demanded that "closer relations with England amounting to a virtual alliance shall not be established." The following year, at the very moment the Senate was ready to vote on the treaty, Devoy circulated an unflattering passage that British Ambassador Bryce had written about the American Senate. In the early hours of March 7, 1912, after prolonged debate, the Senate rejected the treaty.[9]

Shortly after the treaty's rejection, the growing accord between Washington and London was again underscored by the Wilson

---

8. Sir Cecil Spring Rice to Lord Grey, November 13, 1914, in Stephen A. Gwynn, ed., *The Letters and Friendships of Sir Cecil Spring Rice*, 2 vols. (London: Macmillan, 1929), 2: 245. The term "professionals" was used here to describe those Irish Americans who advocated revolutionary measures and physical force to bring about Irish independence.

9. Speech printed in *Gaelic-American*, February 25, 1911. See also Terry Golway, *Irish Rebel: John Devoy and America's Fight for Ireland's Freedom*, 188.

administration's introduction of a bill to repeal the exemption to paying tolls that American ships enjoyed at the Panama Canal. The issue had emerged from the 1901 Hay-Paunceforte Treaty, in which the British had given the United States a free hand in building and fortifying a canal on the condition that all nations would be subjected to toll payments. The United States believed that they were naturally excluded from this condition, whereas the British insisted that the Americans had been included with all other nations and were now reneging on their agreement. The debate surrounding the impasse pitted Irish Americans against the Wilson administration, with the former convinced that the United States was truckling to British maritime power, and the latter believing it an issue of honoring diplomatic pledges.

Throughout 1913, debate raged over the proposed repeal of exemption. Leading the opposition was the "virulently anti-British" Tammany-bred senator from New York, James O'Gorman. He had already incurred the enmity of Wilson himself for helping to shift Tammany's support away from Wilson at the 1912 convention. O'Gorman's reason for opposition to the Panama Tolls Bill was so blatant that even the French observer Jean Jules Jusserand took note that O'Gorman "manifests on every occasion an unyielding hostility toward England." In March 1914, Wilson appeared before the Congress and made an emphatic appeal for the repeal of the exemption. In the aftermath of the president's initiative, Irish Americans mobilized their forces to mount one last defense of the toll exemption. At the end of March, their supporters in New York gathered at Carnegie Hall and sent to Washington resolutions condemning the administration's course of action. In Washington, British Ambassador Sir Cecil Spring Rice was amused to note how feverishly Irish Americans opposed buckling under to the British. Even one of Wilson's staunchest allies in the Senate, Thomas J. Walsh of Montana, railed against the repeal. Despite support from other sectors of the American population, Irish American opposition to the repeal was to no avail. The bill passed in June 1914.[10]

10. On O'Gorman's intransigence over the toll exemption, see the Diary of Josephus Daniels, April 15, 1913, in Link, *The Papers of Woodrow Wilson*, 27:313; Sir Cecil Spring Rice to Sir William Tyrell, January 27, 1914, in ibid., 29:35. Joining O'Gorman in his dislike of Wilson at the time of the

CHAPTER 3

The Panama Tolls controversy confirmed a transparent Irish American dislike for Britain at the time war broke out in Europe. It also highlighted the emerging estrangement between Woodrow Wilson and those Irish Americans whom he felt were allowing their abhorrence for British power to cloud their commitment to the American government's foreign and domestic policy. Two months later, during his address at the unveiling of a statue of Commodore Jack Barry in Franklin Park in Washington on May 16, 1914, Wilson assailed the motives and loyalties of those Irish Americans who had opposed him. After praising the Irish-born Barry for his bravery and valor, he impugned the patriotism of some Irish Americans by suggesting that though Barry was Irish, "his heart [had] crossed the Atlantic." Moreover, the president insinuated that the test of all Americans, irrespective of their "ancient affections," was whether or not they acted according to American interests "on this side of the sea." He claimed that "some Americans need hyphens in their names, because only part of them have come over." After dismissing the propriety of the hyphen in the realm of American thought, Wilson moved towards his conclusion that Irish Americans who did not emulate Jack Barry were less than 100 percent Americans:

> "This man [Barry] was not an Irish-American; he was an Irishman who became American. I venture to say if he voted, he voted with regard to the questions as they looked on this side of the water and not on the others side; and that is my infallible test of a genuine American—that when he votes or when he acts or when

1912 convention were Tammany boss Charles F. Murphy and sachem Daniel F. Cohalan. Cohalan was an active leader in the Clan-na-Gael. See Stanley Coben, *A. Mitchell Palmer* (New York: Columbia University Press, 1963), 62–63; Jean Jules Jusserand to Gaston Doumergue, February 7, 1914, in Link, *The Papers of Woodrow Wilson*, 29:233. Condemnation of Wilson's appeal can be found in *Irish World*, March 28, 1914. Spring Rice also noted that the Home Rule bill "doesn't seem to soften" Irish American attitudes toward the Panama Tolls issue. See Link, *The Papers of Woodrow Wilson*, 27:349. Senator Walsh's opposition can be found in William T. Pigott to Thomas J. Walsh, March 24, 1914, *T. J. Walsh Papers*, Library of Congress.

he fights, his heart and his thought are nowhere but in the center of the emotions and the purposes and the policies of the United States.[11]

While most Irish Americans and the Catholic press were virtually silent in response to Wilson's remarks, professional Irish Americans excoriated Wilson for what appeared to be an insult. Noting that Wilson apparently lost sight of the fact that he was in Franklin Park at the invitation of prominent Irish Americans, John Devoy observed that it "required a peculiarly mean man to abuse courtesy," and that Wilson indulged himself in a "mean and unwarrantable attack on the citizenship of the race of which Commodore Barry came." Devoy believed that Wilson was nursing a grudge from the Panama Tolls controversy and deplored the fact that Wilson "used Jack Barry as a club to hit Jack Barry's countrymen of today because they oppose him in a political controversy." The enmity that came to characterize the relationship between the professional Irish and Woodrow Wilson throughout the Great War began with this flap over Jack Barry's statue.[12]

The progress of Irish freedom and whether it would be expressed within or apart from the United Kingdom had an immense impact upon Irish American attitudes toward World War I. The lines drawn over the Home Rule struggle had revealed sharp divisions within the Irish American community that would increase throughout the war. Moderate Irish American leaders like John Quinn, Bourke Cockran, and Michael Ryan had been delighted by the introduction of a promising Home Rule Bill in 1911. By April 1912, the bill had been read a third time in Parliament, and Irish excitement on both sides of the Atlantic increased as details for its imminent implementation were negotiated.

---

11. John M. Blum, *Joe Tumulty and the Wilson Era*, 69; *Address of President Wilson at the Unveiling of the Statue of Commodore Jack Barry,* May 16, 1914 (Washington, DC: Government Printing Office, 1914).

12. Thomas V. Shannon linked Wilson's remarks on hyphenism to Irish American neutrality in the war that had just broken out. Referring to Wilson's statements as "Yankee prudery, and not worth the slightest attention," Shannon claimed that the "fact that our citizens are of various nations is the surest guarantee that America will give her entire sympathy to none of them." See *New World,* September 18, 1914. Devoy's remarks were printed in the *Gaelic-American,* May 23, 1914.

CHAPTER 3

However, neither the Irish nor the Irish Americans took into consideration the sentiments of the predominantly Protestant six northern counties of Ulster. Their economic ties, religious affinities, and political loyalties mandated continued inclusion in the United Kingdom. With some evident support from Tory sympathizers in Parliament, and under the bold leadership of Sir Edward Carson, they began to collect arms to resist Home Rule by forming the Ulster Volunteers. To counter the mobilization of force in the north, Irish Catholics in the south organized their own volunteer force, and the fragile peace that John Redmond had labored so long to construct began to disintegrate. Mounting tensions finally gave way to violence on July 14, 1914, when gun shipments arrived at the Irish port of Howth near Dublin. British attempts to interdict the delivery of a measly 900 antiquated Mausers failed, but as the King's Own Scottish Borderers returned to their barracks in Dublin, they were accosted by civilians along Bachelor's Walk. The regulars fired into the unarmed crowd and bayoneted one man, resulting in the deaths of four civilians and the wounding of nearly forty.[13]

Near universal condemnation for these killings rained down upon the British government from the Irish American community. If Shane Leslie held Carson ultimately responsible for the outbreak of bloodshed, John Quinn felt Redmond was to blame for not having insisted in the first place that Ulster be prohibited from arming itself. From the editorials of the *Gaelic-American*, stinging attacks fell upon the British government and the failed policies of the Home Rule Party's chief, John Redmond. In a rare moment of solidarity, even Irish American Catholic editors could agree with Devoy's denunciations of the British. While it is not surprising that the hostile anti-British Irish American editor Joseph P. O'Mahoney shared the grisly details of the deaths on the front page of the *Indiana Catholic*, even moderate Irish American Catholic editors expressed repugnance for this atrocity.[14]

---

13. Edward Cuddy, *Irish-Americans and National Isolationism, 1914–1920* (New York: Arno Press, 1976), 42–43. The conservative intellectual Shane Leslie thought that Carson's intervention had dashed hopes for resolving the Irish issue. See Shane Leslie, *The Irish Issue in Its American Aspect* (New York: Macmillan, 1917), 47.

14. John Quinn to AE Russell, November 9, 1914, *John Quinn Papers*, New

OUTBREAK OF GREAT WAR AND NEUTRALITY

Publisher and editor Fred Sharon of the *Catholic Messenger* of Davenport, Iowa, described the Bachelor's Walk killings as "wanton and inexcusable" and could only hope that the gross stupidity of the act might "call the British government and Tory Ulsterites to their senses." Francis P. Smith of the *Pittsburgh Catholic* portrayed the incident as a "dastardly murder ... in thorough keeping with the interminable acts of bloody cruelty."[15]

Notwithstanding the violence of early summer, the Home Rule bill became law in September 1914. In the time between the Bachelor's Walk incident and the passage of the bill, England had declared war and, as a result, the execution of the bill was suspended so that Ulster could cooperate in the war effort. As for Redmond, he pledged the support of all Ireland for the empire in its hour of peril. In October 1914, Redmond went beyond his earlier pledge to defend Ireland's shores with his Volunteers. Now, instead of freeing British soldiers to fight the war in France, he offered to recruit Irishmen for the battlefields of Europe. According to Edward Cuddy, Redmond's offer to furnish the British army with the flower of Ireland's youth totally decimated Irish American support for the Home Rule Party.[16]

While there is evidence to suggest that Redmond's actions cost him a considerable degree of Irish American support, this assertion overlooks continued encouragement from many quarters within this community. As expected, the Clan-na-Gael thoroughly repudiated Redmond's intentions to assist the British Empire; the organization had rejected Home Rule ever since the bill had been introduced in 1911.[17] One of the Clan's chief aims during the year 1914 had been

York Public Library; *Gaelic-American,* June 13, 20, 27, 1914; *Indiana Catholic,* July 31, 1914.

15. *Catholic Messenger,* August 4, 1914; *Pittsburgh Catholic,* July 30, 1914.
16. Cuddy, *Irish-Americans and National Isolationism,* 44–47.
17. The three principal leaders of the Clan-na-Gael who championed physical force solutions for Ireland's liberation were Devoy, McGarrity and Cohalen. Devoy's role in this effort can be easily traced in the pages of the *Gaelic-American,* which, since the research for this study was conducted, have been set in a digital format. Much of his correspondence with the IRB and other Sinn Fein notables in Ireland can be found in William O'Brien and Desmond Ryan, eds., *Devoy's Post Bag,* 2 vols. (New York: C. J. Fallon, 1948). These volumes have also been

CHAPTER 3

to disassociate Irish Americans from Redmond and to discredit the Home Rule bill, which they thought fell short of their goal of complete independence. In a variety of editions of the *Gaelic-American* throughout the summer and fall of 1914, John Devoy smeared Redmond and fulminated against his use of the Irish Volunteers in the service of Britain. After Redmond promised to defend Ireland in order to free British troops for France, the *Gaelic-American* headlined an article on Redmond's perfidy by exclaiming: "Assures the British Government That The Irish Volunteers Will Betray Their Country By Holding It for England While Her Rotten Army is Fighting."[18]

Backing for Redmond among more moderate Irish Americans also suffered because of his support for recruitment. As president of the United Irish League (UILA), Michael J. Ryan had been a steadfast champion of Redmond and his Parliamentary Party and for years had opposed the more radical elements of the Clan-na-Gael. As a politician who hoped to further his own ambitions, he had no stomach for those like Joseph McGarrity of Philadelphia who advocated physical

---

digitized. The traditional source for McGarrity is Sean Cronin, *The McGarrity Papers: Revelations of the Irish Revolutionary Movement in Ireland and America, 1900–1940* (New York: Anvil Books, 1972). This has been digitized by Villanova University. Cohalen's papers, as well as several pamphlets and addresses, are housed in the Manuscript Division of the New York Public Library. His involvement in the events leading up to the Easter Rising have been most recently discussed in Michael Doorley, "Judge Cohalen and American Involvement in the Easter Rising," in Grey, *Ireland's Allies,* 151–64.

18. F. M. Carroll, *American Opinion and the Irish Question, 1910–1922,* 46–47; *Gaelic-American,* August 8, 1914. Note that the *Irish World*, after the death of Patrick Ford in 1913, adopted a more "professional" outlook about Ireland under the direction of his sons. The Fords joined Devoy in condemning Redmond for his decision to recruit Irishmen on England's behalf. See *Irish World,* September 26, 1914. When in May 1914 Philadelphia's *Public Ledger* reported that the city's Irish population was ecstatic at the prospect of Home Rule for Ireland, Philadelphia businessman and Clan chieftain Joseph McGarrity resolved to undermine such a settlement. See Dennis Clark, *The Irish in Philadelphia: Ten Generations of Urban Experience* (Philadelphia: Temple University Press, 1973), 149. One historian who suggests that Redmond's call for aiding the British Empire seriously undermined Irish American support is David Brundage, *Irish Nationalists in America: The Politics of Exile, 1798–1998* (New York: Oxford University Press, 2016), 142–45.

force as the only means to achieve Ireland's liberation. Sensing that England would not postpone Home Rule for long, Ryan threw himself into raising thousands of dollars for moderate constitutional solutions to Ireland's woes. If the Clan could produce several hundred enthusiastic supporters at political rallies in Philadelphia, Ryan could count upon tens of thousands of contributors, many of whom were the "Irish bourgeoisie and the steady workmen in the decent parishes across the city." Ryan's unequivocal backing of Redmond, however, ended when the latter started to recruit Irishmen for the British army. In October 1914, Ryan informed Redmond that Irish American funding would evaporate now that he was directly giving succor to England. Ryan's withdrawal of support was not linked to a rejection of the moderate course of action in 1914 as much as it was a repudiation of Redmond's alignment to London's war efforts. Redmond had carelessly risked Irish American support in his linking Ireland's fortunes to the British Empire. Despite divisions in America as to how Irish autonomy would be inaugurated, there was little interest in departing from a course of neutrality.[19]

In Washington, Spring Rice was quick to comprehend the divisions existing among Irish Americans in the fall of 1914. Writing to Foreign Minister Sir Edward Grey in November, he intimated that his sources had revealed that the "Labour Unions and the Irish are almost entirely on our side ... the professional Irish, and leaders of the Sinn Fein party are against us, but do not carry their parties with them." He concluded by forecasting that there was "practically no chance of united actions between Germans and Irish." The divisiveness that Spring Rice perceived apparently carried over to fundraising efforts among the various Irish American societies. In some instances, it was

19. Dennis Clark, "Intrepid Men: Three Philadelphia Irishmen, 1880–1920," in Meagher, *From Paddy to Studs,* 104–5; Denis Gwynn, *The Life of John Redmond* (London: Burns, Oates and Washburne, 1932), 418. Redmond, much like Devoy, understood the absolute importance of Irish American backing. One publication's dedication page included a toast "from Ireland to Irishmen in America," sent by John E. Redmond, MP. This toast was printed in cursive style, first in Gaelic, then in English, and read, "United we stand, divided we fall." See Shane na Gael, *Irish Toasts* (Boston: H. M. Caldwell Co., 1908).

reported, that requests were made for conflicting purposes. Accusations also abounded as to where the money was actually going.[20]

The assertion that the bottom dropped out of support for Redmond does not seem to have accounted for the Catholic Church's unwavering support for him and Home Rule. When Harvey Cassidy, editor of the *Catholic Sun*, and James K. McGuire, former mayor of Syracuse, collaborated on editorials reproaching Redmond's character, the local ordinary, Bishop John Grimes, had them both censured. Similarly, when the United Irish League's "Redmond Branch" continued to support Home Rule, McGuire felt compelled to part company with them. When Shane Leslie and other Irish Americans financed the publication of a new magazine, *Ireland*, to counteract "German-financed" Irish news and to promote backing for Home Rule, it was claimed that Cardinal Gibbons viewed it favorably and would soon be contributing an article. The normally reserved Gibbons did not stop at supporting efforts to buoy provincial efforts for Home Rule. In a postscript to a note circulating copies of Cardinal Desire-Joseph Mercier's pastoral letter, he wrote Redmond:

> I wish to tell you ... of my admiration and gratification when you proved your sterling loyalty by urging your fellow countrymen to support their government in the crisis through which it was passing. Your words were most timely and golden and have added immeasurably to the esteem in which you are held by right thinking men.

This sentiment was reflected in the views of the Baltimore *Catholic Review*, published under the cardinal's aegis, which applauded Irish "fealty to the Union."[21]

20. Cecil Spring Rice to Lord Newton, November 13, 1914, in Stephen A. Gwynn, *The Letters and Friendships of Sir Cecil Spring Rice*, 2:245. See also Wittke, *The Irish in America*, 274.
21. Beadles, "The Syracuse Irish," 237–41; Carroll, *American Opinion and the Irish Question*, 46; James Cardinal Gibbons to Sir John Redmond, MP, February 17, 1915, *The Gibbons Papers*, Archdiocesan Archives of Baltimore; *Baltimore Catholic Review*, September 26, 1914.

OUTBREAK OF GREAT WAR AND NEUTRALITY

Gibbons's reference to the "right thinking men" betrayed a marked conservative bent to Irish American Catholic thought regarding the progress of Irish self-government and the proper role of Irish American nationalism. Neither was Redmond's support among most Catholic newspapers diminished by his support for the British at the beginning of the war. In fact, it was greatly praised in many Catholic journals and papers by Irish American editors who were quick to divorce themselves and their loyal readership from professionals like Devoy, Cohalan, and McGarrity. To be sure, there were those like O'Mahoney of the *Indiana Catholic*, who seriously doubted the wisdom of Redmond's decision, uncertain that those Irish who supported Home Rule would "Die for England's glory." At the close of 1914, O'Mahoney challenged "those conservative Celts" in the United States for their "having been duped," claiming that these folks wanted other Celts to sing "God Save the King" and "Britannia Rules the Waves." Meanwhile, the slightly less venomous *Freeman's Journal* considered Redmond's recruitment efforts as too great a price for the passage of the Home Rule bill.[22]

The great majority of the Catholic press, however, echoed Gibbons's praise for Redmond. Contrasting the *Freeman's Journal*'s dour appraisal of Redmond's support of the empire was another New York Catholic paper, edited by the Reverend John L. Whelan, who headlined an editorial, "Nationalist Ireland is for the British Empire." "This is a bitter pill for some professional fire-eaters in America," Whelan admitted, "but it is a good thing for Ireland." William Hughes of the *Michigan Catholic* was certain that "Irish blood" could be "depended upon where Britain battles ... and these brave soldiers have never been found wanting when Duty called." Dr. Thomas P. Hart of Cincinnati also applauded Redmond's action, declaring that "with extraordinary courage and presence of mind, Redmond saw the psychological moment to place Ireland by the side of the British Empire in the gigantic struggle just beginning." Observing that the Home Rule bill had been signed in September 1914, Hart inferred that

---

22. *Indiana Catholic,* September 4, 1914, December 4, 1914; *Freeman's Journal,* October 10, 1914.

CHAPTER 3

it "puts her [Irish] people in a position of advantage ... to continue their campaign for ultimate independence."[23]

Praise for Redmond flowing from so many Irish American Catholic editors revealed not only a glowing endorsement for the moderate-conservative approach of Home Rule but a widening rift between mainstream Irish American Catholic thought and the more radical approach of the Clan-na-Gael and their affiliates. The voluminous encomiums for Redmond and Home Rule clearly revealed the belief that Ireland should act responsibly and prove its worthiness for autonomy by coming to the aid of the empire in its distress. While it would be wrong to suggest that this was indicative of outright support for Britain, or of any changes in the non-intervention posture of Irish Americans, it certainly did not demonstrate any antipathy for the British. Equally evident in their approval of Redmond was disdain for the professional Irish Americans who were counseling the Irish to use the empire's woes to their own advantage. Indeed, the acrimony reserved for the professionals by the Irish American Catholic press far exceeded their criticism of Britain in 1914.

The professionals' tarring of John Redmond struck an irritating chord among most Catholic editors. In Milwaukee, Humphrey Desmond called Redmond "the adroit Irish leader," and endorsed Redmond's "good sense" in trying to "increase rather than diminish friendship for the Irish cause." Dismayed by radical Irish Americans crying "Hoch der Kaiser," he feared that such treachery would undermine English voters' confidence in the Home Rule settlement. Weeks later, Desmond declared that, while he did not share Redmond's zealous efforts to recruit for the British army, "there is no reason for any excitement among Irish-Americans." He hastened to add rather astringently that "Sein [sic] Fein circles in Ireland (led by such great unknowns as Sir Roger Casement), and Clan-na-Gael objectors in this country, may be disregarded as negligible quantities, both as regard numbers and mental perspective."[24]

---

23. Brooklyn *Tablet*, September 19, 1914; *Michigan Catholic*, September 24, 1914; *Catholic Telegraph*, August 13, September 24, 1914.

24. *Catholic Citizen*, October 10, December 5, 1914. Father Phelan in St. Louis echoed this theme when he snidely remarked that all the Irish nationalists of

OUTBREAK OF GREAT WAR AND NEUTRALITY

Desmond was joined by many others in condemning the professionals for their attack upon John Redmond and the potential threat it posed to the Home Rule Bill. Fred Sharon in Davenport, Iowa, claimed that it was virtually impossible to conceive of Ireland as anything other than a "constituent part of the British Empire," and criticized the plans of those "alleged friends of Ireland" who would have a German army invade Ireland, as the "rankest kind of rank nonsense." He reminded his readers that this was not the time to "turn their backs on England and welcome as their masters the Germany of the Kulturkampf—a nation that has persecuted Catholics." Sharon continued to hammer away at the professionals, noting that the newly elected president of the Ancient Order of Hibernians, Joseph McLaughlin, was catering to ideas expressed by the Fords of the *Irish World*. Charging that McLaughlin "sought to influence the friends of Ireland in this country against the men and measures which they had supported," Sharon proceeded to extol the former US ambassador to Chile, Patrick Egan, for his unflagging support of Home Rule. He dismissed anything that McLaughlin said on behalf of the Hibernians by quipping that the Hibernian president's views represented "only his own ... which are erroneous at that."[25]

Just as many Irish Americans did not reject Redmond's Home Rule efforts despite his call for Irish enlistment, there is little to suggest in late 1914 that the Irish had soured on Redmond either. According to British historian Richard Grayson, Redmond's recruitment appeal enjoyed a 93 percent approval rating throughout the breadth of Ireland, among both unionists and nationalists. Over two hundred thousand Irishmen swelled the ranks of the British army, and many fought and died on the battlefields of the Great War. Moreover, at least thirty-five thousand Dubliners enlisted in the army, and as fate would have it, many of them, on leave home, were the first to respond to the Easter Rising insurgency in 1916.[26]

St. Louis shouted "Hoch der Kaiser"—"all six of them—count 'em." See *Western Watchman,* September 10, 1914.

    25. *Catholic Messenger,* September 10, 1914, January 7, 1915.

    26. Richard Grayson, *Belfast Boys: How Unionists and Nationalists Fought and Died Together in the First World War* (London: Continuum Books, 2009),

CHAPTER 3

Irish Americans, the Church, and the Policy of Neutrality

The same rancorous divisions that beset the Irish American community over the course of Irish nationalism carried over into their attitudes toward the outbreak of war in the summer of 1914. Even though the Clan-na-Gael has been touted to be representative of Irish American opinion, there does not seem to be much by way of corroborating evidence. When German armies began crossing the plains of Belgium, it appeared as though the sagging fortunes of the Clan might revive. They did, but only with a treasury amounting to about $50,000. As Clan Chieftain John Devoy somberly admitted, "it was a small amount with which to start an insurrection."[27] Despite the penury of the Clan, they devised not only to discredit John Redmond and the Home Rule movement but also to expand cooperation with the Germans. Additionally, they would insist upon a true and strict observance of US neutrality and plan a possible armed overthrow of the British in Ireland.

Devoy experienced little compunction in linking Ireland's interests to those of imperial Germany. In fact, there had been a great deal of cooperation between Irish Americans and German Americans in their attempts to stymie British imperialism. Support for an alliance of German and Irish societies dated back to 1907, when the Hibernians joined hands with the German Central Alliance to combat the signing of the *Entente Cordiale*. Ostensibly pledging themselves to fight against the passage of new discriminatory immigration laws, their principal aim was to prevent the United States from entering any binding alliances with European nations, especially Britain. When the

---

8–10. See also Richard Grayson, *Dublin's Great Wars: The First World War, the Easter Rising and the Irish Revolution* (Cambridge: Cambridge University Press, 2018), 4.

27. Dr. William Carroll to John Devoy, February 7, 1913, in William O'Brien and Desmond Ryan, eds., *Devoy's Post Bag, 1871–1928*, 2 vols. (Dublin: C. J. O'Fallon, 1956), 2:403–404. Link has noted that of the 4.5 million Irish Americans in 1914, most of them were anti-British and that "hopes for a German victory were as sincere as they were widespread." See Link, *The Struggle for Neutrality*, 22. Devoy's lament can be found in John Devoy, *Recollections of an Irish Rebel* (New York: Brentano, 1929), 393.

war broke out in 1914, both the Clan-na-Gael and the American Truth Society joined in this federation of societies. The latter organization was founded in 1912 by a fervent radical, Jeremiah A. O'Leary, who remained largely a loner despite his organization's merger with the United Irish Societies in 1914. Years later George Sylvester Viereck, publisher of the *Fatherland* (the largest German American newspaper of the time) remarked that O'Leary was not "pro-German," but suggested that he was only concerned that British influences were too strong in the United States and that the ultimate aim of Britain was to reduce the American nation to "an integral part of the British Empire." All the same, O'Leary enjoyed limited influence and, other than his celebrated repartee with Wilson over the president's re-nomination in 1916, he proved no more than a minor "thorn in the flesh of the administration."[28]

On August 15, the *Gaelic-American*'s headline triumphantly glowed with news that the Irish Volunteers and citizenry of New York had assembled in Celtic Park, Long Island, in order to "Declare They Stand With Germany." Behind the show of Irish support for the Germans, real efforts at backing up this declaration were soon put forth. Evidence suggests that important members of the Clan were in touch with one another, and that the emerging consensus was that some dramatic intervention in Ireland should be planned. From Philadelphia, Joseph McGarrity, the city's most prominent Clan member, who had earlier quarreled with the moderate Michael Ryan, indicated that he supported the idea of a German invasion of Ireland to oust the British. The old rebel John Devoy began establishing contacts with Germans in the United States, leading up to his meeting with German ambassador Count Johann von Bernstorff in late 1914. At that meeting, Devoy

28. Devoy, *Recollections of an Irish Rebel*, 401; James Child Clifton, *The German-Americans in Politics, 1914–1917* (Madison: University of Wisconsin Press, 1939), 6–7; Michael J. Kelley, "Biographical Sketch," in Jeremiah A. O'Leary, *My Political Trial and Experiences* (New York: Jefferson Publishing, 1919), 13–27; George Sylvester Viereck, *Spreading Germs of Hate* (New York: Scribner's Sons, 1930), 97. Michael Kazin correctly discerned that "most Irish Catholics were too preoccupied with their own internal quarrel" to reach consensus on sides to choose in the Great War. See Kazin, *War Against War: The American Fight for Peace* (New York: Simon & Schuster, 2017), 101.

CHAPTER 3

requested military aid, pointing out that it would be money well spent for both parties concerned.[29]

Other Irish American organizations that promoted radical goals in line with the Clan came forward with further expressions of Irish American solidarity. While New York remained the locus of Irish American efforts to aid Irish liberation, there was considerable support for these aims elsewhere, particularly in the Midwest. The St. Louis Committee of Irish Nationalists extended their sincere wishes for the success of Kaiser Wilhelm at their meeting on September 8. In Indiana, O'Mahoney headed up a movement of Irish Americans throughout the state to oppose British policies and, while his influence may be questioned, a study of public opinion in Indiana observed that most Irish Americans favored Germany at this early stage in the Great War. Because of the large population of Germans in the Midwest, the press (especially the Catholic papers) there tended to treat Germany more sympathetically than papers on the East Coast.[30]

Far and away the most significant effort to usher in a new era of Irish freedom by soliciting German aid was that of a native Protestant Irishman, Sir Roger Casement. Destined to become the most pathetic of Ireland's freedom fighters during the Great War, Casement had been awarded a knighthood for his humanitarian efforts in the Belgian Congo and in a remote region of the Amazon River Valley called Putumayo. Over time, Casement became disenchanted with British policy in Ireland, resulting in his retirement from public service in 1913 and his dedication to working for Irish freedom with the assistance of Devoy, McGarrity, and Judge Daniel F. Cohalan. Casement happened to be in the United States in July 1914 raising funds to arm the Irish Volunteers when the European order began to unravel.[31]

29. *Gaelic-American,* August 15, 1914; Marie V. Tarpey, *The Role of Joseph McGarrity in the Struggle for Irish Independence* (New York: Arno Press, 1976), 83; Devoy, *Recollections of an Irish Rebel,* 403.

30. John C. Crighton, *Missouri and the World War, 1914–1917* (Columbia: University of Missouri Press, 1947), 97; Cedric C. Cummins, *Indiana Public Opinion and the World War, 1914–1917* (Indianapolis: Indiana Historical Bureau, 1945), 56–57; Dean R. Esslinger, "American Catholicism and Irish Attitudes," *Catholic Historical Review* 53 (June 1967): 200–201.

31. For an excellent treatment of Casement's work for the British Foreign

OUTBREAK OF GREAT WAR AND NEUTRALITY

The outbreak of war spawned an outpouring of schemes from Casement's pen. He was convinced that British imperialism was not only shackling the prosperity and freedom of Ireland, but also damaging the fortunes of both Germany and America. According to Devoy, and very much against his wishes, Casement put out feelers to the German government by expressing sentiments favorable to the Reich in an address given on August 25, 1914. To the Kaiser, Casement voiced hope that Germany would thrash Britain, and praised the Germans for fighting to preserve European civilization against British cupidity. Casement's crowning project was his intention to sail to Germany to establish a military brigade from Irish soldiers in the British army whom the Germans had taken as prisoners of war. In return, Casement would exact a promise from Berlin that the Germans would seek as one of their explicit war aims the separation of Ireland from the British Empire. Additionally, Casement expected that the Germans would furtively furnish Ireland with arms, munitions, and German officers to lead an Irish revolt, should the opportunity arise.[32]

It was Devoy's opinion that Casement was naïve about the prospects of convincing the Germans to agree to such specific commitments. Only McGarrity was excited over Casement's plans. Despite Devoy's misgivings, Casement eventually went to Germany under vague promises from Berlin that if, and when, German troops invaded Ireland, they would bring about an end to British rule. In recalling an interview with Arthur Zimmerman, Germany's Under-Secretary of State for

---

Office, see Roger Sawyer, *Casement: The Flawed Hero* (London: Routledge, Kegan Paul, 1984); *Daily Express* (London), November 19, 1920, a clipping found in the Casement Papers, New York Public Library. For dispatches from von Bernstorff to Berlin, revealing Casement's connection to Devoy and Cohalan, see *Documents Relative to the Sinn Fein Movement* (London: His Majesty's Stationery Office, 1921).

32. Casement's plans were spelled out in two separate scenarios entitled, "How Ireland Might Help Germany," and "How Germany Should Help Ireland," manuscript dated August 20, 1914, *Casement Papers,* New York Public Library. On McGarrity's enthusiastic support of Casement, see Maua Anand, Andrew S. Hicks, & R. Bryan Willits, "The Man in Philadelphia: Joseph McGarrity and 1914," in Miriam Nyhan Grey, ed. *Ireland's Allies: America and the 1916 Easter Rising* (Dublin: University College Dublin Press, 2016), 109–123.

CHAPTER 3

the Foreign Office, Casement underscored Germany's declaration of "goodwill" towards Ireland, in which Berlin only wished "national prosperity and national freedom" for Ireland. In return, Casement made his formal offer to form the Irish brigade. Casement's plans for these shock troops of the Irish cause came to naught; he simply could not convince enough Irishmen to join. In fact, it was said that his presence in the prisoners' compound was so unwelcome that after a while he tired of the project altogether.[33]

Unable to initiate the overthrow of British rule via American or German intervention in 1914, professional Irish Americans turned their attention to other means of furthering the cause of Irish freedom. They became involved in both containing and countering the strong pro-Allied bias of the American press. This involvement expanded once the British severed transatlantic cables belonging to Germany. The professionals had much ground to make up. For as one observer noted, "while England had enjoyed American favor since 1909, Germany had fallen from the good graces of most Americans."[34]

Undaunted by such pessimism, Devoy leaped into the fray to offset British censorship of European news, and was joined in his effort by the Fords of the *Irish World*. Week after week, they railed against the

---

33. In fact, Devoy felt that Casement was "very emotional and as trustful as a child." He also resented Casement's impetuous, ill-conceived decisions, which frequently, in Devoy's opinion, "embarrassed the cause." See Devoy, *Recollections of an Irish Rebel*, 406; Casement to Under-Secretary of State, Foreign Office, Berlin, 23 December 1914; and Zimmerman to Sir Roger Casement, 28 December 1914, *Casement Papers*, New York Public Library; James W. Gerard, *My Four Years in Germany* (New York: Doubleday, 1917), 141.

34. Particularly biased American newspapers, according to the professionals, were the *New York Herald, New York Times, New York World, New York Evening Post, New York Tribune, Chicago Herald,* and *Providence Journal*. See John Gaffney, *Breaking the Silence: England, Ireland, Wilson and the War* (New York: Horace and Liveright, 1930), 2; Cushing Strout, *The American Image of the Old World* (New York: Harper & Row, 1963), 158. Another review of public opinion found "Prussian militarism" and "monarchical divine right as the most disliked and feared traits," and the "United States through a long series of incidents came gradually to have a feeling of fear, suspicion and distrust of Germany and her motives." See Clara F. Schieber, *The Transformation of American Sentiment Toward Germany, 1870–1914* (Boston: Cornhill Publishing, 1923), 266, 284.

OUTBREAK OF GREAT WAR AND NEUTRALITY

British-influenced American press and eventually found a useful ally in the papers of the William Randolph Hearst syndicate. Hearst bucked the tide of pro-Allied papers and endorsed a rigid policy of neutrality and non-intervention. While the *Gaelic-American* and *Irish World* enjoyed only a limited and selective readership, the Hearst papers sold daily in cities across the nation. The constant theme of the professional Irish American press in the initial months of the war was to hail German contributions to Western Civilization while belittling British pretensions of altruism in entering the war. They also sought to offset the prevailing disparagement of German militarism by pointing out that the greatest threat to America did not come from the German army as much as it did from British domination of the world's shipping lanes.[35]

The professionals also joined hands with the Germans in 1914 to woo American favor away from the Allies by way of propaganda. Unfortunately for them, early German efforts did not prove efficacious, as the Germans had little understanding of American customs or the language. Relying upon unwieldy tomes rather than handy pamphlets, the awkward German efforts were clumsy and unsophisticated. Even the ever-fretful British ambassador Spring Rice informed the British Foreign Office that German propaganda was so poor in quality, appearing so rigid and dogmatic, that it "almost made England popular in America." Grimly, von Bernstorff validated Spring Rice's dim view of German handiwork and noted that British propaganda was superior in its understanding American idiom and character.[36]

Despite the prodigious contribution of the two Irish American newspapers and O'Leary's American Truth Society, Irish American agitators were not generally successful in convincing other Irish American Catholics to endorse the professionals' views. To be sure, on some occasions, and over some incidents, Catholic newspapers were eager to join the professionals' chorus against British manipulation

---

35. Count Johann von Bernstorff, *My Three Years in America* (New York: Charles Scribner's Sons, 1930) 288; *Gaelic-American,* June 14, October 17, 1914; *Irish World,* October 24, 1914.

36. James Morgan Reed, *Atrocity Propaganda, 1914–1917* (New York: Yale University Press, 1941), 142–43; Spring Rice to Lord Newton, October 21, 1914, in Stephen A. Gwynn, 2:239; von Bernstorff, *My Three Years in America,* 57.

of the press. However, the professionals ultimately failed to swing Catholic opinion to their side for numerous reasons, not the least of which was their failure to identify Irish interests with the triumph of German arms over Britain. Such identification ran against the strong non-interventionist stand of most Irish American Catholics and tended to ignore major dissatisfaction with the conduct of German armies in the war.[37]

Irish propaganda efforts during this time were further plagued by financial backing that proved to be "rather anemic." In his analysis of ethnic attempts at currying American favor, George Sylvester Viereck singled out Irish propaganda as prone to hyperbole, remarking that "frequently it was too violent to be convincing." Although they were certainly a vocal minority in 1914, the professionals did not represent the majority of Irish Americans. By their own admission, they were disorganized, faction-ridden, and hampered by poor finances and small membership. They lacked the support of mainstream Irish Americans, most critically the Catholic Church, as well as both wealthy and middle-class Irish. Their early efforts were blunted by these handicaps in addition to their investing too much hope in a victorious and magnanimous German government. By the end of 1914, they had failed to overcome both the indifference most Irish Americans demonstrated for Irish freedom and their distaste for violent tactics.[38]

The failure of the professionals to capture the endorsement of the Catholic Church in 1914 proved to be a serious setback for their hopes to persuade the majority of Irish Americans to their cause. Nowhere did they fail more abysmally than with the Irish American hierarchy of the American Church. Given the power and influence exercised by that hierarchy, the position they adopted toward the hostilities in

37. *America,* November 28, 1914; *Indiana Catholic,* August 28, 1914; *Catholic Register,* August 8, 1914; Buckley, *The New York Irish,* 36.
38. US General Staff, Military Intelligence Division, *Propaganda in Its Military and Legal Aspects* (Washington, DC: Executive Division of General Staff, USA, n.d.), 57; Viereck, *Spreading Germs of Hate,* 25. An example of professional Irish literary license is one of Devoy's editorials, in which Britain is described as the "modern Attila, the Scourge of God, the curse of the world, the incarnation of greed, her avarice and insolence are only equaled by her conscienceless cupidity." See *Gaelic-American,* March 27, 1915.

OUTBREAK OF GREAT WAR AND NEUTRALITY

Europe was critical in the formation of official Church policy. With a decidedly vertical authority structure in place, what the bishops proclaimed was likely to be reiterated by their local clergy, as well as by their diocesan newspapers. In turn, these verdicts would be handed down to a respectful, if not always thoroughly accepting, laity.

Perhaps the best testimony to this power was tendered by John Devoy, who enjoyed a somewhat adversarial relationship with the Catholic Church. In his recollections years after the war, he admitted that the Clan-na-Gael suffered for lack of support from the hierarchy in the cause of Irish independence until well after the Easter uprising of 1916. Devoy pointed to Cardinal O'Connell's supportive speech at Madison Square Garden in 1919, months after the end of the war, as the first significant sympathy expressed for the nationalist cause by the hierarchy. According to Devoy, it was not until the Irish Convention in February 1919, when "Cardinal Gibbons, who had up to then opposed the advanced movement (but had never attacked it) ... with twenty-eight bishops ... gave his blessing to the movement," that hierarchical support became explicit. Without this vital endorsement, the nationalist cause languished during the war years.[39]

It is not surprising that the hierarchy, in 1914, did not approve of radical efforts to overthrow British rule in Ireland by applauding Britain's enemies. In fact, there were those among the hierarchy who, in the years leading up to the war, fell in line with the Anglo-American *rapprochement* of the early twentieth century. Foremost among them was James Cardinal Gibbons, the dean of the American hierarchy. While the exact reasons for his Anglophile leanings are still unclear, one might surmise that the ever-cautious Gibbons was doing his best to align Catholic action, especially among Irish American Catholics, with mainstream American political and diplomatic praxis. In any event, in 1896 he eagerly joined Cardinals Herbert Vaughan of England and Michael Logue of Ireland in proposing a permanent tribunal of arbitration as a replacement for war between English-speaking nations.

With the passing of time, Gibbon's fondness for the English only seemed to increase. Of Gibbons's address at Westminster Cathedral

---

39. Devoy, *Recollections of an Irish Rebel,* 126–27.

CHAPTER 3

on St. Patrick's Day in 1907, Roger Casement, the tragic figure of the 1916 Easter Rebellion, wrote:

> No English imperialist ever lifted his horn higher than this Catholic arch-jingo prelate ... to tell an audience ... of Irishmen and women, who, or whose fathers, had been expelled from their native land by English laws and British rapacity that we also have a "common heritage of civil and political freedom," ... this is indeed out-TIMESING the Times.

Casement's comments rambled onward to abrade Gibbons for his crediting the English for the most recent Catholic revival in Britain and for his inordinate praise of the late Queen Victoria. In closing, Casement was so befuddled by this address that he could not reconcile the fact that the Catholic prelate was of Irish extraction.[40]

Casement's critical assessment of Gibbons, irrespective of his inclination towards hyperbole, does not seem far from the mark, when as late as 1913 Gibbons was eagerly promoting "closer and more amicable relations between England and this country." In expressing his regrets for being unable to attend the hundredth anniversary of the signing of the Peace of Ghent ending the War of 1812, he waxed eloquent about the similarities between the governments of Great Britain and the United States. In hailing the might of Britain's empire and her Royal Navy, he mused that a harmonious relationship between the two countries would be "a blessing, not only to these two great Powers, but to all the nations of the civilized world." He concluded by enjoining that "Britannia and America join hands across the Atlantic" to pledge a "sacred oath of peace," which would bond Americans and Britons in avoiding any "blood shed in fratricidal war." That Gibbons was so favorably disposed towards the British point of view, and that he would likely be positioned to influence Catholic opinion, explains

---

40. John Tracy Ellis, *The Life of James Cardinal Gibbons* (Milwaukee: The Bruce Publishing Company, 1963), 2:84; Remarks by Sir Roger Casement on Cardinal Gibbons' Address at Westminster Cathedral, March 17, 1907, *Casement Papers,* New York Public Library.

OUTBREAK OF GREAT WAR AND NEUTRALITY

why Sir Gilbert Parker, head of British propaganda efforts in the United States, forwarded the cardinal "official papers" favorable to the English position in the war.[41]

Considering Gibbons's steadfast support of Redmond and the Home Rule solution, as well as his pattern of admiring the British, it might appear odd that he was not more outspoken when the war broke out in 1914. However, this is largely what happened and, it would seem, others in the episcopate followed suit. Such silence was most likely the result of a desire to maintain the strict and impartial neutrality urged by President Wilson and cherished by mainstream America. The hierarchy also seemed motivated by a desire to keep the peace within its own culturally diverse constituency by, in effect, endorsing the view expressed by the Reverend John P. Noll of *Our Sunday Visitor*—that there were inherent hazards in voicing strong or inflamed opinions regarding the belligerents in the war. Moreover, it appeared safer to focus on the deplorable situation in Mexico at that particular moment.[42]

These considerations animated the pleas for peace issued by the hierarchy. In Boston, Cardinal O'Connell declared Sunday, October 4, 1914, as "Peace Sunday" and instructed his clergy and laity to offer their prayers at Mass for the speedy conclusion to the European bloodletting. Beyond this proclamation, and the Boston *Pilot*'s policy of condemning the war as altogether heinous, no noteworthy attention was paid to the outbreak of the war in this diocese. In New York, which was the hotbed of Irish American nationalist activity, Cardinal Farley did not dwell on the inauguration of the Great War. As John P. Buckley has noted, Farley "kept ... officially neutral by refraining from any public comments, by enjoining his priests to silence, and by impartially sponsoring relief drives for the war sufferers in both camps." If during the first few months of the war Farley's private

---

41. James Cardinal Gibbons to Alton B. Parker, April 27, 1913, and Sir Gilbert Parker to James Cardinal Gibbons, October 7, 1914, *Gibbons Papers*, Archives of the Archdiocese of Baltimore.

42. "An Appeal by the President, Presented in the Senate, August 19, 1914," in Ray Stannard Baker and William E. Dodd, eds. *The Public Papers of Woodrow Wilson*, 6 vols. (New York: Harper Brothers, 1925–1927), 1:157–58; *Our Sunday Visitor*, December 6, 1914.

papers revealed anything, they underscored his preoccupation with interceding on behalf of the sorely distressed Catholic Church in Mexico. In this work, he was greatly assisted by his fellow prelate in Baltimore—Cardinal Gibbons.[43]

The preponderantly Irish American clergy took positions on political and national matters much in keeping with the hierarchical cues. The priesthood was as much a career as it was a calling, and for a priest to express opinions contrary to his ordinary was tantamount to professional suicide. Political expression by clerics, especially regarding controversial topics, was viewed dimly by the hierarchy. One Catholic newspaper of the time published the conventional wisdom that the "Catholic Church is always a house of worship and never a political rostrum," and the priest who elected to preach politics "would speedily be taken to task by his bishop." The Catholic Church was not, after all, a democracy.[44]

To be sure, there were individual priests who took strong stands on the matter of Irish American nationalism and, by way of inference, upon the outbreak of war in Europe. Priests of longstanding popularity, and/or those serving under ordinaries not particularly preoccupied with control, were given leeway for personal expression. Perhaps the most notable cleric who vigorously defended radical measures was Father Peter Yorke in San Francisco. An advocate of Sinn Fein, Yorke believed that Redmond was out of tune with the movement of events and that his parliamentary Home Rule Party had sold out to the British. Despite his Anglophobia, Yorke did not go so far as to wish the Germans success; he called for strict adherence to neutrality, although for reasons of his own and not in subservience to the hierarchical mandate.[45]

In St. Louis, Father Timothy Dempsey, enormously popular for his work with the destitute and homeless, was also dismayed with the course of Irish American Catholic opinion as expressed in the

---

43. Boston *Pilot*, October 3, 1914; Buckley, *The New York Irish*, 54; Cardinal Gibbons to Cardinal Farley, October 16, 1914; Father Laboure to Cardinal Farley, October 20, 1914, quoted in Buckley, 55–56.

44. *Catholic News*, May 29, 1915.

45. Joseph Brusher, *Consecrated Thunderbolt: Father Yorke of San Francisco* (Hawthorne, NJ: Joseph F. Wagner Publishers, 1973), 156–60.

OUTBREAK OF GREAT WAR AND NEUTRALITY

Western Watchman, the former domain of the recently retired Father David S. Phelan, an inveterate foe of American nativism. When Phelan argued that since Home Rule was practically assured, Irish American agitators should tone down their assault on Redmond, Dempsey would have none of it. Writing to Joseph P. O'Mahoney, editor of the *Indiana Catholic*, Dempsey expressed his sincere hope that "we never see the fulfillment of a certain Irish leader's promise that when the Old Land gets Home Rule she will be the most loyal part of the British Empire."[46]

In the main, however, few priests appeared to stray far from the official Church position. While it is indeed true that Catholics of Irish descent did have significant differences with the way the British government dealt with their ancestral home, it "seems not to have been voiced through the Churches but through the various Irish and Irish-American societies." In the one standard study of the differences between Catholic and Protestant clergymen in the early years of the war, Ray Abrams concluded that Catholic priests "were in their pulpit utterances, loyal to the president, and refrained from the type of criticism so prevalent among the Protestant churches." Most Irish American Catholic editors played an integral role in muting the alluring sound of the war tocsin among its readers. Irrespective of the eventual line of sympathy that any of the papers adopted toward the European belligerents, editorials and articles featured in the early months of the war called for neutrality and cool reason.

The popular national devotional magazines were the most dispassionate in their reporting of the beginning of the Great War. Spiritual in nature, they generally avoided articulating any editorial opinions on the war and quickly adopted a policy of prayerful vigilance and impartiality. When a devotional publication uncharacteristically expressed a strong opinion, it was only to condemn war as "folly" and to exhort its readers and the public at large to "preserve the strident neutrality" as requested by the Wilson administration.[47]

---

46. Crighton, *Missouri and the World War*, 98; *Indiana Catholic*, September 11, 1914.

47. Ray H. Abrams, *Preachers Present Arms: The Role of the American Churches in World Wars I and II, with Some Observations on the Vietnam War*

CHAPTER 3

As for the most popular national Catholic newspaper, *Our Sunday Visitor*, Father John P. Noll largely left news of the war outside of the paper altogether. When his initial mandate for neutral thought appeared insufficient to his readers, he published his official policy on the war in which he explained the inherent dangers of any paper attempting to take sides in an immigrant nation such as the United States. Declaring that it would be "risky business" for any publisher or editor to betray specific sympathies, he predicted that the editor who did would "receive a good scolding from many of his readers and the cancellation of subscriptions." Making good on his pledge, Noll assiduously avoided any further news of the war.[48]

It would be incorrect to suggest that all Catholic newspapers and Irish American Catholic editors were devoid of partisanship once the guns of Europe began firing in 1914. Richard Tierney, SJ, editor of the prestigious *America*, was one who favored the Central Powers of Germany and Austria-Hungary. From the outset, Tierney was skeptical of German responsibility for the outbreak of war and was infuriated by reports of German atrocities, insisting that they were "utterly unworthy of belief," and that Germany "is not a nation of barbarians." Sensing that Americans were being served up biased news coverage, he vowed to provide his readers with a counterpoise to British-monopolized reporting.[49] In the main, however, papers that appeared to defend Germany in the early months of the war conditioned their remarks by supplications for neutral thought and behavior among their readers. Chicago's Catholic newspaper, the New World, under the direction of Father Thomas V. Shannon, repeated President Wilson's plea for peace. Similarly, the Freeman's Journal initially tried to offset pro-British

(Scottsdale, AZ: Herald Press, 1969), 32; *Sacred Heart Review*, September 1914; *The Franciscan Herald*, September 1914; *Ave Maria*, August 15, 1914.

48. *Our Sunday Visitor*, August 30, 1914.

49. Tierney, a Jesuit, was so outspoken in his convictions that it might account for Spring Rice's remarks that, as a religious order, the Jesuits "are one man on the side of Prussia." See Stephen A. Gwynn, *Letters and Friendships of Sir Cecil Spring Rice*, 2:245; *America*, August 15, August 29, September 5, 1914. Tierney's bias was so pronounced that one of his readers suggested that the publishing site of the periodical should be moved from New York to Berlin to reflect the pro-German slant. See *America*, October 31, 1914.

sympathies by presenting Germany's side in the conflict—in an attempt to eradicate German culpability so that neutrality would remain the only valid course of action.[50]

Clearly, the most vitriolic attack upon the British was voiced by Joseph P. O'Mahoney's *Indiana Catholic*. While exhorting his readers to the standard of neutrality, he took pains to point out, somewhat presciently, that despite the fact the US State Department was pro-British, Catholics should follow the dictates of the dying pontiff, Pius X, to be absolutely neutral and dissociated from the conflict. He predicted that Britain, having promoted the war out of "sheer jealousy" of Germany's growing power, would have to go through a period of "sack cloth and ashes" before the war ended.[51]

Most Catholics, however, adopted a clear neutral posture at the beginning of the Great War, one that coincided with the American national sentiment of the time. Catholic editors such as Thomas O'Flanagan fixed attention on the American dimension of the ever-widening conflict in Europe. Noting that the president's plea for neutrality was "timely and patriotic," he cajoled his audience to "place a higher value on the boon of American citizenship," recommending that all Americans should undertake a "careful reading, or re-reading of the president's address." Milwaukee's Humphrey Desmond indicated that the only side he was advising Catholics to take was the "side of peace and opposed to war."[52]

Newspapers that demonstrated a degree of pro-Allies sympathy joined others in recommending a strict course of neutrality. Smith's *Pittsburgh Catholic* enjoined readers of "divers nationalities to preserve the peace," reminding them that they "foreswore all fealty to the lands of their nativity" when they took up American citizenship. He also insisted that it was neither "timidity nor cowardice" to plead for the "neutral tongue." Irish American Catholic editors in Hartford, Milwaukee, Pittsburgh, Detroit, San Antonio, Baltimore, Cleveland, and Brooklyn unequivocally condemned war as folly and pleaded with their readers to reject all trappings of the martial spirit and to

50. *New World*, August 21, 1914; *Freeman's Journal*, August 22, 1914.
51. *Indiana Catholic*, August 28, 1914.
52. *Catholic Transcript*, August 20, 1914; *Catholic Citizen*, August 22, 1914.

CHAPTER 3

remain calm. Desmond put it most directly when he counseled that consideration needed to be shown all citizens, irrespective of their ethnic extraction. He suggested that everyone should "concede them the right to sympathize with their representative mother lands in the great conflict going on."[53]

The accord that nearly all representatives of the Catholic press reached over a neutral course of action for American Catholics did not extend to assigning culpability for the war's outbreak. Most of the press appeared to agree with the Boston *Pilot*'s verdict that the "cause of the war in Europe is at best, not clear at the present time to use here in America, and judgment should be suspended." All the same, there were serious defections from this cautious policy. The Reverend John Burke of the Paulist publication *Catholic World* was one who demurred from exercising caution. From the moment German armies went on the march in August, Burke was quick to hold Germany accountable and at fault. According to Burke, underlying German war guilt was her will to dominate Europe and her insatiable envy of British colonial possessions. Citing German militarism as the perennial unbalancing factor in recent European history, Burke saw in Kaiser Wilhelm the incarnation of malevolent Prussian designs for conquest. In building up the German army and navy to challenge British power, Burke contended, the Kaiser was to blame for having "encouraged the war spirit" to flourish. He was concerned that if the Kaiser prevailed in this contest "military ideas will dominate not only Europe but the world." On the other hand, an Allied victory would ensure that "effectual steps shall be taken to secure permanent peace." Having sated himself with a thorough evisceration of the Prussians, Burke turned his attention to condemning the Austrians. Had they not been so unrelenting in their demands upon Serbia, and had they acted like Britain and France in

---

53. *Pittsburgh Catholic,* August 20, 1914; *Michigan Catholic,* August 27, 1914; *Catholic Messenger,* September 17, 1914; Boston *Pilot,* August 22, 1914; *Catholic Universe,* August 7, 1914; *Michigan Catholic,* August 6, 1914; Baltimore *Catholic Review,* August 29, 1914; *Southern Messenger,* August 20, 1914; *Catholic Transcript,* August 13, 1914; *Fortnightly Review,* September 15, 1914; *Catholic Citizen,* August 22, 1914.

attempting to resist the expansion of hostilities, Burke contended, then matters would never have devolved into such a nightmare.[54]

As seen earlier, Richard Tierney's *America* stood in sharp contrast to Burke's *Catholic World* over which power was responsible for the outbreak of the war. Other significant Irish American Catholic editors who joined Tierney in attempting to present the Central Powers' position were O'Mahoney, Shannon, and the more secular Fords of the *Irish World*. The vituperative O'Mahoney led their charge with a vigorous defense of Germany, noting that nothing could be believed in the American press, given British censorship and pro-British sentiment. He squarely pinned blame for the war's outbreak on England; "she promoted the war in Europe so that while others were doing the fighting, she might destroy Germany's commerce." Aside from the professional Irish press, O'Mahoney's *Indiana Catholic*, Tierney's *America*, and, on occasion, Shannon's *New World*, there were few others willing to take up the cudgel for Germany in 1914.[55]

Even outside official Church circles, the vast majority of Irish American Catholics stood well to the conservative side of the Clan-na-Gael in 1914. As noted previously, most Irish Americans continued to support Home Rule, even though their ardor was somewhat lessened by Redmond's overt enthusiasm for defending the British Empire. Neither prominent nor ordinary Irish American Catholics adopted the furtherance of radical nationalistic goals in any large numbers. Scores of prominent Irish Americans rejected the aims of the professionals, and in several cases loaned their time and efforts to balancing Irish America's views of the Great War.

David I. Walsh, the first Roman Catholic governor of Massachusetts, was one who resisted the efforts of those who tried to enlist support for radical purposes. Faced with a sizeable Irish American Catholic

---

54. Boston *Pilot*, November 14, 1914. See also, *Catholic Transcript*, August 6, 1914; Denver *Catholic Register*, August 27, 1914; and Kansas City *Catholic Register*, September 5, 1914. Burke's indictment of the Germans can be found in *Catholic World*, October 1914. Editor Fred Sharon validated Burke's fears of German designs in the war. See *Catholic Messenger*, August 13, 1914.

55. *Indiana Catholic*, November 13, 1914.

CHAPTER 3

population in Massachusetts, he was conscious of their traditional hatred for Britain, but he was also cognizant that he governed many pro-British "blue bloods." Wisely, Walsh adopted a course of action that was "carefully neutral." In his official capacity, he refused to attend "fervid meetings to raise funds for the Irish Volunteers" or social functions geared to raise money for Allied causes. His formal posture was to side with Woodrow Wilson and William Jennings Bryan in their pleas for absolute neutrality. James Michael Curley, mayor of Boston, meekly announced support of Britain's cause. The *Gaelic-American* took note and hurled invectives such as "yellow dog" and "contemptible cur" Curley's way, and then curtly disowned him.[56]

Just as New York City provided the nexus for professional agitation in 1914, it also served as home to those who resisted its influence. Except for Judge Daniel F. Cohalan, most of Tammany Hall's sachems steered clear of the war issue and followed Charles Francis Murphy's lead, which was non-interventionist in the extreme. One clear opponent of the professionals in 1914 was the peerless orator and New York congressman, Bourke Cockran. Asked by Joseph McGarrity of Philadelphia how he felt about convening all the Irish societies to make a formal declaration over the war, he advised that it was not a wise idea to call such a convention and said he believed it necessary to eschew any "attitude as citizens in the deplorable war now devastating the fairest countries of Europe." He further remonstrated that he did not think it advisable to classify any Americans along the lines of ethnic origin, and that no action should be undertaken "which might be construed abroad as indicating that Americans are divided upon racial lines, religious lines, sectional lines, or lines of any kind of description."[57] Cockran's non-interventionist policy alone was not enough to alienate him from the professionals. It was his unqualified rejection of their advocacy for Germany that did. Even though Cockran,

---

56. Dorothy G. Wayman, *David I. Walsh: Citizen-Patriot* (Milwaukee: Bruce Publishing, 1952), 75; *Gaelic-American,* August 1, 1914.

57. Bourke Cockran to Maurice Donnelly, October 2, 1914, *Bourke Cockran Papers,* New York Public Library. Devoy recalled that in the years 1914–1915 both John Quinn and Bourke Cockran were "not in agreement with our policy." See Devoy, *Recollections of an Irish Rebel,* 406.

OUTBREAK OF GREAT WAR AND NEUTRALITY

like Michael Ryan of Philadelphia, had become disenchanted with Redmond's eagerness to recruit Irish soldiers for the British army, he appreciated that England stood for civilized virtues while "Prussian militarism could succeed in reversing the progressive tendencies of the last two centuries."[58]

The war was barely underway when John Quinn joined the ranks of those opposing the professionals' love of all things German. Quinn's deep and abiding interest in the arts made him an ardent supporter of the French. His own difficulties with Church censorship made him immune to Church criticism regarding the anti-clericalism of the French government. His sense of acquired respectability, his "qualified Irishry" as it were, made him shudder at those who appealed to the baser instincts of violence and revolution. He made these sentiments known to his friend AE Russell in November 1914, intimating that "I have no sympathy with the Irish in this country and in Ireland who are on the side of Germany." In December, Quinn elaborated upon his scorn for the Germans and his admiration for the British and French:

> If I were an Irishman I would have been on the side of England because I prefer English civilization to German civilization; England's idea of freedom to Germany's idea of imperialism and military government; individual freedom to bossism; French culture and French ideas to German sentiment and German beer.

For those who urged a Teutonic occupation of Ireland, Quinn had disparaging words. Admittedly, Quinn averred, the Germans might teach the Irish industry, order, efficiency, economy, and cleanliness, but the Irish would quickly become "mighty sick of German assimilation, of German kultur ... they would flee the land in terror."[59]

---

58. Bourke Cockran to Moretan Frewen, July 30, 1914, *Bourke Cockran Papers*, New York Public Library.

59. John Quinn to AE Russell, November 1914, *John Quinn Papers*, New York Public Library; John Quinn to Douglas Hyde, December 31, 1914, in *John Quinn Papers*, New York Public Library. Interestingly, Roger Casement, whom Quinn had boarded in his apartment for a month in 1914, had appealed to Quinn

CHAPTER 3

Bourke Cockran and John Quinn were not alone in their strident opposition to the attempt made by the professionals to engender pro-German sympathies among Irish Americans. Other prominent Irish American Catholics, such as J. C. Walsh, Jerome Griffin, Patrick Egan, and the Anglo-Irish Catholic Shane Leslie, also strove to convince their co-religionists to ignore radical rhetoric. Joining them were most Irish American financiers and industrialists who were clearly disposed toward the British because of their own commercial interests. Ordinary Irish American Catholics clasped hands with others in declaring that some of their own had become dupes of German propaganda. Irish American societies, such as the Hibernians, were sharply divided over what endorsement, if any, they should make concerning the war in 1914. The Friendly Sons of St. Patrick remained staunch supporters of Home Rule and American citizenship; they too, turned a deaf ear to the pleas of the professional Irish Americans to favor the Germans. The transparent lack of support for radical measures from both Irish societies and prominent Irish Americans, excepting a select few, leads one to conclude, as did Carl Wittke, that the "silent majority was not necessarily in agreement with the professional German American or Irish-American leaders." Furthermore, as Wittke has correctly observed, "many Irish and German-Americans belonged to no organizations of a political character."[60]

That fewer Irish Americans maintained an affiliation with secular societies seems consistent with earlier observations that Irish American Catholics were weaning themselves away from a strictly immigrant

---

to provide legal counsel for the selling of rifles to the Irish Volunteers. By the end of 1914, Quinn had written off Casement as useless to the Irish cause. See Roger Casement to John Quinn, August 24, 1914, and John Quinn to Douglas Hyde, December 31, 1914, in *John Quinn Papers,* New York Public Library.

    60. The *Catholic Messenger* repudiated the election of John McLaughlin in its January 7, 1915, edition for his adoption of radical principles. Most state chapters of the Hibernians adopted pledges like that of Texas, one that was absolutely neutral in its opinion on the Great War. See *Southern Messenger,* October 15, 1914; *131st Anniversary Dinner of the Society of the Friendly Sons of St. Patrick in the City of New York, March 17, 1915, Hotel Astor* (New York: published by the Society, 1915), 26–27; Wittke, *The Irish in America,* 275–76.

OUTBREAK OF GREAT WAR AND NEUTRALITY

identification and were gravitating toward a zealous Catholic and patriotic American one. This would explain the ever-increasing membership in parochial societies such as the Knights of Columbus. It also might account for the apparent reluctance of most Irish American Catholics to become involved in the incipient imbroglio over favoring one belligerent or the other in 1914. Unlike the Ancient Order of Hibernians and other ethnic Irish organizations, which linked Irish Americans with the great nationalist heroes of Ireland's past, the Knights of Columbus "was an ethnic organization in which the struggle for Catholic legitimacy was fought by the rules of the American battlefield." The ingrained conservatism that this struggle fostered was revealed in the leadership of the organization, which was markedly upper middle-class, successful and very respectable.[61]

Catholic newspapers, which regularly reported on the activities and the meetings of the Knights during the first few months of the war, revealed nothing of their deliberations with respect to the war itself outside their repeated endorsements of the president's call for neutrality. Other than this specific stand, minutes of the Knights' meetings include purely parochial concerns such as charity auctions, membership drives, parade participation, social events and news, financial reports, and the like. It appeared that their charter's dual pledge of responsible, loyal citizenship and respectable, pious Catholicism compelled them to obey the direction handed down to them by civil and religious leadership.[62]

Other factors related to the European belligerents also played a role in shaping Irish American attitudes toward the war in late summer and fall of 1914. Preeminent among all considerations was the impact of Germany's violation of Belgian neutrality. Even though many Catholic papers appeared to buck the national trend by favoring the Central Powers in the days leading up to the war, the violation of Belgium's neutrality and Germany's subsequent plundering of landmarks dimmed

61. Christopher Kaufmann, *Faith and Fraternalism: The History of the Knights of Columbus, 1882–1982* (New York: Harper & Row, 1982), 71.
62. See *Michigan Catholic,* August 20, 1914; *Catholic Messenger,* August 20, 1914; Boston *Pilot,* August 22, 1914; Brooklyn *Tablet,* August 29, 1914; Baltimore *Catholic Review,* August 29, 1914.

the glow of German gallantry. In addition, it tended to raise the overall estimation of Belgium's new allies, France and Britain.[63]

The German invasion of Belgium made matters difficult for those Irish Americans and the handful of Catholic editors who had conspicuously favored the German cause in the early weeks of the war. Undaunted, John Devoy discounted Britain's dutiful declaration of war as a response to Germany's violation of Belgian neutrality. He insisted that both Britain and France had themselves planned to move through Belgium and were only thwarted in this endeavor by Germany's celerity. Invoking the old bromide that "the best defense is an active offense," Devoy countered stories of German atrocities by condemning British imperialism and relating that Germany would have to go far to match the cruelty that the Belgians had inflicted upon natives in the Congo. Reflexively, O'Mahoney rushed to the aid of the professionals' interpretation of the Belgian issue by verifying that the French had already violated Belgium's neutrality by massing their troops on the border. He trivialized stories of German atrocities, featuring instead accounts of German kindness to priests and other Catholic prisoners of war. O'Mahoney dismissed Belgian woes by declaring, "Yes, Germany is in Belgium because if she hadn't gone in there England would, with 400,000 men to strike Germany in the rear."[64]

Most of the other Catholic papers suspended judgment until complete information was available and assurances could be made that reporting on the situation in Belgium was not being manipulated by British censorship. They were aware that the Royal Navy had snipped the transatlantic cables emanating from the European continent, resulting in nearly all news being filtered by London. Moreover, the celebrated American journalist Richard Harding had rushed to Belgium

63. Esslinger, "American Catholicism and Irish Attitudes toward Neutrality, 1914–1917," 200–201.

64. *Gaelic-American,* September 19, September 26, 1914; *Indiana Catholic,* September 7, 1914. Tierney also questioned the veracity of these atrocity reports. See *America,* September 26, 1914. German American attempts to explain the invasion of Belgium, particularly Viereck's *Fatherland,* could not convince Americans that Germany was forced to do so. See Felice A. Bonadio, "Failure of German Propaganda in the United States, 1914–1917," *Mid-America* 41 (January 1959): 45–47.

and was dispatching reports to New York. A certifiable Anglophile, Harding presented colorful corroboration of German rape, wanton destruction, and frightful atrocities. Father Whelan, like so many other Irish American Catholic editors, lamented the destruction of the Louvain and hoped that justification for such an action would be issued from Berlin. In the main, the violation of Belgium's neutrality generated a significant measure of sympathy for both Belgium and her allies. Cardinal Gibbons was a close friend of the heroic Cardinal Mercier of Belgium and was also fond of the Belgian royal family; he immediately headed efforts to organize a massive relief drive among American Catholics.[65]

Some publications, however, did not spare Germany blame for the atrocities. Catholic editors had a penchant for expressing themselves in colorful, florid, even imaginative ways, somewhat of a sectarian version of yellow journalism. Father Burke, a notable supporter of the Allies, hailed the "heroic resistance" of Belgium and warned of the "dark dangers" of German militarism. William Hughes apparently let his imagination get the better part of him when he implausibly asserted that the atrocities were the handiwork of "bloody Hessians." Recalling that it was the Hessians who as mercenaries (under Oliver Cromwell and then the Hanoverian kings) had committed "unspeakable" and "wanton deeds" in both Ireland and America, he suggested that it might well be the "progeny of these brutal German soldiers who are responsible for the devastation of Catholic Belgium."[66]

There were other factors that, affected the attitudes Irish Americans developed in the first few months of the war. And although they generally paled in comparison to the violation of Belgian neutrality and the atrocities that followed, they still entered the discussion concerning the belligerents. The war highlighted Catholic animosity towards

---

65. See Charles Belmont Davis, ed., *Adventures and Letters of Richard Harding Davis* (New York: Charles Scribner's Sons, 1917); Brooklyn *Tablet*, September 5, 1914; Will, *The Life of Cardinal Gibbons*, 2:805.

66. *Catholic World*, October 1914; *Michigan Catholic*, October 1, 1914. Shortly before his retirement, Father Phelan opined that it was the fault of German Protestants: "[They] chopped up Catholic Germany in the Reformation ... they've done the same in Louvain." See *Western Watchman*, September 17, 1914.

CHAPTER 3

France for her propensity toward anti-clericalism. Especially irksome to the Church had been the government's expulsion of religious orders in 1904. When the battles spilled onto French soil, several Catholic editors were quick to exact literary revenge. As might be expected, those papers unfavorably disposed to the Allies took great pains to point out the continued insensitivity of the French government to its Catholic populace. The redoubtable O'Mahoney matched German atrocity stories with imputations of his own involving the French government's malevolence toward the Catholic Church. In yet another swipe at the French, the *Catholic News* gleefully reported that "now even the atheistic civil authorities are thanking their lucky stars that the nuns, they once expelled, have come back to take care of the wounded soldiers." The effect these anti-French exposures had in shaping Irish American Catholic attitudes is difficult to ascertain. Some Catholic editors were eager to distinguish between the government of France and the "loyal Catholics" of that country. That the war was destroying French civilization provided an ambivalent satisfaction among American Catholics; many felt that France was paying a steep price for its earlier outrages against the Church.[67]

The charge that Catholics favored the Central Powers because of the traditional Catholic bond between the papacy and the Hapsburg dynasty lacks substance. It is true that there was some concern in the British Foreign Office that German and Austrian influence at the Vatican needed to be counteracted. Consequently, they established a delegation to the Holy See and appointed Sir Henry Howard, of old English Catholic stock, as the first minister. Catholic papers in the United States took little note of the business. One paper that did, Whelan's Brooklyn *Tablet*, complimented the British for their choice of Howard, remarking that "there are ways of doing things ... and this has been done in the right way." American Catholics did look to the papacy as a possible disinterested mediator of the war in Europe. When Pius X died in August 1914, one Catholic editor attributed his passing to heartbreak over the European war. While the pontiff undoubtedly was anguished over Catholic nations at war with one another, his general deteriorating

---

67. *Indiana Catholic,* September 7, 1914; *Catholic News,* January 2, 1915.

health had much more to do with his demise. New papal initiatives to arbitrate peace would be left to his successor, Benedict XV.[68]

One fundamental reason that Irish American Catholics clung to a policy of strict neutrality in the first few months of the war is that they found themselves amid an identity crisis. Were they Irish or Irish Americans? Or were they, in fact, Americans with Irish ancestry. It would appear that most Irish Americans, especially those of later generations than the first-generation immigrant, refused to take sides among the European belligerents. Any other choice would alienate other immigrant ethnicities in America, native-born Americans, and the American government—the latter two ever watchful for signs of disloyalty among the immigrant population. The Catholic Church, which presided over a polyglot of ethnic Catholics, was ever conscious of the explosive character of ethnic factionalism and insisted that the faithful toe the line of absolute neutrality.[69]

As 1914 ended, it became clear that Irish Americans were divided in their opinions regarding the war. On one extreme, the Clan-na-Gael represented a notoriously active minority that promoted a collaborative policy with Germany and a verbal attack upon those who entertained pro-Allied sentiments. They remained a distinct minority as the New Year 1915 beckoned, because they failed to harmonize their faction-ridden membership and supplement their anemic financing. Moreover, their early attempts at merging Ireland's freedom with Germany's defeat of Britain never captured the imagination of the Irish American community at large. This pro-German position also undermined their efforts when news of German-inspired atrocities began to circulate in the United States. The bulk of Irish American Catholics resisted the entreaties of the professional Irish. Many of

---

68. Thomas Hachey, ed., *Anglo-Vatican Relations, 1914–1919: Confidential Annual Reports of the British Minister to the Holy See* (Boston: G. K. Hall, 1972), xvi–xxi; Brooklyn *Tablet,* January 2, 1915; Baltimore *Catholic Review,* August 22, 1914; Kansas City *Catholic Register,* August 6, 1914.

69. Shannon, *The American Irish,* 132, 145; Mona Harrington, "Loyalties: Dual and Divided," in Michael Walzer, Edward T. Kantowicz, John Higham, and Mona Harrington, eds., *The Politics of Ethnicity* (Cambridge, MA: Harvard University Press, 1980), 94.

CHAPTER 3

them expressed sympathy for the Allies and believed in 1914 that America's place was far away from the European battlefields. Many of these Irish Americans had no affiliation with Irish social and political clubs, as they increasingly invested their energies and leisure in strictly American and Catholic organizations.

The influential Irish-led Catholic Church immediately adopted a position of absolute neutrality regarding the war. Responsible for the maintenance of harmony and accord between millions of people in various ethnic groups, it adhered to a non-interventionist policy. As such, it was understandable that they rejected the professionals' attempts to lure Irish American Catholics into a pro-German orbit. But their vehement resistance to the professionals' agenda reveals more important motives. Striving for acceptance and respectability, the Church felt compelled to reject appeals to the revolutionary principles of the Clan-na-Gael. Church support for the Home Rule Party reflected an entrenched conservatism among Church leadership, as well as a decided effort to mirror the nation's amelioration of differences with Great Britain. In the case of Cardinal Gibbons, it bordered on an unqualified admiration for the British. In any event, concern for acceptance and respectability prompted many Irish American Catholics to adhere to the government's policy of neutrality in the war. In turn, Catholic organizations and Church-affiliated societies demonstrated their devotion to the Church by following hierarchical directives. In this context, it became eminently possible to remain both good Catholics and patriotic Americans.

CHAPTER 4

NEUTRALITY UNDER STRAIN IN 1915

The only thing more amazing than the speed with which the German juggernaut raced across the plains of Belgium and northern France in early August 1914 was the fact that it came to such a screeching halt on the Marne in the early fall of that year. The war was about to settle down on the western front for the next four years. Despite the fond hopes of some Americans, particularly German Americans and their Irish American confederates, the conflict soon took on the ponderous countenance of trench warfare, and with that, all predictions for a swift and decisive end to the war evaporated.

As Arthur S. Link has pointed out, 1915 was a time when basic American public attitudes toward the Great War in Europe were shaped. It also marked a time when the Wilson administration attempted to "lay the foundations of American neutrality and sought to find accommodation to the ever-encroaching maritime systems of Great Britain and Germany."[1] In shaping their own attitudes towards the war in Europe throughout this year, Irish Americans and the American Catholic Church often found themselves not only at odds with Wilson's articulation of neutrality but also at variance with each other, as the same divisions that had splintered unanimity at the inception of the war continued to invest its ranks. As the year unfolded, Irish American reaction to events would reveal conflicting views toward the war in Europe as well as illuminate the sharp differences within the Irish American and Catholic community itself.

---

1. Arthur S. Link, *The Struggle for Neutrality*, vii.

CHAPTER 4

Mexican Problem Continues

The tumult that had long characterized the domestic political climate of Mexico continued to manifest itself throughout 1915. While the war in Europe slowly acquired a position of grave importance throughout this period, its prominence was generally eclipsed by Catholic fixation upon the travails of the Church in Mexico. Indeed, American Catholic clerics and newspapers increasingly despaired of the course the revolution was taking in Mexico. Huerta's ouster had never been accepted by the American Catholic hierarchy, and when in April 1915 it appeared as though Venustiano Carranza was on the brink of triumphing over the other contenders for power, Catholic protests intensified.[2] In the vanguard of protest once again strode the formidable Reverend Francis C. Kelley. In a publication entitled *The Book of the Red and Yellow*, Kelley described in lurid and sanguinary detail Carranza's campaign of anti-clericalism: desecration of churches; seizure of ecclesiastical property; expulsion of religious orders and priests; murder of clerics and nuns; and the impressment of seminarians into the revolutionary armies. Kelley's expose was supported by many Catholic editors, who released a stream of condign censure for anti-clerical depredations unleashed in Mexico in the wake of Huerta's exile. One such editorial charged Carranza's rival Pancho Villa with a determination to "exterminate Catholics" and claimed that hundreds of Sisters of Charity had been forced to forfeit their virginity to the rapine of Villa's bandits.[3]

In January 1915, Kelley obtained access to the White House through the sympathetic intervention of an Irish American, Dudley Field Malone, a special agent of the State Department. Providing a series of unsolicited reports, followed by two meetings with Secretary of State William Jennings Bryan and one with Wilson himself, Kelly tried but failed to overcome their skepticism that the atrocity stories

---

2. At least one editor, Father John F. Whelan, posited that the Masons were responsible for Huerta's downfall. See Brooklyn *Tablet,* February 6, 1915; Link, *The Struggle for Neutrality,* 468.

3. Brooklyn *Tablet,* February 20, 1915; Francis C. Kelley, *The Bishop Jots It Down* (Boston: Little, Brown, 1939), 187; *Indiana Catholic,* October 30, 1914.

he was always alluding to were truthful. Kelley, though somewhat comforted by the president's interest in the issue, was shocked by Wilson's glib remark comparing the Mexican Revolution to the French one of 1789. Kelley recalled the president musing that he hoped "that out of the bloodletting in Mexico some such good may come."[4]

Despite Kelley's persistence throughout the spring of 1915, the Wilson administration refused to budge from its position of non-intervention in Mexican affairs. When Kelley tried to offer actual policy statements for the president, and in one case, specifically recommended the introduction of yet another reactionary Mexican general to the unsettled situation, Bryan and Wilson concurred that the cleric had taken too many liberties. In a letter to Bryan, Wilson reiterated his conviction that "no other position is possible for us, and I think the whole country will agree with us, and not with Father Kelley."[5]

Wilson may well have asserted that the entire nation agreed with his posture on Mexico, but he clearly did not consider the strong opposition from the American Catholic Church. Throughout the spring, a flood of petitions, letters and resolutions from individual Catholics and societies condemning the religious persecutions in Mexico flooded the State Department. Conspicuously absent from this wave of protest was the voice of Cardinal Gibbons, who continued to urge restraint as late as August 1915. Reports indicated that Gibbons understood that Wilson was faced with complex diplomatic problems in handling the Mexican troubles and wished to give the president the latitude necessary to resolve the issue. While he strenuously opposed any US military incursion into Mexico, Gibbons hoped that Wilson would consider increasing the pressure upon the Constitutionalist forces under Carranza to forego their anti-clerical measures. However, as the fall of 1915

---

4. Dudley Field Malone to Woodrow Wilson, January 18, 1915, in Arthur S. Link, *The Papers of Woodrow Wilson*, 32:86; William Jennings Bryan to Woodrow Wilson, February 18, 1915, in *The Papers of Woodrow Wilson*, 32:248–49; Francis C. Kelley to Woodrow Wilson, February 23, 1915, in *The Papers of Woodrow Wilson*, 32:279–81; Kelley, *The Bishop Jots It Down*, 191.

5. Link, *The Struggle of Neutrality*, 9; William Jennings Bryan to Woodrow Wilson, April 19, 1915, in Link, *The Papers of Woodrow Wilson*, 33:30; Woodrow Wilson to William Jennings Bryan, April 21, 1915, in *The Papers of Woodrow Wilson*, 33:52.

CHAPTER 4

progressed, Carranza's hold upon Mexico strengthened and beckoned formal US recognition. At the same time, Wilson had become convinced that a certain degree of hostility towards the powerful Catholic Church in Mexico had become inevitable, and that the American hierarchy were espousing unrealistic reactionary alternatives. Despite the outspoken opposition of American Catholics, the Wilson administration formally recognized the Carranza government in October.[6]

Carranza's recognition unleashed a torrent of abuse in the Catholic press. In Philadelphia, John J. O'Shea noted that recognition marked a "sad declension in the esteem in which the Catholic world has been taught to hold it." Later, this same newspaper applauded Secretary of State Lansing's opinion that the Mexican government was not living up to its promises to cease persecutions of Catholics. Describing the situation south of the border as the "Mexican mess," O'Shea printed the Mexican hierarchy's assertion that it had never conspired to overthrow the Madero government. The *Catholic Standard and Times* also quoted Special Correspondent Raymond Carroll of the *New York Sun* that the Mexican revolutionaries "only fight to ravish women and steal what is loose from the land, and they know nothing of the sixth, seventh or eighth commandments." The frequently vitriolic Reverend M. J. Foley of the *Western Catholic* accused Wilson as having "taken the monster of lust, murder and sacrilege, Carranza, to his great, comprehensive, liberty loving(?) bosom and canonized him." The Jesuit Richard Tierney had just concluded one edition of *America* by admonishing Wilson that "Carranza's recognition will be an open insult to 16,000,000 Catholics in the United States," when he had to criticize the president the next week for encouraging Carranza to "proceed on his diabolical course."[7]

---

6. Ellis, *The Life of James Cardinal Gibbons,* 2:217; Richard Lee Metcalfe to Woodrow Wilson, c. August 14, 1915, in Link, *The Papers of Woodrow Wilson,* 33:200, n.1; Woodrow Wilson to Edith Bolling Galt, August 18, 1915, in *The Papers of Woodrow Wilson,* 33:242. John Patrick Buckley has suggested that Cardinal Gibbons sought to influence Spring Rice to pressure Wilson to acquiesce to the Catholic position. See Buckley, *The New York Irish,* 58.

7. *Catholic Standard and Times,* October 23, 1915, December 18, 2015; *Western Catholic,* October 23, 1915; *America,* October 16, 1915, October 23, 1915.

NEUTRALITY UNDER STRAIN IN 1915

In the face of Catholic criticism over Wilson's recognition of the Carranza government, the administration attempted to refute allegations that atrocities were being committed on a wholesale basis by the Mexican government. This refutation became even more offensive to American Catholics, because it was proffered by the one Roman Catholic in the administration—Wilson's personal secretary, the Irish American Catholic Joseph Tumulty. In response to an open letter written by a prominent New York Catholic named James J. McGuire, Tumulty defended the administration's record on the Mexican matter and claimed that "no official record" of atrocities existed. Moreover, he chided McGuire for needlessly trying to inflame public opinion over the Mexican revolution. By this time, Father Kelley had given up all hope that the Wilson administration cared anything for the Mexican Church. Aided by Tierney's *America*, Kelley assailed Tumulty's claims and flatly declared that he could submit irrefutable evidence that atrocities in Mexico were rampant.[8]

By January 1916, even Cardinal Gibbons's patience with administration policy was exhausted. Noting that the cardinal was a loyal supporter of the government, the *Pittsburgh Catholic* insinuated that "provoking facts must be palpably apparent" for His Eminence to criticize the president's policies. In a reprint of an interview conducted with the *New York Times*, Gibbons was reported to have said:

> With no desire to embarrass President Wilson, rather having every wish to aid in all endeavors to bring peace and quiet to the people of Mexico, I cannot be blind to the fact that the ultimate destruction of all authority in that land is the logical result of the policy of this administration from its very inception.[9]

---

8. Joseph P. Tumulty to James McGuire, November 29, 1915, *Tumulty Papers*, Library of Congress. McGuire's letter to Tumulty was published in the *New York World*, November 27, 1915; Blum, *Joe Tumulty and the Wilson Era*, 92; *America*, December 4, 1915.

9. See *Pittsburgh Catholic*, January 20, 1916.

CHAPTER 4

In the acerbic exchange of opinions in this matter, Wilson came to the defense of his Secretary and at one point claimed to understand the truth of the situation by "hearing a sufficiently large number of liars talk about it." Wilson's remarks were seen as a veiled attack upon the hierarchy of the American Catholic Church. Throughout February and March 1916, Catholic editors leveled sharp rebukes against the Wilson administration. Further remonstrations were forestalled in March 1916 when Pancho Villa launched his infamous raid against Columbus, New Mexico and forced Wilson to look differently at the Mexican problem. In the following month, the Easter uprising in Dublin vaulted European affairs to the forefront of the attention of American Catholics, especially those of Irish ancestry.[10]

Other Distractions

In addition to the Mexican dilemma, pressing matters involving Catholic concerns within the United States continued throughout 1915 to deflect the attention of the Church and its press organs from the European war and Ireland's plight The ongoing crusade against anti-Catholic bigotry and the trumpeting of the superior nature of Catholicism, featured in endless guest articles and editorials, were rarely crowded off the pages of the weekly Catholic press. Even the great flap caused by the release of the blockbuster film *The Birth of a Nation*, D. H. Griffith's cinematic glorification of the Ku Klux Klan in the Reconstruction era, celebrating the victory of white supremacy and the castigation of black Americans, did not receive much attention from the hierarchy or the Catholic press. No Catholic papers specifically endorsed the film, yet few condemned it. Most telling was the absence of any reaction from Boston's Cardinal O'Connell. Having assumed control of the *Pilot* in 1908, O'Connell's conservative policies no longer pandered to any liberal Americanist agenda. Thus, the *Pilot* generally fell silent on racial matters. In April 1915, the film was first shown in Boston, the home of old-line abolitionism and

10. Wilson quoted in *New York Times*, January 28, 1916; Arthur S. Link, *Wilson: Confusions and Crises, 1915–1916* (Princeton, NJ: Princeton University Press, 1964), 204.

a small but vocal African American community. Organized protests compelled Griffith and his promoters to seek endorsements from prominent persons in the Boston and Massachusetts area, including an appeal to Boston's Irish American and Catholic mayor Michael Curley to thwart any attempts to have the movie banned in Boston. Curley, realizing that this was not a political fight worth the risk of personal involvement, declared the film morally inoffensive and permitted its showing. Protests both mild and violent swirled around Boston for several weeks in the spring of 1915.

The conspicuous absence of any condemnation of Griffith's film seems even more despicable since prominent members of the American hierarchy had gone on record as having condemned the conventional racism of the era. John Ireland, for one, had earlier attended a national African American League meeting in St. Paul in which he condemned segregation and the disenfranchisement of all colored peoples. Cardinal Gibbons, although an advocate of Booker T. Washington's patient "accommodationist" approach to Negro advancement, had worked behind the scenes to further racial equality. Throughout 1909–1910, Gibbons had helped defeat a scheme to disenfranchise Maryland's black voters in his own backyard. Nonetheless, the American hierarchy and virtually all the Catholic press organs ignored the controversy generated by the public showing of the *Birth of a Nation*. In Boston, where the public viewing of the movie was quite controversial, Cardinal O'Connell remained mute and instructed the editor of diocesan newspaper, the *Pilot*, to ignore the controversy altogether. Instead, the paper launched into diatribes against playwrights George Bernard Shaw and Charles R. Kennedy for producing works that were blasphemous and insidious in their attacks upon the American Catholic Church. The paper also conducted a rather innocuous character study, extolling the virtues of Chief Justice Roger B. Taney, a slave-holding Marylander during the antebellum era, whose pronounced attachment to Catholicism, the *Pilot* maintained, "put him at the very forefront of the American Catholic editorial laity."[11] Griffith's film is said to

11. See Dick Lehr, *The Birth of a Nation: How a Legendary Filmmaker and a Crusading Editor Reignited America's Civil War* (New York: Public Affairs, 2014), 178–80. See also Boston *Pilot*, March 23, 1915.

CHAPTER 4

have inspired William Joseph Simmons of Georgia to proclaim the resurrection of the Ku Klux Klan later that year. On Thanksgiving night 1915, Simmons and a handful of "Kluxer" acolytes climbed Stone Mountain outside of Atlanta and burned a huge Christian cross. One must wonder if Catholic editors came to regret their silence over *Birth of a Nation* once the robed and hooded Klan grew to enormous proportions and began to thunder against immigrants and Catholics in the following decade.

Perhaps another existing cultural dynamic helps to explain the tepid response of the American Catholic Church to the resurgence in racial bigotry. The Irish and free Black Americans had a shared history of racial antagonism dating back to the antebellum era, mostly over competition for employment as manual labor, but charged by tribal hatred. Throughout the nineteenth century, Irish Americans had been demonized by nativists for being as uncivilized as Native Americans or the tribal peoples of Africa, the characterizations replete with comparisons of Irish and Africans as both indolent and childlike, with uncontrollable passions. By the close of the century, the Irish had been spurred to lay claim to a set of cultural characteristics that would make them respectable and capable of exercising the rights of responsible citizenship. While declining to fully embrace the dominant WASP culture, the Irish understood that to gain acceptance in American society "they had to look with loathing on everything the native whites loathed."[12] Another recent study suggests that while the Irish in America may well have been victimized throughout the nineteenth century, they soon emerged as notable defenders of white supremacy and that Irish Americans "must be recognized as both victims, and inescapably, oppressors."[13]

---

12. Bruce Nelson, *Irish Nationalists and the Making of the Irish Race* (Princeton, NJ: Princeton University Press, 2012), 6–10.

13. Sean Connolly, *On Every Tide: The Making and Remaking of the Irish World* (New York: Basic Books, 2022), 10. Connolly extends this thesis to cover Australia, and to a slightly lesser extent, New Zealand and Canada.

NEUTRALITY UNDER STRAIN IN 1915

Defining Neutrality

In 1915, Irish American Catholics were undoubtedly interested in the events unfolding south of the American border, but their concerns were both broader and more complex than those of the Church hierarchy. At the dawn of 1915, the impact of the European war, with its attendant tales of death, mayhem, atrocity, and destruction, had registered deeply and wholly with Americans. Just as Wilson's policy of neutrality was frequently fashioned by actions taken by Great Britain and Germany, Irish American opinions concerning the war were equally reactive in nature. In their case, Irish Americans generally responded to the way the Wilson administration interpreted, implemented, and adhered to the official policy of neutrality as promulgated by the government in the late summer 1914. In his annual address to Congress in December of that year, Wilson proclaimed that the country was "at peace with all the world," confident that war could not reach American shores, buffered as the country was by a veritable oceanic moat. Yet while neutrality was theoretically sound, in practice it was a thing of fragility.[14]

Despite Wilson's dedication to neutrality, several factors conspired to challenge his willingness and ability to adhere to it. The most persistent threats to absolute and impartial neutrality were the vagaries of public opinion. As noted earlier, the culmination of years of improved relations with Great Britain, coinciding with both accurate and exaggerated reports of German depredations in Belgium, along with news of Germany's fondness for unrestricted submarine warfare, spawned a diminution in goodwill towards Imperial Germany. Popular opinion, which had been trenchantly neutral, began tilting towards the Allied cause by 1915. Specific acts of German "barbarism" in 1915 might have intensified American indignation, but they only served, in truth, to reinforce an already established pro-Allied preference. At least this was the general tone of the country's secular press.[15]

---

14. Wilson quoted in A. Scott Berg, *Wilson* (New York: Simon & Schuster, 2013), 334–37.

15. *Literary Digest* 50 (April 24, 1915): 937. Even when the United States sent its sharply worded note to the British government over her violations of neutral rights in October 1915, most American newspapers gave only grudging support. See Link, *The Struggle for Neutrality,* 687–88.

CHAPTER 4

Skillful British propaganda by Sir Gilbert Parker, and later by Sir William Wiseman, increased this bias by creating a favorable portrayal of the Allied cause. Since the British censored news from the front, it was not surprising that Americans were fed a steady diet of Prussian brutality and treachery. News of the Allied war effort underscored its altruism and valorous motivations. British propaganda suggested that the Allies were carrying on a valiant defense of liberties and democracy while Americans stood idly by, refusing to assume their responsibilities.[16]

It would be misleading to suggest that the Allies did nothing to generate resentment in America during the period between January 1915 and March 1916; the most notable irritant was British interference with American shipping rights.[17] But it was Germany that committed the gravest acts meriting censure and condemnation by Americans. In February 1915, the German government announced that a war zone had been drawn around the British Isles and that any vessel entering that area, irrespective of its nationality, registry, or designation, was subject to possible sinking by German U-Boats. And it would not be long before the Germans put teeth into that warning. Meanwhile, in May, the *Bryce Report* was published, detailing the German atrocities committed in Belgium. It bolstered the perception that Imperial Germany, the "Hun," was a menace to western civilization. While German Americans and many Irish Americans refused to believe the full truth of the Bryce

---

16. Charles Seymour, *American Neutrality, 1914–1917* (New Haven, CT: Yale University Press, 1935), 147; W. B. Fowler, *British-American Relations, 1917–1919: The Role of Sir William Wiseman* (Princeton, NJ: Princeton University Press, 1969), 9–11; James D. Squires, *British Propaganda at Home and in the United States, 1914–1917* (London: Cambridge University Press, 1935), 69–76. Parker continued to feed Cardinal Gibbons information on the Belgian situation, describing in detail the "terrible devastations and desolation of innocent Belgians." See Sir Gilbert Parker to James Cardinal Gibbons, December 1, 1914, *Gibbons Papers,* Archives of the Archdiocese of Baltimore.

17. Britain's ambassador to the United States, Sir Cecil Spring Rice, noted that once Germany announced its intention to refrain from sinking unarmed passenger liners, negative attention would be drawn to British restrictions on trade. See Spring Rice to Lord Grey, January 13, 1916, in Gwynn, 2:309.

NEUTRALITY UNDER STRAIN IN 1915

Commission findings, many Americans were shocked at both the extent and horrific nature of the reported atrocities.[18]

Germany's proclamation of unrestricted submarine warfare shocked Woodrow Wilson. He cabled the Imperial German government and expressed his incredulity that Germany would even think to employ submarines against neutral merchant ships. He warned that he would hold Germany to a "strict accountability" for any incident in which an American ship was sunk or in which Americans were injured or killed. Furthermore, he declared that the United States would "take any steps that might be necessary to safeguard American lives and property and to secure to American citizens the full enjoyment of their acknowledged rights on the high seas." His strident prose took a few German leaders by surprise, but did nothing in the short term to alter Germany's decision, and her determination to bring Great Britain to her knees.[19]

Wilson's tough stance on German policy belied his expressed dedication to absolute neutrality, something not lost on the professional Irish Americans. Although he proved publicly stalwart in his commitment to impartial neutrality, Wilson's private disclosures revealed that his sympathies rested with the Allies. Reflecting on British sentiments that they were fighting America's war for Americans, Wilson even admitted as much to his secretary Joseph P. Tumulty. In a thoughtful assessment of Wilson, historian Henry F. May contends that as a "custodian of culture ... [Wilson] shared, at least from 1915 and probably earlier, the almost instinctive certainty that the cause of the Allies was that of civilization." May concluded his study of Wilson's neutrality by proposing that all that held Wilson back from committing the nation to hostile neutrality and probable intervention as early as 1915 was his "vacillating conscience" and his insistence that "it had to be absolutely right ..." Wilson's psychological or

---

18. See Robert H. Ferrell, *American Neutrality* (New York: W. W. Norton, 1975), 461; *Literary Digest* 50 (May 29, 1915): 1257–59; *Colliers,* June 5, 1915.

19. Telegram, William Jennings Bryan to German Foreign Office, via James W. Gerard, February 10, 1915, in US Department of State, *Papers Relating to the Foreign Relations of the United States, 1915.*

CHAPTER 4

intellectual convictions notwithstanding, it was certainly and painfully obvious to his many critics that "neutrality as the President practiced it meant American acquiescence to British control of the seas and the outpouring of munitions and war supplies from the United States to the Allied countries."[20]

Those who immediately surrounded and advised Wilson, and who most likely exerted the greatest degree of influence upon him, were equally sympathetic to the Allies. Once Secretary of State William Jennings Bryan resigned on June 7, 1915, over what he perceived to be an altogether too stern approach taken by Wilson over the *Lusitania* sinking, his replacement, Robert Lansing, completed the ranks of the Anglophiles surrounding the president. In a private moment, Lansing mused that it was only a matter of time before the US must join hands with the Allies, as the German government was "utterly hostile to all nations with democratic institutions ... [and] those who compose it see in democracy a menace to absolutism and the defeat of the German ambition for world domination."[21] The president's close advisor Colonel Edward M. House was one with Lansing in his conviction that American interests were inextricably tied to the Allies, fearing in late 1915 that if they were "to go down in defeat ... we would follow in natural sequence." Perhaps it was this sentiment that led House to convince London that the US government would never contemplate making a serious issue over British violations of neutral rights on the high seas.[22]

If staying the neutral course was a challenge to the Wilson administration, it was a *sine qua non* for Irish American Catholics—professionals, moderates, and conservatives alike. From the outset of the war, Irish Americans were constantly forming leagues and congresses whose purpose was to reinforce the administration's

20. Joseph P. Tumulty, *Woodrow Wilson As I Know Him* (Garden City, NY: Doubleday, Page, 1921), 231; Henry F. May, *The End of American Innocence* (Chicago: Quadrangle Press, 1964), 383; Link, *The Struggle for Neutrality,* 161.

21. Quoted in Robert Lansing, *War Memoirs of Robert Lansing* (Indianapolis: Bobbs-Merrill, 1935), 21.

22. Quoted in Daniel Smith, ed., *American Intervention, 1917: Sentiment, Self-Interest or Ideals?* (Boston: Houghton Mifflin, 1966), 29; Edward Cuddy, *Irish-Americans and National Isolationism, 1914–1917* (New York: Arno Press, 1976), 73.

commitment to neutrality. They closely monitored the government's evolving definition and praxis of neutrality and attempted to dissuade the nation from its preference for the Allies. Many Irish Americans linked arms with German Americans throughout 1915 to demand *de facto* rather than *de jure* neutrality, as they were convinced that the administration had acquiesced to British maritime power and the bristling business in war munitions conducted with the Allies.[23]

While moderate Irish Americans and Catholic editors occasionally sanctioned efforts to protest Wilsonian neutrality, the bulk of agitation came from a minority of Irish Americans within the professional Irish camp. On December 1, 1914, a meeting of 16,000 American Irish and Germans in Chicago founded the German-Irish Central Legislative Committee for the Furtherance of American Neutrality, in large part to protest the continued brisk trade in war material with the British by supporting an embargo. Although it was uncertain whether Joseph McLaughlin, president of the Ancient Order of Hibernians, always spoke for most of his membership, he undoubtedly struck a chord among them when he criticized the establishment that prays "for peace one day and ships cannons, rifles and explosives to England on six days of the week."[24]

Measures for an embargo introduced in Congress by German American representatives from the Midwest went down in defeat. Similarly, national sentiment did not sustain Irish American beliefs that an embargo had to be an *a priori* condition of impartial neutrality. Nonetheless, efforts to persuade Congress to pass an arms embargo continued throughout 1915. Jeremiah A. O'Leary of the American Truth Society took the lead by earmarking those Congressmen who opposed the embargo for defeat in the next election. However, international law, precedent, profits, and the staunch opposition of the administration doomed these efforts.[25] In St. Louis, another congregation of German

---

23. Clifton J. Child, "German-American Attempts to Protest the Exportation of Munitions of War, 1914–1915," *Mississippi Valley Historical Review* 25 (December 1938): 354.

24. Quoted in the *Irish World,* February 13, 1915.

25. Link, *The Struggle for Neutrality,* 161–64; *Congressional Record,* 64th Congress, 3rd Session, Part I, Vol. 53, 4016; Edward Cuddy, "Irish-American

CHAPTER 4

and Irish Americans met on January 10, 1915 to form a local branch of the Armed Neutrality League. The leadership consisted of lawyers, educators, businessmen, and a few pastors of Catholic and German Evangelical or Lutheran churches. While radical Irish Americans cooperated with the League and with the German American Alliance, most with moderate views supported the Allies as a means of proving that Ireland would stand by its commitments and was thusly fit for self-government.[26]

Although for different reasons, mainstream and institutional Irish American Catholicism supported the professionals' efforts to sustain the neutral course. In Cincinnati, Dr. Thomas Hart asseverated that "our neutrality is strained to the limit by the evident partiality of the daily press toward the side of the Allies." Similarly, Father John L. Whelan, compelled to defend himself of the charge that he was favoring Germany, asserted that he was "not pro-Germany and anti-England." He did, however, call for "fair play," and admonished the *New York Evening Sun* and other papers for their decidedly pro-Allied bias.[27] More pointed than attacks upon the press were charges against the government for dealing in the profitable munitions trade. Yet few moderate Catholic papers, other than the *Tablet*, printed such accusations. Such moderation did not afflict Joseph P. O'Mahoney of the *Indiana Catholic and Report*, who boldly maintained that if the United States would stop shipping war goods to the Allies the war would quickly end. Later, when incensed over the milquetoast protest delivered to Britain over the interruption of US commerce on the high seas, O'Mahoney caustically declared that "Great Britain knows our rights but she also knows who is in the Secretary of State's office and the rest is easy."[28]

Propagandists and American Neutrality, 1914–1917," *Mid-America* 49 (June 1967), 261–62. Note that Congressional supporters of embargo measures included moderate Irish Americans, such as Senators Thomas J. Walsh and James O'Gorman, as well as Representatives William J. Cory and Michael Burke of Wisconsin and Thomas Gallagher of Illinois. See *Congressional Record* 64th Congress, 1st Session, Vol. 53, 509, Appendix 932, and 145, 1671–75, 8914, Appendix 53.

26. Crighton, *Missouri and the World War,* 91–97.
27. *Catholic Telegraph,* April 1, 1915; Brooklyn *Tablet,* March 22, 1915.
28. Brooklyn *Tablet,* April 3, 1915; *Indiana Catholic and Report,* May 7, 1915, June 22, 1915.

NEUTRALITY UNDER STRAIN IN 1915

If the British placed a premium on influencing American public opinion, German Americans and Irish Americans did not shrink from the contest and did not yield gracefully to the British in the arena of propaganda. From the very onset of the war, efforts were launched to capture the minds of the American people and to dissuade the Wilson administration from its pro-Allied posture. Noted psychologist and professor Hugo Munsterberg of Harvard University set the tone in November 1914 when he tried to persuade the president to adhere to the strict neutrality he professed. Referring to recent congressional elections, Munsterberg claimed that Irish Americans were beginning to defect from the Democratic standard because they resented the administration's favoritism toward the Allies. Daniel F. Cohalan collaborated with Gaelic language expert Kuno Meyer, a German scholar, in trying to appeal to moderate Irish American sympathies. Meyer's prominent lecture series, entitled "The Golden Age of Irish Civilization and Its Influence on Germany," however contrived at points, highlighted how the histories of Germany and Ireland were unmistakably intertwined.[29] In early 1915, Bernhard Dernburg, a German banker turned politician, arrived in the United States to work with German ambassador von Bernstorff. Whereas the ambassador thought the quality of propaganda under Dernburg's direction materially improved, it would have been ineffective without the collaboration of Irish American agitators such as Devoy and Cohalan. On their own, the Germans proved largely inept at the art of propaganda in America; therefore, according to one student of the subject, they "were led by their Hibernian Allies ... [for] the political ascendancy of the Irish gave them an ascendancy over all other racial groups."[30]

Professional Irish Americans were better at propaganda than German Americans in sheer quantity and literary quality. Financed

---

29. Hugo Munsterberg to Woodrow Wilson, November 7, 1914, in Link, *The Papers of Woodrow Wilson*, 31:277–78; Carl Wittke, *The Irish in America* (Baton Rouge: Louisiana University Press, 1956), 277; George Sylvester Viereck, *Spreading Germs of Hate* (New York: Scribner's Sons, 1930), 233.

30. Johann von Bernstorff, *My Three Years in America*, 35–37; Frederick Luebke, *Bonds of Loyalty: German-Americans and World War I* (DeKalb: Northern Illinois University Press, 1974), 21; Viereck, *Spreading Germs of Hate*, 223.

CHAPTER 4

in part by German funding, James K. McGuire, a former mayor of Syracuse and fervent Irish nationalist, sought to offset pro-British propaganda by accusing England of "serving up the news for the world." Repeating the standard shriek of the professionals, he tried to persuade his readers that British maritime power was a direct insult to the United States. Bowing to the interests of his Catholic audience, McGuire presented the Kaiser as a model statesman of peace and religious tolerance. Whatever the actual appeal to Catholic audiences may have been, McGuire would claim in the introduction to his second book, one that again extolled the virtues of Germany, that his first book "received upward of 1200 letters of endorsement from the clergy," and added that, "they must have spoken the views of most of their parishioners."[31]

Whereas McGuire's views reflected the professionals' inflated hopes that a German victory over Britain would ensure Irish freedom, only a handful of Catholic newspapers even came close to this conclusion. The best that these anti-British papers could do was to paint Germany in the best light. Richard Tierney's *America* favorably portrayed the German government's relations to Catholicism by comparing it to that of the French. Branding the French government as "atheistic," Tierney condemned it for questioning the patriotism of religious orders within France. Simultaneously he praised the German Center Party for its suppression of a vulgar poem circulating throughout Germany entitled, *Hassgesang gegen England*, as a "chant of hate." Declaring that the war was to be waged with "no bitterness" or "passionate hatred," Tierney reported that the Centrists expressed sentiments that were in "full conformity with the wishes of the Holy Father and indeed with the demands of our Faith."[32]

---

31. It was reported that $22,000 for publishing costs had been fronted by German Americans for McGuire's efforts. See US Congress, Senate, Sub-Committee on the Judiciary, *Hearings, Brewing Liquor Interests and German Propaganda,* 2nd and 3rd Sessions, 1919, vol. 1, 1392, 1396–1398, 1504; James K. McGuire, *The King, The Kaiser and Irish Freedom* (New York, Wolfe Tone, 1915), 29–32, 219, 275; James K. McGuire, *What Germany Could Do for Ireland* (New York: Wolfe Tone, 1915).

32. *America,* April 17, 1915.

NEUTRALITY UNDER STRAIN IN 1915

In Indiana, O'Mahoney supported McGuire's generous appraisal of the Kaiser in an article titled "The Pope and the Kaiser," in which he regaled his readers with vignettes of the German military being kind to priests and other Catholic prisoners of war. Both the *Freeman's Journal* and the *New World* were particularly fond of printing pictures smuggled out of Germany in which Germans or Austrians were constantly portrayed attending the liturgy of the Mass. In another snapshot, Kaiser Wilhelm is seen decorating fifteen sisters of the Franciscan Order with Iron Crosses for their selfless efforts in military hospitals. Contrary to actual Catholic feeling towards Germany's other ally, the Turks, the *Freeman's Journal* featured a flattering photograph of Turkish officers with a caption praising them for their stout defense of the Dardanelles.[33]

Moderate Catholic thought, though unswerving in its adherence to neutrality, rejected the propagandist extremes of both sides, particularly the "insidious goals" of the professional Irish Americans. Moderates, such as John Quinn, reviled intemperate propagandizing and scoffed at the Kuno Meyer lecture series. Summarily assessing Meyer's mission as an abject failure, he declared that "nine out of ten here are in sympathy with the Allies and nothing that England is likely to do will change that feeling." Quinn further revealed that on one occasion he had confronted a certain Frank Harris for his public lecture on German virtues and English vices, offering the assessment that a "hundred Harrises could not change public opinion in this country, 90% of which is with the Allies."[34] Quinn's moderation reflected the opinions of many members of the Society of the Friendly Sons of Saint Patrick. At their annual dinner meeting in 1915, they greeted New York Mayor John Purroy Mitchel's endorsement of the Home Rule measure with great applause. Later in the year, Quinn confided to William Butler Yeats that he despaired of Roger Casement's mission in Germany and expressed contempt for the professional agitators who were goading

---

33. *Indiana Catholic*, January 22, 1915; *Freeman's Journal*, June 19, 1915, October 15, 1915; *New World*, July 9, 1915, October 15, 1915; *Freeman's Journal*, June 14, 1915.

34. Quinn is quoted in Alan Himber, ed. *The Letters of John Quinn to William Butler Yeats* (Ann Arbor: University of Michigan Research Press, 1983), 148–50.

CHAPTER 4

Casement on to such frivolous extremes. Comparing Casement to the tragic hero of 1798, Quinn voiced pity for Sir Roger, believing he was the "incarnation of Wolfe Tone."[35]

Most Catholic editors agreed with Quinn's disparagement of the professionals' efforts to sway public opinion significantly towards the German cause. Fred Sharon of Iowa's *Catholic Messenger* commended the various Hibernian divisions throughout the United States, as well as the United Irish Society of Philadelphia, for their continued support of Redmond and Home Rule as the only sensible course of action. Vowing that he had only entered the Irish imbroglio when the Clan-na-Gael misrepresented Irish American opinion, Sharon begged his fellow American Celts not to allow any "dissension in the ranks," as they "owe their first and last allegiance to our government." Sharon's views on the wisdom of the Home Rule settlement were echoed by Father John Burke in the *Catholic World*, who deplored the "misrepresentations" of not only the Protestant extremist Sir Edward Carson, but Sir Roger Casement and Professor Kuno Meyer as well.[36]

Out of Milwaukee Humphrey Desmond scorned the professionals' attempts to press for Irish freedom by violent means. Claiming that it "was the inalienable right of a small section of every nationality to be adequately foolish at times," he contended that this privilege could not be "denied even the Irish." Specifically identifying John Devoy and Joseph McGarrity by name, he condemned the Clan-na-Gael for their efforts to raise arms and munitions for a rebellious army in Ireland. Francis Smith reminded his readers in the Pittsburgh diocese that extremists of any variety were dangerous. Labeling it as shameful for men "to go up and down the country, lecturing and denouncing our attitude as a selfish one as they view it from their racial predilections," he defended the course of the US government's position of strict neutrality. In a parting shot at extremists, Smith described Theodore Roosevelt as "violently righteous." Indeed, Colonel Roosevelt and Dr.

---

35. See *131st Anniversary Dinner of the Society of the Friendly Sons of St. Patrick*, 26–27. For what it is worth, the Clan-na-Gael believed that eight out of ten Irish Americans favored Germany over Britain; Quinn is quoted in Himber, *The Letters of John Quinn to William Butler Yeats*, 176.

36. *Catholic World*, May 15, 1915.

NEUTRALITY UNDER STRAIN IN 1915

Bernhard Dernburg had "points in common," he awkwardly opined, "[They]are matched in talk, suffocating, poisonous gases belching from oral trenches, and no respirators to escape the fumes."[37]

The *Lusitania*

In February 1915, Germany announced it would begin a policy of unrestricted submarine warfare in a zone encircling the British Isles. On May 7, off the Old Head of Kinsale, U-boat commander Walter Schwieger torpedoed the Cunard liner *Lusitania*, sending it to the ocean floor with the loss of 124 American lives. No other event in the war, including the German invasion and plunder of Belgium, the relentless bombardment of Antwerp, or the destruction of the library at Louvain angered the American people more. The sinking of the *Lusitania* was perceived by Americans as a heinous murder ordered by the German government; Germany had now become what many had been contending all along—"an outlaw among civilized nations."[38]

Despite some exceptional anti-German hysteria that swept the nation, reactions from the Wilson administration and Capitol Hill were generally guided by a desire to maintain a neutral course. Whereas the number of American lives lost in the case of the *Lusitania* was without precedent, there had been several fatalities at sea already recorded. One American had died aboard the passenger-cargo liner *Falaba* off the coast of Ireland on March 28, 1915. While national opinion became predictably incensed over the *Falaba* incident, neither Wilson nor Bryan could agree on the technicalities and language of a diplomatic protest, and one that was never sent. In the time elapsing between the sinkings of the Falaba and the Lusitania, the American vessel the U.S.S. *Cushing* was attacked by a German plane on April 29, sustaining little damage and no loss of life. Two days later, however, the American tanker the *Gulflight* was torpedoed, and in the melee that ensued, the captain suffered a fatal myocardial infarction and two crew

---

37. *Catholic Citizen,* December 4, 1915; *Pittsburgh Catholic,* May 20, 1915.
38. Link, *The Struggle for Neutrality,* 372–73. For the virtually unanimous condemnation of this action in the American press, see *Literary Digest* 50 (May 15, 1915): 1133–34.

CHAPTER 4

members drowned in the Irish Sea. Again, as in the case of the *Falaba*, official American reaction to these assaults upon neutral shipping, and the loss of American lives, could not crystallize before the sinking of the *Lusitania* superseded all other considerations.[39]

Despite the State Department's note to the German government in February 1915, indicating that the U.S. would hold Germany "strictly responsible" for the loss of American lives and property within the declared war zone, Wilson stood for calmness and deliberation in the wake of the *Lusitania* sinking. Vacillating between a pacifism urged by his secretary of state and a need to palliate bruised national honor, Wilson sent three increasingly stern diplomatic protests to the government of Germany. In response, William Jennings Bryan resigned, because he perceived the language in the first two notes to be so harsh that it might provoke the Germans into a confrontation. Meanwhile, former President Theodore Roosevelt, speaking for many pro-Allied people, excoriated Wilson for his pusillanimous letter-writing campaign.[40] Wilson, for all his uncertainty, continued to reflect the national mood, which was desirous of maintaining the peace at all costs. Despite the initial wave of outrage and repugnance for Germany's audacity, Spring Rice correctly assessed the national sentiment of America in the early summer 1915 when he suggested to his superiors in London that "the prevailing sentiment is undoubtedly for peace ... not perhaps at any price but peace at a very considerable price."[41]

Irish Americans were dragged into the maelstrom of political activity prompted by Germany's recourse to unrestricted submarine warfare. Those most adversely affected by the German strategy were the professionals and their German cohorts. Dr. Dernburg was

39. *Literary Digest* 50 (April 10, 1915): 789–91; *Lansing Papers*, 1:365–84; *New York Times*, "Gave No Warning to American Ship," May 4, 1915, p. 1.

40. Department of State, *Papers Relating to the Foreign Relations of the United States, 1915, Supplement, The World War* (Washington, DC: Government Printing Office, 1928), 98; *Lansing Papers*, 1:395–401, 422–50; Theodore Roosevelt to A. H. Lee, June 17, 1915, in Elting E. Morison, ed., *The Letters of Theodore Roosevelt*, 8 vols. (Cambridge, MA: Harvard University Press, 1951–1954), 8:937.

41. Cecil Spring Rice to Lord Grey, June 23, 1915, in Stephen A. Gwynn, 2:274.

NEUTRALITY UNDER STRAIN IN 1915

in Cleveland when word of the *Lusitania*'s fate reached the United States. Unwisely, Dernburg commented to the press that the sinking of the British liner was defensible in that the ship was carrying contraband of war, which made it an auxiliary cruiser of the British navy. Von Bernstorff quickly issued a statement to the *New York Times* to offset Dernburg's bluntness in which he lamented the loss of life but laid responsibility for the tragedy at the doorstep of the British Admiralty. Bernstorff claimed that the British strategy of submitting the German populace to starvation by blockade had compelled the German navy to undertake drastic measures. Years later, the German ambassador reflected that the *Lusitania* affair was a pivotal point in the propaganda war for American opinion. From May 1915 onward, Bernstorff recalled, American sentiment became irretrievably surrendered to the Allied cause.[42]

No one was more acutely aware of the potential disaster impending in American opinion of Germany than John Devoy. Immediately following the sinking, he argued that the British had acted reprehensibly by permitting civilians to sail into a war zone upon a "Floating Arsenal" when the Germans had made their intentions clear to everyone concerned. The Fords of the *Irish World* argued in much the same way as Bernstorff had done. They contended that the British navy and merchant marine had resorted to such extreme means by arming their ships and sanctioning the ramming of submarines that U-boat commanders had little choice but to attack without warning.[43] In addition to condemning British naval warfare and defending German retaliation, the professionals strove to minimize the damage done to American public opinion and to ensure that pro-Allied enthusiasts did not sway the Wilson administration from its commitment to absolute neutrality. Several days after the *Lusitania* sinking, a telegram was sent to the White House stating that the State Department should wire the British steamship *Transylvania* to warn it to disembark American passengers before entering the war zone. The telegram's signatories included James T. Clark, president of the United Irish Societies, Patrick H. O'Donnell, president of the Irish Fellowship Club, and

42. Bernstorff, *My Three Years in America*, 106.
43. *Gaelic-American*, May 15, 1915; *Irish World*, May 15, 1915.

CHAPTER 4

Horace L. Brand, Chairman of the German-Irish Central Legislative Committee.[44]

Within a month of the sinking of the *Lusitania*, the United Irish Societies and the German Alliance combined efforts by forming another movement to preserve neutrality, called the Friends of Peace. On June 24, 1915, a large rally of both Irish and German Americans gathered at Madison Square Garden to demonstrate for peace. Notably present were the Irish American firebrand Jeremiah A. O'Leary of the American Truth Society and recently resigned Secretary of State William Jennings Bryan. At a later Friends of Peace meeting in Hoboken, New Jersey, at which O'Leary gave the keynote address, one spokesman summed up the meeting's verdict on the *Lusitania* by defending Germany's right to fire upon the liner. As far as the Americans who were drowned were concerned, "they were themselves to blame for being so silly as to sit upon a keg of powder." In Chicago, the meeting of the Friends of Peace was judged to be a failure. It was poorly attended, as organized labor, including many Irish Americans, was dissuaded from attending the meeting by labor leader Samuel Gompers.[45]

The potential hazard of the *Lusitania* sinking and the effect it might have on diplomatic relations with Germany sent the professionals grasping for straws. When Secretary of State Bryan, whom the *Gaelic-American* and *Irish World* had alternately vilified in the past with disparaging epithets, such as "Billy Sunday humbugger," and "grape-juice clown," resigned over the strong wording of Wilson's *Lusitania* notes, he was hailed as a great statesman by the professionals. Encouraged by Bryan's defection from Wilson's cabinet, the professional Irish American press continued to heap abuse upon Wilson's diplomatic notes to Berlin and to condemn American trafficking in war munitions to the Allies.[46]

---

44. William Jennings Bryan to Woodrow Wilson, May 13, 1915, in Link, *The Papers of Woodrow Wilson,* 32:185.

45. Bryan soon realized that he was being exploited by pro-German sympathizers and promptly disengaged from the movement. See Child, "German-American Attempts to Protest the Exportation of Munitions of War, 1914–1915," 75–81; *New York Times,* August 31, 1915; Luebke, *Bonds of Loyalty,* 121.

46. Wittke, *The Irish in America,* 278–79; *Irish World,* June 12, 1915, June 19, 1915.

NEUTRALITY UNDER STRAIN IN 1915

Altogether different was the response of other Irish Americans, especially the Church's hierarchy, to the maritime crises of 1915. When pressed for his opinion of the *Lusitania* tragedy, Cardinal Gibbons expressed what would prove to be the consensus of all moderate and conservative Irish American Catholics; he spoke of shock and horror at the loss of lives yet also of the need for acting coolly and rationally. In the *New York Times* he said:

> I feel the greatest sorrow for this terrible tragedy ... [but] the American people must be calm and prudent. It is best to leave the destinies of the nation in the hands of the President and the Government. Popular sentiment is not a standard to be followed too hastily.[47]

When Wilson, in a speech in Philadelphia on May 10, rejected force as a means of seeking redress and declared himself as "being too proud to fight," Cardinal O'Connell of Boston wrote the president a congratulatory letter. The normally taciturn Cardinal Farley of New York vociferously condemned the sinking of the *Lusitania* as "absolutely without justification ... the most appalling thing in my life." Although unable to make sense out of the tragedy, Farley exhorted his faithful to follow the position taken by the president. "I am sure all good Americans approve of his stand in the Lusitania affair," he contended, "as well as his efforts to maintain strict neutrality throughout the war."[48]

The stand taken by the hierarchy over the *Lusitania* established a pattern of response throughout 1915 and 1916 about naval warfare. In the weeks following the *Lusitania* sinking, when pro-Allied advocates were encouraging harsh sanctions against the Germans, the hierarchy pleaded for calmness and caution. When the British freighter *Arabic* was sunk on

---

47. *New York Times,* "Gibbons Urges Calmness," May 5, 1915, p. 4.
48. Albert Shaw, ed. *The Messages and Papers of Woodrow Wilson,* 2 vols. (New York: Review of Reviews, 1924), 1:114–18; William Henry Cardinal O'Connell to Woodrow Wilson, May 11, 1915, in Link, *The Papers of Woodrow Wilson,* 33:159; Farley is quoted in *New York Times,* "Stands by President," May 15, 1915, p. 6.

CHAPTER 4

August 15, 1915, with the loss of two American lives, Gibbons once again rallied to the peace standard. He warned that "war is a terrible thing," and that Americans should "not lightly jump into the strife that is tearing the world to pieces." His greatest admonition, however, was reserved for those adventurists who carelessly risked their lives traveling on ships clearly tagged for danger. "A true lover of America," he insinuated, "should not sacrifice personal whims when the honor and peace of the nation hang in the balance." And in what can only be judged as a reproof of those who held intemperate opinions on the matter, he requested that they refrain from expressing themselves so forcefully, since doing so would impede progress and complicate the situation.[49]

Immediately following the *Arabic* sinking, Pope Benedict XV enjoined Gibbons to reveal to the administration that the Holy See had convinced Berlin to desist from sinking ships in the future. While the *New York Times* and *Baltimore Sun* saw a much broader peace initiative in a September meeting between Gibbons and Wilson, it was, in fact, only designed to soften the bellicose attitudes emerging in America over the *Arabic* crisis.[50] In the main, the Catholic press reflected the position of the hierarchy in the greatest threats to the preservation of American neutrality throughout 1915 and early 1916. Even before the sinking of the *Lusitania*, Francis P. Smith of the *Pittsburgh Catholic* railed against the torpedoing of the *Falaba* and encouraged the government to register a protest in Berlin about the perfidious action. More than that Smith could not condone, for any hasty action "that might inflame public opinion" further was to be eschewed at all costs. Omaha's Father Gannon condemned Germany's attack upon the *Gulflight* as a violation of international law and concurred with Thomas O'Flanagan in Cincinnati that "Germany owes us reparation for the *Cushing* and the *Gulflight*."[51]

---

49. Gibbons quoted in *New York Times,* August 25, 1915. Convinced that Wilson was following the correct course of action, Gibbons praised him for his restraint in the *Arabic* crisis. See Memorandum of James Cardinal Gibbons of His Interview with Woodrow Wilson, September 2, 1915, *Gibbons Papers,* Archives of the Archdiocese of Baltimore.
50. Ellis, *The Life of James Cardinal Gibbons,* 2:231–32.
51. *Pittsburgh Catholic,* April 15, 1915; *True Voice,* May 7, 1915, May 14, 1915; *Catholic Transcript,* May 13, 1915.

NEUTRALITY UNDER STRAIN IN 1915

The reaction of Irish American Catholic editors to the sinking of the *Lusitania* continued to reveal the division within their ranks. Virtually all papers deplored the senseless loss of life among those on the great liner, yet they could not agree completely as to who was responsible. Particularly revealing was the scant attention the sinking received among those papers that had traditionally displayed pro-German sympathies. The respected *America* featured an article with a German explanation for the sinking, which then veered into a disclaimer that English prisoners of war were being mistreated by Germans. A. Brendan Ford's *Freeman's Journal* lamented the loss of life but added that American had been warned and should have taken heed. Joseph P. O'Mahoney contemptuously brushed off the affair by remarking that it was "an incidental phase of the harvest of death reaped daily in the awful war." Frequently an ally of the professional press, the *New World* was unusually critical of Germany's action, noting that all Ireland was on England's side in this matter and that America had a "higher duty ... to speak out for the rest of the non-warring world."[52]

The measure of the *Lusitania* tragedy can be seen in the number of papers that abandoned their strictly neutral stance for a swipe at Germany. Predictably, the Reverend John Burke of the *Catholic World* condemned Germany and ruefully remarked that it had the singular good effect of bringing home the "real character of German warfare." Observing that the "world stands aghast at the *Lusitania* horror," Father Gannon in Omaha calculated that Germany's purpose was to "startle the world and strike terror by the ruthless sacrifice of life rather than to destroy the ship itself." And in Hartford, Thomas O'Flanagan declared that Germany should respond favorably to US demands; after all, he reasoned, "she was the aggressor when she struck a blow which civilization calls foul." When the *Arabic* was disabled by a German torpedo, O'Flanagan assessed that "one successful battle is worth more to Germany now than the respect and approval and the applause of all the peoples of the world."[53]

52. *America*, May 15, 1915; *Freeman's Journal*, May 15, 1915; *Indiana Catholic and Record*, May 21, 1915; *New World*, May 21, 1915.

53. *Catholic World*, June 11, 1915; *True Voice*, May 14, 1915; *Catholic Transcript*, May 20, 1915, August 26, 1915.

CHAPTER 4

Despite expending considerable vitriol at Germany's expense, most moderate Catholic papers lined up behind the hierarchy's banner of neutrality. Even O'Flanagan was perplexed as to who was to blame for the *Lusitania*, suggesting that the "blame rests mainly between Germany that fired the first shot, and England that dared her to fire." The Reverend John Whelan expressed "horror" over the loss of life and feared that this incident might pull America into war with Germany, implying that this would be a misdirected course of action.[54] Most enjoined their readers not to permit passions to cloud their judgments. Again, O'Flanagan attempted to draw a comparison between the jingoism following the *Maine* disaster and the spirit cropping up in the aftermath of the *Lusitania* sinking. Calling pro-Allied supporters "war-howlers" for their harsh demands on Germany over the *Lusitania*, he advised his readers that the warmongers of 1898 had "erred egregiously in the case of the Maine." O'Flanagan's pragmatic appeal to reason was repeated by the *Catholic Messenger*, which hoped the crisis would be "met with cool, sensible, consummate wisdom after deliberate investigation." Dr. Hart in Cincinnati exhorted the president to avoid "hasty and indiscrete action," and when the *Arabic* was attacked in August, he called for "temperance in speech." Noting that Cardinal Gibbons believed that the "*Arabic* incident weighs as a feather to the awful calamity of war," he recommended heeding Wilson's "salutary request for neutrality." Most Catholic editors pointed with pride to the fact that their co-religionists exercised moderation over the *Lusitania* episode. Francis P. Smith claimed that "reason and self-control were everywhere in evidence ... and there was no jingoism rampant in this country upon the sinking of the *Lusitania*." Another editor proudly compared Catholic reaction to that of American Protestants, charging that in the latter's pulpits "unrestrained denunciation of the German government was the keynote of most sermons" on the Sunday following news of the sinking. By contrast, "only words of calmness were heard" from Catholic lecterns.[55]

54. *Catholic Transcript,* May 13, 1915; Brooklyn *Tablet,* May 22, 1915.
55. *Catholic Transcript,* May 13, 1915; *Catholic Messenger,* May 13, 1915; *Catholic Telegraph,* May 13, 1915, September 2, 1915; *Pittsburgh Catholic,* May 20, 1915; *Ave Maria,* May 22, 1915.

NEUTRALITY UNDER STRAIN IN 1915

So dedicated were many Catholic editors to the cause of neutrality that they adumbrated the *Lusitania* tragedy by burying it deep within the pages of their editions or ignoring it altogether. For instance, Kansas City's *Catholic Register* eschewed any commentary on the sinking of the great liner, other than to include the remarks made by the Church's hierarchy. Given the enormity of the *Lusitania* calamity, it would have seemed appropriate to have highlighted this story in at least one of the two editions of the paper published after news of the sunken liner had been made public. And a simple desire to avoid stirring up ethnic passions does not seem to be an adequate justification. Rather, it would appear as though the editors of many Catholic newspapers remained fixated on advancing an agenda they deemed entirely more important than the disturbing news emanating from the European war. The priority in most Catholic papers was a militant defense of Catholicism against the railings of nativist detractors. The *Catholic Register* headlined its May 13 edition with a banner headline, "Isn't It Time to Squelch 'Pastor Russell'?" The Protestant clergyman in question was infamous for his assault upon Catholics. The paper determined that it was more important to excoriate the pastor's questionable morality (lately revealed in divorce proceedings in which his wife had been granted a decree based upon cruelty and adultery) than to elaborate upon the matter of the *Lusitania*. The paper's assault upon Pastor Russell reached its climax when it described Russell as a "jellyfish," noting that if he were "attracted to a damsel and she accepts his advances, he tarries; if she rejects him then he drifts on to other waters." The following week the *Catholic Register* took on another bastion of nativism, by headlining with an "Open Letter to the *Menace*," gashing it as a "miserable publication" and accusing it of a "loathsome campaign of iniquity." Responding to the *Menace*'s scurrilous diatribe against the work of the Good Shepherd nuns, the paper labeled the attack as an "appeal to religious bigotry, prejudice and backwoods ignorance," concluding that "no man pays his intelligence any compliment in accepting seriously your insane tirades of abuse against Catholics." The same edition printed a lengthy article hailing the work that Catholic priests were doing for "Civic Uplift Movements." And a full-page story and supportive advertisement was devoted to complimenting Humphrey Desmond of Milwaukee's *Catholic Citizen*, and his assistant Scannell O'Neil, for their serial column "Cock and Bull Stories," an expose and refutation of routine Protestant critiques of Catholic scandals, such as "What Goes on in the Nunneries." Clearly, the Catholic press was infinitely more interested in asserting the American Catholic position in the United States than stoking bellicose inclinations regarding the Great War or the physical force liberation of Ireland.[56]

The reactions of the more moderate spokesmen of the Irish American Catholic community seemed to have more in common with the official Church position than they did with the professionals. Bourke Cockran's disparaging remarks concerning Prussian militarism were penned only two months after Commander Schwieger sent the *Lusitania* to the ocean floor. At the same time, however, Cockran's dedication to maintaining the peace was consistent with the hierarchy's recommendations. Although representing a minority position, clamors for war prompted by the sinking of the *Lusitania* and other ocean-faring vessels inspired Cockran to undertake a late fall speaking campaign across the nation, promoting international pacifism. He was so committed to this work that he was eventually named a Knight of St. Gregory at the behest of Cardinal Farley.[57]

The *Lusitania* affair made an extremist out of John Quinn. He was no longer willing to disguise his contempt for the Germans. Writing to an associate, he described the Germans as acting like demons and said that the very worst should be expected of them. "I am in favor of boycotting them in this country," he charged, and "making them ashamed of their nationality and their blood and their names." Unlike Bourke Cockran and other advocates of peace, Quinn was disenchanted with Wilson's pusillanimous confrontation with the Germans in the months following the sinking. In July he wrote his friend William Butler Yeats that Wilson was a "physical and moral coward." His harsh characterization of the president was remarkably like former

---

56. *Catholic Register* (Kansas City), May 13, 1915, May 20, 1915, May 27, 1915.

57. Bishop Patrick Hayes to Bourke Cockran, July 3, 1916, *Cockran Papers*, New York Public Library.

NEUTRALITY UNDER STRAIN IN 1915

President Theodore Roosevelt's description of Wilson.[58] Others in the Irish American political limelight, such as Senators Thomas Walsh of Montana and James D. Phelan of California, adopted a cautious approach to the situation. Senator James A. O'Gorman of New York, a veteran Anglophobe, tried to avoid questions concerning the *Lusitania*. He did point out, however, the "folly of our urging hasty or precipitate action by our Government." While it cannot be said with certainty that he was sincere in his sentiments, O'Gorman expressed confidence in the "wisdom and patriotism of the President ... to safeguard every American interest."[59]

The Knights of Columbus, which was heavily Irish American and was the largest Catholic fraternal organization in the United States, took its marching orders from the Church and remained strictly neutral in its positions on the Great War and Irish aspirations for freedom. From the onset of the war, and throughout the period of American neutrality, the Knights concentrated on its fraternal obligations and the defense of the faith from nativist attacks. When the *Lusitania* went down, many of the state chapters of the Knights were holding annual conventions. Once the hierarchy framed the proper Catholic response, the Knights ventured to offer similar expressions, although they were always couched in stirring and impassioned patriotic pledges of loyalty to the government. From Colorado, it was reported that the "Columbus Knights" had approved Wilson's course in upholding the nation's dignity.[60]

Earlier sympathy for Germany's cause was compromised to the point of evaporation by the loss of lives aboard the *Lusitania* and other merchant vessels in 1915 and early 1916. In Butte, Montana, a rugged mining town of the west where radical Irish American organized labor

---

58. John Quinn to Gwen John, June 7, 1915, *John Quinn Papers*, New York Public Library; Quinn's letter to William Butler Yeats is found in Himber, *The Letters of John Quinn to William Butler Yeats*, 176.

59. O'Gorman quoted in *New York Times*, "Knights of Columbus Loyal," May 25, 1915, p. 3. Senator Phelan offered similar advice to his Catholic constituents in *The Monitor*, May 15, 1915.

60. *New York Times*, May 25, 1915. Additional expressions of support for Wilson by the Knights can be found in the *Catholic Messenger*, May 13, 1915; *Catholic Citizen*, May 22, 1915; Boston *Pilot*, May 15, 1915; and *Catholic Transcript*, May 20, 1915.

CHAPTER 4

was championed, Anglophobia remained persistent. Yet by 1915 some of the earlier demonstrations of pro-German support were beginning to erode. The Hibernians there, whom some of the younger Irish American radicals suspected were a "branch of the Knights of Columbus," began to hesitate in their open espousal of Germany, for fear it would run counter to the policy of the American government. The last fervid expression of Hibernian solidarity with Butte's German and Austrian communities was displayed in the St. Patrick's Day parade in 1915—two months before the *Lusitania* was sunk. In the state of Maine, where one study of public opinion found Irish Americans generally supportive of the Central Powers in 1914, a reaction against Irish American agitators, particularly O'Leary and the American Truth Society, developed after the tale of the *Lusitania* circulated.[61]

What became increasingly manifest after the sinking of the *Lusitania* is that the gap existing in the ranks of Irish Americans widened. Nowhere was this division more apparent than when John Devoy's *Gaelic-American* censured Cardinal Gibbons for his continued friendliness towards John Redmond and for his involvement in various international movements to the exclusion of working for Irish freedom. Similarly, when Jeremiah O'Leary assaulted Wilson and Lansing for their continued tolerance of British interference in American neutral rights on the high seas, many Americans resented his harassment of the administration. One testy response came from a certain Joshua O'Leary of Worcester, Massachusetts, who argued that the "other O'Leary" was "representative of only a small section of the Irish race," and pronounced that the agitator's latest telegram to the administration was "simply disgusting to patriotic American citizens as well as to all intelligent and sincere friends of Ireland."[62]

---

61. David M. Emmons, *The Butte Irish: Class and Ethnicity in an American Mining Town, 1875–1925* (Urbana: University of Illinois Press, 1989), 348, 359. Despite the expressed disapproval of the local ordinary, Bishop John Carroll, strong leadership and support for the professional Irish position came from priests, especially Fathers Michael Hannon and James English. The study of Maine's opinion in 1915 is found in Edwin Cottrell, *How Maine Viewed the War* (Orono: University of Maine Press, 1940), 51.

62. *Gaelic-American*, April 1, 1916; *New York Times*, November 15, 1915.

NEUTRALITY UNDER STRAIN IN 1915

A broad spectrum of Irish American Catholics felt it was sheer folly for Americans to travel on belligerent ships into the war zone. John Devoy believed that only a ban upon such perilous traveling was the way to preserve peace. Cardinal Gibbons largely concurred with Devoy when he opined that it was an act of great selfishness to sacrifice the nation's welfare out of a whim to travel abroad. When in March 1916 resolutions aimed at barring Americans from such travel were introduced into Congress by Representative A. Jeff McLemore and Senator Thomas P. Gore, a substantial number of Irish American lawmakers backed their passage. George Sylvester Viereck claimed that a "brilliant young Irish-American poet and politician" named Sheamus O'Sheel gave McLemore the idea for the resolution. As it turned out the resolutions were tabled in committee, when Wilson enforced party discipline to secure the necessary "nay" votes.[63]

A lull in Germany's commitment to unrestricted submarine warfare occurred between the sinking of the *Arabic* in August 1915 and the attack upon the French steamer Sussex in March 1916. The apparent suspension of attacks might have pleased Wilson, and the uninterrupted interference of the British navy may have continued to bruise American sensitivities, but Germany's sinking of the *Lusitania* had made an indelible impression on American public opinion. The impression was deepened by reports of widespread German sabotage and conspiracies against American firms involved in the munitions trade with the Allies. In July 1915, a German American sympathizer planted a bomb that exploded in the Senate cloak room of the Capitol Building. A day later this same German loner barged his way onto the estate of J. P. Morgan, well known for obtaining loans for the Allies, and seriously wounded the great titan of industry and finance. Under the direction of Captain Franz von Rintelen, attempts were made to recruit Irish American stevedores to place incendiary bombs on freighters transporting munitions to Britain. Later in the year, accounts

---

63. *Gaelic-American,* March 4, 1916; *Catholic Transcript,* May 25, 1915. Gibbons is quoted in *New York Times,* August 25, 1915. Link, *Confusions and Crises,* 167–78; Crighton, *Missouri and the World War,* 108; Viereck, *Spreading Germs of Hate,* 104–5; Woodrow Wilson to William Gibbs McAdoo and Albert Sidney Burleson, March 2, 1916, in Link, *The Papers of Woodrow Wilson,* 36:239.

of numerous intrigues were played up in the press and served to an eager public. On December 1, 1915, Secretary of State Robert Lansing informed von Bernstorff that passports were being revoked for two military attaches, Captain Karl Boy-Ed and Captain Franz von Papen, and they would be asked to return to Germany immediately. Both had been implicated in conspiracies to violate American neutrality. American estimation of Germany sank even deeper.[64]

Reports of intrigues, sabotage, and conspiracies, as well as sophisticated propaganda efforts, played a substantial role in developing American attitudes toward the belligerents. However, the graphic scenes of carnage and death from the battlefields and the high seas were the principal elements molding American views during 1915. More subtly, and more curiously, the war also fostered a climate in which many of the attitudes and opinions held by Irish American Catholics prior to the war underwent varying degrees of reinforcement or redefinition.

Throughout 1915, the war had forced many Irish Americans and Catholics to articulate where they stood in relation to one another and to the nation. By 1915 it was clear that Irish American Catholics were not uniform in their political and social views on the war in Europe and the means of Irish liberation. More than that, they nurtured a grievance about their own status in an America that was still culturally Protestant and patently hostile towards them. Insecure and resentful, Irish American Catholics exhibited a defensiveness on one hand, and an assertive, even militant, posture on the other to justify their inclusion in American society. The defensive quality of their justifications revealed the resilient underlying paradoxes at the

---

64. Mild irritation over Britain's interference with American trade can be found in the *Lansing Papers,* 1:304–5, 447–48. That the US relationship with Great Britain had become strained, see Sir Cecil Spring Rice to Lord Grey, January 13, 1916, in Stephen A. Gwynn, ed., *The Letters and Friendships of Sir Cecil Spring Rice,* 2:309. Reports of German sabotage and intrigue can be seen in the *New York Times,* "Move to Punish Plotters," November 22, 1915, "2,000,000 Spent: Boy-ed here on German Plot," November 24, 1915, p. 1. See also Carroll, *American Opinion and the Irish Question,* 49. On the recall of Boy-Ed and von Papen, see Memorandum by the Secretary of State of an Interview with the German Ambassador (Bernstorff), in *Lansing Papers,* 1:86.

root of their experience at this period in the United States. As Irish Americans resented suspicions about their loyalty and patriotism, they made certain that they were second to none in trumpeting their love and devotion to the country. In this respect they were bold, assertive, and confident. At times, however, Irish American Catholics, seeking acceptance into the larger and somewhat amorphous Anglo-Saxon society, detested the fact that they had to endure what they perceived to be callous aspersions on their character and morality and retreated into a sanctuary of communal support.

Perhaps the greatest manifestation of increased Irish American Catholic sensitivity centered upon the revival of questions concerning their loyalty and patriotism. For Irish Americans, particularly the professionals, the opening salvo of the "hyphen war" had been fired by President Wilson in his speech dedicating the memorial to Commodore Barry in Franklin Park. From that date to the election of 1916 the debate over the hyphen raged and drew all segments of the Irish American Catholic community into the fracas. For his part, Wilson kept the issue dangling in front of the American public in most of his addresses. In May 1915, Wilson greeted several thousand newly naturalized citizens in Philadelphia with the admonition that, while a person might still "love the home of his birth and the nation of his origin," he ought to dedicate himself "to the place to which you go." Declaring that America did not consist of groups, and that a person who considered himself as belonging to another national group had clearly not made the transition into becoming American, he deplored any "man who goes among you to trade upon your nationality as not a worthy Son to live under the Stars and Stripes." Two months later Wilson put words into action by creating a National Americanization Day, falling on Independence Day 1915. The explicit goals of Americanization were to foster the use of the English language among immigrants, to highlight American standards of living, and to promote the virtues of American citizenship.[65] By October 1915, the acrimony between

---

65. Address to Several Thousand Foreign-Born Citizens after Naturalization Ceremonies, Philadelphia, May 10, 1915, in Shaw, *The Messages and Papers of Woodrow Wilson,* 1:115–16; Edward G. Hartmann, *The Movement to Americanize the Immigrant* (New York: AMS Press, 1967), 114–33.

CHAPTER 4

Wilson and his hyphenated detractors was intense. Taking advantage of yet another opportunity to assail hyphenated Americans, Wilson told a gathering of the Daughters of the American Revolution, a group that hardly needed such instruction, that "there have been some among us who have not thought first of America, who have thought to use the might of America in some matter not of America's origination." He further educated his receptive audience about the greatly exaggerated strength of the hyphenate by declaring that "the number of such is, I am sure, not large ... [and] those who would seek to represent them are very vocal, but they are not very influential."[66]

When Jeremiah O'Leary's telegraphic scoffing at US failures to remain totally neutral began arriving at the White House and State Department, both Wilson and Lansing decided to accelerate the crusade. Wilson ended the year by denouncing the hyphen in an address before a joint session of Congress on December 7. Claiming that there were those who "have poured the poison of disloyalty into the very arteries of our national life," he denounced them as having "sought to bring the authority and good name of our government into contempt." Then, in the most emotionally charged moment of his oration, he moved that "such creatures of passion, disloyalty and anarchy must be crushed out."[67] Wilson's assault upon the hyphenated American generated a flurry of protest and prompted a wave of patriotic assertions and demonstrations by the Irish American Catholic community. While the furor over the hyphen did not peak until later in 1916, there was no lack of defensive posturing and words from the mouths and pens of Irish Americans in 1915. In some ways, this was one of the very few issues that unified the Irish American community, although the tone and measure of the arguments employed tended to separate the professionals from the mainstream.

Predictably, the professional press did not permit any of Wilson's assaults on Irish American patriotism to go unanswered. As noted

---

66. President Wilson's Address to the Daughters of the American Revolution, Washington, October 11, 1915, in Shaw, *The Messages and Papers of Woodrow Wilson*, 1:124–26.

67. Ward, *Ireland and Anglo-American Relations*, 99–100; Link, *Confusions and Crises*, 36.

earlier, they mounted a blistering attack on Wilson when he first introduced a hint that Irish American were disloyal in the Commodore Barry memorial speech. Following each of Wilson's addresses in which he impugned the loyalty of Irish American citizens, the professionals lashed back with vigorous denials and branded his remarks as vicious, cruel, and unfair. One of the professionals' allies in the religious community, Richard Tierney, SJ, of *America*, went so far as to suggest that the "world is more apt to suffer from exaggerated and excessive patriotism than from its dearth." One genuinely neutral editor was pushed to the point of exasperation, asking his readers how the president could "justify the term of Scotch-Irish and object to the term German-American or Irish-American."[68]

Mainstream Irish Americans, especially those within the Catholic sphere, devoted less energy to confronting the administration over these insults, and more to waging a comprehensive defense of Irish American and Catholic loyalty and patriotism. The headline of one Catholic newspaper, "Catholic Church Stands for Law and Order," was repeated in so many words in practically every religious newspaper at one time or another. Another paper not only protested "attaching a stigma to the time-honored and honorable hyphenated adjectives of nationality," but provided its readers with a history of the Fighting Irish 69th Regiment of New York, extolling its courage, loyalty, obedience, and all other patriotic virtues imaginable. Cardinal Mundelein of Chicago proposed in May 1916 to "thoroughly Americanize the Catholic school system in Chicago," so that "there shall no longer be Irish-Americans, German-Americans ... but only real Americans." As if intending to satisfy Wilson personally, Mundelein added that, "we intend to take the hyphen out of the parochial school system in Chicago."[69]

The Knights of Columbus rallied to the defense of both Irish Americans and American Catholicism. Following each of Woodrow Wilson's speeches, which generally intertwined patriotic exhortations

68. *Gaelic-American*, May 23, 1915; *Irish World*, October 16, 1915; *Gaelic-American*, February 20, 1915, October 23, 1915; *America*, April 22, 1915; *Catholic Transcript*, December 30, 1915.
69. *Brooklyn Tablet*, August 14, 1915; *Catholic Transcript*, June 29, 1916; Shanabruch, *Chicago's Catholics*, 187–88.

with baleful references to hyphenate disloyalty, the Knights applauded the president for his patriotic utterances while ignoring the insults. When the president designated July 4, 1915, as the first National Americanization Day, the Knights responded enthusiastically. In Brooklyn, the *Tablet* predicted: "Throngs Expected at K of C Celebration," and anticipated that an "elaborate program for patriotic exercises at Prospect Park" would be forthcoming. A week later, the paper reported that the featured orator, the Honorable William D. Cunningham, "spoke of the part that Catholics, particularly Irish Catholics, had to do with the development of this country."[70] This sentiment reverberated through the Knights of Columbus meetings across the country, as evidenced in a report from the Shenandoah Council of Iowa, which reflected that Catholics had from the beginning of the nation to the present day "mingled their blood with that of Protestants on every battlefield in the cause of liberty."

The *Gaelic-American* could not endure the way the Knights responded to Wilson's speeches, and Devoy condemned them for condoning the administration's attacks on Irish Americans.[71] Unfortunately for John Devoy and the Clan-na-Gael, they were swimming against the current on this issue. When Fred Sharon of the *Catholic Messenger* averred that "no one called Phil Sheridan a "hyphenated" American when he thundered down the Valley of the Shenandoah," he was only reflecting in a small way the near obsession Irish Americans displayed in grounding their current loyalty to flag and country in the military history of the United States. At the 1915 annual banquet of the American Irish Historical Society, guests were regaled by all the speakers on the dais, including Senator James D. Phelan of California, about the heroic exploits of Irish Americans dating back to the American Revolution.[72]

70. *New York Times,* O'Connell Praises Speech," May 12, 1915, p. 7; Brooklyn *Tablet,* July 3, 1915, July 10, 1915.
71. *Catholic Messenger,* January 28, 1015; *Gaelic-American,* October 23, 1915.
72. *Catholic Messenger,* April 1, 1915; "Address of General Peter W. Meldrim at the Seventeenth Annual Banquet of the Society," in Edward Hamilton Daly, ed., *Journal of the American Irish Historical Society* (New York: Published by the Society, 1915), 14:98.

NEUTRALITY UNDER STRAIN IN 1915

In San Francisco, the Knights of St. Patrick extolled Irish Americans not only for their past deeds of bravery and loyalty but also for the "new testimony to the spirit of patriotism" that they were displaying. One speaker noted that the only thing that surpassed Irish American "pride in our ancient lineage is our pride in our citizenship in the American Republic." When the well-respected Society of the Friendly Sons of St. Patrick met for their annual dinner in March 1915, the mayor of New York, John Purroy Mitchel, was greeted with loud applause when he revealed that he knew of no one who "has ever seriously questioned" the loyalty of Irish Americans. The approbation with which this comment was received was exceeded only by that accorded an actor named Wilton Lackaye, when he blurted out that he "should be the last man in the world to be in favor of hyphenated movements ... as far as I am concerned, I would just as soon shoot an Irishman as a German if they came menacing New York." The following year, the theme of the dinner was "Americanization," in the word emblazoned on a large illuminated American flag floating over the dais. After the president of the Society opened up the festivities by announcing that "we bow to none in love and loyalty to the United States," Senator Phelan keynoted the evening by asserting that "certainly the Irish have the right to claim this land as their own," and concluded his oration to tremendous cheering with a pledge that, "in a contest of loyalties between the Old Land the New Land," Irish Americans would "espouse the cause of the New."[73]

The same sensitivity attached to allegations of Irish American disloyalty carried over into responses to any criticism of their honor and respectability. The war frequently offered a context in which these real or imagined slights could be challenged. Although all representatives of the Irish American Catholic community expressed resentment toward those who denigrated the Irish nationality, the professionals generally

---

73. Address by the Honorable Thomas J. Lennon at the Banquet of the Knights of St. Patrick, San Francisco, March 17, 1915, *Journal of the American Historical Society,* 14:309–313; *131st Anniversary Dinner of the Society of the Friendly Sons of St. Patrick in the City of New York, March 17, 1915, Hotel Astor* (New York: Published by the Society, 1915), 25, 52. An account of the 132nd Anniversary Dinner was published by the Society the following year, 7, 13, 22.

proved too consumed with their revolutionary interests on Ireland's behalf to devote much attention to this task. The Irish American Catholic press eagerly filled the void. One of the more intriguing responses found in the Catholic press swirled around one of the most enduring popular songs of the war—"It's a Long Way to Tipperary." In a letter to the *Indiana Catholic*, the Reverend James H. Cotter, former editor of the *Buffalo Catholic Union and Times*, expressed disgust over the use of this song as an English recruitment tool, observing that it hinted at the "stupidity of the Irishman," and that it flouted the "inconstancy of the Irish woman." Cotter was quickly commended by O'Mahoney, who applauded his "censure of the miserable composition called Tipperary—a song of the London slums."[74]

Irish American Catholics also highlighted the difference between Ireland's superior moral mettle, despite being a prostrate country, and the moral and social degeneracy of the dominant English Protestant culture. With prudish gloating, Catholic writers and editors cited reports of questionable validity that the "cause of intemperance is on the decrease in Ireland," whereas in England it was on a sharp rise. Similarly, Catholic editors cited such inconsequential events as the closing of a prison in Ireland as an indication that Gaelic crime was on the wane. One editor reported in a similar vein that the "absence of indictable offenses is really notable and is decidedly creditable to the Christian morality of Ireland's people." This same editor referred to a favorable speech given by former President William Howard Taft at a St. Patrick's Day banquet in Chicago as proof positive that "Irishmen are not anarchists."[75]

The Irish were not only more law-abiding and sober than their English counterparts, but also possessed a superior sexual morality, according to Irish American Catholics. Another journalist could not resist reporting that in England there were supposedly 30,000 unmarried women who were pregnant as a result of the quartering

---

74. *Indiana Catholic,* January 15, 1916. Arthur Preuss echoed Cotter's sentiments by condemning the tune as a "slur on the morality of the Irish people in London." See *Fortnightly Review,* January 1, 1915.

75. *Michigan Catholic,* December 3, 1914; *Southern Messenger,* July 29, 1915; *Ave Maria,* April 29, 1916.

of soldiers in their midst. The same could not be said of Ireland, claimed the writer, even though Ireland was as much an armed camp as England. Contending that "nobody has heard of such a scandal" in Ireland, the article concluded with the questionable but mordant verdict that the "mouths of those who prate about the higher morality among Protestants than Catholics should be closed forever."[76]

Such exertions on the part of the Irish American Catholic press revealed an overly sensitive and defensive posture. The New York *Catholic News* was very clear on this matter when it pointed out that the "Irish can take a joke on themselves more good-naturedly than many other races, but they do hate to be openly and senselessly insulted." While quick to dissociate itself from the more radical elements of their community, mainstream Irish American opinion also divorced itself from the so-called "Shoneen Irish" who saw "little to be proud of in their ancestry," and who quickly traded in their Irish lineage for acceptance into Protestant society.[77]

The Catholic press's defense of Irish virtue served a vital community function. When Catholic editors portrayed the Irish as a moral, responsible, and well-adjusted group, Irish American Catholics emerged as a model of respectability. Irish American and Catholic editors hoped that the impression they were creating was one of an Irish people worthy of governing themselves and that their emigres in America were likewise a worthy people. As for the hyper-patriotism in the press, this was intended to prove that the Irish American was, had always been, and would ever be loyal to the country of their adoption. By their proclamations of patriotism, mainstream Irish American Catholics were making it very difficult for themselves to deviate from positions that the government was adopting during the crisis of neutrality.

The year 1915 had proved difficult for professional Irish Americans, as they fell far short of reaching the goals they had set when the war began. John Redmond and the Home Rule settlement were far from

76. Denver *Catholic Register,* May 20, 1915.
77. *Catholic News,* January 1, 1916; *Michigan Catholic,* March 25, 1915. The term "Shoneen" was coined by an Irish cultural nationalist, D. P. Moran. It was used pejoratively to describe those Irish Catholics who aped English customs and mannerisms. See Emmons, *The Butte Irish,* 352.

CHAPTER 4

disgraced in the estimation of most Irish Americans, and the strict neutrality expected of the American government floundered in favor of continued munitions commerce with the British. Moreover, the Germans and their operatives in the United States failed to convince most Americans, and for that matter, even mainstream Irish American Catholics, that a German military victory was in the best interests of either Ireland or the United States. Even if these stark realities could have been ignored, the impact of the Belgian atrocity stories and the hysteria generated by revelations of German sabotage and intrigue made the promotion of a pro-German stance even more arduous. Yet more devastating than all these factors were the negative American reactions to Germany's adoption of unrestricted submarine warfare.

More than any other stricken vessel, the *Lusitania* symbolized the horror of submarine warfare and fixed in American minds the barbarity of its perpetrators. Americans were appalled by the gruesome images of the sunken liner. The specter of bloated corpses floating in the Irish Sea and the ghoulish visages of children in coffins, depicted in grisly detail by newspapers, nullified whatever sympathy German and Irish American propagandists had secured. If the British proved annoying by intercepting American ships and seizing contraband, their activities paled in comparison to the slaughter of innocents by submarines. This harsh reality was not lost upon that wily veteran of Sinn Fein, John Devoy, who admitted that the *Lusitania* affair had hurt the cause deeply and that the movement was "going to have a hard time, owing to the new situation." It may be fair to suggest that the Germans and their Irish American allies never fully recovered from the sinking of the *Lusitania*. Despite the professionals' attempts to explain why Germany had resorted to this form of warfare, they could not efface the horridly visceral images of German cruelty upon the high seas.[78]

Devoy's belief that the preservation of American neutrality was at stake prompted him to call for a convention of Irish Americans in early March 1916, to demonstrate that they were not lining up on the side of

---

78. John Devoy to Joseph McGarrity, May 14, 1915, *Joseph McGarrity Papers,* New York Public Library; Buckley, *The New York Irish,* 44–48; Confidential Circular Letter from John Devoy, January 15, 1916, *Joseph McGarrity Papers,* New York Public Library.

the Allies. In private, the professionals conceded that their cause was suffering much more than they would admit in public. Following the *Lusitania* sinking, Devoy confided to confederate Joseph McGarrity that he had heard of a gathering of influential Irish Americans in New York where it had been mentioned that but for a few radicals, "the whole Irish race here would be lined up on the side of 'humanity and civilization.'" Devoy's convention itself was well attended and the speeches were quite stirring. All the same, many significant members of the Irish American community absented themselves. Bourke Cockran simply refused the invitation. Senator James A. O'Gorman, a veteran Anglophobe, likewise refused. Representative Michael Donohoe, in responding to James McLaughlin of the Hibernians, a group divided over the merits of such a convention, explained that such measures as the convention were bound to undermine John Redmond's efforts.[79] Afterward, John Quinn, never one to mince words, informed Shane Leslie that the convention resembled an "opera bouffe," and that no one other than Clan devotees had participated. For his part, Leslie condemned the Irish Race Convention as a tool of German propaganda, while Francis Hackett of the *New Republic* lamented that the tone of the convention was "too racial." Hackett even refused to endorse the strident denunciation of England that the speeches of Judge John W. Goff and Patrick H. O'Donnell provided. Other Irish Americans registered their objections to the convention in various New York City newspapers.[80]

The Irish Race Convention received no official endorsement from the American hierarchy, although some support was offered in both Tierney's *America* and in Boston's *Pilot*. It also appeared that a handful of Irish American Catholic clergy, mostly from New York, attended

---

79. John Devoy to Joseph McGarrity, May 29, 1915, *Joseph McGarrity Papers*; James A. O'Gorman to Daniel F. Cohalan, March 1, 1916, quoted in Buckley, *The New York Irish*, 53; Michael Donohoe to James McLaughlin, February 19, 1916, *Joseph McGarrity Papers*.

80. John Quinn to Shane Leslie, September 6, 1916, *John Quinn Papers*, New York Public Library; Carroll, *American Opinion and the Irish Question*, 53; Francis Hackett, "A Policy for Ireland," *New Republic* 6 (March 25, 1916): 209–11; *New York Times*, "Irish Want England Humbled, Says Goff," March 5, 1916, p. 7.

CHAPTER 4

the convention. To carry on the work initiated at the convention, a new organization, known as the Friends of Irish Freedom (FOIF) was created. Nominally headed by Victor Herbert, a famous composer of the time, it was ultimately controlled by the Clan-na-Gael. At the FOIF's next convention, they elected Father Peter E. Magennis, a New York Carmelite priest, as their president. Magennis's selection might have been part of the Clan's strategy to broaden its base of support. Unlike the Clan itself, FOIF members were not bound by any oath, and a woman's auxiliary was also formed. While Magennis was clearly assisted in his activities by fellow Carmelites residing at their East 29th Street priory, as well as by a few other Irish American clerics, their efforts attracted the displeasure of higher ecclesiastical authorities.[81]

On its own merits, the Irish Race Convention failed to stimulate the Anglophobia among the Irish American and Catholic community that its planners hoped. To most moderate and informed Irish Americans, the FOIF was nothing but a front for the Clan-na-Gael and most absolved themselves of any connection to it. Despite the trace of apprehension in British ambassador Spring Rice's dispatch to Lord Grey, noting that the "professional Irish politician is against us,"[82] mainstream Irish American and Catholic opinion of Germany and the Clan's agenda had fallen to an all-time low. On the eve of the Easter Rising in Dublin (1916), most Irish American Catholics favored President Wilson's neutral course, and if their sympathies were not fully extended towards the Allies, they were most certainly reeling backwards and away from the Germans.

---

81. Wittke, *The Irish in America;* Sean T. O'Kelley to the Very Reverend Donald M. O'Callaghan, O.Carm., January 8, 1961, and Reverend Lawrence D. Flanagan, O.Carm., to Eamon de Valera, December, 1962–January 1963, quoted in Alfred Isaacson, O. Carm., ed., *Irish Letters in the New York Carmelites' Archives* (Boca Raton, FL: Vestigium Press, 1988), 24, 35–36.

82. Sir Cecil Spring Rice to Lord Grey, January 13, 1916, in Gwynn, *Letters and Friendships of Sir Cecil Spring Rice,* 2:309. Even in Butte, normally a bedrock of Irish nationalism, James Connolly, a socialist, labor organizer, and fervent Irish nationalist, had a difficult time rousing Irish American Catholic strikers with his "Hoch der Kaiser" appeals. See Emmons, *The Butte Irish,* 352–53.

CHAPTER 5

IRISH AMERICAN CATHOLICS AND THE 1916 EASTER REBELLION

Although traditionally considered to have caused a significant shift in Irish American attitudes toward Irish nationalism and the European war,[1] events in the middle six months of 1916 did little to alter the gradual dissolution of American neutrality or energize demands for immediate Irish independence. Neither the pathetic failure of the Easter Rising nor the savage British reprisals in its wake succeeded in consolidating divergent opinions within the Irish American and Catholic communities.

1916: Mexican Revolution

In March 1916, American Catholic interest in international affairs remained fixed upon the relentless spasms of revolution-wracked Mexico. This was, as always, a far safer focus for criticism of the Wilson administration's policies, for both the American hierarchy and the Catholic press, than the course of the European war. Pancho Villa's audacious sortie into American territory had stunned the nation and galvanized the Wilson administration into adopting an interventionist and punitive course of action. By the end of the month, General John

---

1. Alan J. Ward, *Ireland and Anglo-American Relations, 1899–1921* (Montreal: McGill University Press, 1969), 63–78; Charles C. Tansill, *America and the Fight for Irish Freedom, 1866–1922* (New York: Devin-Adair, 1957), 224–25.

CHAPTER 5

J. Pershing had penetrated 350 miles into Mexican territory in pursuit of the bandit-revolutionary Villa.[2]

Predictably, American Catholics sedulously criticized the administration's handling of the Mexican crisis. Reflecting the nearly unanimous opinion of the Catholic press was Richard Tierney's succinct verdict that the situation in Mexico was the inevitable consequence of the administration's ill-advised policies. Catholic opinion in general continued to fume over Joseph Tumulty's earlier denials of Mexican atrocities as well as the belief that Wilson had branded Father Clement X. Kelley and various members of the hierarchy as "liars."[3]

Pershing's force, which continued through June 1916 to hopelessly roam the Mexican countryside in search of the elusive Villa, eventually drew the ire of Venustiano Carranza and the Mexican citizenry. For a brief while, it appeared as though war might break out between the two countries, something the German government duly noted. American Catholic reaction to this possibility was ambivalent, and in many ways offered an insight into the way American Catholics would react to similar circumstances a year later. While displeased with the administration's policies regarding Mexico for fully two years, Church leaders still encouraged their faithful to support the administration's decision to send the punitive expedition into Mexico. Father John L. Whelan articulated the mainstream Catholic position when, in directing an editorial toward Wilson, he declared that while Catholics would fight for a president who hopefully would retain that position but a few more months, they would do so only because "Catholics are loyal citizens."[4]

This appeal to sterling citizenship, despite profound skepticism of the prevailing foreign policy, matched the response of the largest Catholic lay organization—the Knights of Columbus. In what proved to be a precursor to a more expanded endeavor a year later, the Knights elected to mirror YMCA efforts along the Mexican border by establishing their own centers providing religious and social services

---

2. Arthur S. Link, *Wilson: Confusions and Crises* (Princeton, NJ: Princeton University Press, 1964), 208–217.
3. *America,* April 1, 1916; Denver *Catholic Register,* January 11, 1917.
4. Brooklyn *Tablet,* July 1, 1916.

for American soldiers. To fulfill the Knights' mission of diffusing anti-Catholic bigotry, these centers provided services free of charge and opened them up to soldiers of all religious affiliations. Despite the official Catholic censure of the government's policies toward Mexico, the Knights welcomed the chance to prove that "a man can be a devout Catholic and a loyal patriot."[5]

As the summer waned, hostilities lessened between the United States and the Mexican insurgents. By the end of August, both sides were searching for a peaceful solution that would lead to the eventual departure of American forces from northern Mexico. With military operations in Mexico tapering off, American Catholic disaffection with the Wilson administration continued to fester, particularly when the president snubbed proposed Catholic candidates and appointed John R. Mott, the leader of the YMCA, as his final choice for membership on the Joint American and Mexican Peace Commission. While Wilson's Mexican policies remained a source of contention to American Catholics throughout the campaign of 1916, it appeared that some degree of stabilization had been achieved by that fall. Despite incredulity in some Catholic quarters, the Mexican government made a display of curbing the excesses of anti-clericalism and guaranteeing the integrity of the Church. Hence, American Catholic displeasure toward Wilson over the Mexican imbroglio softened somewhat, at the same moment that European and Irish affairs began to require greater concern and scrutiny.[6]

Germany Resumes Unrestricted U-Boat Warfare

While events in Mexico throughout early 1916 helped to deflect American Catholic attention away from the European war, German depredations on the high seas and acts of sabotage within the United States continued to spark the outrage of, and subsequent rebuke by, the American government and its citizenry. Such actions consistently hampered efforts by the Clan-na-Gael and other sympathetic Irish

---

5. "Guardsmen on the Border," *Columbiad* 23 (October 1916): 15; "Along the Mexican Border," *Columbiad* 23 (November 1916): 18.

6. *New World*, September 22, 1916; *America*, October 16, 1916.

CHAPTER 5

Americans to promote German interests in the United States, serving only to bolster the nation in its commitment to a neutral course of action.

When the unarmed French passenger ferry *Sussex* was torpedoed on March 24, 1916 in the English Channel, injuring several Americans, diplomatic relations between Washington and Berlin were nearly ruptured. Secretary of State Robert Lansing advised Wilson that the "time for writing notes discussing the subject has passed." Declaring that the "honor of the United States and the duty of the government to its citizens" required a decisive response, Lansing suggested that von Bernstorff be handed his passport and the United States immediately sever diplomatic relations with Imperial Germany. Colonel Edward M. House, Wilson's informal political and diplomatic advisor, was inclined to believe that the bottom was out of the tub and that the time had arrived when diplomatic protests and notes to the Germans had run its course. When the Germans failed to provide sufficient explanations to the administration by mid-April 1916 regarding the *Sussex* incident, a declaration of war against Germany seemed likely.[7]

While the torpedoing of the *Sussex* hardly matched the sinking of the *Lusitania* for sheer terror and loss of life, it did represent a culmination of incidents involving German aggression and was viewed in the United States as a major provocation. That war with Germany might be a distinct possibility in the wake of the *Sussex* affair did not appear to be lost upon Germany's advocates among the Irish American professionals. Whereas John Devoy chose to gloss over the *Sussex* matter, A. Brendan Ford's *Irish World* scurried to provide an explanation, claiming, rather lamely, that a British mine was most likely to blame. When Wilson, even when staying the hand of his more bellicose advisors, forwarded his stern *Sussex* note to the German government, Ford claimed that the president was so partial to the British that he was out to abet their interests by prohibiting German use of the submarine altogether. In any event, the contretemps was avoided when the German government responded with another pledge to curtail unrestricted submarine warfare for the foreseeable future.[8]

---

7. Secretary of State to President Wilson, March 27, 1916, *Lansing Papers*, 1:537–39; Link, *Confusions and Crises*, 249.

8. *Irish World*, April 1 and 26, 1916. Germany's announcement on May 4,

If the professionals were alarmed by the potential negative impact of Germany's apparent resumption of unrestricted warfare, the American Catholic Church continued to press for calm and prudent responses. Some papers no longer remained sanguine about the preservation of peace and neutrality. William A. McKearney of the *Catholic Universe* in Cleveland forecast that "it appears like war with Germany ... we have been reduced gradually to a nation without a backbone in our dealings with other nations, and it is a relief that finally we have met the issue." As a cautionary measure, McKearney counseled his readers to demonstrate kindness to German Americans, while reminding all Catholics that their "first duty is to support the government with our whole strength."[9]

Whatever fears McKearney and other Catholic editors entertained regarding the possible severance of diplomatic relations with Germany, they wholeheartedly endorsed efforts by the pontiff, Benedict XV, to intercede with the warring parties, particularly Germany, to avert America's entry into the war. From the outset of the Great War, there had been widespread American Catholic support for neutrality. Given the increasingly pro-Allied tenor of overall American opinion, even the professionals had established the maintenance of American neutrality as the only supportable position; they had never harbored illusions that the United States would enter the war on the side of the Central Powers. This would explain why Pius X's call for peace in the summer of 1914 was so vigorously applauded in both the American Catholic and Irish American communities.

Pius's successor, Benedict XV, undertook greater efforts to persuade the belligerents to sue for peace, and repeatedly offered his services to mediate differences between the warring nations. One such effort was occasioned by the German attack upon the *Sussex*. In May 1916, Benedict communicated to Wilson his plea that the American leader refrain from any precipitous action to enforce the sanctions outlined in the president's April 18 note to Berlin. In a draft reply to the pope's initiative, Wilson expressed his appreciation for the "friendly sentiment

1916 that it would curtail unrestricted submarine warfare was commonly referred to as the Sussex Pledge. The German government renounced it in January 1917.

9. *Catholic Universe,* April 21, 1916.

CHAPTER 5

of broad humanity" espoused by the pontiff and assured Benedict that matters between Washington and Berlin "had already entered upon a stage of satisfactory understanding" before he had even received the pontiff's missive.[10]

Sympathy for Germany's cause suffered further setbacks when repeated acts of German subversion and sabotage within the United States came to light throughout 1916. In addition to instigating strikes among dock workers who loaded munitions aboard ships bound for England, German agents, with some Irish American collaboration, had committed over two hundred acts of sabotage against ships, factories, canals, and bridges by 1916. The most spectacular incident occurred on Black Tom, a New Jersey island in New York Harbor, on July 30, 1916. In the early morning hours, explosions rocked the harbor and uncontrollable fires consumed the largest munitions depot in the United States. The first explosion, at 2:08 a.m., was the most devastating. It sent fragmentary debris long distances. Some lodged in the uplifted torch-bearing arm of the Statue of Liberty, while others wedged into the clock tower of *The Jersey Journal* building. Windows were shattered in Manhattan and Brooklyn, and several of the stained-glass windows of St. Patrick's Cathedral were destroyed. People within twenty miles of Black Tom were reportedly knocked out of their beds. The Brooklyn Bridge shuddered in the explosions' wake, and people as far away as Maryland and Connecticut were awakened by what they thought was an earthquake. Seven deaths were recorded, and scores in Jersey City were injured.[11]

---

10. Pope Benedict to President Wilson, n.d. and Draft Reply to Pope Benedict XV, May 15, 1916, in *Lansing Papers*, 1:15–16. This was neither the first nor the last occasion that Benedict XV offered to broker peace negotiations to end the war and arrange for a just and equitable settlement. See Terry Philpot, "World War I's Pope Benedict and the Pursuit of Peace," *National Catholic Reporter* (July 19, 2014).

11. For a detailed description of the Black Tom incident and other acts of sabotage, see Jules Witcover, S*abotage at Black Tom: Imperial Germany's Secret War in America, 1914–1917* (Chapel Hill, NC: Algonquin Press, 1989). A year earlier, a deranged, German-born former Harvard professor, Erich Muenter, set off a bomb in the US Senate cloakroom to protest US munitions-makers sending war supplies to the Allies. A day later, he invaded the estate of J. P. Morgan on Long

IRISH AMERICAN CATHOLICS & 1916 EASTER REBELLION

The explosions on Black Tom came hard on the heels of revelations of German and Irish American collaboration in the Irish uprising in April 1916. On April 18, the US Secret Service barged into the New York offices of the German consulate and discovered evidence incriminating several prominent Irish Americans, chiefly Judge Daniel F. Cohalan. In what was popularly known as the [Wolf] von Igel Raid, named after the military attaché stationed in New York following the deportation of Franz von Papen and Karl Boy Ed, government officials seized papers revealing German intentions to land a cargo of arms in Ireland to support an uprising. The matter was not immediately made public, though elements of it trickled out in 1917 after American entry into the war. One of the letters suggested John Devoy's involvement in negotiations with the Germans about a planned uprising in Ireland around Easter Sunday. He was just getting over his horror at being summoned to a Federal court in Manhattan eleven days before the raid to testify about a German plot to blow up the Welland Canal in Canada. The feisty old Fenian warrior admitted that he left the courtroom that day rattled and frightened, even though he had wriggled off the hook. Fortunately, his one letter did not come home to roost, but it convinced him that the American government was fully aware of his nefarious activities.[12] He remained defiant enough to deplore the raid upon von Igel's office as a violation of both international and domestic law and intimated that Attorney General Thomas W. Gregory, whom Devoy believed to be both an anti-Irish and anti-Catholic bigot, was the genius behind the caper.[13]

Island, with the idea of holding him hostage until the arms trade was halted. He did manage to shoot Morgan, slightly wounding him, before he was subdued and jailed. Shortly after, he was found dead in his cell from an apparent suicide.

12. Terry Golway, *Irish Rebel: John Devoy and America's Fight for Irish Freedom* (New York: St. Martin's Press, 1998), 230–31. In visits to the German consulate before the raid, Devoy had implored von Igel to tidy up his cluttered desk.

13. *Gaelic-American*, April 22, 1916. In a related matter, it was reported that some members of the Clan held talks with Sikhs to conspire in toppling the British Empire in India. Details of this collaboration were revealed in the Hindu German Conspiracy trials held in San Francisco in 1917–1918. See Matthew Erin Plowman, "Irish Republicans and the Indo-German Conspiracy of World War I," *New Hibernia Review* 73 (2003): 81–105.

CHAPTER 5

Devoy, in fact, suspected that Woodrow Wilson had personally authorized the raid. Hailing Wilson as "the meanest and most malignant man who ever filled the office of the President of the United States," Devoy cited Wilson's longstanding and implacable hatred of Judge Cohalan as the fundamental motivation for the raid. Other than Devoy's personal recollection, there was a profound absence of any commentary in any of the Irish American publications. Virtually no other prominent Irish Americans offered their opinions as to the genesis of the raid, leading one to surmise that they believed it would be better to remain silent rather than fan the flames. Catholic publications in the main were likewise mute about ascribing responsibility for the intrusion on the German consulate. Among Catholic publications, only Tierney's *America* ventured the opinion that the British Government appeared to have had "some foreknowledge of the uprising."[14]

Given the dramatic enormity of the Black Tom bombing, it is somewhat surprising that suspicion of German intrigue did not redound to Germany's discredit. Certainly, the responsibility for the sabotage of a huge munitions warehouse filled with explosives bound for Great Britain could only have been lost on the most obtuse Americans. Yet the government did not exploit this dastardly act (just as it purposely delayed publication of the papers seized in the von Igel raid) to alter their strict position of neutrality. Wilson, gearing up for a reelection campaign, knew that the country would not countenance any serious militant posturing that would compromise American neutrality. Moreover, on July 11, the British had inexplicably and ill-advisedly issued a formal blacklist that applied to eighty-five American firms and

---

14. John Devoy, *Recollections of an Irish Rebel*, 470; *Gaelic-American*, April 22, 1916; *America*, May 6, 1916. Tansill claimed that the fact that "Cohalan was anti-English was enough to damn him in Wilson's eyes," and was convinced that the State Department handed over all pertinent information regarding the planned rebellion to the British. Countering this claim with an impressive array of evidence is Max Caulfield, who contends that the British took no precautions that suggested they had been apprised of this information. In any event, the issue was moot, as the British had already cracked the German code for messages relayed between Berlin and the Clan-na-Gael in New York. See Charles C. Tansill, *America and the Fight for Irish Freedom, 1866–1922* (New York: Devin Adair, 1957), 193–94; Max Caulfield, *Easter Rebellion* (London: Four Square Books, 1965), 36.

individuals. The blacklist marked the culmination of recent Allied war measures, vastly increasing American public criticism of the Allies and somewhat deflecting the usual condemnation of the Central Powers.[15]

The secular press, especially that in New York City, devoted considerable attention to the destructive fallout from the Black Tom explosions. In particular, the *New York Times*, a decidedly pro-Allied organ, suggested the incident might be an act of German sabotage. However, in the days following the explosion, doubt existed as to its cause. Reports that a disaffected Jersey City immigrant laborer was found lurking in the vicinity of the island were added to the admission that several smudge pots had been lit by two night watchmen trying to ward off mosquitoes. Consequently, even the *Times*, willing to speculate on the cause of the explosions, withheld judgment until a full investigation was conducted. Meanwhile, professional Irish publications gave scant attention to the incident. Attempting to mitigate the bombing's fallout for the Germans, the *Irish World* faulted the armament industry and the government for allowing such an immense cache of munitions on the New Jersey shore in clear violation of that state's laws.[16]

It is hardly surprising, then, that Catholic publications refused to cast aspersions on the Germans, or anyone else for that matter. The further west that one went, the more muted Catholic papers became. New York area papers did give detailed descriptions of the explosion's impact, particularly on Catholic churches and institutions. In the pages of the Brooklyn *Tablet*, *Catholic News of New York*, and Hartford's *Catholic Transcript*, meticulous accounts of the damage to St. Patrick's Cathedral, parish churches, and parochial schools in Manhattan and Brooklyn, and of the heavy damage to the Polish church of Our Lady of Czestochowa in Jersey City, were served up to their readers. Catholic papers may have meekly hinted at the inherent dangers in storing weapons of war in a peaceful country, but they refused to condemn anyone lest it ignite war fever and jeopardize

---

15. Daniel Smith, *Robert Lansing and American Neutrality, 1914–1917* (New York: Da Capo Press, 1972), 141.

16. *New York Times*, "Ruins Disclose Disaster's Cause," August 1, 1916, p.1; "Jersey City To Ban Munitions," August 2, 1916, p.1; *Irish World*, August 3, 1916.

CHAPTER 5

American neutrality. They seemed satisfied to accept the uncertainty about the incident's cause.[17]

There was little, then, in which the Clan-na-Gael could take heart, in the days leading up to the Easter uprising. German submarine strikes against Allied and neutral shipping had generated palpable ill-will in the United States. In light of these actions, the professional Irish American press could muster only timid and lackluster arguments that Wilson's *Sussex* notes were but a pretense for supporting British control of the Atlantic shipping lanes.[18] The distorted logic clouding the thinking of radical Irish Americans did not afflict German leaders. In May 1916, they responded to Wilson's entreaties by pledging to refrain from attacking merchant vessels without giving proper warning. They also assured the American government that every effort would be made to rescue passengers and crews of stricken ships. While the Germans qualified their pledges by linking adherence to them with England's abandonment of her illegal activities upon the high seas, Wilson was reasonably satisfied and accepted the response with minor clarifications. For the time being, war between the United States and Germany had been averted.[19]

If the professionals labored unsuccessfully to defend Germany's right to self-defense, they also derived little satisfaction from their efforts to mold Irish American and Catholic opinion. In March, the Executive Committee of American Irish Societies, which included the New York Municipal League of America, the Ancient Order of Hibernians Board of Erin, and a host of other Irish American benevolent societies, denounced the convocation of John Devoy's Irish Race Convention. This was a pointed jab at the meeting, which had been convened in New York, included over two thousand Irish Americans, and created a new organization to carry on the mission, named the Friends of Irish Freedom (FOIF). Noting that Devoy intended to use it as a "propaganda tool," the committee assailed him for "his violent attack on American neutrality and his transparent

---

17. Brooklyn *Tablet*, August 4, 1916, *Catholic News of New York*, August 5, 1916, and *Catholic Transcript*, August 5, 1916.
18. *Irish World*, April 29, 1916.
19. Link, *Confusions and Crises*, 275–78.

attempt to intimidate the Washington Government."[20] Meanwhile, Catholic responses were largely tepid to Devoy's entire effort. Some papers with leanings toward the professionals printed favorable reviews of the Convention's proceedings.[21] Most Irish American Catholic editors, however, expressed exhaustion with the tone of the professional press. Father John L. Whelan attacked Devoy and the Fords of the *Irish World* for their constant ranting of "To Hell with England," as a ploy to peddle subscriptions. When news of the tragic results of the Easter uprising reached the United States, Milwaukee's Humphrey Desmond sneeringly quipped that it was a "disappointing denouement of the recent Irish Race Convention in New York." Contemptuous of Devoy's fundraising attempts at the Convention, Desmond mused that for all the purported money raised, "we expected to see a moving picture of an Irish insurrection ... once more John has deceived us."[22]

The Easter Rising and Fallout

If the crusade for Irish freedom in the United States languished in the doldrums of apathy in early April 1916, along with any hope of improving Germany's moral reputation, both causes were brought back into focus by the outbreak of rebellion in Dublin on Easter Monday, April 24, 1916. Largely judged a singular folly initially, this poorly orchestrated insurrection and its subsequent suppression were deeply absorbed by Irish Americans and provided a context in which this widely diverse community's position towards the war in Europe and Irish nationalism might have radically shifted.

20. Quoted in *New York Times*, "Irish Pledge Aid To The President," March 2, 1916, p. 5. The history of FOIF is ably presented in Michael Doorley, *Irish-American Diaspora Nationalism: The Friends of Irish Freedom, 1916–1935* (New York: Four Courts Press, 2005), 21–59.
21. *Freeman's Journal*, March 11, 1916; *Indiana Catholic and Record*, March 11, 1916.
22. Brooklyn *Tablet*, May 5, 1916; *Catholic Citizen*, May 16, 1916. Devoy had certainly inflated the significance of the convention, describing it as one of the greatest and most representative of Irish Americans that had taken place in the United States. See *Gaelic American*, March 11, 1916.

CHAPTER 5

The outbreak of war in August 1914 had placed the entire progress of Irish freedom in abeyance. The Empire's war effort had wrought a tenuous alliance between England's Conservative and Liberal parties, which effectively robbed John Redmond's Irish party of the political maneuverability and clout necessary to enact the Home Rule measure. Further hopes for Home Rule were eroded when its most implacable foe—Sir Edward Carson of Ulster—was promoted to a post in the London coalition government. With few other options available, Redmond pledged Ireland's support for the British Empire, in the hope that when victory was achieved a grateful Britain would fully endorse Home Rule. Although roundly denounced by a vocal minority both in Ireland and Irish America, Redmond's strategy was hailed as prudent and just. However, by early 1916, with Irish casualties mounting and the specter of Irish conscription looming larger, a heightened sense of apprehension and unrest had sewn itself into the Irish national fabric. Yet despite these untoward signals, most Irishmen were opposed to open rebellion.[23]

While Redmond labored to establish credit with the British government to draw upon after the war, the small and weak, though greatly determined, Sinn Fein Party continued its pursuit of separation. Taking advantage of the escalating disaffection with Irish involvement in the war and the absence of countless Redmond supporters serving in Irish regiments in France, the military council of the Irish Republican Brotherhood [IRB] decided to stage a rebellion on Easter Monday 1916. In February of that year, the plotters stepped up their communications with the Clan-na-Gael in New York. John Devoy, Daniel Cohalan and Joseph McGarrity of Philadelphia had always dreamed of taking advantage of British absorption with the European war to bring about Irish independence. Hoping for German assistance, they reestablished contacts with the German diplomatic corps in the United States.

From the outset of the war, the professionals, in their discussions with Berlin, underscored their need for arms and a cadre of capable German officers to assist them.[24] From August 1914 until Easter 1916,

---

23. Eunan O'Halpin, *The Decline of the Union: British Government in Ireland, 1892–1920* (Syracuse, NY: Syracuse University Press, 1987), 111.
24. O'Halpin, *The Decline of the Union,* 112–13; Devoy, *Recollections of an Irish Rebel,* 403.

IRISH AMERICAN CATHOLICS & 1916 EASTER REBELLION

myriad coded messages passed between Clan conspirators and Berlin concerning the raising of money and the alluring prospects for direct German aid. But diminished hopes for German succor had already been demonstrated by the desultory progress of Roger Casement's mission in Berlin. Not only had his efforts to raise an Irish regiment among the ranks of Irish prisoners of war ended in abject failure, but it dawned upon Casement that the Germans had no intention of rendering adequate assistance for a full-scale rebellion in Ireland. Their only interest, he claimed, was to deceive Irish Americans and encourage their agitation within the United States.[25] Casement's dour pessimism echoed sentiments shared by Clan officials in the United States. Writing in typically cryptic fashion to Bulmer Hobson, Secretary of the Irish Volunteers, Joseph McGarrity doubted that the Germans would risk sending a sizeable landing force in Ireland's favor, as he feared that the "sea serpent [Britain] is too strong in his naval strength to permit strangers to come in large numbers."[26]

Notwithstanding the many factors militating against success, not the least of which was the Clan-na-Gael's inability to furnish enough arms and munitions, the military council of the IRB agreed to a general mobilization of the Irish Volunteers for Easter weekend. The ill-starred rebellion immediately began on a poor footing when Roger Casement, despite much advice to the contrary, boarded a German submarine that dropped him and a couple of associates off the Irish coast at the Bay of Tralee. So convinced was he that the uprising had virtually no chance of success, Casement traveled to Ireland with the ostensible purpose of convincing his compatriots of the futility of the effort and was captured

---

25. Casement Diary, March 17, 1916, *Casement Papers,* New York Public Library.

26. Joseph McGarrity to Bulmer Hobson, 1915, *Joseph McGarrity Papers,* New York Public Library. For McGarrity's role in planning the uprising with Roger Casement in 1914, see Maura Anand, Andrew S. Hicks, & R. Bryan Willits, "The Man in Philadelphia: Joseph McGarrity and 1914," in Grey, *Ireland's Allies,* 109–123. Michael Doorley concludes his insightful examination of Judge Daniel Cohalen with the verdict that, while his later relationship with de Valera was tempestuously suspect, his "decisive contribution to the American dimension of the Easter Rising is unambiguous." See Doorley, "Judge Cohalen and American Involvement in the Easter Rising," in Grey, *Ireland's Allies,* 163.

CHAPTER 5

and arrested on April 21, shortly after coming ashore On the same day, the disguised German steamer *Aud*, carrying a modest supply of arms for the intended uprising, was intercepted by the Royal Navy in the Irish Sea. While being escorted into Queenstown harbor, her crew promptly scuttled the vessel, sending the stash of arms to a watery grave. In view of these developments, Eoin MacNeill, commander of the Irish Volunteers, published a notice in Dublin's *Sunday Independent* canceling the general mobilization that had been scheduled for Easter Sunday. For all intents and purposes, the Rising appeared aborted.[27]

That an uprising would occur under such adverse conditions never dawned upon British authorities at Dublin Castle. Assured that Casement was already in route to a London prison and that the dreaded mobilization had been canceled, the British garrison in Dublin relaxed its vigilance. Shortly before noon on Easter Monday, a determined radical element of the Sinn Fein party rose up in arms. Seizing several strategic locations within the city, including the General Post Office, the rebels held sway for a few days until British reinforcements under the command of Sir John Maxwell came surging up the Liffey, bringing sufficient firepower to induce an inglorious surrender by the insurgents. Granted plenary powers to suppress the uprising, Maxwell brutally crushed resistance and summarily executed sixteen rebel leaders. Maxwell's zeal quickly produced such an outpouring of Irish outrage, including that of John Redmond and John Dillon of the Nationalist party, that it eventually prodded London to quash its Dublin commander's reprisals.[28]

Irish Americans reacted viscerally to the Dublin uprising and its denouement and suppression. Once again, conflicting responses underscored sharp divisions within this community, with mainstream Irish American Catholics lining up in sharp contrast to the more radical

---

27. Although most of the Irish Volunteers stood behind Redmond's commitment to the British Empire, a force of nearly 7,000 refused to do so. Maintaining the designation "Volunteers," this was the forced expected to respond to the general mobilization. See O'Halpin, *The Decline of the Union*, 105, 113; Leon Broin, *Dublin Castle and the 1916 Rising* (New York: New York University Press, 1971), 82–83.

28. Leon Broin, *Dublin Castle and the 1916 Rising*, 123–27.

elements of Irish American society. Rather than serve as a catalyst for unifying Irish American and Catholic attitudes toward the evolution of Irish independence and the Great War itself, the Dublin uprising seemed only to exacerbate disunity, and it utterly failed to avert the dissolution of American neutrality.

As news of the uprising dribbled into the United States, it was initially greeted with general disbelief and dismay by the Irish American Catholic community. And before the reports of General Maxwell's brutal reprisals were revealed, the Irish American community was incredulous that such a foolhardy enterprise had taken place. The irrepressible John Quinn vented his disgust with the "horrible fiasco" in a letter to the English author Joseph Conrad when he branded the rebellion as "sheer lunacy." John B. Crimmins, former president of the American-Irish Historical Society, glibly thundered that "Sir Roger is crazy." Chicago's representative of Redmond's Nationalist Party somberly predicted that the rebellion "is bound to fail." A hastily called emergency session of the New York Council of the UIL of America resolved that the Dublin insurrection was no more than an "insane attempt at rebellion," and expressed continued support for Redmond's Home Rule movement. When a small group of radical Irish American demonstrators attempted to disrupt the proceedings, they were unceremoniously ejected by a lone police officer named Charles J. Clancy.[29]

Other prominent Irish Americans lamented the outbreak of rebellion, not only because it was ludicrous, but because it jeopardized the cause of Home Rule for which Redmond and Dillon were diligently pressing forward in the British Parliament. Francis Hackett of the *New Republic* was one Irish American who was disenchanted with the news of the uprising. Claiming that there was "no chance of material victory," Hackett condemned the rebellion as not only imprudent but

29. John Quinn to Joseph Conrad, May 11, 1916, *John Quinn Papers,* New York Public Library; Crimmons and Barry are quoted in the *New York Times,* "Sink German Ship Off Irish Coast, Catch Casement," April 25, 1916, p. 1; "Fate of Sir Roger Casement," April 25, 1916, p. 7. the meeting of the United Irish League was reported in the *New York Times,* "One Clancy Quells Irish Uprising," April 29, 1916, p. 1.

CHAPTER 5

"wild and futile" as well. Joseph C. Walsh, editor of *Ireland*, deplored the uprising as a repudiation of the sentiments of the vast majority of Irish people, particularly their civil and religious leaders.[30]

Similar moderate and conservative sentiments were repeated in the Catholic press by Irish American editors. McKearney of Cleveland's *Catholic Universe* endorsed Life magazine's version of the rebellion as a "crazy outbreak, timed to the hour of England's peril, dangerous, hapless, and pitiable," and added his own opinion that while some might have called the victims "martyrs or fools ... we must acknowledge that their activities have injured rather than helped the cause of a free Ireland." William A. Hughes in Detroit declared that the "affair was clumsily managed, started at an inopportune hour and encouraged by men who kept well without the sniper's bullets." Blaming the Rising on "over-zealous youth and men, harangued by curb-stone agitators," Hughes feared that it would be perceived as "malice and treason." In San Antonio, William Campbell bemoaned the insurrection as "all other judicious friends of Ireland have already done." He expressed a prevailing concern in Irish American and Catholic circles that the rash actions of a "handful of disloyal Irishmen in Dublin" would offset the "thousands of patriotic Irish soldiers who are doing and dying in the ranks of the Allies."[31]

Mainstream Irish American Catholic disenchantment was not entirely reserved for those of the IRB who responded to the call to arms on Easter Monday. They expressed a significant measure of disgust and contempt for those Irish Americans perceived as having encouraged the insurrection. And for their duplicity and lackluster support of the rebellion, the Germans, too, were heavily criticized. With his customary circumspection, Cardinal Gibbons confided to British ambassador Sir Cecil Spring Rice that "all respectable Irishmen condemned [the] revolt in unqualified terms," fearing, however, that if the British government failed to manage the aftershocks of rebellion carefully, there would be

---

30. *New Republic,* May 6, 1916, May 13, 1916. Walsh quoted in *New York Times Magazine,* April 30, 1916, pp. 27, 59.
31. *Catholic Universe,* June 2, 1916; *Michigan Catholic,* May 4, 1916; *Southern Messenger,* May 16, 1916.

the "danger of manufacturing martyrs of American use." The extremely reticent Cardinal James Farley of New York immediately censured the Friends of Irish Freedom for stirring up rebellion in Ireland, indicating that he had disapproved of this society from its inception. Patrick Egan, former United States ambassador to Chile, enjoined the assembly of the UILA to resolve that the Dublin plot was the design of an unsupported minority faction, "egged on by a group of pro-German plotters upon American soil, financed and otherwise aided by Germany, who seem willing to sacrifice their native—aye, and their adopted country—to make a Germany holiday."[32]

The handful of Catholic editors that were normally supportive of the professionals' agenda resigned themselves to offer muted sympathy for Ireland's plight in the wake of the rebellion, but conceded that they could not support the uprising itself. The one notable exception was the fiery Irish nationalist Father Peter Yorke of San Francisco. In his independent newspaper *The Leader*, Yorke hailed the uprising as Ireland's declaration of war on England and applauded the revolutionaries for their "willingness to sacrifice all for the motherland."[33] Yorke had long since soured on Redmond's Home Rule solution and in San Francisco's Catholic newspaper, the *Monitor*, he castigated the Jesuit editor of *America* for that priest's denunciation of the Rising as dogmatically insulting to God. Cleverly, Yorke posited that the "vagaries of the theologians in the Irish revolution make us sympathize with the old lady that lost her purse ... God help me," she says, "I only hope a theologian won't find it." Most Catholic editors, however, endorsed John Redmond's indictment of those Irish Americans who had encouraged young Irishmen "into this insane

---

32. Gibbons is quoted in Carroll, *American Opinion and the Irish Question*, 64; Farley is quoted in John Patrick Buckley, "The New York Irish: Their View of American Foreign Policy, 1914–1921," 80. Egan is quoted in *New York Times*, "Troops Crush Revolt in Dublin," April 26, 1916, p. 1.

33. *The Leader*, April 29, 1916. Several other Catholic papers—*The Freeman's Journal, Catholic News,* and Boston *Pilot* emphasized the misfortune that had befallen Ireland, while doubting the wisdom of the Rising. Other than Yorke, only O'Mahoney, with minimal exposition, gave unqualified support for the Easter uprising from the outset. See *Indiana Catholic and Record,* May 5, 1916.

CHAPTER 5

and anti-patriotic movement while they have remained in the safe remoteness of American cities."[34]

From the editorials of the *Catholic Messenger* of Davenport came some of the most stinging attacks on Irish Americans who promoted the Easter uprising. Flailing away at the "ill-advised propaganda" of Clan-na-Gael leaders in the United States, the paper asserted that it "resulted in the slaughter of their incredulous dupes in Ireland." When it became public knowledge that the American government intended to investigate whether the Clan's activities were in violation of neutrality laws, the *Catholic Messenger* applauded the decision.[35] On the other side of Iowa, Father Peter Gannon in Omaha colorfully and sneeringly captured the opinion of many Catholic editors when he favorably compared the actions of those who died in the uprising to the role played by the Clan-na-Gael:

> They certainly stand on a higher plane in public estimation than the contemptible blowhards of New York and other American cities who urged them on ... these fools and fakirs can be proud of their work. True Irishmen, loyal to the principle of rational liberty ... have nothing but contempt for men who urge others to enter in a campaign of armed insurrection while they themselves are careful to keep three thousand miles between them and the scene of the conflict.[36]

Cincinnati's Thomas O'Flanagan expanded upon Gannon's condign censure by aiming at some of New York City's clerics. Noting unanimous disapproval of the rebellion in Irish religious circles, he inveighed against the "wisdom of a few New York priests" who ventured to think that their opinions of what was best for Ireland "may outweigh that of the hierarchy and priesthood of Ireland."[37]

    34. Pamphlet, *Strong Words from Mr. Redmond, Treason to the Home Rule Cause* (London: Sir Joseph Causton & Sons, 1916), 5. Yorke is quoted in Brusher, *Consecrated Thunderbolt*, 168.
    35. *Catholic Messenger*, April 27, 1916, May 4, 1916.
    36. *True Voice*, May 5, 1916.
    37. *Catholic Transcript*, May 4, 1916.

IRISH AMERICAN CATHOLICS & 1916 EASTER REBELLION

The Germans did not escape the derision of Catholic editors either. For both their feeble support of the rebellion, which all but assured its failure, and their transparent display of opportunism, they were soundly criticized. Humphrey Desmond caustically employed biblical metaphor when he claimed that "Casement was vomited up by a submarine much as the whale disgorged Jonah." He concluded his assessment of the rebellion by laconically observing that while the Irish were renowned for bravery and the Germans for their efficiency, the "recent German invasion of Ireland and the ensuing Dublin uprising are not the best proofs of either proposition." Other moderate Irish Americans were equally quick to dispel any notions that Germany was Ireland's friend. P. T. Barry insisted that Irishmen were not in league with the Germans and had "long ago cast their lot on the side of the Allies and are fighting for them." Desmond, fully concurring with Barry's assertion, noted that the "only real rising that day ... were the masses of Irish who went about their usual daily work." And in Cincinnati, O'Flanagan railed against those who thought "Germany cares a whole lot for Ireland." Once Germany's purposes were achieved, he averred, "she would fling Ireland sheer into the jaws of the British lion."[38]

If John Devoy and others in the Clan-na-Gael were dismayed by the hostile reception that news of the Dublin uprising received in Irish American and Catholic circles, they were delighted by the revulsion that greeted reports of General Maxwell's bloody dispatching of rebel leadership. For the first time during the war, all segments of the Irish American Catholic community were unified in their denunciation of British brutality. But this common loathing did not necessarily translate into a unified commitment to any direct changes in Irish American and Catholic policies with respect to the future direction of a free Ireland. Moderate and conservative Irish American Catholics remained detached from the Clan's agenda, particularly the idea of supporting an Irish-German coalition. While some moderates were weaned from the Home Rule cause, there remained a solid measure of support for it in many quarters, most notably in the American Catholic Church. To the extent that the Dublin executions moved many

---

38. *Catholic Citizen,* May 6, 1916, May 13, 1916; Barry quoted in *New York Times,* April 27, 1916; *Catholic Transcript,* April 27, 1916.

CHAPTER 5

Irish Americans back into the rigid neutrality that had been slowly dissolving since the outbreak of the war, they merely afforded the Clan breathing room to resume assailing the American government's perceived pro-Allied trajectory.

It was hardly surprising that the Irish American community became incensed by the execution of Irish rebels following the insurrection. American opinion in general reflected shock and disgust with British savagery in meting out punishment upon the Irish. The *Literary Digest*'s survey of American editors revealed virtual unanimity in condemning the executions and cited the *Washington Post*'s terse verdict of British actions as "stupid and vengeful." British reprisals even horrified some of the nation's leading Anglophiles. In a letter to the *New York Evening Post*, novelist William Dean Howells remarked that "in giving way to her vengeance, England has roused the moral sense of mankind against her ... she has left us who loved her cause in the war against despotism without another word to say for her."[39]

Summary British justice may not have rendered all her American friends speechless, but it did edge popular opinion back towards adherence to strict neutrality. Having earlier believed that Americans largely sympathized with Britain's wartime plight in Ireland, Walter Lippmann, editor of the *New Republic*, declared that the "Dublin executions had done more to drive Americans back to isolation than any other event since the war began." In his frequent reports to the British Foreign Office, Spring Rice could find little in American opinion to suggest that sentiment towards Great Britain was anything but hostile and contrary. The British ambassador's counterpart, Johann von Bernstorff, was finally able to report optimistic news to his superiors, noting that American opinion "was more favorable owing to the influence of the Irish executions."[40]

---

39. *Literary Digest*, 52 (May 6, 1916): 1263–65, 1355; Howells is quoted in Arthur S. Link, *Campaigns for Progressivism and Peace* (Princeton, NJ: Princeton University Press, 1965), 13.

40. *New Republic* 7 (July 29, 1916): 321–22; Sir Cecil Spring-Rice to Lord Grey, May 10, 1916, May 19, 1916, May 30, 1916, in Stephen A. Gwynn, ed., *The Letters and Friendships of Sir Cecil Spring Rice*, 2 vols. (London: Macmillan, 1929), 2:327, 331, 334; Bernstorff, *My Three Years in America*, 264.

IRISH AMERICAN CATHOLICS & 1916 EASTER REBELLION

In the wake of the reprisals, Irish Americans quickly mobilized their forces to condemn the severity of British suppression. A meeting of the New York Council of the UILA, representing eighty-eight branches and affiliated societies, passed a resolution deploring the "heartrending executions of the last few days." Patrick Egan, who offered the resolution, reiterated his condemnation of those Irish Americans who had encouraged the rebellion, noting that "ninety-eight percent of all Irishmen were not in sympathy with the revolt ... and if anyone should be shot it should have been John Devoy who hatched the whole nefarious scheme here in New York and was personally responsible for it." He concluded, however, with a fervent plea to the British government that their "wisdom and humanity may promptly stay the sword of retaliation and that no more blood will stain the record of Ireland's present situation."[41]

The equanimity in the UILA's resolution was not as evident in other mass meetings of Irish Americans in the weeks following the uprising's suppression. On May 14, a capacity crowd flocked to Carnegie Hall in New York to hear a host of prominent Irish Americans condemn British actions in unequivocal terms. Most representative of mainstream Irish American outrage was the address of the quintessential Catholic orator and New York congressman, Bourke Cockran. Despite his professed admiration for the British judicial system, Cockran was so unnerved by British cruelty as to remark:

> For more than thirty years, I was one who believed ... it was the part of wisdom for Irishmen to forget ... at least forgive and try to forget—the wrongs and oppression extending over seven centuries, inflicted by England on Ireland in the hope that in the better

---

41. Quoted in *New York Times,* May 6, 1916. Egan, once a fervent revolutionary back in Ireland, a member of the IRB, and treasurer of the Irish Land League, had fled Ireland for the United States in 1882. Quickly ingratiating himself with the Republican Party, he was rewarded with the diplomatic post as ambassador to Chile. But by the turn of the century, Egan had thrown his hat in with Redmond and the Home Rule movement, and was a fierce enemy of Devoy and the advanced party.

CHAPTER 5

day which we believed to be dawning these two nations might be able to unite in productive co-operation for the benefit of both, and now behold the bitter refutation of our arguments ... the foulest deeds that ever discredited English rule are exceeded in this latest massacre.[42]

Other speakers at the Carnegie Hall meeting assailed British repression in equally strident tones. Referring to the "fifteen martyrs" of Ireland, New York Supreme Court Justice Edward J. Gavegan predicted that the "battle of Dublin will go down in history as the first and only victory in the war won by British troops." According to accounts of the meeting, both Devoy and Judge Cohalan were positioned prominently upon the stage, and that "frequent hisses" were heard when John Redmond's name was mentioned.[43]

Similar expressions of anger were reported at other gatherings of Irish Americans throughout the United States. In San Francisco, Peter Yorke and six other priests were noted as attending a meeting of the Irish Patriots, where expressions of sympathy for Ireland and disgust for Britain filled the hall. In Rochester, New York, the local branch of the Friends of Irish Liberty passed a resolution denouncing British justice as "deliberate murder" and vowed that "England must be held to strict accountability when the fortune of war places the power in Irish hands." Buoyed by such rhetoric, John Devoy felt comfortable enough to blurt out that the "British would rue the day" for their foul deeds and went on to malign John Redmond for undermining efforts to achieve Irish independence. In a final stab, he scolded Woodrow Wilson for having apprised the British of Irish plans to rebel.[44]

---

42. William Bourke Cockran, speech delivered at Carnegie Hall, New York, 1916, *Bourke Cockran Papers,* New York Public Library. Cockran was mindful that he had been heckled by several Irish Americans in an audience while speaking at a 1915 rally.

43. As reported in the *New York Times,* "Irish Pay Tribute to Dublin Rebels," May 15, 1916, pp. 1–2.

44. *The Monitor,* May 6, 1916; Resolution of Friends of Irish Liberty quoted in the *New York Times,* "Irish As Allies of Germany," May 15, 1916, p. 2; *Gaelic-American,* May 6, 1916.

The mounting surge of indignation among Irish Americans extended itself into political action. Congressmen from districts where Irish American and Catholic votes counted significantly introduced resolutions in the House of Representatives, petitioning the British government to refrain from any further executions. Similar pressure was exerted upon the State Department to employ its influence in mitigating British punishment of rebels holding dual Irish and American citizenship. Even the reserved John Quinn tried to intervene with Spring Rice to reduce Eoin MacNeill's sentence to life imprisonment, since "he did more to break up the uprising than anyone." Fortunately for MacNeill, London had already applied the brakes to summary executions, and in a trial by peers, his death sentence was commuted to imprisonment.[45]

The telling damage generated by the executions was the disaffection sown in mainstream Irish American and Catholic circles with respect to longstanding British promises of Home Rule and the much-vaunted altruistic motives of the Allies. Although it is arguable that Redmond's Home Rule advocacy was dealt a death blow by the draconian measures adopted by Maxwell in the wake of the rebellion, the avalanche of criticism in Irish American and Catholic arenas was beyond doubt. It was in evidence when Michael Ryan, president of the UILA, a bulwark of mainstream Irish-Americanism, cabled Redmond:

> Irish executions have alienated every friend and caused resurgence of ancient enmities. Your lifework destroyed by British brutality. Opinion widespread that promise of Home Rule was mockery."[46]

---

45. See House Resolutions 235, 244, 245, May 12, 1916, 1st Session, in 53 Cong. Rec. 7899, 8358, 8427 (1916); Carroll, *American Opinion and the Irish Question,* 63; John Quinn to Shane Leslie, June 7, 1916, *John Quinn Papers,* New York Public Library. Leslie was of the Anglo-Irish landowning class, a convert to Catholicism, ardent supporter of John Redmond and Home Rule, and a diplomat and writer. In his capacity as a literary figure, he became an intimate of John Quinn.

46. Edward Cuddy, "Irish-American Propagandists and Neutrality, 1914–1917," *Mid-America* 49 (June 1967): 259.

CHAPTER 5

Within two months of the news of British reprisals, the Ancient Order of Hibernians, who had always vacillated between the constitutional course and the more radical agenda of the Clan-na-Gael, rescinded all support for Redmond.[47]

Conservative and moderate Irish American Catholics expressed similar concern for the fading prospects of achieving Home Rule. In Chicago, P. T. Barry cabled Redmond with the forlorn appraisal that the "rebellion won condemnation, the executions sympathy, even among the native Americans." Shane Leslie pointed out to Redmond that while the "rising called out sympathy for you except in a small circle ... [the] executions enabled that circle to spread their ripple further than they had hoped or dreamed." Both John Quinn and Francis Hackett were equally appalled by the stupidity of the British. Quinn had hoped that the British would have demonstrated greater intelligence by not emulating German barbarity, while Hackett suggested that the British had not drawn as much cold blood in their handling of the rebellion in South Africa as they had in Ireland.[48]

The handful of Irish American Catholic editors who had previously voiced support for the overthrow of British rule in Ireland by any means now brandished their pens in defense of the martyred rebels. Even moderates, such as Thomas V. Shannon, spurned England's posturing as the "champion and defender of the liberties of smaller nations." Pointing to the "historic brutality" of England in South Africa, India, and Ireland, he compared her to the proverbial leopard, which "does not change its spots." The *Catholic News* out of New York concluded that England has made it "impossible for genuine Irishmen to regard her as anything but the enemy of their race." In support of its verdict, the same paper described in gory detail how noted rebel leader Francis Skeffington was engaged in assisting a wounded British officer

---

47. Ryan quoted in Gwynn, *Letters and Friendships of Sir Cecil Spring Rice,* 2:500; John O'Dea, *History of the Ancient Order of Hibernians and Ladies Auxiliary,* 3 vols. (Philadelphia: National Board of the A.O.H., 1923), 3:1499–1500.

48. Barry quoted in Carroll, *American Opinion and the Irish Question,* 65; John Quinn to Joseph Conrad, May 13, 1916, *John Quinn Papers,* New York Public Library; Francis Hackett, "The Irish Revolt," *New Republic* 7 (May 13, 1916), 14–36.

when he was arrested and later executed. The accompanying editorial contemptuously dismissed the circulating opinion that "England isn't as brutal as in years gone by," by retorting that England "is the same old ruthless England." In Indiana, O'Mahoney not only condemned the executions, but also assailed moderate Irish Americans for their timidity in defending Ireland. Labeling some men of Irish blood as "Tories who would have probably endorsed Benedict Arnold," he boldly asserted that they were a "very small element" who did not represent the views of "any living Irish society in the nation."[49]

Irish American Catholic editors who had previously written of the Irish question in very temperate tones suddenly abandoned this approach. Tierney's *America,* no friend of the British, took the occasion to caustically blast the British, concluding that the history of England and Ireland reiterated one ageless theme: "a narrative of savagery and blood, met by intrepid patriotism and unswerving fidelity to the teachings of Jesus Christ." Father Whelan sadly reflected that since the uprising had been quickly and almost effortlessly suppressed, there had been no need for such vengeance on the part of the British. Characterizing British policy as "astoundingly stupid ... [the] work of weak men," he predicted that this action would accord Britain the "alienation of the sympathies of many men and women all over the world."[50]

The executions of Irish rebels most assuredly earned the enmity of the *Pilot* in Boston, now directly controlled by William Cardinal O'Connell. In fact, O'Connell's desertion from Home Rule and his subsequent endorsement of a free and completely autonomous Ireland can be traced to his outrage over the executions. In a departure from its usually restrained reporting of international news, the June 3 edition of the paper printed a collection of articles from both the secular and religious press condemning British atrocities, headlined: "England Arraigned at the Bar of Humanity." O'Connell's venom was not reserved for the British alone; his paper viciously assailed those "English subsidized papers" in the United States that presented the

49. *New World,* May 19, 1916; *Catholic News,* May 6, 1916; May 20, 1916; *Indiana Catholic and Record,* May 5, 1916.
50. *America,* May 29, 1916; Brooklyn *Tablet,* May 20, 1916.

uprising as the work of malcontents. In particular, he attacked the Boston Transcript, as ever "so faithful to the Union Jack ... the Koran of the Brahmins."[51]

With moderate and conservative Irish American Catholic editors joining the chorus of denunciation of British reprisals, the ranks of Irish America were massed against the British. Father Peter Gannon observed that while the insurrection failed to garner the support of Irish America, the "cruel infliction of the death penalty ... has exerted a feeling of horror everywhere ... and there will henceforth be little sympathy for the cause of England among Irishmen in America." In Philadelphia, Father Edward P. Spillane argued in the *Catholic Standard and Times* that since the rebel leaders had laid down their arms "to spare further effusion of blood," they should not have been "butchered by court-martial process." The now ailing editor of the *Michigan Catholic*, William Hughes, was equally exasperated by this "latest British, brutish murder," and warned Britain that such action would "rally every Irishman worthy of the name around the holy cause" for which the rebel leaders had lost their lives.[52]

Even John Burke of the *Catholic World*, the one Irish American editor with decided sympathy for the Allies, delivered one of the most stinging rebukes of British policy. Britain's treatment of the rebels was "atrocious," and her use of arbitrary court-martials to execute them was reminiscent of the draconian methods of Lord Castlereagh a century earlier:

> Whenever the English Government has to deal with Ireland, it shows a pitiful, blundering sense of misunderstanding and oftentimes of injustice which shocks the world.[53]

Notwithstanding the hyperbolic and vituperative reaction from moderate Irish Americans over British actions in the wake of the uprising, no

51. Boston *Pilot,* June 3, 1916, July 1, 1916.
52. *True Voice*, May 12, 1916; *Standard and Times* (Philadelphia), May 20, 1916; *Michigan Catholic,* May 25, 1916.
53. *Catholic World,* June 6, 1916.

substantial solidarity emerged among the Irish American Catholic community concerning the future direction of Irish nationalism. When Michael Ryan had cabled John Redmond that his life's work had been destroyed by British actions, he was more correct than he may have realized. In early 1917, even Redmond admitted as much.[54] Nonetheless, moderate Catholic editors proved reluctant to abandon Redmond and Home Rule through the summer and fall of 1916, even though they may have privately concluded this cause moribund. From Iowa's heartland, Fred Sharon surmised that had England enacted Home Rule at the outset of the war, the uprising would have been averted. Campbell's *Southern Messenger* insisted that even though the British had acted badly in the affair, Redmond's cautious course remained the "one hope and security of a free future for poor Ireland." Dr. Thomas Hart echoed Campbell's sentiment that the quick enactment of Home Rule would be a judicious move on Britain's part. Claiming that the British government "is in a bad odor all over the world," she could still salvage her sterling reputation by moving forward with Home Rule. And O'Flanagan articulated a view common among many Catholic editors that there could still be a silver lining in all this tragedy:

> If the present European struggle does not prove to England that she needs Ireland and both countries are to place their highest hopes in mutual friendship and good will, then she is blind indeed.[55]

The Easter Rising and the anguish over British insensitivity in meting out justice, along with the announcement of Britain's blacklisting of American firms, had lowered the estimation of Albion in many American eyes. Her continued tampering with the United States mail system, despite Secretary of State Robert Lansing's formal protests,

---

54. Not until the American entry into the Great War and Wilson's statements on the right of self-determination for all people did Irish American and Catholic solidarity emerge. Only then did the disparate views within the community merge, as will be discussed in a later chapter.

55. *Catholic Messenger*, June 1, 1916; *Southern Messenger*, June 3, 1916; *Catholic Telegraph*, June 8, 1916; *Catholic Transcript*, May 11, 1916.

CHAPTER 5

did not improve the matter. Such behavior not only adversely affected Anglo-American relations, but also tended to reaffirm the neutrality over the European war that had heretofore been tilting towards the Allies. Even the Anglophile Lansing became concerned with Britain's conduct during the middle months of 1916. He wrote Wilson that he was afraid "that London does not appreciate that the tide of resentment is rising very high in this country and that there is a tendency to demand drastic action by this Government." In his response, Wilson instructed Lansing to urge US Ambassador to the Court of St. James, Walter Hines Page, to convey to the British "a very clear impression of the lamentable and dangerous mistakes they are making."[56] But more damage had occurred in the meantime.

The Trial and Execution of Sir Roger Casement

British favor in the United States continued to erode during the lingering trial and subsequent execution of Sir Roger Casement. Whereas the British execution of rebel leaders in May might have been a hasty or impulsive action, the Casement trial differed considerably. It dragged on for three months for the entire world to evaluate. While the earlier executions caused an explosion of unbridled indignation, Casement's trial and death allowed Irish American reaction to simmer slowly to a boil. Irish Americans, joined by many others, thought Casement's case warranted greater and more deliberate consideration than the fate of the rebels summarily executed in Dublin. Many Irish Americans believed that Sir Roger's humanitarian service in the British Foreign Service, which had earned him a knighthood, entitled him to a reprieve. Others pleaded that Casement's very service to the British Crown in the jungles of the Congo and the Peruvian Amazon had exacted such a psychic toll upon him as to render him mentally irresponsible in recent years. Most Irish Americans, however, felt as did Judge Cohalan, that to execute Casement "did not seem within the bounds of even British stupidity."[57]

---

56. Secretary of State to President Wilson, September 22, 1916, and President Wilson to Secretary of State, September 29, 1916. *Lansing Papers,* 1:314, 1319.

57. John Quinn, "Roger Casement, Martyr," in *New York Times Magazine*

IRISH AMERICAN CATHOLICS & 1916 EASTER REBELLION

It was apparent to many that to carry out Casement's death sentence would be a supreme blunder for the British. Even the nervous Spring Rice had detected well before Casement's trial that there was a danger of making him a martyr. He advised Lord Grey that the "Germans here look forward with great interest to his execution, of which they will take full advantage." In Philadelphia, important Clan leader Joseph McGarrity was beside himself with incredulity. Upon hearing of the outcome of Casement's trial, in which Casement was found guilty of treason, Judge Cohalan refused to believe that the death sentence would be carried out. While disclaiming that England would spare Casement's life as a matter of mercy or justice, England would stay the execution, he argued, to "show the neutral world that she was not always bloodthirsty and had occasional spells when her actions did not belie her words." In this matter, even Cohalan's bitter adversary, John Quinn, voiced concurrence. He wrote his friend Shane Leslie: "I don't think Casement will swing."[58]

During the summer of 1916, considerable energies were expended by Irish Americans to intervene on Casement's behalf. Understanding that the most efficacious way to affect this intercession was through official channels, Irish American societies cajoled the US government to plead with the British for clemency in Casement's case. Responding to pressure from their Irish American constituents, members of Congress drafted various resolutions beseeching Wilson to intervene. On July 22, Senator James E. Martine of New Jersey introduced the first Senate resolution, imploring Wilson to request a stay of execution for Casement. Perhaps with an eye towards the upcoming fall elections,

---

(August 13, 1916): 1; *New York Times,* "Connects Cohalan With Revolt Fund," May 28, 1916, p. 5.

58. Sir Cecil Spring Rice to Lord Grey, May 30, 1916, in Stephen A. Gwynn, ed., *The Letters and Friendships of Sir Cecil Spring Rice*, 2:336; Cohalan quoted in *New York Times,* June 30, 1916; John Quinn to Shane Leslie, July 22, 1916, *John Quinn Papers,* New York Public Library. The English seemed determined to convict Casement for his treasonous activities and even tinkered with the definition of treason to convict him. Moreover, copies of Casement's diaries, dubbed the *Black Diaries,* that had been seized in Casement's London residence, exposing him as a practicing homosexual, were privately circulated as to turn away would-be supporters.

CHAPTER 5

Congress passed a more forceful resolution a week later, with the Senate voting 46 to 19 in favor, with 30 abstentions. The resolution was rushed to the White House, where it joined numerous personal appeals for clemency that had been forwarded to the president.[59]

Likely the most prominent appeals made to the president came from Michael F. Doyle, a successful Philadelphia lawyer hired to conduct Casement's defense. He was convinced that Wilson would be able to influence London to grant full clemency. After presenting his reasons for asking the president to weigh in on Casement's behalf, Doyle, a faithful Democratic party regular, assured Wilson that he looked forward to being "of great service to him during the campaign." Senator James D. Phelan of California saw to it that the clemency appeal drafted by the Knights of St. Patrick in San Francisco made its way directly to Wilson's attention.[60]

In New York, John Quinn joined other prominent Irish Americans in pleading with Lord Grey that Casement's death sentence be commuted. Through his connections with Spring Rice in Washington, Quinn was able to have an appeal cabled to London. After proclaiming support for British efforts in the war, it suggested that a policy of clemency for Casement would be a great salve for the wrongs committed by all in this unfortunate crisis.[61]

As expected, Casement's execution on August 3 unleashed a torrent of protest from Irish Americans. Senator Phelan, who had labored intensely to obtain a reprieve, asked the administration to explain why the transmission of the Senate resolution had been delayed. In the State Department, Counselor Frank L. Polk acknowledged receipt of a telegram from James K. McGuire mirroring Phelan's inquiry. To few people's surprise, the Clan-na-Gael accused the administration of

---

59. Senate Resolutions 237 and 241, July 22 and 29, 1916, 64th Congress, 1st Session, in 53 Cong. Rec., Part II, 11429, 11770–73 (1916).

60. Michael Francis Doyle to Joseph P. Tumulty, July 6, 1916, in Link, *The Papers of Woodrow Wilson*, 37:503–514; *The Monitor*, July 8, 1916.

61. John Quinn to Shane Leslie, July 21, 1916; John Quinn to Joseph Conrad, August 2, 1916, *John Quinn Papers*, New York Public Library. Note that neither Leslie nor Conrad was receptive to these appeals. Despite their fondness for Roger Casement, neither of them could overlook his blatant treasonous activities.

purposefully delaying the transmission of the Senate resolution because Wilson did not want to embarrass the British government. The charge was not baseless. When a group of earnest congressmen channeled a petition on Casement's behalf to the president's chief secretary, Joseph Tumulty, Wilson curtly demurred, remarking that it would be "inexcusable to touch this." John Devoy was nearly apoplectic over Wilson's refusal to intervene with the British government, insinuating with possible accuracy that the president was a confirmed nativist at heart. He unleashed a shower of invective, charging that Wilson hated the Irish "with the implacable hatred of an Ulster Orangeman—the stock he comes of." Devoy then took aim at the president's lineage by cleverly noting that Wilson's father was a Southern Presbyterian minister who, when loyal Irishmen fought to save the Union in the Civil War, labored to destroy it, with the Reverend Wilson "desecrating a Christian pulpit ... railing in favor of human slavery."[62]

While Irish Americans remained puzzled over the administration's failure to help Casement, they were quick to excoriate Britain's part in the process. Joseph McLaughlin in delivering the opening address of the Maryland state convention of Hibernians, flatly asserted that "Casement was murdered." The following day, the assembled Hibernians passed a resolution demanding a full investigation be conducted as to why the Senate resolutions were not forwarded in time to the British government. In one of his reports to Lord Grey, the ever-fretful Spring Rice noted that while news of Casement's demise was being digested quietly by most Americans, "Irish and German parties are working the Casement case underground for all it is worth, and I fear the consequences may be grave."[63]

A similar vein of disgust coursed through John Quinn's eulogy for Casement that appeared in the *New York Times Magazine*. Observing

---

62. Wilson quoted in Tansill, *America and the Fight for Irish Freedom*, 210. *Gaelic-American*, August 12 and 19, 1916. Despite his temperate rhetoric, Wilson's private sympathies betrayed his Anglophilia and his policies generally reflected this sentiment. See Kazin, *War Against War*, 22–23.

63. The proceedings of the Maryland state convention of Hibernians were reported in the *New York Times*, August 26 and 27, 1916; Sir Cecil Spring Rice to Lord Grey, August 31, 1916, in Gwynn, 2:344.

CHAPTER 5

that England even refused to deliver Casement's body to his relatives for burial, instead pitching it into a common pit, Quinn sardonically commented that the quicklime that was corroding his body was performing a similar service to the "English claim that she is fighting for humanity." As perturbed as Quinn appeared to be over Britain's barbarity, he could not pass up an opportunity to malign Germany's role in the affair. He maintained that "a final and deeper infamy remains to be exposed." Perhaps, he argued, "England sprang the trap that took his life ... [but] Germany pushed him into that trap." If England was "pitiless" in executing Casement, then "Germany's act was infamous." Quinn's friend, Francis Hackett of the *New Republic*, echoed Quinn's indictment by somberly noting that if England continued to treat the Irish with such naked contempt, she could expect "further acts of rebellion."[64]

Although the Catholic press suppressed commentary during the period of the trial itself, it joined the chorus in denouncing Casement's execution. The normally restrained *Pilot* proclaimed that "another martyr has been added to the long roll of the Irish patriotic dead." Answering its own question, "Why do Irishmen Hate England?" the paper tartly responded that "once again has England answered the question and answered it in the only way she knows—by the sword." The moderate Thomas V. Shannon of Chicago's *New World* blandly suggested that the "execution of Sir Roger Casement was logical and stupid," adding that "it might prove to be the sorriest day's work that England ever did." Even Tierney's *America* fondly eulogized Casement by declaring that he "loved his ideal, and spoke his devotion in love's highest terms, and sweetest tone, sacrifice." And William Hughes, who frequently lambasted the Clan-na-Gael and other avid nationalists for their support of Germany, did not mince words in vilifying the British. Likening the British government to "bull-hounds" who "lap their jowls in clean Irish blood," he presented Casement as the apotheosis of Christian martyrdom in his "suffering the modern crucifixion on a British gibbet."[65]

---

64. *New York Times Magazine* (August 13, 1916); Francis Hackett, "In Contempt of Ireland," *New Republic* 8 (August 19, 1916): 94.

65. Boston *Pilot*, August 12, 1916; *New World*, August 11, 1916; *America*, August 12, 1916; *Michigan Catholic*, August 10, 1916.

IRISH AMERICAN CATHOLICS & 1916 EASTER REBELLION

Irish American Catholics in 1916

Though many divisions riddled the ranks of prominent and articulate members of the Irish American community, it proves difficult to assess where their sympathies lay by the summer's end in 1916. Even the campaign and election months later did not signal a definitive referendum on Irish issues among Irish American Catholics. They probably reflected the same ambivalence that affected the better-known members of their community.

By 1916, the sure but slow advancement of Irish American Catholics into mainstream American society, as demonstrated in their economic, occupational, and political empowerment, had still not provided a positive context for understanding their attitudes toward Irish affairs or the European war in general. In the public sphere, prominent, successful, and respectable Irish Americans could be found supporting vastly divergent positions on these matters—and all were convinced that the larger community shared their views. Both Daniel Cohalan and Joseph McGarrity, an influential politician-judge and a wealthy businessman, respectively, supported Irish freedom by a violent overthrow of the British government. Even knowing that they were but spokesmen for a minority of their community, both believed that it was only a matter of time and circumstance before others would come around to their positions. Conversely, John Quinn and Francis Hackett were equally strident in their support of Home Rule, and their marked espousal of the Allied cause was transparent. Despite his disdain for the myopic intellectualism of the Catholic clergy, Quinn was convinced he spoke for the vast majority of Irish American Catholics.

Divisiveness within the ranks of the Irish American Catholic community went far beyond the factional bickering of their more voluble members. The struggle between moderates and avid nationalists for the support of the larger community betrayed a significant degree of uncertainty and apathy. While the mass meeting at Carnegie Hall featured a capacity crowd, such meetings were convened irregularly and were not indicative of sustained support. Nor did such mass meetings, like those held at the war's outbreak, the Irish Race Convention of March 1916, or even the one at Carnegie Hall, reap financial dividends

CHAPTER 5

for the nationalist cause. In a letter to Joseph McGarrity, Michael J. Jennings, Treasurer of the Clan-na-Gael, detailed the meager fiscal footing of the organization in early 1916. In July, when Devoy forwarded $5,000 to Michael Doyle for Casement's defense, he was only able to do so by drawing upon credit from the sale of his own recently deceased brother's estate. Considering the incessant outrage over the British execution of Irish rebels, as well as the impending trial of Roger Casement, it appears odd that the Clan was unable to tap into grassroots Irish American support.[66]

Further evidence that the mutterings of Anglophobia did not necessarily translate into determined action was the refusal of powerful Irish American politicians to adopt decisive postures on the Irish issues. As noted earlier, James Michael Curley in Boston assiduously avoided partisan involvement in the issue of Irish independence and had already drawn the ire of ardent Irish American nationalists for his pro-Allied sympathies. Charles F. Murphy, at the zenith of his power in Tammany Hall politics in New York City, also remained largely apathetic to these international issues. Murphy, sensitive as ever to the concerns of his own constituency, saw that attention to the more mundane needs of urban life had been the real key to his extraordinary success. Murphy's apparent indifference to the Irish struggle of 1916 irritated those Irish Americans supportive of Irish independence. At a meeting of the Irish Women's Council, Father Patrick O'Donnell urged Irish Americans to quit voting the Democratic ticket until it was "purged of all those who were under suspicion of having part in the betrayal of Ireland." Descrying Murphy as the Democratic leader "who graces the St. Patrick's Day parade by marching at the head of it," O'Donnell disparaged Murphy's grip on New York congressmen who might otherwise have voted for resolutions barring munitions trade with the Allies. The simple reason for this sorry situation, O'Donnell asserted, was that the urban boss was the "back of all the manufacture of munitions in this country." What O'Donnell may have overlooked is that Murphy's Irish American constituency was more interested in

---

66. Michael J. Jennings to Joseph McGarrity, February 24, 1916, *Joseph McGarrity Papers*, Library of Congress; Devoy, *Recollections of an Irish Rebel*, 496.

their stake in America than the cause of Irish independence. Murphy, the quintessential politician, was not obtuse.

The Catholic hierarchy in the United States reacted to news from Ireland and Europe in a line parallel to that of the ambivalent Irish American community at large. It is difficult to ascertain where most Irish American Catholics stood on the issues generated by the failed Dublin uprising. The influential hierarchy generally refused to be drawn into any inflammatory debate over the affair and clearly encouraged their faithful to do the same. Given the authoritative structure of church discipline, with its strong emphasis on absolute obedience, few priests strayed from the instruction tendered by their appointed superiors. The few outspoken clerics, like Peter Yorke, Timothy Dempsey of St. Louis, and the small coterie of priests in the New York archdiocese who supported the overthrow of British rule, frequently ran afoul of their local ordinaries. Though these clerics appeared to be popular with their parishioners, their voices were muffled by the appeals of most priests and the Catholic press for moderation and restraint.[67]

Strict obedience to hierarchical directives remained the cornerstone of the most popular Irish American Catholic fraternal organization—the Knights of Columbus. Despite their distinct Irish identification at this time, the Knights maintained a monumental silence throughout the spring and summer of 1916, eschewing commentary on Irish and European affairs in favor of local and parochial concerns.[68] That the Knights were occasionally the target of Devoy's *Gaelic-American* and other Irish-American firebrands for their absolute and unquestioning loyalty to conventional forms of civil authority suggests that they were not to be counted among those fomenting rebellion in Ireland.[69]

Rather than become embroiled in the divisive politics of the Irish question, the institutional Catholic Church in the United States sought to alleviate the suffering resulting from the ill-fated Dublin uprising. In

67. John C. Crighton, *Missouri and the World War, 1914–1917*, 98.
68. Of the four Catholic papers (Boston *Pilot*, Brooklyn *Tablet*, *Catholic Messenger*, and *Indiana Catholic and Record*) that regularly printed summaries of the K of C meetings, none revealed any commentary regarding the Dublin uprising or its suppression except to mention relief efforts underway.
69. *Gaelic-American*, October 23, 1915.

CHAPTER 5

a letter addressed to his priests, Cardinal Farley of New York ordered a collection to be taken up at all Masses on July 9 for the victims of the Irish rebellion. With the exhortation that "Christian charity imposes on us all ... but especially on those of us of Irish blood," he commanded his priests to collect money for the establishment of an Irish Relief Fund. While obliquely intimating that England's suppression of the rebellion had induced widespread misery in Ireland, he enjoined his priests to refrain from offering any opinions upon the way the British had handled the matter. In San Francisco, Archbishop Edward Hanna personally presided over meetings of the Irish Relief Crusade, which garnered over $10,000 in its first week's effort. In other dioceses, fairs and bazaars contributed substantially to the growing amounts of cash available for relief distribution. By the close of July, Church-sponsored fund-raising efforts had netted over $100,000 in Irish relief.[70]

The hierarchy's refusal to cast opprobrium on Britain's role in the suppression of the Irish rebellion was consistent with its commitment to the Americanization of its own faithful, including Irish American Catholics. The Americanist prelates instinctively understood that fanning the flames of anti-British passion was not in the interests of promoting Catholicism as inherently harmonious with American patriotism. It was better to be somewhat distanced from the hue and cry of Irish nationalists, lest Catholics be deemed more interested in their native land than their adopted one. Rather than explicitly condemn the cause of human misery or confront the conflicting forces involved, the American Catholic Church opted to palliate the suffering generated by conflict and change. In the case of the Irish question, the hierarchy shunned political considerations and directed Church efforts toward relief. The Church also kept these fundraising endeavors strictly separate from those conducted by Irish American societies and organizations. In particular, the Church eschewed any connection with the Clan-na-Gael or its offshoot, the Friends of Irish Freedom.

---

70. Farley is quoted in the *New York Times,* July 10, 1916. For Farley's dilemma over how to react to British barbarity, see Kate Feighery, "Timely and Substantial Relief: New York's Cardinal John Farley and the 1916 Easter Rising," in Grey, *Ireland's Allies,* 286–87; *Michigan Catholic,* August 24, 1916; *Pittsburgh Catholic,* January 18, 1917; Carroll, *American Opinion and the Irish Question,* 79.

IRISH AMERICAN CATHOLICS & 1916 EASTER REBELLION

Evidently, the institutional Church's relief efforts received far greater support among Irish American Catholics than those of secular or fraternal organizations. In Syracuse, for instance, the Friends managed to raise a mere $600, whereas Irish-born Bishop John Grimes produced $10,000 with but minimal effort on his part.[71]

Cardinal Gibbons not only sounded out the opinions of his own Irish American Catholic faithful but felt compelled to balance them with the interests of the transnational Church centered in Rome of which he was a prominent spokesman. He instinctively understood that Benedict XV was averse to anything that smacked of revolutionary tumult anywhere in the Western world. A regular correspondent with the effective primate of Ireland, Michael Cardinal Logue, Gibbons was able to take his cue from this Irish cleric who had long been a staunch supporter of Home Rule and an opponent of radical Irish nationalism. Logue was a consistent advocate of peaceful constitutional means to inaugurate gradual steps to effect Irish autonomy within the British Empire. In the wake of the Easter Rising and British reprisals, Logue continued to counsel patience and caution. As late as 1917, when Britain considered the implementation of conscription in Ireland, Logue advised the young men of Ireland not to overreact but to wait for instruction from the Irish hierarchy. Observing that Irish Catholics were bound by civil law and moral compunction to oppose conscription, he counseled that "they should not take the matter into their own hands or get into any foolish movement." These reservations could not have been lost upon Cardinal Gibbons.[72]

The Catholic press, controlled as it was by Irish Americans, reflected the same ambivalence and political diversity over the Irish issue in the summer of 1916. While local ordinaries gave some latitude

---

71. While the three American cardinals (Gibbons, Farley, and O'Connell) refused to soundly condemn British actions, they quickly assumed leading roles in the Irish Relief Fund effort. Farley accepted the position of honorary chairman, while Gibbons joined him later as honorary president. See *New York Times*, "Organize for Irish Relief," May 18, 1916, 6. For further information on Bishop John Grimes' episcopacy, see Beadles, "The Syracuse Irish."

72. Katherine Finlay, "British Catholic Identity during the First World War: The Challenge of Universality and Particularity" (DPhil thesis, Wolfson College, Oxford University, 2003).

CHAPTER 5

to the press to express more strident positions, the leash given them appears to have been quite short. Certain papers, such as the *Freeman's Journal*, the *Indiana Catholic and Record*, and *Yorke's The Leader*, hardly needed the provocation of the rebel executions to adopt more rigorous positions toward the violent overthrow of British rule in Ireland. These papers had, from the outbreak of the war in 1914, made their pro-German and anti-British feelings patently clear. Only the Boston *Pilot*, motivated by a more animated Cardinal O'Connell, seemed to adopt a more militant Irish nationalism after Britain's suppression of the Irish rebellion.[73] The overwhelming majority of the Catholic press continued to toe the hierarchical line by adhering to an impartial attitude toward the Irish issue and how it affected sympathies toward the European belligerents.

Britain's longstanding political and religious oppression of Ireland, highlighted by the executions following the uprising, made it nearly impossible for Irish American Catholic editors to avoid criticizing her in the summer of 1916. All the same, an aversion to the Germans and a wary approach toward Irish Americans agitators tended to blunt this criticism and reinforce neutral postures. Most Irish American Catholic editors viewed the executions that summer primarily as a political blunder on England's part that made it difficult to accept her avowed altruism in the Great War. Some, like Humphrey Desmond in Milwaukee, though outraged by British brutality, continued to hold the Clan-na-Gael and Sinn Fein factions principally responsible for the uprising and the deprivation that followed. This ambivalence over the Irish issue was best expressed in William Hughes's exasperated claim that, while the "moral indignation of the world" might have been aroused by British barbarism, "we say this not by way of venting anti-British spleen, but as a true friend of England who would save her from herself."[74]

---

73. In an editorial on Casement's execution, the paper concluded that "England by their deaths has justified the growing sentiment that the sword is the only answer to the sword." See Boston *Pilot*, August 12, 1916.
74. *Catholic Messenger,* August 10. 1916; *Catholic Citizen,* June 2, 1916, September 30, 1916; *Michigan Catholic,* August 3, 1916.

IRISH AMERICAN CATHOLICS & 1916 EASTER REBELLION

It would appear, then, that the middle months of 1916 were simultaneously cathartic and unremarkable for the Irish American Catholic community with regard to the Easter Rising, its heavy-handed suppression, and its aftermath. Some historians have assessed the events of 1916 as the major stimulant for an upsurge of support for physical force to effect Irish freedom. And it is virtually inarguable that a more militant form of Irish nationalism became the consensus sentiment among Irish Americans, at the expense of Redmond's constitutional nationalism.[75] Much to Devoy's delight, FOIF membership started to climb, reaching a peak in 1919 with some 275,000 members. These gains, however, were mostly made in 1918 and 1919, when America's entry into the war and Wilson's articulation of the self-determination of all peoples, accompanied by the collapse of Redmond's Irish Parliamentary Party, permitted Irish American Catholics to rally around a new agenda. This was not the case in the late summer 1916. In fact, Devoy's delight was tarnished somewhat by the refusal of moderate Irish Americans and the Catholic Church to jump on the bandwagon of his ardent nationalist movement. Moreover, there remained in the summer of 1916 but little support for German assistance in bringing about a free and independent Irish republic. Irish American attention was now diverted from the drama of the Easter Rebellion and directed towards the presidential election in the fall.

---

75. David Brundage, "In Time of Peace, Prepare for War: Key Themes in the Social Thought of New York's Irish Nationalists," in Ronald H. Bayor and Timothy J. Meagher, eds., *The New York Irish* (Baltimore: Johns Hopkins University Press, 1996), 325–33. Meagher tempers Brundage's assertion that FOIF membership exploded in the wake of the Easter Rising by pointing out that it did not do so until after the war. Meagher, *The Columbia Guide to Irish American History*, 119; Kevin Kenny, "American-Irish Nationalism," in Lee and Casey, eds., *Making the Irish American*, 294–95.

CHAPTER 6

1917:
Toward a Declaration of War

The Election of 1916

On September 29, 1916, Jeremiah O'Leary, president of the American Truth Society, an anti-British and pro-German organization, cabled a derisive telegram to Woodrow Wilson, implying that the president was losing his party's support because of his pro-British policies. Pointing to the renomination of Democratic Senator James E. Martine of New Jersey as one of several signs that Democratic voters no longer wanted "any truckling to the British Empire," O'Leary jeeringly asked Wilson when he planned to "respond to these evidences of popular disapproval." Refusing to be intimidated, the president fired a terse response to O'Leary and, in doing so, chose to take an aggressive stand against Irish American agitators and their confederates. The telegram read: "Your telegram received. I would feel deeply mortified to have you or anybody like you vote for me. Since you have access to many disloyal Americans and I have not, I will ask you to convey this message to them."[1] Not only was Wilson's rebuke ingenious; it would frame the debate in the upcoming election and the months to follow.

---

1. O'Leary's telegram was printed in *New York Times,* "Wilson Wants No Disloyal Vote Cast On His Side," September 30, 1916, p. 1. Wilson's response is found in Link, *The Papers of Woodrow Wilson,* 8: 285. Martine, a rather undistinguished one-term senator, was noted for his Progressive policies, with particular interest in labor unrest in the mining concerns. He was not particularly anti-British, and Wilson supported his unsuccessful reelection bid in 1916. Exactly what O'Leary intended to make of his renomination is unclear.

1917: TOWARD A DECLARATION OF WAR

The heated exchange between the ordinarily *sangfroid Wilson* and the hyperbolic O'Leary in the fall of 1916 marked a significant modification in Irish American strategies regarding the war, Irish liberation, and the position of Irish American Catholics within the United States. Both the professionals and moderate Irish American Catholics had come to an understanding, however inchoate, that the United States was edging towards intervention in the European war and that it most likely would be on the side of the Allies and not the Germans. In response, Irish American factions would redouble their efforts to support adherence to absolute neutrality so long as it was possible. The professionals came to the realization that unstinting belief that the Germans were a viable force in the liberation of Ireland was fleeting at best. Their best option was to continue to trumpet the virtues of neutrality and to denigrate the altruism of Great Britain. Conservative, moderate, and Catholic Irish Americans recognized the slide to the Allied cause just as the professionals did, but sought to accommodate themselves to the new geopolitical realities. Rather than champion the cause of Irish freedom at the expense of Great Britain, Irish American Catholics strove to prove their absolute loyalty to the government of the United States, wherever that allegiance might lead them.

The issues that dominated the campaign and election of 1916 were as complex as they were myriad. Both presidential candidates, Woodrow Wilson and Charles Evans Hughes, not only faced critical domestic matters, but also had to articulate how the nation would continue to deal with a warring world that threatened its cherished neutrality. For Irish Americans in particular, the Wilson administration's record in navigating a neutral course over the previous two years became a preeminent issue.

Irish Americans of all stripes were still perplexed over the administration's role in the delayed transmission of the Senate's resolution seeking clemency for Roger Casement. Among the many inquiries into the matter, none was more indicative of the extent of this concern than that of Michael F. Doyle, the Philadelphia lawyer who had been hired as legal counsel in the Casement treason trial. He wrote Tumulty, expressing fear that the Republicans were planning to make a campaign issue out of the resolution and that an official explanation of the matter needed to be extended. Lecturing the president's secretary

CHAPTER 6

that, had "careful and sympathetic handling" of this matter been employed, the furor over the executions could have been avoided, Doyle reminded Tumulty that the "great bulk of Catholic and those of Irish descent are opposing the President." Tumulty's official assurance that the resolution had in fact been delivered to London on time, though greeted with a degree of skepticism in some Irish American quarters, did at least mitigate the discontent in the community at large.[2]

The noticeable strain in Woodrow Wilson's relationship with Irish Americans was not initiated by the confusion surrounding the July 29 Senate resolution. Wilson's difficulty with the general hyphenate issue had a history, rooted in his remarks at the unveiling of the John Barry statue in Franklin Park in May 1914, which had first led him into open conflict with many Irish Americans. When war broke out in Europe a few months later, illuminating the difficulties of maintaining a neutral position in an immigrant nation like the United States, the president and some Irish Americans were drawn into an escalating feud. In a Memorial Day address on May 30, 1914, Wilson continued to hammer away at the anti-hyphen theme. Using this national holiday honoring the nation's war dead as the occasion for his remarks, and garbed in a mantle of self-righteousness, the president proposed:

> The United States has again to work out by spiritual process a new union ... when men shall not allow old loves to take the place of present allegiances; when men must, on the contrary, translate that very ardor of love of country of their birth into the ardor of love for the country of their adoption ... America must come first in every purpose we entertain.[3]

Although Wilson hardly needed any encouragement in his provocative confrontation of the hyphen, it was his secretary, Joseph Tumulty, who recommended "Americanism" as one of the central planks in

---

2. Joseph P. Tumulty to Michael Francis Doyle, October 14, 1916, in Link, *The Papers of Woodrow Wilson,* 38:443–45.
3. Ray S. Baker and William E. Dodd, eds., *The Public Papers of Woodrow Wilson,* 6 vols. (New York: Harper and Brothers, 1925–1927), 2:193.

1917: TOWARD A DECLARATION OF WAR

the party's platform. Tumulty very likely inherited the idea from a telegram he received from Wisconsin Senator Paul O. Husting. Representing a hugely immigrant state, Husting suggested to Tumulty that "Americanism" should be introduced in the upcoming Democratic convention to be held in St. Louis in June 1916. The senator recommended that the central idea should be that "we should accept the challenge of the German alliance ... and that the issue should be clearly understood as being between those who stand for America only and those who stand for some other country first."[4]

This suggestion found its way squarely into the party's platform several days later. Declaring Americanism as the "supreme issue of the day," the Democratic Party proclaimed that "America must show itself not as a nation of partisans but a nation of patriots." As for those who would arouse foreign prejudices "in disregard of our own country's welfare," the Democrats condemned them or anything else that was calculated to "divide our people into antagonistic groups." The platform was greeted with general approbation by those in attendance at the convention. That the Democratic Party fully embraced the anti-foreign tone of the platform might explain in part why a resolution introduced by Irish American delegate Martin Lomasney of Massachusetts was so unceremoniously rebuffed. Lomasney, a Boston ward-heeler and political kingpin, attempted to coax the Party into recognizing and approving the "demand of the Irish people for their independence." Although the delegates were clearly irritated with Lomasney's impertinence, they listened carefully to his resolution. Despite this courtesy, the delegation quickly voted to refer the resolution to committee, where it was tabled and excluded from the final draft of the platform.[5]

When Irish American delegates like David I. Walsh, outgoing governor of Massachusetts, "stood with Wilson" in repudiating

---

4. Paul O. Husting to J. P. Tumulty, June 12, 1916, *Joseph P. Tumulty Papers*, Library of Congress. Husting, an immigrant from Luxembourg, was one of Wilson's most loyal and pro-Allied supporters. His death in a hunting accident at the hands of his brother in October 1917 cost Wilson a key ally in the Senate during the vote on the League of Nations. See *New York Times*, October 22, 1917.

5. Official Report of the Proceedings of the Democratic National Convention, St. Louis, June 14, 15, and 16, 1916, 122–23, 131–33.

CHAPTER 6

hyphenated Americans, the administration decided to pursue a more aggressive posture in promoting Americanism as a central campaign issue. As the summer of 1916 advanced, Tumulty grew incensed by the tone of some Irish American propaganda and with reports of German-supported acts of sabotage. For his part, Wilson applied himself with relish to promoting Americanism. In his address to the nation on Flag Day 1916, Wilson underscored his antipathy to "hyphenated Americans" by pointing out that "there is a disloyalty active in the United States, and it must be absolutely crushed." In his address on the issue of citizenship at the opening of the Conference on Americanization held on July 13, 1916, he used the occasion to assail disloyal agitators who were trying to pull the nation's sympathy toward foreign interests. Finally, at Shadow Lawn, an estate in New Jersey, in his acceptance speech for the nomination as the Democratic presidential candidate, Wilson placed himself in sharp contrast to "hyphenated Americans." He declared that he neither sought the favor nor feared the displeasure "of a small alien element among us which puts loyalty to any foreign power before loyalty to the United States."[6]

Wilson's attacks upon the hyphenated element in American society struck a clear, dark, and resonant chord in the Irish American and Catholic communities in 1916. The increasing vehemence of these assaults had captured the fancy of the nation at large and was forcing Irish Americans to clarify their loyalties. These attacks caused the Irish American Catholic community a great deal of distress and anxiety. They found themselves trapped in a perplexing situation, fearing that they would appear disloyal to the government should they press Ireland's cause too strenuously or attack the president himself. Their responses to this dilemma once again highlighted the rich diversity and divergent opinions within the community itself.

Irish Americans who had agitated for a free and independent Ireland, and who had railed against the administration over its

---

6. Blum, *Joe Tumulty and the Wilson Era*, 102; "Flag Day Address, June 15, 1916," and "Address on Citizenship at Washington Before the Conference of Americanization, July 13, 1916," in Baker and Dodd, *The Public Papers of Woodrow Wilson*, 2:209, 251; Address Delivered at Shadow Lawn, New Jersey, September 2, 1916, in Baker and Dodd, 2:283.

1917: TOWARD A DECLARATION OF WAR

pro-British policies, felt the sting of Wilson's condemnation most acutely in the campaign of 1916. In fact, they had deeply resented Wilson's intimations of their disloyalty ever since the war started in 1914. Their resentment over the president's acceleration of attacks propelled them to strike back at the administration. Learning of Wilson's nomination for a second term, John Devoy stretched the vernacular with his indictment of the lamentable proceedings at the Democratic Convention:

> The Convention in St. Louis was the most shameful exhibition in American history of slavish subservience to a man of discredited moral character, without political convictions, who has prostituted his office to the service of England and brought racial strife among the American people for ignoble personal ends.[7]

Later in the campaign season, Devoy attempted to turn the hyphenate issue against the president himself. He pointed out that the very ethnics whose loyalty Wilson was impugning in 1916, the Irish and Germans, had fought for the Union, whereas Wilson's ancestors had sought to dismember it.[8]

Devoy's accusation that Wilson had introduced ethnic strife into the American social fabric was a theme worked frequently by those Irish Americans who opposed the administration. Jeremiah O'Leary, who had recently engaged in a telegraphic bout with the president, attempted to tap into Irish American fears of renewed anti-Catholic bigotry when he produced a pamphlet responding to Wilson's terse telegram of September 29:

> It is the contention of Mr. O'Leary that the President attacked not him but his name as an appeal to the bigoted and know-nothing elements in the United States. Mr. O'Leary contends that the President's

7. *Gaelic-American*, June 24, 1916.
8. *Gaelic-American*, October 21, 1916.

CHAPTER 6

attacks, in view of the fact that the President has shown
a decided antagonism to Irish and Catholic matters, is
an attack upon the Irish race in America.[9]

The Catholic press was equally distressed to see anti-Catholic tones injected into the campaign's rhetoric. In a local election in Cleveland, Ohio, the *Catholic Universe*, departing from its normal policy of impartiality, recommended a certain Mr. Eugene Quigley as a candidate for office, noting that "issues of bigotry and anti-Catholicism were at stake." Father Whelan of the Brooklyn *Tablet* admitted that Catholics faced a real conundrum in the upcoming November election for president. Calling Wilson the "Presbyterian who hobnobs with nun-killing Carranza," and stating that "Baptist Hughes," was intimately "connected with anti-Catholic bigots," Whelan recommended the lesser of two evils; he reluctantly urged his readers to consider voting the Presbyterian ticket.[10] In both of these cited cases, and in countless others dotting the pages of Catholic newspapers, the paramount issue in the fall of 1916 was unwarranted attacks on Irish-Americans and Catholics by Protestant nativists. The cause of Ireland, and even the great issue of American neutrality, were clearly secondary considerations. Irish American Catholics were to be clearly identified and touted as American patriots.

Moderate and conservative members of the Irish American Catholic community were equally perturbed and distressed about insinuations of their disloyalty to the nation as suggested by the campaign's anti-hyphenate rhetoric. Mainstream Irish American Catholics, in a manner not unlike more strident professional Irish compatriots, rejected implications of divided allegiance. In effusive patriotic terms, they immediately pointed to their community's past contributions to the building and defending of their adopted country. The speeches delivered at the 1916 annual dinner of the Society of the Friendly Sons of St. Patrick in the City of New York reflected this sentiment. The

9. *A Statement Issued by the American Truth Society in Defense of Its President Against an Unjust Attack Made upon Him by the President of the United States, 1916*, pamphlet, New York Public Library

10. *Catholic Universe*, November 3, 1916; Brooklyn *Tablet*, July 1, 1916.

1917: TOWARD A DECLARATION OF WAR

keynote of the evening, as indicated by the recording secretary, William J. Clarke, was "Americanism." Noting that six hundred diners "joined heartily in the singing of the national anthem ... [and] concluded with a rousing cheer," Clarke recorded that "the health of the President of the United States was drunk among a scene of great enthusiasm." Speaking to the assembled members at the dinner, Senator James Phelan of California asserted that while many immigrants had been stigmatized as hyphenates, "certainly the Irish for all their contributions have the right to claim this land as their own." To a standing ovation, he proclaimed that the "men who have come from Ireland and their descendants are loyal to the flag." Phelan was followed on the speaker's dais by former Minnesota senator Charles A. Towne, who observed that the evening had clearly instilled in the hearts of all assembled a "recrudescence of patriotism." In grandiloquent style, he polished off his speech by confessing to his audience, which included Irish American composer George M. Cohan, "that I am one of those old-fashioned Fourth of July, American flag patriots."[11]

The Catholic Church, equally sensitive to the hyphenate stigma, also responded with declarations of patriotic loyalty. In his 1916 book *A Retrospect of Fifty Years*, Cardinal Gibbons used the occasion of his golden jubilee of ordination to remark upon the need for Catholic patriotism in an election year. "Patriotism implies not only love of soil and of fellow citizens," he gushingly argued, but would also involve a citizen's willingness "to consecrate his life ... in defense of altar and fireside, of God and Fatherland." The cardinal reminded his readers that "love of country shows itself ... by the observance of law and the good use of political rights." Good Catholics, therefore, could express their loyalty to the nation by respecting the "flag that symbolizes the country, and the chief magistrate who represents it." Nor was Gibbons alone within the hierarchy in advancing the patriotic line. In the *New York Times Magazine*, Bishop James A. McFaul of Trenton presented the American Federation of Catholic Societies as extending the "right hand of fellowship to citizens of every creed who would maintain the

---

11. *132nd Anniversary Dinner of the Society of the Friendly Sons of St. Patrick in the City of New York, March 17, 1916, Hotel Astor* (New York: Published by the Society, 1916), 7, 20–22, 28.

CHAPTER 6

ideals of the Republic." Hailing the Catholic as "no alien in the United States," McFaul argued that Catholic ancestors had joined with men of other creeds in fighting "for the liberty of the nation."[12]

Irish American Catholic anxiety was not alleviated by any assurance that there might be a more attractive candidate than Wilson. The Republican Party adopted an equally strident position on the hyphenate issue. While Charles Evans Hughes was reasonably restrained in his rhetoric, he could not silence the dominant Republican figure in the campaign—Theodore Roosevelt. Roosevelt's renegade entrance into the political race in 1912 as an independent might well have cost the Republicans the White House that year, and made him *persona non grata* in the Party, but his cooperation in 1916 was considered indispensable if the Republicans were going to defeat Wilson. At a very early point in the Great War, Roosevelt had rallied to the Allied cause, and he doggedly assailed the Wilson administration for its tepid and pusillanimous response to German aggression. At the height of the hyphenate crisis in 1916, Roosevelt wrote an impassioned work entitled *Fear God and Take Your Own Part*, in which he appealed to all patriotic Americans to band together and prepare for the arrival of war. When that moment arrived, there would be no room left in the United States for the hyphenated American. Whereas Hughes's relative silence on the loyalty issue generally attracted disaffected Democratic Irish American and German American voters, the attraction was greatly diminished by their view that Roosevelt would ultimately fashion Hughes's foreign policy.[13]

Roosevelt's ardent and bellicose support of the Allies, coupled with his unrestrained assaults upon allegedly disloyal hyphenates, heightened the fears among German Americans and most Irish Americans who might otherwise have crossed party lines to vote for Hughes. In a letter brought to Tumulty's attention, a German American physician, J. C.

---

12. James Cardinal Gibbons, *A Retrospect of Fifty Years* (New York: John Murphy, 1916), 299–303.

13. Theodore Roosevelt, *Fear God and Take Your Own Part* (New York: George H. Doran, 1916), 138–64; Louis L. Gerson, *The Hyphenate in Recent American Politics and Diplomacy* (Lawrence: University of Kansas Press, 1964), 65–66.

1917: TOWARD A DECLARATION OF WAR

Vorbeck, validated this fright by intimating that Roosevelt's increasing ties to Hughes were causing many of his fellow German Americans to reconsider their loyalties to the Republican Party. Echoing a growing sentiment in German American and Irish American circles, Vorbeck stated that "Wilson is the safest candidate." Similarly, George Sylvester Viereck noted in *The Fatherland* that "every time Roosevelt opens his mouth, Mr. Hughes loses 10,000 votes." In what must be considered the most stinging and surprising rejection of the Hughes candidacy, the German ambassador von Bernstorff openly supported Wilson.[14]

To a large extent, Wilson's strained relationship with Irish Americans was offset by Roosevelt's greater militancy over the hyphenate issue and the former president's eagerness to make cause with the Allies. Ambivalence in this matter did not deter some of the more ardent Irish American professionals, such as Jeremiah A. O'Leary, from making overtures to the Republicans. In the middle of September, O'Leary led a small delegation of Irish Americans to a meeting with Hughes in New York, and apparently came away satisfied with the Republican's commitment to neutrality. Hughes's subsequent claim that he had unwittingly met with extremists, and made no promises, did not dislodge the adverse publicity he received in the press.[15]

The specter of Roosevelt looming over Charles Evans Hughes made many Irish Americans fearful that a Republican victory was tantamount to entering the Great War. It was only with great reluctance that even John Devoy, given his unmitigated hatred for Woodrow Wilson, came to Hughes's standard. A month before the election, Devoy mulled over the sad choice between "one [Roosevelt] who attacks you openly and in front with a raised club; and the other [Wilson] who stabs you in the back and unaware with a poisoned dagger." If ardent Irish American

---

14. J. C. Vorbeck, M.D., to the Honorable James A. Reed, July 13, 1916, *Joseph P. Tumulty Papers,* Library of Congress; Viereck is quoted in Thomas Kerr, "German-Americans and Neutrality in the 1916 Elections," *Mid-America* 43 (April 1961): 101; Bernstorff, *My Three Years in America,* 300.

15. Michael Kelley, "Biographical Sketch," in Jeremiah A. O'Leary, *My Political Trial and Experiences* (New York: Jefferson Publishing, 1919), 37–42; Merlo J. Pusey, *Charles Evans Hughes,* 2 vols. (New York: Columbia University Press, 1963), 1:355.

CHAPTER 6

nationalists commended Hughes's candidacy to the Irish American community, they did so with significant misgivings and because of their irreconcilable differences with Woodrow Wilson.[16]

Moderate and conservative Irish Americans, notwithstanding their real differences with the Wilson administration, resolved their ambivalence over the election much more readily than fervent Irish American nationalists. As a whole, they remained in the Democratic fold. Thomas J. Walsh, credited with the "able management" of Wilson's western campaign, believed that Irish American Catholics must remain loyal to the Wilson ticket to avoid legitimizing criticism that they courted foreign interests. Francis Hackett was joined by fellow Irish American Herbert Croly of the *New Republic*, in seizing upon the hyphen issue as a reason to continue supporting Wilson. Both condemned O'Leary's effort to lobby Irish American votes over to Hughes and denounced the Republican candidate for not having rejected O'Leary and his ilk.[17]

Singular dedication to the Irish cause, along with his inveterate hatred of Woodrow Wilson, may have forced a hesitant Daniel Cohalan finally to announce his support of the Republican ticket, but such devotion did not inspire most other Irish American politicians to do the same. John Quinn, counselor to Charles F. Murphy, the political boss of New York City's Tammany Hall, was occupied with bashing the Germans for their treacherous role in the Casement affair and screening several "threatening letters" from them. Quinn's support for Wilson was a foregone conclusion. Other New York politicians remained steadfastly in the Democratic camp. While Wilson and Tammany

---

16. *Gaelic-American,* October 7, 1916.
17. Josephine O'Keane, *Thomas J. Walsh: A Senator from Montana* (Francestown, NH: Morchall Jones, 1955), 72; T. J. Walsh to Claude G. Bowers, September 8, 1916, *T. J. Walsh Papers,* Library of Congress; Herbert Croly, "The Two Parties in 1916," *New Republic* 8 (October 21, 1916): 286. Croly was a third-generation Irish American and did not appear to have any religious convictions. All the same, his *New Republic,* an intellectual weekly, assailed Catholicism often and viciously. For example, see the September 2, 1916, editorials. "Short of entering the war on England's side," groaned the Fords, "the Administration has done everything for England that an English viceroy might do." See *Irish World,* June 24, 1916.

1917: TOWARD A DECLARATION OF WAR

Hall had never enjoyed a cordial relationship, their mutual interests in maintaining Democratic solidarity compelled them to cooperate. According to Tumulty, former New York governor Martin Glynn campaigned vigorously for Wilson and defended the administration's record on neutrality. Wilson's campaign manager in the East, Vance McCormack, reportedly had a "delightful conference" with Charles Francis Murphy, in which the latter assured the administration that the Democratic vote would turn out on Election Day.[18]

Irish American politicians and progressives with national stature also lined up behind the Democratic ticket. Bourke Cockran, despite his disappointment over the administration's handling of Mexican affairs, stood squarely behind the president. In a lengthy memorandum on the European war, Cockran elaborated why Wilson was more likely than Hughes to keep the United States out of that conflagration. Progressives like Governor Edward Dunne of Illinois, New York Supreme Court Justice Victor Dowling, and Bainbridge Colby praised Wilson for keeping the nation on a neutral course and actively promoting enlightened legislation. Even William Jennings Bryan, who had earlier resigned from the administration over the president's handling of the *Lusitania* crisis, actively campaigned for Wilson in the western states. And although Senator Thomas P. Gore and Representative Jeff McLemore had opposed Wilson over trading policies with the Allies, they, too, joined the Wilson bandwagon.[19]

Although domestic and political concerns dictated continued support of the Democratic ticket by Irish Americans, there were other matters that threatened voter turnout in November. Most Irish American Catholics continued to deplore the president's policies in Mexico. Whereas a certain degree of stability was emerging from the anarchy in that troubled nation, American Catholics remained displeased with the administration's record in Mexico. The most vocal

18. John Quinn to Hon. John P. Cohalan, September 9, 1916, *John Quinn Papers,* New York Public Library; Joseph P. Tumulty, *Woodrow Wilson as I Know Him,* 185. McCormack is quoted in *New York Times,* "Dares Hughes To Say Roosevelt is Right," October 3, 1916, p. 10.

19. *New York Times,* October 3, 1916; Bourke Cockran, Memorandum on the War, September 22, 1916, *Bourke Cockran Papers,* New York Public Library; Ward, *Ireland and Anglo-American Relations,* 136.

CHAPTER 6

critics of the administration, however, tended to be extremists, such as Father Francis C. Kelley, or those Irish Americans who already nursed other implacable differences with Wilson. Disenchanted with the reception he had received from the Wilson administration in 1915, Father Kelley deserted the Democratic Party and chose to back Hughes in 1916. His own *Extension Magazine* featured a scathing attack upon Wilson's bungling of the Mexican issue and commended Hughes for his "clear-cut and definite position," a stance that the clairvoyant Kelley must have detected better than Hughes himself. Kelley's invective aimed at Wilson was vicious enough that Senator T. J. Walsh, an active Wilson campaigner, was compelled to write Cardinal George Mundelein of Chicago to complain about it. Father Edward Flannery, chaplain to the Connecticut chapter of Hibernians, who had earlier outlined in a letter to Joseph Tumulty ideas for improving Wilson's image with Irish American voters in New England, joined Kelley in defecting from the Democratic Party upon hearing that Wilson had failed to nominate a Catholic to the peace commission on Mexican affairs. The resentment was compounded when Wilson appointed YMCA leader John Mott to head the commission. Upon hearing of Mott's selection, Flannery sent an ultimatum to the president, demanding an explanation. Should Wilson fail to provide one the priest threatened to instruct "every Irish Catholic in the state of Connecticut to vote against" the Democratic ticket.[20]

Wilson's chances of keeping the solid Irish American Catholic vote in the Democratic fold were again jeopardized when rumors began circulating around the country of his alleged discourtesies to Catholic officialdom. Particularly damaging was the story that he had insulted Cardinal Gibbons by addressing him at a reception at the White House as "Mr. Gibbons." Additionally, it was rumored that he had treated Archbishop John Ireland with similar disrespect, and that

---

20. Gaffey, *Francis Clement Kelley and the American Catholic Dream* (Washington, DC: The Heritage Foundation, 1980), 36–37; T. J. Walsh to George Cardinal Mundelein, September 13, 1916, *T. J. Walsh Papers,* Library of Congress; J. P. Tumulty to Woodrow Wilson, with Enclosure, August 25, 1916, in Link, *Campaigns for Progressivism and Peace,* 38:83. Rev. Edward Flannery to J. P. Tumulty, August 24, 1916, *Joseph P. Tumulty Papers.*

he had refused on "religious grounds" to attend the Pan-American Thanksgiving Day Mass in both 1915 and 1916. To round out the circle of rumor-mongering, it was reported that he had refused to receive Monsignor Giovanni Bonanzo, the Apostolic Delegate, who was conveying a message to him from Pope Benedict XV. Gossip begat gossip that the entire hierarchy, particularly Cardinals Gibbons and O'Connell, were conspiring to defeat Wilson in the election, and that Gibbons had remarked that "any Catholic who votes for Wilson should be damned." Tumulty recognized the grave consequences of allowing these falsehoods to go uncontested. When Wilson prepared a memorandum in which he denied having casually addressed Cardinal Gibbons, Tumulty saw to it that it was circulated to Democratic leaders, who used it effectively. The cardinal himself was prevailed upon to make a similar denial in the *New York World*, declaring himself wearied by this persistent falsehood and vowing that he would never tell Church leaders to instruct Catholics how to vote.[21]

The application of such political salves appeared to produce a salutary effect upon Wilson's candidacy as Election Day approached. The Catholic press increasingly reflected a more impartial stance towards the candidates. Shannon of the *New World*, a frequent critic of the administration, pulled up short of endorsing Hughes in his election editorial. While he admonished his audience not to vote "along strict party lines ... to save jobs," he encouraged Catholics to "cast a thoughtful, conscientious vote." Yorke's *Monitor* declined to endorse either candidate, indicating that there did not appear to be any difference between them. The *Pittsburgh Catholic* declared that "the *Catholic* advocates neither political party but stands for American manhood." Several papers refuted all rumors afoot that the Catholic clergy were actively campaigning for Hughes. The *Michigan Catholic* printed excerpts from the *New York World*'s article in which Gibbons emphatically denied that Catholics were organizing to defeat Wilson. And in Cincinnati, Dr. Thomas Hart indignantly denied that priests and bishops were seeking the defeat of "one of the candidates for the presidency of the United States."[22]

21. Link, *Campaigns for Progressivism and Peace*, 130–34.
22. *New World*, October 27, 1916; The *Monitor*, November 4, 1916;

CHAPTER 6

Thomas O'Flanagan's editorial in the *Catholic Transcript* was further evidence that the administration's efforts to improve its image with Irish Americans and Catholic voters in general were succeeding. Resenting the implication that Irish American Catholic votes were simply there for the Republican Party's taking, O'Flanagan declared that they were "not notoriously for sale ... to the highest bidder." By pointing out that many German American papers "have developed unwonted interest in the affairs of Ireland and the Irish people," he summarily rejected the notion that Irish Americans would be "susceptible of the rankest flattery" being doled out to them. While refusing to endorse either candidate, O'Flanagan concluded with a few words of advice to the Germans and their obstreperous Irish American allies:

> Nothing that German capital can command will make self-respecting Irishmen or Catholics turn from Wilson to Hughes or from Hughes to Wilson. They are able to think and we hope they are able to vote according to their intelligence and conscience. The American Irish and Catholics think they know how to vote; they are not for sale, thank you.[23]

On November 7, 1916, Americans reelected Woodrow Wilson. While losing much of the industrial Northeast to Hughes, Wilson did well enough throughout the rest of the nation, particularly in the far western states, to capture victory. Wilson's triumphs in Ohio and California offset setbacks in Illinois, New York, Massachusetts, Pennsylvania, New Jersey, and Connecticut. These states had voted Republican since 1896 and would continue to do so through 1924. The loss of these Northeastern states where Irish Americans voted in great numbers convinced post-election analysts that many of these voters crossed party lines to cast their ballots for Hughes. Indeed, the professional Irish American press tried to salvage a moral victory by spinning a tale

---

Pittsburgh Catholic, August 10, 1916; *Michigan Catholic*, November 2, 1916; *Catholic Telegraph*, October 26, 1916.
   23. *Catholic Transcript*, October 12, 1916.

1917: TOWARD A DECLARATION OF WAR

that Irish American voters in these industrialized states should have secured the margin of victory for Hughes.[24]

Despite the radical Irish American press's wishful thinking that Irish and Catholic voters had significantly influenced the Republican victories in the large industrial centers of the Northeast and Midwest, little evidence exists to substantiate this claim. Several studies of Irish American voting patterns throughout the United States have demonstrated very little defection from the Democratic ranks. In a study of several assembly districts in Manhattan with heavy concentrations of Irish American voters, John P. Buckley discovered that while Wilson did not poll as well as he had in the 1912 election, he nonetheless carried these districts handily. Edward Cuddy's study of voting results in Irish American wards in Buffalo revealed that more votes were cast for Wilson in 1916 than in 1912, indicating that he had not made enemies in the community during his first term. In the most extensive study of Irish American voting patterns in the election of 1916 yet produced, William M. Leary, Jr., provided similar evidence that in several urban centers such as, Boston, New York, New Haven and San Francisco, where the Irish voted in strength, Wilson fared significantly better than any other Democratic candidate had done since 1904 or would do again until Al Smith's candidacy in 1928. In his review of ward voting in Boston, Leary found that Wilson received percentages in Irish American wards comparable to those that the popular Irish American Catholic Governor David I. Walsh had achieved in 1914. And another study revealed that in Cook County, Illinois, a place that normally voted Republican, Democrats polled better in 1916 than they ever had before.[25]

Despite many grievances against the Wilson administration, including his handling of the Mexican crisis, his apparent truckling

---

24. S. D. Lovell, *The Presidential Election of 1916* (Carbondale: Southern Illinois University Press, 1986), 155–56; *Irish World*, November 18, 1916.

25. Buckley, *The New York Irish*, 103; Edward Cuddy, "Irish-Americans and the 1916 Election: An Episode in Immigrant Adjustment," *American Quarterly* 21, no.2, Part 1 (Summer 1969): 236; William M. Leary, Jr., "Woodrow Wilson, Irish-Americans and the Election of 1916", *Journal of American History* 54 (June 1967): 57–72; Edgar Eugene Robinson, *The Presidential Vote, 1896–1932*, rev. ed. (New York: Octagon Books, 1970), 79–81.

CHAPTER 6

to the British Empire, and his perceived assaults upon hyphenated Americans, Irish American Catholics remained largely faithful to the Democratic standard if not to the president himself. The reasons for this behavior are varied and complex. Perhaps Bourke Cockran summarized the community's dilemma best when, in refusing to stump for Wilson, he declared that "between voting for a candidate and taking the platform to urge his election there is a difference and it is the source of my perplexity."[26] Clearly, Irish Americans and many Catholics were not enthusiastic in their support of Wilson; this, however, did not dissuade them for casting their votes for him.

The president's chances for victory were most certainly assisted by the inept, insipid, and uninspiring challenge from his opponent Charles Evans Hughes. Even Hughes's principal cheerleader, Teddy Roosevelt, is said to have been so distraught by the milquetoast pronouncements of his candidate that he confided to a friend that the only difference between the bearded Hughes and the shorn Wilson was a matter of a shave. Hughes's ambiguity, coupled with Roosevelt's anti-hyphenate and bellicose rhetoric, frustrated some of his admirers in the professional Irish camp. The *Irish World* took umbrage with the "anglomaniac advisors" surrounding Hughes while the candidate himself engaged in "talking twaddle." Devoy was flummoxed by Roosevelt's influence with Hughes, colorfully noting that "Roosevelt is going around like a braying jackass denouncing better men than himself because they insist that the United States shall not be made a tool of England." After all the returns were tabulated, Democrats who had defected to the Republican banner derisively blamed Roosevelt for having "contributed more than any other person in America" to Wilson's triumph. Moreover, Hughes's efforts were afflicted by troubles unrelated to Irish American interests or his stand, whatever it was, on neutrality. In the final weeks of the campaign, he slighted Hiram Johnson, the popular California progressive, and consequently lost an important endorsement in a pivotal state, which helped carry Wilson to victory. Unlike Wilson, Hughes did not have able campaign managers, such as Walsh and McCormack, and his campaign was frequently mismanaged

---

26. Quoted in James McGurrin, *Bourke Cockran: A Free Lance in American Politics* (New York: Charles Scribner's Sons, 1948), 292.

as a result. Hughes was also unable to dodge the image of being too tangibly associated with the rich and privileged classes.[27]

Hughes's connection to Roosevelt made Irish Americans wary of the future course of American foreign policy. While they had little faith in Woodrow Wilson, as one Irish American observed, that "they had even less faith in Hughes." Unable to resolve these ambiguities, Irish Americans made "no concerted effort ... to defeat Wilson." Hughes exasperated even his most avid Irish American supporters. Jeremiah O'Leary, who would no more have voted for Wilson than would Charles Evans Hughes, blamed the Republican candidate's defeat on his vacillation over neutrality. In light of Hughes's ambiguous position on this matter, O'Leary argued that Wilson won the Republican states on the Pacific coast "where the feminine influence was thrown to his support under the supposition that he had kept us out of the war and would continue to do so."[28]

Wilson did not retain Irish American votes solely because Hughes's candidacy was so transparently unattractive. There were compelling economic and domestic issues in which the Democratic Party tended to represent important Irish American interests. Wilson's loss of several industrialized states of the North should not be construed as a rejection by labor. In virtually every state in the Union, organized labor voted the Democratic ticket. In several of the states that Wilson lost, the Republican margin of victory was razor thin and tended to reflect a strong suburban and rural Republican turnout, which offset Democratic majorities in the industrialized cities. Moreover, as Leary has pointed out, these states traditionally voted Republican in national elections, excepting 1912, when Wilson captured them at the expense of a fractured Republican ticket. In California, a key state in Wilson's victory column, which delivered but a slender four-thousand-vote

27. *Irish World*, October 7, 1916; *Gaelic-American*, October 21, 1916; Cuddy, "Irish-Americans and the Election of 1916," 237; Pusey, *Charles Evans Hughes*, 1:362–363.
28. John D. Spillane, "The Irish Movement in the United States since 1911," in William Fitzgerald, ed., *The voice of Ireland: a survey of the race and nation from all angles by the foremost leaders at home and abroad, Dublin, 1923* (London: John Heywood, 1924), 229; Kelly, "Biographical Sketch," 44–48.

majority, organized labor worked diligently on Wilson's behalf. The beloved Father Peter Yorke, a tireless champion of labor and radical Irish nationalism, may have cast his vote for Hughes, but that did not seem to work the magic among Irish American wards in the city of San Francisco that came out heavily in favor of Wilson. Despite the skepticism of some prelates within the Catholic hierarchy regarding "progressive fads," evidence suggests that Irish American Catholic workers may have rejected these sentiments and voted quietly in their own best interests. Second- and third-generation Irish American Catholics might have experienced a sentimental pull upon their hearts for Irish liberation, and they may have deplored the very idea of American coziness with Great Britain, but they voted in their interests as Americans. The Democratic ticket was infinitely more identified with the passage of progressive legislation that improved the quality of the work environment than was the Republican Hughes. During the campaign season itself, Wilson had signed two bills regulating the length of the working day and the conditions under which children could be employed in the labor force. He had delivered on the "bread and butter" issues most pertinent to the Irish American laboring class.[29]

No matter how much Irish American Catholics resented the administration's pro-British sympathies and imputations of Irish American disloyalty, there was no denying that the president had kept the nation out of the war. With Hughes and his henchman, the Anglophile Roosevelt, as the only alternative, Wilson emerged as the more credible peace candidate. When those giddy New York Democrats hailed Roosevelt as having contributed more than anyone else to the president's victory, they were merely reflecting the sentiments of the Irish American Catholic community. While it may have struck many

29. Leary, "Woodrow Wilson, Irish-Americans and the Election of 1916," 66; McCaffrey, *The Irish Diaspora*, 145. For example, Cardinal O'Connell called progressive reform movements, "silly talk." Holding morality as the highest virtue, he was convinced that "to thousands of people, forced by circumstances to live in crowded districts, clean hearts are far more important than clean streets." Quoted in Brooklyn *Tablet*, January 20, 1917. The working-class city of Worcester, Massachusetts also turned out a strong Democratic majority in the election of 1916. See Timothy Meagher, *Inventing Irish America*, 297; Link, *Campaigns for Progressivism and Peace*, 55–60, 83–92.

1917: TOWARD A DECLARATION OF WAR

Irish Americans as ironic that they would support a candidate with whom they had experienced such a tempestuous relationship, it appeared too dangerous to shrug off their allegiance to the Democratic Party and vote the Republican ticket. Like Bourke Cockran, many Irish American candidates were willing to subordinate their disappointment with the Wilson administration's policies in the hope of preserving the peace. It seems very fitting that the most memorable and widely used campaign slogan of that year, "He Kept Us Out of War," was coined by Irish American Catholic and former New York governor Martin Glynn.[30]

Campaign reports and election feedback suggested that Wilson's peace platform proved attractive to Irish American Catholic voters, as well as to other ethnic immigrant populations. Despite assertions that Catholics were conspiring to engineer Wilson's defeat in several states, particularly Indiana, evidence to the contrary defied these claims. In Missouri, Catholic leaders worked to counteract the movement against the president and contributed to Wilson's carrying the state with a margin greater than that of his 1912 victory. One of Wilson's campaign managers, Senator Walsh, was repeatedly apprised by confidants, not only in Missouri but in the crucial state of Ohio, that the administration's peace platform was paying big dividends. From Boston, British consul F. P. Leay reported to the London office after the election that both the Hibernians, who were expected to vote for Hughes, and the Knights of Columbus had strongly supported Wilson. In Syracuse, Wilson's 1916 plurality in heavily Irish American districts was four full percentage points higher than it was in 1912. Allegiance to the Democratic Party and the peace candidacy were identified as the principal reasons for this increase. To claims that the Catholic Church was working against the Wilson ticket, his chief biographer, Arthur Link, could respond that only Oregon was a legitimate example where the clergy actively worked to defeat him.[31]

---

30. Pusey, *Charles Evans Hughes*, 1:364; Cuddy, *Irish-Americans and National Isolationism*, 120.

31. For a denial that Indiana's Catholic clergy were conspiring against Wilson, see *Our Sunday Visitor*, November 1, 1916; Creighton, *Missouri and the World War*, 151–55. For Walsh's data, see Edward F. Gottra to T. J. Walsh, October 7, 1916, M. J. Faistt to T. J. Walsh, October 24, 1916, and James T. Carroll to T.

CHAPTER 6

For Irish American Catholics, the election of 1916 was but another milestone on the road to integration and inclusion within American society. It was not, however, a craven submission to assimilation, as Irish Americans entered the mainstream on their own terms and for their own reasons. Most Irish American Catholics proved willing to overlook real grievances with the Wilson administration to vote the Democratic ticket. For reasons that were vital to their own interests as Americans, they were beginning to shed a degree of their strictly Irish identity and were approaching American society as respectable Catholics and Americans. The hyphenate issue, while it offended many Irish American Catholics, had the effect of galvanizing efforts by the community to assert their absolute allegiance to the United States. As one observer noted, Irish Americans had to select between their own interests as Americans, and the "interests of the leaders of Irish-American nationalism ... and their interests as Americans prevailed." Try as they did, leading Irish American nationalists failed to rally the community at large to their agenda in 1916. In the end, they had "little effect on the Irish vote."[32]

The Road to War

Many Americans, including those of Irish ancestry, assumed that Wilson's campaign boast of having kept the United States out of the war was a pledge to pursue that same course once reelected. In the months spanning the election and the United States' declaration of war, the ability to maintain this course became steadily more difficult. The inexorable movement towards intervention severed another of the few tenuous strands of unity remaining among Irish American Catholics in

---

J. Walsh, October 23, 1916, *T. J. Walsh Papers,* Library of Congress; Carroll, *American Opinion and the Irish Question,* 84, n.2; Beadles, *The Syracuse Irish,* 260; Link, *Campaigns for Progressivism and Peace,* 161. There were some inflated charges that Denver's *Catholic Register* was acting as if it were an agent for the Hughes ticket.

    32. Donald H. Akenson, *The United States and Ireland* (Cambridge, MA: Harvard University Press, 1973), 44; R. A. Burchell, "Did the Irish and German Voters Desert the Democrats in 1920?: A Tentative Statistical Answer," *Journal of American Studies* 6 (August 1972): 155.

1917: TOWARD A DECLARATION OF WAR

late 1916. In the months leading to April 1917, Irish Americans labored under the conflicting imperatives of fervently desiring peace and dutifully embracing the advent of hostilities. Even during the final weeks of the campaign of 1916, the direction of the European war heightened this growing sense of tension and anxiety. When the German High Command began stationing submarines off the Atlantic coast of the United States to torpedo Allied shipping in October 1916, the *Catholic Transcript* revealed the strains of maintaining neutrality. Noting that the transfer of warfare from European to American waters did not make this war "one whit more our own," and still insisting that the war was a European concern and not an American one, the paper's editor O'Flanagan nonetheless argued that "if needs be, we will defend our rights."[33]

The fear that defending American rights would lead the United States into a war with Germany sent the professionals scurrying to defuse any militant statements, such as that by O'Flanagan. They continued to assail Great Britain at every turn with the hope of reinforcing neutral attitudes within the Irish American community. The Fords of the *Irish World* applauded efforts by Representative John J. Fitzgerald of Brooklyn to place an embargo on food shipments to England. In a graphic political cartoon, cynically captioned "The Hand Across the Sea," the *Irish World* featured John Bull's greedy, grasping paw clutching America's harvest while emaciated Americans stood by starving. The *Freeman's Journal* validated this assessment by sardonically remarking that "piles upon piles of provisions are ready to be shipped, whilst thousands of Americans are barely subsisting on the necessities of life." When the Germans made overtures to initiate peace negotiations in December, the *Freeman's Journal*, also controlled by the Ford family, glibly forecast that if nothing came of this offer, the "moral responsibility" for the continuance of warfare would be "upon England and her Allies." When the Allies rejected Germany's offer, the paper quickly reminded readers of its earlier judgment.[34]

Despite her overtures, Germany's cause in the United States suffered another serious setback in Irish American and Catholic circles

---

33. *Catholic Transcript*, October 12, 1916.
34. *Irish World*, December 2 and 9, 1916; *Freeman's Journal*, December 16, 1916, January 6 and March 17, 1917.

CHAPTER 6

when reports circulated that the Germans were using Belgian deportees as forced labor in Germany. The Kaiser's government had never recovered from the stigma attached to it by the atrocities committed in the first few weeks of the war as German troops pushed through helpless Belgium. Although this most recent practice was forcefully condemned in both the national and Catholic press, Germany's remaining friends in the Irish American and Catholic press rushed to her defense. O'Mahoney, a consistent friend of the Germans, argued that many Belgians "refused to return, being completely satisfied with their work and pay." Faintly praising Germany's magnanimity by her willingness to "right a wrong when it is pointed out to her," O'Mahoney, in a thinly veiled reference to the British, claimed that "there are those who never admit they are wrong." Tierney in *America* also attempted to defend Germany by weakly arguing that the "wages were good," disingenuously adding that the Germans had initiated this labor program to "counter the demoralizing effects of continuing idleness" among the Belgians.[35]

While attacks on Great Britain had always been a strategic element of the professional Irish American press, they now took every opportunity after the election to sustain Wilson in his mandate to preserve peace. There was general support in the Irish American community for Wilson's second attempt to arbitrate a peace settlement in January 1917. On the 22nd of that month, Wilson gave his famous "Peace without Victory" address. In it he enjoined the European powers to forsake unrealistic postwar aims, as well as to ensure the rights and liberties of all nations. While some Irish Americans disagreed with the particulars of Wilson's suggestions, they did warmly endorse his plea for peace. Although it would not be until after the United States entered the war that Wilson fully articulated the aim of self-determination for all peoples, the seed of this idea was planted in the minds of many Irish Americans and before long would signal a strategic shift with respect to advancing claims for Irish liberation.[36]

---

35. *Catholic World,* December 9, 1916; *Catholic Transcript,* November 30, 1916; Denver *Catholic Register,* January 4, 1917; *Indiana Catholic and Record,* December 29, 1916; *America,* November 25, 1916.

36. *Gaelic-American,* January 27, 1917. Even Jeremiah O'Leary, Wilson's

1917: TOWARD A DECLARATION OF WAR

Wilson's attempt to negotiate a peaceful settlement to the European war were brushed aside when the British rejected the offer and the Kaiser's government decided it must attempt to win the war outright before the great power across the Atlantic had a chance to join it. To wit, the Germans announced on January 31 that they would resume unrestricted submarine warfare against Allied and neutral shipping. Convinced by his military advisors that Americans would be unable to contribute effectively to the Allied war effort in the short term, the Kaiser elected to renege on the Sussex Pledge and gamble on breaking the military stalemate on the western front. Three days later, the Wilson administration severed diplomatic ties with Imperial Germany, and Count von Bernstorff was sent packing. For Irish Americans, the diplomatic rupture did not bode well for the maintenance of neutrality. Most segments in the community nevertheless continued to hope that a declaration of war could be averted.

Radical Irish American nationalists counseled against the growing martial spirit in the nation. With the possibility of war now imminent, the professional press abandoned its brief rapprochement with the Wilson administration and accused it of "un-neutral action," for seeking "war with Germany for doing with the submarine the same thing England is doing with battleships and cruisers." Earlier, John Devoy had contended that the German resumption of unrestricted submarine warfare was not a legitimate reason for war, and that the president was culpable for having placed such "unreasonable demands" upon its use. A national conference of Irish organizations meeting in New York issued a statement cautioning against any American involvement with the Allies that would contribute to the continued "subjugation of Ireland, India and Egypt to English rule." The professionals also appealed to arguments that financiers and munitions manufacturers were manipulating popular opinion in favor of the Allies for their own selfish, self-aggrandizing purposes. The *Irish World* bemoaned the immorality of American lives being sacrificed "in order to safeguard Mr. Morgan's rotten investment," and

---

implacable adversary, applauded the president's initiative. See Kelly, "A Biographical Sketch, 62.

CHAPTER 6

followed up the next week by mocking Wall Street for having "bet on the wrong side of the European war."[37]

Catholic papers sympathetic to the aspirations of the Clan-na-Gael and the professional press also attempted to warn their readers about jingoist propaganda. Wary of Britain's naval strength, the *Freeman's Journal* cautioned that American succor to the Allies would ensure English emergence from victory as "absolute in trade as she is now in her rule of the seas." Rather than ignore Germany's controversial renewal of submarine warfare, this same paper conjectured that it was the "only way Germany has of fighting back." Shannon of Chicago's *New World* exasperatedly advised his readers that Wall Street was rejoicing over the diplomatic rupture with Germany because stock gamblers "believe they are entering upon an era of stock speculations which will put millions in their pockets." Reviving Dr. Samuel Johnson's old bromide about patriotism being the "last refuge of the scoundrel," Shannon pointed out that "true patriotism for Americans ... is to be loyal to the Constitution." But the handful of Catholic editors who continued to rail against Britain and the avarice of American commerce were swimming against the tide—and rather knew it, even while they persisted in doing so.[38]

For most Catholic newspapers, the diplomatic break with Germany marked a cathartic moment in their assessments of the new geo-political reality. Without entirely forsaking the cause of American neutrality, Catholic sentiment, particularly among Irish American editors, drifted towards coming to terms with the probability of war with Germany. Still, some papers continued to resist overt demonstrations of militarism. While urging prudence and restraint, these papers were conspicuous in expressing full-blown patriotic sentiment. Father C. F. Thomas of the Baltimore *Catholic Review*, basking in the approval of Cardinal Gibbons, made it clear that his paper had "no views on the controversy," and that it was "neither for nor against the Allies,

37. *Gaelic-American,* February 10 and 24, 1917; *Documents Relative to the Sinn Fein Movement,* 28; *Irish World,* February 17 and 24, 1917.
38. *Freeman's Journal,* February 3 and 10, 1917; *New World,* February 10, 1917.

neither for nor against the Central Powers." At the same time, Thomas was unequivocal in venturing the opinion that "as Americans ... we have no hesitation to say that we should be found among the most patriotic and American ... for with us patriotism is no mealy-mouthed platitude." In Milwaukee, Humphrey Desmond, in a diocese heavily populated by German Americans, iterated similar ambivalence over the new direction in the European war by acknowledging that while it was understandable that Germany had been driven to deploy submarines, the United States could not permit it to do so unopposed.[39]

Many other Catholic newspapers started to shed their entrenched positions on neutrality in favor of confronting the decision Germany had taken on unrestricted submarine warfare. Dr. Hart proclaimed that there was "but one course for Catholic citizens to pursue, unswerving devotion to the United States; wholehearted loyalty to the Government at Washington." Urging Catholics to "stand by the President through thick and thin," Hart concluded that to do "anything less is treason to God and country." The *Catholic Messenger* decided that "Germany herself has forced the existing relations upon the United States," and lectured its readers that "now is the time to stand behind the government." Father Whelan's consistent optimism that neutrality could be preserved gave way to desperation once diplomatic relations with Germany were severed. "Despite whichever way our sympathies have heretofore gone as to the nations at war," intoned Whelan, "with the severance of diplomatic relations with one side, they must now remain suspended." Most revealing in Whelan's commentary, however, was his morbid and tortured assessment that America and Germany would soon be mortal enemies:

> Our present course of war is with the Germans. Yet how we love them—the German people—our brothers in Christ. We may have to kill them, while they kill us."[40]

39. Baltimore *Catholic Review,* February 10, 1917; *Catholic Citizen,* February 10. 1917.

40. *Catholic Telegraph,* March 8, 1917; *Catholic Messenger,* February 8, 1917; Brooklyn *Tablet,* February 10, 1917.

CHAPTER 6

There were, moreover, significant defections from the strictly neutral positions previously held by some Irish Americans. The rush to assert loyalty to the government during the diplomatic crisis of the winter of 1917 signaled a significant departure from opinions held mere weeks before. The most startling metamorphosis was that of Jeremiah O'Leary. After the administration's decision to sever diplomatic ties with Germany, O'Leary felt compelled to declare, however qualified, his patriotic priorities. Fulminating that he did not want anyone to make a mistake as to where he stood, O'Leary expounded in a somewhat equivocating manner, that if the United States went to war with Germany, "whether justly or unjustly, wisely or unwisely, for better or worse," his "heart and soul, and my life, if need be, are at her service." The FOIF, while encouraging Wilson to remain neutral, countenanced the real possibility of war with Germany and hoped to piggyback Irish freedom as part of the war commitment. Perceived as vacillating during a national crisis by an ever-mounting number of other Irish Americans, the FOIF found itself criticized for framing policies that were not "based upon solely American considerations." And the Ancient Order of Hibernians, heretofore tepid at best in their support of the administration, now pledged their complete support. Such a display of patriotic allegiance from former detractors prompted Wilson to respond to their president, Joseph McLaughlin:

> Your generous offer of February 5th, pledging to the Administration, the unswerving loyalty of the two-hundred and fifty-thousand members of the Ancient Order of Hibernians, is very heartening to me, and I thank you and them for their inspiring reassurance.[41]

---

41. O'Leary quoted in Kelly, "Biographical Sketch," 72; *New York Times*, February 11, 1917; *Catholic Messenger*, February 15, 1917. Wilson's response to the Hibernians was printed in *Pittsburgh Catholic*, February 15, 1917. In May 1917, the FOIF organized a petition to be sent to the president and the Congress "with an alleged 500,000 American signatures," which concluded that the "only final settlement must be the complete independence of Ireland." See Michael Doorley, *Irish-American Diaspora Nationalism*, 65.

1917: TOWARD A DECLARATION OF WAR

Significant attitudinal shifts were beginning to find their way into print from some of Wilson's staunchest Irish American critics in the press. O'Mahoney, an inveterate opponent of the administration's neutral policies in the past, continued to call for caution and prudence, but he intimated that should war break out, "all American citizens must be as one man, united behind our common government." He further stipulated that the government could rely upon Irish Americans in any conflict by flatly declaring that no one could "question the loyalty of the Irish race in America to the American flag and American institutions." Tierney's *America* departed from its longstanding adherence to neutrality, as it could not stomach Germany's renewal of unrestricted submarine warfare. Tierney summed up his position by quoting erstwhile presidential hopeful Charles Evans Hughes's statement in the *New York Sun* that "we are all Americans, standing loyally behind President Wilson." The New York *Catholic News*, an occasional critic of Great Britain, also adopted a patriotic stance in this diplomatic crisis. Averring that this was "no time for discussion," one of its leading editorials bluntly instructed readers that "President Wilson has acted, and every American citizen must now support him."[42]

While Catholic spokesmen remained hopeful that hostilities could be averted, the diplomatic crisis of February 1917 revealed their willingness to sanction force if required. Many leading Irish American Catholics had become advocates of American preparedness despite their non-interventionist inclinations. Cardinal Gibbons, along with Bishop Ireland, was one of the most prominent. Staunchly opposed to preparedness throughout 1915, Gibbons had discerned a shift in the national mood on this issue by 1916. The *Lusitania* crisis had propelled the administration into regarding as vital the nation's ability to defend its interests. This urgency led to the resignation of Secretary of War Lindley Garrison from the cabinet in February 1916, largely a result of his opposition to strengthening the nation's defensive capabilities. Gibbons's conversion to the preparedness cause began in early 1916 with his approval of universal military training to foster patriotic unity

---

42. *Indiana Catholic*, February 8 and March 16, 1917; *America*, February 10, 1917; *Catholic News*, February 10, 1917.

CHAPTER 6

and fuse together the disparate ethnic groups in the nation. The cardinal was keenly aware that his faithful comprised most of these foreign elements. In February 1916, Gibbons declined to endorse a petition circulated by the Reverend Frederick Lynch, Secretary of the Church Peace Union, which argued against the president's preparedness campaign. Gibbons evidently saw the connection between preparedness and patriotism, as well as the advantages attached to promoting these concepts among Catholics. Apparently, Gibbons was so successful at promoting preparedness that even the jingoist Teddy Roosevelt applauded his efforts.[43]

Gibbons was not the sole Irish American Catholic prelate to boost the preparedness campaign. Archbishop John Ireland of St. Paul, a former chaplain in the Civil War, and a close acquaintance of Roosevelt, dismissed as inconsequential fears that as the war dragged on the United States might not be able to remain neutral. The Catholic press had for some time debated the risks of preparedness, and many editors had resolved as early as the *Lusitania* and *Sussex* crises that preparation was more desirable since it seemed "more likely that we may become involved." Meanwhile, the Knights of Columbus did their share in the preparedness campaign by increasing the number of "patriotic exercises" in which "Catholic patriotism and loyalty to the nation were repeatedly offered to the nation." By remarking that "there is only one place for the United States and that is to be first," the renowned non-interventionist Bourke Cockran approved Wilson's contention that the United States should upgrade its naval capabilities. In such a context, it was hardly surprising that Irish American Catholics were willing to go to war following the disruption in diplomatic relations with Germany in early 1917. Such sentiment was perhaps best captured in the remarks of the chairman of the Knights of Columbus Commission on Religious Prejudice, Colonel P. H. Callahan, at a St. Patrick's Day dinner in Louisville, Kentucky, when he proposed that if war was necessary, he

---

43. Link, *Confusions and Crises,* 51–54; Allen Sinclair Will, *The Life of Cardinal Gibbons, Archbishop of Baltimore* (Baltimore: E. P. Dutton Press, 1922), 2:812; Ellis, *James Cardinal Gibbons,* 2:232; Theodore Roosevelt to James Cardinal Gibbons, August 11, 1916, *Gibbons Papers,* Archives of the Archdiocese of Baltimore.

would be ready and would "demand of you Irishmen here assembled to join this Irish Brigade and fight to uphold freedom."[44]

Imperial Germany's resumption of unrestricted submarine warfare in February 1917 had finally forced the Wilson administration into a position of intransigence from which there was little hope of retreating. Britain's judicial excesses in the 1916 Dublin uprising, and her continued harassment of US shipping, though irritating, paled in comparison to the human carnage wrought by the submarine. Invoking horrid memories of the *Lusitania* and other stricken vessels, Germany's strategic decision to resume indiscriminate sinking of Allied and neutral ships propelled the United States into the war in April 1917. The administration's decision to sever diplomatic relations with Germany forced Irish American Catholics, as it did all Americans, to profess their loyalty to the nation. Irish American Catholics aligned themselves with the administration's aggressive stance toward the Germans and prepared for war.

Even though most Irish Americans recognized the inevitability of hostilities, and that the nation was on the brink of war, some still pressed the non-interventionist cause. Professional Irish Americans spearheaded this effort in the dwindling weeks between the severance of diplomatic relations with Germany and the declaration of war. When, in the heat of patriotic effusiveness following the diplomatic break with Germany, pro-Allied sympathizers petitioned all Americans to sign a pledge of loyalty to the nation's defense, the *Gaelic-American* balked at such an attempt "to plunge this country into war for England's benefit." When Daniel Cohalan and several other prominent members of the Clan-na-Gael refused to profess this specific pledge of loyalty, the *Irish World* supported the Clan by reasoning that "to pledge loyalty to any official in a Republic, no matter how highly placed, is virtually treason to the Republic."[45]

44. Archbishop John Ireland to James Cardinal Gibbons, December 28, 1916, *Gibbons Papers*, Archives of the Archdiocese of Baltimore; *True Voice*, May 25, 1915; *Catholic Universe*, April 21, 1916, *Catholic Standard and Times*, April 8, 1916; Brooklyn *Tablet*, January 6, 1917; *Pittsburgh Catholic*, March 1, 1917; *Catholic Telegraph*, March 8, 1917; McGurrin, *Bourke Cockran: A Free Lance in American Politics*, 292. Callahan is quoted in *Pittsburgh Catholic*, March 29, 1917.

45. *Gaelic-American*, March 17, 1917; *Irish World*, March 24, 1917.

CHAPTER 6

A couple of Irish American Catholic prelates, for reasons entirely different than the Clan-na-Gael's, were also alarmed by what they felt was excessive militancy. Cardinal O'Connell observed that "hysterical flag waving" was not in the best interests of the country, especially when egged on by those so eager to rush to Britain's aid. The *Pittsburgh Catholic* printed a sermon by Bishop Michael Gallagher of Grand Rapids, Michigan, in which he indicated that there was "little or no sentiment in the country for war, and the President is deceived by the munitions managers and their press, when he thinks the people are clamoring for bloodshed." Many other Irish American Catholic editors added their voices of restraint by printing the text of Washington's Farewell Address, warning the country to avoid entangling alliances with foreign powers."[46]

Notwithstanding these voices of caution, the irrevocable slide towards war proceeded. Public outrage with Germany reached its zenith in March when the press reported some of the initial casualties of that nation's indiscriminate attacks upon American shipping. Tolerance for Germany was then virtually destroyed when the American government publicized the infamous Zimmermann Telegram. Sent by Foreign Minister Arthur Zimmermann over cables controlled by the British, it incredibly offered the Mexican government the restoration of lands seized by the Americans in the Mexican-American War if Mexico attacked the United States and distracted her from full involvement in the Great War. The profound stupidity of Zimmermann's overtures to Mexico left even the professional Irish American press stunned. While most Catholic papers made but brief mention of the Zimmermann plan, Tierney, who had resisted condemning Germany in the past, greeted the news with indignation, noting that at the very same time she was professing a desire to maintain friendly relations with the United States, the "Foreign Office at Berlin was taking measures to involve this country in war with Mexico and Japan." John Quinn was so apoplectically incensed by the Zimmermann Telegram that he wistfully

---

46. Boston *Pilot*, March 19, 1917; *Pittsburgh Catholic*, March 22, 1917; *Freeman's Journal*, February 24, 1917; *Catholic Telegraph*, February 23, 1917; *Pittsburgh Catholic*, March 22, 1917. In 1920 Bishop Gallagher was elected president of FOIF.

1917: TOWARD A DECLARATION OF WAR

declared that his one fear was the "the war will stop before we get into it." The vast majority of Irish Americans, while lining up behind the administration, still hoped that war could be avoided in March 1917. These hopes were shattered in April.

Woodrow Wilson went before a joint session of Congress on April 2, 1917 to seek a declaration of war against Imperial Germany and the Central Powers. He was not denied. In his address, directed largely to potentially disloyal German Americans and their sympathizers, Wilson made it clear that perfidy on their part would not be tolerated. Any disloyalty, Wilson intoned, would be "dealt with with a firm hand of stern repression." He doubted there would be any significant treason "except from a lawless and malignant few."[47]

Although resigned to the course of action dictated by America's declaration of war, the professional Irish American press did not initially greet this announcement without grumbling. Realizing that it was no longer feasible to promote Ireland's liberation via German military victory, the professionals embraced the inevitable, but harangued against any collusion with the British. The *Irish World* lamented that Wilson's address merely completed the administration's longstanding devious design of rushing into war to help "paint the map of the world British red." Later, the Fords caustically posited that the US' unwitting entry into the war was a capitulation to Cecil Rhodes's fatuous goal of returning the United States to the fold of the British Empire.[48]

John Devoy also succumbed to the nation's declaration of war, but unlike the Fords, he rejected the idea that the US would fight Britain's battles. Specifically referring to his life's mission of freeing Ireland, he instructed his readers that "this government of freemen gives no aid to England in stamping out the aspirations of the Irish people for freedom."[49]

---

47. *America,* March 10, 1917; John Quinn to Douglas Hyde, March 14, 1917, *John Quinn Papers,* New York Public Library; "Wilson's Address to Congress Advising That Germany's Course Be Declared War Against the United States (Delivered in Joint Session, April 2, 1917)," quoted in Shaw, *Messages and Papers of Woodrow Wilson,* 2:382.
48. *Irish World,* April 7 and June 23, 1917.
49. *Gaelic-American,* April 7, 1917.

CHAPTER 6

Despite their suspicion of the impending Anglo-American alliance, most professionals rallied to the flag. At another gathering at Carnegie Hall, marking the first anniversary of the Easter uprising, Daniel Cohalan led the assembled crowd in voicing "its unswerving loyalty to the United States of America." Cohalan and Devoy's acquiescence to the American war effort, and their personal pledges of loyalty to the state in the eventuality of war with Germany, were so pronounced as to disappoint fellow Clan-na-Gael member Joseph McGarrity, presaging a division in the ranks of the professional Irish Americans. Having recently professed his loyalty to the United States in the event of war with Germany, Jeremiah A. O'Leary made good on his promise to serve by offering his legal expertise to the government, though it would be a promise he would not keep. In Syracuse, James K. McGuire, who had actively promoted the expansion of the Friends of Irish Freedom in upstate New York, and who authored two books arguing that a German victory would be a boon to both Ireland and America, suddenly became an articulate advocate for "American First." Like Devoy and Cohalan, McGuire became "patriotic in both word and deed."[50]

Traditional Clan-na-Gael allies in the Catholic press joined other Irish Americans in expressing their support, albeit restrained, for the declaration of war. Tierney appeared resigned to the inevitable when he breezily quipped that "at last our country is at war." Disappointed by Germany's decisions in the months leading up to April, he concluded that "war is not our choice: strife has been thrust upon us by repeated and wanton violations of our rights." A. Brendan Ford of the *Freeman's Journal* observed without much enthusiasm that, since "Congress has declared that this country is at war," and since the Chief Executive will

---

50. Cohalan quoted in Brooklyn *Tablet;* Sean Cronin, *The McGarrity Papers* (Tralee, County Kerry, Ireland: Anvil Books, 1972), 27; Kelly, "Biographical Sketch," 66–67; Beadles, *The Syracuse Irish,* 264. Despite his implacable disdain for the British, Cohalan seemed to be bowing to the inevitable as early as January 1917, when he delivered an address at Carnegie Hall. "No men of any race," he declared, "have shed their blood more freely, or even recklessly, than have the men of our breed." Quoted in Michael Doorley, "Judge Daniel Cohalan: A Nationalist Crusader Against British Influence in American Life," *New Hibernia Review* 19, no.2 (Summer/Sambreadh 2015): 120.

1917: TOWARD A DECLARATION OF WAR

"execute that decree," it was the obligation of those "who appointed them both ... to do our part in fulfilling that law." After complimenting Montana Representative Jeannette Rankin for her "gutsy vote" against the declaration of war, Thomas V. Shannon solemnly announced that the nation was at war despite a divided House vote of 373–50. O'Mahoney of the *Indiana Catholic and Record* flatly stated that the declaration of war was the "last word" on the subject. However, unable to resist a parting shot at those Americans who had advocated intervention in the war, the sardonic editor quipped that "those who are anxious to get rid of the Hohenzollerns and Hapsburgs should not forget the Guelphs when they are cleaning up."[51]

If hardened Irish American nationalists were singing a somewhat restrained patriotic chorus of Americanism in April 1917, it is hardly startling that moderate and conservative Irish Americans and Catholics were outdoing themselves in patriotic, even chauvinistic, fervor. Most Irish Americans were unreserved in their support for the government and acknowledged it openly and repeatedly in public demonstrations. In the public sector, prominent Irish Americans stepped forward with resounding declarations, pledging not only their personal commitment to the nation's cause but that of their compatriots as well. Despite his prior non-interventionist leanings, the elder statesman of the Irish American community, Bourke Cockran, applied crusading zest to his endorsement of Wilson's war message. Noting the president's "lofty conception of the law," Cockran claimed that "posterity will hold this address to be the weightiest uttered by any public man since Urban II preached the first crusade at Clermont-Ferrand more than eight-hundred years ago."[52]

Bourke Cockran's adorned message of support for the president was merely a small sample of the voluminous encomiums heaped upon the president's call for war offered by prominent Irish Americans in public life. Catholic Senators John Phelan and Thomas J. Walsh strongly endorsed the declaration of war, though House Representative

---

51. *America,* April 14, 1917; *Freeman's Journal,* April 17, 1917; *New World,* April 14, 1917; *Indiana Catholic and Record,* April 6, 1917.

52. Bourke Cockran to Joseph P. Tumulty, April 13, 1917, *Bourke Cockran Papers,* New York Public Library.

CHAPTER 6

Jeff McLemore, an Irish American Protestant, was one of the few who voted against it. Most Irish American Catholic legislators, including John T. Fitzgerald, who had earlier opposed food shipments to the Allies, elected to sustain the president in his resolve and to allow the use of congressional facilities for the "recruiting of men, the development of economic resources or the relief of those to whom the war will bring distress."[53]

In New York, Mayor John Purroy Mitchel, who had been an ardent supporter of the Allied cause since the beginning of the war, had emerged as a leading spokesman for the preparedness campaign in the wake of the *Lusitania* crisis. The war's declaration inspired him to declare the first week of May 1917 as "Navy Week," during which he challenged his constituents to exceed the enlistment quotas established for them. Mitchel's fellow New Yorker, John Quinn, saw in Congress's declaration the culmination of hopes he had harbored since 1914. Long believing that a defeat of German arms was in both America's and Ireland's interests, Quinn wasted little time in lofty rhetoric but set out actively to aid the cause. Seeing a successful settlement of the Irish question as a vehicle to unify Irish American support of the Allies, Quinn headed a delegation of New York Irish Americans that met with British minister Arthur Balfour during his visit to Washington. He proudly wrote Theodore Roosevelt that the delegation would be comprised of a most eclectic and ecumenical representation, with two Catholic priests, representing Catholic Irishmen, two prominent Irish

---

53. See *Congressional Record*, 65th Congress, 2nd Session, April 5, 1917, 55 Cong. Rec., Part I, 261, 412–13 (1917). It is difficult to distinguish Catholics from Protestants by Irish surnames alone. In the Senate, none of the six who voted against the declaration of war bore Irish surnames. In the House, in addition to McLemore, Representatives Keating and Connelly were the only members with Irish surnames who voted against the declaration. Keating was Catholic. Connelly's religious affiliation could not be determined. In the House, Representatives Sullivan, O'Shaughnessy, and Walsh were identifiable Catholics. Representative McLaughlin was a Protestant. The religious affiliation of Representatives McFadden, Dempsey, Glynn, and Gallagher could not be ascertained. All these members voted for the declaration of war. Fitzgerald's remarks can be found in Edwin Kilroe, Abraham Kaplan, and Joseph Johnson, *Tammany: A Patriotic History* (New York: Democratic Committee, 1924), 59.

1917: TOWARD A DECLARATION OF WAR

American Protestants, and "Morgan J. O'Brien and myself, representing American neutral Irishmen, but nationalists."[54]

With the break in diplomatic relations with Germany, mainstream Irish American organizations and societies rapidly fell in line with the administration's view of the European conflict. The declaration of war merely tapped a latent ultra-patriotism awaiting an opportunity for expression. From across the nation, various chapters of the Ancient Order of Hibernians endorsed the decision to enter the war. Despite the contention in David Emmons's study of Butte, Montana's Irish American community that "the American declaration of war broke the heart of Irish America," this city's Irish American contingent was, nevertheless, willing to express its fidelity to the president's decision. In New York, the Friendly Sons of St. Patrick passed a resolution offered by Senator James A. O'Gorman at their quarterly meeting on May 3, vowing their "unequivocal support to the President and Commander-in-Chief."[55]

The most effusive display of patriotism and Americanism in April 1917 came from the American Catholic Church and press. Throughout the years of American neutrality, both the hierarchy and the Irish American Catholic press maintained a cautious policy of aloofness and detachment from partisan views on the war. Conscious of its own multicultural composition, and conscientiously sensitive to accusations of disloyalty during the anti-hyphenate campaign, the Church assiduously refused to take sides in the European conflict. The declaration of war liberated the American Catholic Church from these self-imposed restrictions and provided a timely opportunity to

---

54. *New York Times,* "Catholics Pledge Loyalty to Nation," April 20, 1917, p. 6; John Quinn to Theodore Roosevelt, May 1, 1917, *John Quinn Papers,* New York Public Library.

55. Several of these declarations were approvingly reported in Catholic newspapers. See *Catholic Messenger,* April 19, 1917; *The Monitor,* April 19, 1917; *Pittsburgh Catholic,* April 26, 1917; Boston *Pilot,* April 21, 1917. It should be noted that in Butte, while there was little enthusiasm among Irish Americans for the declaration of war, and that several of the local priests were supporters of physical force Irish nationalism, the local ordinary, Bishop John Carroll of Helena, was a strong supporter of Americanism. See Emmons, *The Butte Irish,* 360–61. See also Telegram, Michael Baxter, President of the American Irish Club of Butte to Thomas J. Walsh, April 2, 1917, *T. J. Walsh Papers,* Library of Congress.

prove that American Catholics, irrespective of their native lands, were American citizens of the highest order.

Cardinal Gibbons was in the vanguard of Irish American Catholic support for the president and the nation. Within days of the president's appeal to Congress, and before the actual vote declaring war, Gibbons outlined how Catholics were to respond to the impending crisis. He importuned all American citizens to do their duty and to uphold the president and the legislative department in the "solemn obligations" that confronted the nation. Acts, more than words, were the crucible of one's loyalty and citizenship, Gibbons stated. "Absolute and unreserved obedience to his country's call," was his fundamental message. The following day, in an interview with the *New York Times*, Gibbons expanded upon his views on the responsibilities of American Catholic citizenship as it related to bearing arms in defense of the country:

> Above all else we must be loyal to our country ... there should be no hesitancy on the part of able-bodied men in answering the call that has gone forth to man the ships that protect our shores. I hope Catholic young men will step up and take their places in the front ranks ... they should obey whatever our Congress decides is for the good of the country.[56]

Independently, various Irish American prelates also rushed to support the government and proclaim American Catholic patriotism. In Charleston, South Carolina, Bishop William T. Russell, in tones reminiscent of the days of royal absolutism, instructed Catholics that, as "God is the author of every just government ... from Him all powers derive their authority," the president and Congress "rule by this divine right ... and the citizen is bound to uphold the authority of the state in obeying its laws and by defending it if need be with his life." Bishop John P. Farrelly of Cleveland reflected hierarchical sentiment

---

56. Richard C. Murphy and Lawrence J. Mannion, *The History of the Society of the Friendly Sons of St. Patrick in the City of New York* (New York: J. C. Dillon, 1962), 438; Gibbons' Statement on the Outbreak of War, April 5, 1917, copy in the *Gibbons Papers,* Archives of the Archdiocese of Baltimore.

1917: TOWARD A DECLARATION OF WAR

when he responded to the president's call by declaring that there was "no government in the world today more entitled to the loyalty and devotion of its Catholic citizens than is that of the United States."[57]

Cardinal John Farley of New York, who had walked a political tightrope for several years over any favoritism displayed toward Germany and the ensuing debate over the best course for Irish liberation, quickly made his call to arms in a circular read in all churches in the Archdiocese. At one point, Farley stated that while he had hoped "peace could [have] come by arbitration and diplomacy ... it would seem, however, that no permanent peace can be hoped for except through the defeat of German arms in the field or the repudiation of the Prussian autocracy by the German people themselves." His clever condemnation of Prussia, a state where Lutherans dominated, did not salve the wounded pride of Germans in New York, nor did it spare him the indignation of ardent Irish American nationalists. Farley intoned that Catholics would rush to heed the call to arms, as Catholic manhood and American citizenship required such. He quashed any allegations regarding the lack of Catholic patriotism by noting that "every branch of the service is filled with Catholics, and it is the testimony of all who are qualified to judge that their patriotism, their efficiency, their orderly and soldierly conduct are of the highest type."[58]

Coincidentally, a convocation of archbishops was in session at the Catholic University of American in Washington, D.C. in the days following the declaration of war. In unison, the assembled prelates offered "their most sacred and sincere loyalty and patriotism to our country, our government and our flag." Acknowledging with gratitude the many freedoms Catholics had enjoyed under the American flag, the

---

57. Bishop Russell's comments were quoted in the *New York Times,* May 14, 1917; Circular Letter, John P. Farrelly, to the priests of the Diocese of Cleveland, April 9, 1917, copy in the *Gibbons Papers,* Archives of the Archdiocese of Baltimore. Farrelly was appointed by Mayor Harry L. Davis to the Cleveland War Commission and ordered English to be spoken at all German churches and schools in the diocese. See Nelson J. Callahan and William F. Hickey, *The Irish-Americans and Their Communities in Cleveland* (Cleveland: Cleveland State University, 1978).

58. Farley is quoted in Kate Feigherty, "Timely and Substantial Relief," in Grey, *Ireland's Allies,* 287. See also *New York Times,* "Farley Endorses War," April 22, 1917, p. 6.

CHAPTER 6

archbishops pledged the unstinting loyalty of every American Catholic citizen. Noting that they were inspired by neither hate nor fear, "but by the holy sentiment of truest patriotic fervor and zeal," the bishops stood ready and committed, as did their flocks, "to cooperate in every way possible with our President and National Government to the end that the great and holy cause of liberty shall triumph." Then, perhaps, betraying the innate insecurity of a suspect religion and culture, the archbishops declared:

> Our people now, as ever, will rise as one man to serve the nation; our priests and consecrated women will once again, as in every former trial of our country, win by their bravery and heroism, and their service, new admiration and approval.

Wilson was effusive in his thanks for the "very remarkable resolutions" made by the bishops at Catholic University, finding it consoling that "men of such large influence should act in so large a sense of patriotism and so admirable a spirit of devotion to our common country."[59]

Perhaps the most unexpected hierarchical outburst of patriotism came from Cardinal O'Connell of Boston. Throughout the period of American neutrality, he had often been a critic of the pro-British American press, and as late as March 1917 had warned the nation of "hysterical flag-waving." Upon hearing of the declaration of war, however, O'Connell abandoned his criticism and revealed in his instructions to Boston's faithful a patriotism bordering on jingoism. "There is but one sentiment possible today," he commanded, and "that is absolute unity." The country was at war now and needed every "man, woman, and child ... to strengthen her, to hearten her, and to stand faithfully by her until her hour of glorious triumph shall arrive."[60]

---

59. Open Letter of the Catholic Archbishops of America, April 1917, copy in the *Gibbons Papers,* Archives of the Archdiocese of Baltimore; Woodrow Wilson to Cardinal Gibbons, April 27, 1917, in Link, *The Papers of Woodrow Wilson,* 42:145. See also Dohen, *Nationalism and American Catholicism,* 148–49.

60. Boston *Pilot,* April 14, 1917.

1917: TOWARD A DECLARATION OF WAR

The hierarchy found willing and able allies in the Catholic press for the promotion of patriotism among its faithful. Several Irish American Catholic editors took a serious view of the outbreak of war and attempted to convince their readers that the conflict had been thrust upon the American people by German aggression. "The struggle is not of our own making," reasoned O'Flanagan, blaming both the renewal of submarine warfare and the recent intrigues of the German Foreign Ministry as reasons why the Germans were culpable for provoking the "armed hostility of the United States." In unveiled cynicism about Representative Jeannette Rankin's vote against the declaration of war, Thomas P. Hart in Cincinnati blandly stated, "We feel sorry for Mrs. Rankin." Burke of the *Catholic World*, the one steadfast supporter of the Allied cause, wrote of the impending outbreak of war with what was tantamount to smug vindication of his longstanding views. Hailing the great truth of the era that the United States had never desired war and had done everything in its power to avoid it, he placed the entire blame for its coming upon the Germans, whom he thought would "stand guilty before the judgment of God not only for its beginning, but for all the murder, the suffering and the bitterness that will follow upon its prosecution."[61]

While some Irish American Catholic editors dwelled on the grim responsibilities facing American Catholics, others were ebullient in expressing patriotic sentiment. Father D. E. Hudson, generally reluctant to venture opinions during the neutral years, now suggested that it was the imperative duty of each citizen "to show as much patriotism as he can, and to refrain from any word or act that would impair the patriotism of others." Humphrey Desmond in Milwaukee concurred in Hudson's patriotic exhortations by quipping, "better a little surplus of effusion than crabbed reserve." And McKearney in Cleveland addressed the need for American Catholics, presumably Irish American ones, to extend a cooperative hand to Great Britain:

> We have great allies, and we must stand or fall with them. There can be no such thing as "hoping the United States wins but that England loses." People in this

---

61. *Catholic Transcript,* April 5, 1917; *Catholic Telegraph,* April 12, 1917; *Catholic World,* April 5, 1917.

CHAPTER 6

country do not love England. We have sound reason for not loving her. But we are fighting the same fight and must win.[62]

While prodding their readers to dizzying heights of patriotic ardor, Irish American Catholic editors could not restrain themselves from brandishing ethnic pride, sometimes at the expense of America's new allies. The Denver *Catholic Register* forecast that the Germans would find the American Navy quite different from the Royal Navy. Boasting that "there are so many Irish in America that our country loves a hot fight," Francis Smith predicted that "it will be utterly impossible to keep Uncle Sam's ships safely hidden in port." In his report of the April 17 meeting of Irish Americans at Carnegie Hall, Whelan in Brooklyn proudly reflected that "there is no stronger throb of patriotism beating in the heart of any American than that which thrills the heart of the American of Irish descent." Upon inspecting military recruitment stations, Whelan, like others, slid into a mawkish display of ethnic pride. Observing the closely packed columns of khaki-clad young men marching with measured steps to their country's call in this hour of need, Whelan claimed that one could not be deceived by their appearances. "They look Irish, they are Irish," he thundered, "the Irish in America are Americans first, last and all the time, and they are ready to fight to prove it." Two months after the war's declaration, an article in St. Louis's Catholic paper, the Western Watchman, in a city with a large German population, Jay Elmer Fox reported on a rally organized by Fathers O'Brien and McFadden. "Our war is a holy war, a crusade for humanity, for the purpose of rescuing homes desecrated by the German barbarians who must be taught the lesson of their lives," Father O'Brien waxed rhapsodically. He finished with the instruction that, Catholics of America should, "[G]o ... and teach these barbarians what American citizens and soldiers are like."[63]

The Knights of Columbus, hesitant to express opinions during the years of American neutrality, now came to the unfettered support of the

62. *Ave Maria*, April 21, 1917; *Catholic Citizen*, April 7, 1917; *Catholic Universe*, April 20, 1917.
63. Brooklyn *Tablet*, May 23, 1917; *Western Watchman*, June 22, 1917.

1917: TOWARD A DECLARATION OF WAR

American government. Presented with the unprecedented opportunity to demonstrate Catholic patriotism, Supreme Knight John Flaherty pledged the aid of nearly a half-million members to the president and nation. As an incentive for enlistment, the Board of Directors fortified this pledge by suspending an "extra-hazardous risks" insurance exemption clause for the war effort. Flaherty's pledge of fidelity was reinforced by the many Knights of Columbus councils throughout the nation. The Admiral Dewey Council in Brooklyn recommended that the two largely ceremonial regiments of Knights be recruited to "full regimental strength" and be drilled so that they could be offered to "President Wilson as the K of C contribution to the volunteer army."[64]

In May 1917, Flaherty presented Wilson plans for tendering tangible assistance to the war effort. Reminding the president that the Knights had sponsored fifteen centers of support at the Mexican front with the support of the American military at the various camps on the southern border, Flaherty promised a greatly expanded expenditure for the looming conflict if Wilson approved. "May we, in modesty, add that we expect to furnish more men for service than any other organization," the Grand Knight proposed, and that "it will be as with the case at the Mexican front, be open to all men in the service." A. G. Bagley, a Knight who had served on the Commission on Religious Prejudice, expressed concern that Irish American radicals were still balking at supporting the war effort. He feared that their actions would "bring the patriotism of Catholics into question." Referring specifically to Father Peter Yorke's nationalist newspaper, the *Leader*, Bagley quoted one edition that branded Wilson as a "Judas Iscariot" for allying American fortunes with Great Britain. Consequently, Bagley offered the ambitious recommendation that the Knights establish quarters in every training camp in the country. He was motivated by the belief that the benefits derived from publicizing the Knights' activities "would counteract" any intimations of Catholic disloyalty."[65]

---

64. Maurice Francis Egan and John B. Kennedy, *The Knights of Columbus in Peace and War,* 2 vols. (New Haven, CT: Knights of Columbus Press, 1920), 2:216–18

65. John Flaherty to Woodrow Wilson, May 23, 1917, quoted in Christopher Kaufmann, *Faith and Fraternalism: The History of the Knights of Columbus,*

CHAPTER 6

Bagley's concerns over potential manifestations of Irish American Catholic dissension were largely unfounded. Opposition to the government from virtually all Irish American quarters had evaporated the moment war was declared. Irish American Catholics of all political persuasions flocked to sustain the president and government through an explosion of patriotic expression. The American declaration of war provided the overall Irish American Catholic community with a unique opportunity to demonstrate their worthiness as American citizens. While ardent Irish American nationalists were forced by America's entry into the war to develop new strategies for expediting Irish freedom, the vast majority of Irish Americans lined up behind the government because, as one observer of the period suggested, "they were more American than Irish ... they could no longer entertain thoughts of German victory."[66]

1882–1982 (New York: Scribner's, 1982), 193; Telegram, A. G. Bagley to William McGinley, April 14, 1917, quoted in Kaufmann, *Faith and Fraternalism,* 193.

66. Joseph P. O'Grady, "Irish-Americans, Woodrow Wilson and Self-Determination," *Records of the American Catholic Historical Society of Philadelphia* 74 (September 1963): 160.

CHAPTER 7

ONWARD CATHOLIC SOLDIERS: The Church and the War, 1917–1918

The entry of the United States into war with Germany in April 1917 marked a watershed in the history of Irish American Catholicism. With only a few insignificant exceptions, Irish American Catholics stood solidly behind the Wilson administration once war had been declared. This was a major development, given their strong aversion to Britain's historical mistreatment of Ireland and their prior steadfast commitment to the neutralist cause. Irish American Catholics willingly chose to suspend these entrenched convictions and positions, and the choice they made suggests that their self-identity had reached a point where explicit overtures on behalf of Irish nationalism had become peripheral and secondary to their interests as Americans. The Irish American and Catholic contributions to the nation's martial spirit, and to the war effort itself, highlighted their willingness to subordinate their distinctly Irish predilections for the good of the nation. Most intriguing is the nearly instantaneous transformation into this militant patriotism. Much as a flip of the light switch illuminates a previously blackened room, most Irish Americans and Catholics abandoned whatever hesitations and misgivings they had previously harbored and threw themselves headlong into an electrically charged explosion of patriotic expression.

The declaration of war had the greatest impact on those in the Irish American community who had been singularly devoted to the goal of wresting Ireland from British dominion. America's entrance into the Great War required a reformulation of traditional strategies for advocating Irish freedom, particularly since fond hopes for a German

CHAPTER 7

victory were no longer tenable. New strategies would also have to be devised along lines that enabled avid Irish American nationalists to espouse Irish freedom without undermining the newly forged alliance with Great Britain. It proved to be a most difficult mission. The nineteen months of active American participation in the war marked the nadir in prospects for fulfilling the aspirations of this segment of the Irish American Catholic community.

Perhaps unwittingly, President Wilson himself may have provided Irish American radicals with a viable strategy for Irish independence, when shortly after the declaration of war, he spelled out the reasons for US entry. With an eye towards the restructuring of postwar Europe, Wilson articulated America's war aims in a way that obliquely foreshadowed the potential future of Ireland. "We are fighting for the liberty, the self-government, and the un-dictated development of all peoples," he solemnly intoned, "and every feature of that settlement that concludes this war must be conceived and executed for that purpose." He emphasized that no people should be "forced under sovereignty under which it does not wish to live."[1]

Irish American professionals were quick to pounce on Wilson's goal of self-determination for all peoples. The *Gaelic-American* issued a statement tying Irish independence to the president's intimation that "America's object is the promotion of Democracy and the restoration of their rights to all the oppressed peoples of Europe." While successful in discovering a basis on which to argue for Irish freedom, the professionals were unwilling to curb their attacks on the

---

1. A copy of this message can be found in the *Joseph P. Tumulty Papers*, Library of Congress. Ironically, Wilson rejected an attempt by Pope Benedict XV to present peace proposals to the warring nations on August 1, 1917. The reasons were myriad. The British and French saw the pontiff's proposals as an attempt to rescue Germany and Austria from total defeat, while Wilson was committed to his own program for postwar Europe, to name but two. Strangely, Wilson's Fourteen Points, announced in January 1918, contained several of Benedict's proposals. Some dissatisfaction was heard in American Catholic circles, but the Church had long hitched its wagon to Wilson's agenda. See Luca Castagna, *A Bridge Across the Ocean: The United States and the Holy See Between the Two World Wars* (Washington, DC: The Catholic University of America Press, 2014), 44–47. See also *National Catholic Reporter*, July 19, 2014.

ONWARD CATHOLIC SOLDIERS

British government. This failure eventually led to the suppression of several Irish American papers, and drew the censure of the greater Irish American Catholic community. Many ardent nationalists could not tolerate the fact that the British were now American allies, and many feared that American assistance in the war would only fortify British imperial aims. The radical press seized every opportunity to warn the nation of English perfidy. Throughout the summer of 1917, these papers complained that the American war effort, both in men and material, would be exploited by the British so that their position would be paramount when the war ended. At one point, the *Irish World* suggested that the British were plotting to lavishly expend American blood at the front so that England could "husband her manpower in a way that will make her military strength tell at the close of the war." Aware that they were adopting a position of dissent within America, the Irish American press championed the cause of civil liberties. Speaking in defense of free speech, John Devoy contended that his own paper was more truly loyal to the United States than the national press, whom he castigated in purple shades as "journalistic prostitutes ... working for England." They might fling charges of disloyalty and treason against "every man who stands for the independence of Ireland," he conjectured, but his paper intended to insist that "President Wilson should make good on his own solemn words."[2]

Vitriol of this magnitude revealed the desperate straits in which the professionals found themselves once *Columbia* clasped hands with *Britannia* in the spring of 1917. And caustic remarks like Devoy's could scarcely escape the attention of the government. In a national environment charged with suspicion for any utterances deemed unpatriotic, fervent Irish American nationalists came under scrutiny and censure. Under the direction of Postmaster General Albert S. Burleson, several Irish American papers were temporarily barred from the mails for printing uncomplimentary remarks concerning America's allies. The *Freeman's Journal* was presumed to be censured for printing an obscure statement of Thomas Jefferson's, to the effect that "Ireland ought to be free." Similarly, Burleson banned the *Irish World* from the mails for predicting

---

2. *Gaelic-American*, June 2, June 16, 1917; *Irish World*, August 14, 1917; *Gaelic-American*, August 18, 1917.

CHAPTER 7

that Palestine would become a British protectorate. O'Leary's satirical publication *Bull*, and Devoy's *Gaelic-American*, suffered similar fates, leading the old Fenian to reminisce later that "no one in open sympathy with Ireland's struggle against her oppressor during 1917 and 1918 was immune from raids." Tierney's *America* barely avoided a postal ban for printing a series of articles by various authors arguing the relative merits of Home Rule versus Irish independence.[3]

Irish organizations closely aligned with the agenda of the Clan-na-Gael were shunted into dormancy by the outbursts of patriotism following the declaration of war. Outside of New York City, the Friends of Irish Freedom essentially suspended all activities for the duration of the war. In New York, members of this organization were intimidated into virtual silence by the clamor of patriots who incited riots to obstruct and discredit anti-British demonstrations. The Ancient Order of Hibernians, which had been inconsistent in its support of the government until early 1917, abruptly announced the postponement of its 1918 annual convention, fearful that their convening might distract from the war effort. Not only did the American Truth Society suspend its activities, for what they were worth, but its founder, Jeremiah A. O'Leary, was accused of obstructing the draft. O'Leary was eventually arrested by government agents, who found him hiding under his car on a chicken farm in Washington State. Meanwhile, when the government released documents seized in the 1915 von Igel raid, Judge Daniel F. Cohalan found himself implicated as a pro-German conspirator. Wilson took a personal interest, and even delighted, in supplying as much incriminating evidence for the Justice Department as was needed to convict his nemesis Cohalan; the judge's personal connections to the Democratic Party barely allowed him to wriggle off the hook. And in Buffalo, the local Clan-na-Gael leader, John T. Ryan, fled the country to escape possible indictment.[4]

---

3. Horace C. Peterson and Gilbert C. Fite, *Opponents of War, 1917–1918* (Madison: University of Wisconsin Press, 1957), 100; Devoy, *Recollections of an Irish Rebel*, 471; see articles appearing in successive editions of *America*, beginning May 12, 1917.

4. Beadles, *The Syracuse Irish*, 264; John Dennis Moore to Woodrow Wilson, August 17, 1917, in Link, *The Papers of Woodrow Wilson*, 43:508–9. The

ONWARD CATHOLIC SOLDIERS

To award this degree of attention to the professional Irish in the wake of the American declaration of war is comparable to damning by faint praise. A minority position during the years of American neutrality, the extreme Irish American nationalist platform completely collapsed by the summer of 1917 when others in the Irish American and Catholic community shunned their positions. Bourke Cockran, representing a broad spectrum of Irish American public figures, stridently argued that continued agitation for Irish freedom was clearly inappropriate for American citizens. In a letter to a constituent in New York that was made public, Cockran argued that once the country had entered the war, it would require the "entire attention" of every American citizen. Consequently, Cockran "declined to discuss the Irish question except in so far as it may affect our part in the gigantic struggle against Germany and her allies." John Quinn not only eagerly accepted an invitation to address New Yorkers at the patriotic exercises celebrating Lafayette Day on September 6, 1917, but saw it as a chance to condemn the so-called "professional Irish-Americans" as "soapbox asses who advertise themselves as friends of Irish freedom." From the plains of North Dakota, Senator Porter J. McCumber railed against the "few Irish agitators," declaring that "whoever attacks Great Britain attacks us." In New York, up-and-coming political giant Al Smith, who would be elected as New York's first Irish American governor in the fall of 1918, refrained from indulging in any talk of Irish freedom during the war. He was willing to support relief efforts for struggling Irish women and children, victims of the war, but his speeches were deemed "lightweight," with none of the revolutionary rhetoric that dominated this debate. Like so many Irish American Catholics, Smith had cultivated a sentiment that was cultural and nostalgic when it came to Ireland's progress, but eschewed pronouncements that were political or nationalistic in tenor.[5]

Hibernians' decision to suspend their convention was found in Patrick McCartan, *With De Valera in America* (New York: Brentano, 1932), 39; O'Leary, *My Political Trial and Experiences,* 149; Woodrow Wilson to Frank Irving Cobb, September 26, 1917, in Link, *The Papers of Woodrow Wilson,* 44:265; F. M. Carroll, *American Opinion and the Irish Question,* 103.

    5. Bourke Cockran to Mr. McCormick, May 2, 1917, *Bourke Cockran*

CHAPTER 7

Among the Irish American Catholic hierarchy, none were more resolved to extinguish dissent against the government than Cardinals Gibbons and Farley. In October 1917, Gibbons accepted the position of honorary chairman of the League of National Unity to foster a vigorous prosecution of the war. In this capacity, Gibbons informed the president that he was working towards the end of convincing any American citizens of the "folly and grave disobedience" of all "unjust and ill-tempered criticism of national policies." In a veiled reference to Irish American nationalists, the cardinal consoled Wilson by asserting that he would see to it that his countrymen understood they might be looking at matters from "only one angle, whereas the government sees it from every viewpoint." Displays of loyalty such as Cardinal Gibbons's even comforted British Ambassador Spring Rice, who had earlier informed his government that "all Irish organizations including the majority of priests are now in the hands of Sinn Feiners." He could now assure London that practically all Irish Americans "were ready to follow Cardinal Gibbons who insisted on sole allegiance to the flag."[6]

Meanwhile, Cardinal Farley in New York effectively suppressed pockets of dissent and fractious antics among his own Irish American Catholic clergy, making it understood that all priests in his diocese were to steer clear of anything that the government might find objectionable. The Irish-born cardinal refused to tolerate any signs of overt Irish nationalism within his diocese, even though the war was beginning to wind down and his own days on earth were numbered. When word reached Farley that Father Peter Magennis, the newly elected president of the FOIF, was distributing Sinn Fein literature out of his parish on New York's lower East Side and was reportedly

---

Papers, New York Public Library; John Quinn to Jacob Epstein, September 12, 1917, *John Quinn Papers,* New York Public Library; McCumber quoted in Carroll, *American Opinion and the Irish Question,* 103; Robert A. Slayton, *Empire Statesman: The Rise and Redemption of Al Smith* (New York: Free Press, 2001), 176.

6. James Cardinal Gibbons to Woodrow Wilson, October 6, 1917, in Link, *The Papers of Woodrow Wilson,* 44:320–321; Sir Cecil Spring Rice to Arthur Balfour, July 13, 1917, in Stephen A. Gwynn, *The Letters and Friendships of Sir Cecil Spring Rice,* 2:407; A Letter and Telegram from Sir Cecil Spring Rice to Arthur James Balfour, January 4, 1918, in Link, *The Papers of Woodrow Wilson,* 45:455.

harboring weapons for revolutionary activity in Ireland, he came down hard on the Carmelite priest, effectively informing Magennis that if he did not cease and desist in these activities, he should seek to repair to another diocese. Adamantly, Farley cracked down on anything in his diocese that smacked of impugning the "loyalty of American Catholics." In March 1918, about the same time as he was corralling the activities of Magennis, Farley questioned the antics of a Monsignor James Power, an ecclesiastical figure prominent among the professional Irish Americans, regarding his activities at All Saints Parish in the Bronx. Farley admonished Power over reports that he was distributing Sinn Fein propaganda in his parish and that the Christian Brothers who taught in the parochial school had turned portraits of Woodrow Wilson to the wall in their classrooms. He forcefully reminded Power that this was not the moment "to permit in or about the church, or any institutions controlled by it, anything to which the United States government could take exception." Farley was eager to avoid the "Irish question" whenever he could, for fear of stirring up more trouble. He was about protecting the New York Catholic Church by proving to its detractors that it was a resoundingly American institution. Farley was ably assisted in this endeavor by the New York area Catholic press. Burke of the *Catholic World*, conspicuous among Irish American Catholic editors for his sustained support of the Allies during the neutral years, assailed the actions of dissenters by acerbically noting that the country has "its due share of the uninformed and ignorant, of the selfish and shirkers, perhaps even of secret traitors, at least among the foreign nationalities." The Brooklyn *Tablet* joined the assault upon the Irish American press by defiantly daring them to express their patently disloyal pro-German sympathies "without pretext or pretenses or subterfuge." There is little wonder then, that agitation for Irish independence was largely shelved by the greater Irish American and Catholic community until after the Armistice was signed.[7]

7. John Patrick Buckley, "The New York Irish," 159–61; Feighery, "Timely and Substantial Relief," in Grey, *Ireland's Allies*, 291. *Catholic World*, May 1917; Brooklyn *Tablet*, August 11, 1917. Farley died in September 1918. His successor, Archbishop (later Cardinal) Patrick Joseph Hayes, the son of Irish immigrants, was installed in March 1919. Circumstances had changed, and Hayes was able to

CHAPTER 7

No one agency within the American Catholic Church played a more constituent part in molding Irish American Catholic opinion during the Progressive Era than the Catholic press. Not only was it the foremost champion defending Catholicism from the assaults of nativist forces, the Catholic press in the main appealed to Irish Americans in Irish societies and local parishes to stay clear of the radical and professional agenda. The Catholic press praised and affirmed Irish American Catholics in their adoption of moderate and conservative views on Irish nationalism.

Notwithstanding the individual efforts of American prelates, such as Gibbons and Farley, the institutional Church lacked a national organization and platform to encourage Catholic support for the war effort. This lacuna was ably filled by the enterprising Paulist priest John E. Burke, the son of Irish immigrants in New York City. In late 1917, Burke organized the National Catholic War Council (NCWC), which gave the American hierarchy a unified voice in determining American Catholic obligations in supporting the administration's direction of war activities. The NCWC was a fully staffed organization in which Burke himself served as general secretary. Other than Cardinal O'Connell of Boston, the Church's other prelates seemed perfectly content and highly cooperative with the Council's direction. The NCWC proved so valuable and effective during the period of the war that it transformed into the National Catholic Welfare Council once the war concluded.[8]

As a rule, Irish American Catholics were largely powerless, and hence quiet, about the wave of anti-German hysteria that erupted in the United States in the months following the declaration of war. Throughout the country, but particularly in the Midwestern states—where German

---

entertain aspirations for Irish freedom along the lines of self-determination. When Eamon De Valera visited New York later in 1919, the archbishop welcomed him and donated a small amount of money to the Irish President's fund. For reasons why the cause of Irish nationalism languished in Cardinal O'Connell's Boston until the end of the war, see Damien Murray, *Irish Nationalists in Boston: Catholicism and Conflict, 1900–1928* (Washington, DC: The Catholic University of America Press, 2018), 1–90.

8. Thomas J. Shelley, "Twentieth-Century American Catholicism and Irish Americans," in Lee and Casey, eds., *Making the Irish American*, 585.

American populations were disproportionately high—bands of patriots and loyalty legions embarked on a purge of all things Teutonic. In St. Paul and Milwaukee, majestic bronze statues of *Germania* that adorned elegantly constructed late nineteenth-century buildings were unceremoniously removed and hauled away. In Cincinnati, a statue of *Germania*, mounted in a cove on a building's façade, found herself remodeled into a facsimile of *Columbia*, with a hastily applied, "*E Pluribus Unum*" etched into her gown. The sign adorning the entrance to the building was covered. Overnight, the *Deutsche Gegenseitige Versicherungs Gesellschaft von Cincinnati* firm was converted to the German Mutual Insurance Company of Cincinnati. In Chicago, the Grant Park statue of the German Enlightenment giant Goethe was vandalized one night. In April 1918, an unfortunate German immigrant, Robert Prager, known for his lackluster support for the war against Germany, was seized by a mob in Collinsville, Illinois, opposite the Mississippi River from St. Louis, and unceremoniously lynched by being hung from a lamp post. The subsequent trial acquitted all the defendants indicted in the incident. One juryman reportedly exclaimed, "Well I guess nobody can say we aren't loyal now."[9]

Perhaps no other state in the Union was more earmarked for scrutiny than Wisconsin. Nearly 60 percent of the population in its principal city, Milwaukee, claimed German ancestry. The nativist Wisconsin Legion of Loyalty undertook a vigorous campaign to identify sources of potential disloyalty and subversion. The Legion produced a map of the state that blanketed in black ten counties on a loop up the shore of Lake Michigan and around Lake Winnebago where loyalties were deemed most suspect. German street names were changed, the pronunciation of German-sounding towns was altered, and intense scrutiny was paid to those contributing to Liberty Loan Drives.

---

9. The fate of the *Germania* statues in Milwaukee, St. Paul, and Cincinnati can be found in *Milwaukee Sentinel*, April 17, 1981; Mary Lethert Wingerd, *Claiming the City: Politics, Faith and the Power of Place in St. Paul* (Ithaca, NY: Cornell University Press, 2003), 162; John Faherty, *Over the Rhine Buildings: German History Scorned No More* (Cincinnati: Cincinnati Enquirer, July 16, 2014), 1–3. Prager's unfortunate fate is found in Ronald Schaffer, *America in the Great War* (New York: Oxford University Press, 1991), 26.

CHAPTER 7

Schools, both public and parochial, were pressured to drop German as a foreign language elective. One professor of German studies at Northland College in Ashland was tarred and feathered by local thugs. The Pabst Theater in Milwaukee was pressured into canceling plays, operas, and symphonic performances that featured composers such as Mozart, Bach, and Beethoven. Members of the Wisconsin Loyalty Legion sent letters to the Pabst owners, pointing out that the company's German entertainment was offensive since the United States was at war with Germany, and concluded by flatly declaring that "German language plays" were of "no appreciable educational value." Both Catholic and Lutheran churches were chided for continuing to conduct services in German. In the Church's defense, one Catholic prelate, Archbishop John Glennon of St. Louis, attempted a meek rebuttal of such measures, noting that, "We are not making war on languages but on false principles." Milwaukee's local ordinary, Bishop Sebastian Messmer, a native of the German-speaking Swiss canton of St. Gallen, could only suggest that Catholics comply with the Americanization efforts that were underway.[10]

Other members of the hierarchy, overwhelmingly Irish American, also remained largely quiescent in the crackdown on German Americans and their remaining Irish American allies. Part of the reason is that, other than Cardinal O'Connell in Boston, all noteworthy anti-Americanist members of the hierarchy had passed away. Archbishop John Ireland had no reservations about actively advancing Catholic participation

---

10. The extensive efforts of the Wisconsin Loyalty Legion can be found in *War History Commission, Loyalty Legion Correspondence and Miscellaneous Papers, 1917–1919, General Correspondence May 1918–April 1919,* Series No. 1706, in Wisconsin State Historical Society. See also Lorin Lee Cary, "The Wisconsin Loyalty Legion. 1917–1918," *Wisconsin Magazine of History* (Autumn 1969), 33–50. Glennon's and Messmer's comments can be found in Milwaukee's Catholic newspaper, *Catholic Citizen,* May 4, 1918. An insightful study of the impact that the Great War had on parochial education can be found in Sister Linda Marie Bos, SSND, "Let Us Act Promptly: School Sisters of Notre Dame and World War I," *Catholic Historian* 12, no. 3 (Summer 1994): 73–86. In the Spring of 1916, Great Relief Bazaars had been held in several American cities to provide aid to German and Austrian widows and orphans of the Great War. This would have been inconceivable one year later. See *Milwaukee Journal,* February 29, 1916.

in the war effort, and shed few tears for the trials and tribulations of German Americans. For decades, Ireland had struggled mightily with German Benedictines at St. Cloud, with Minnesota's St. John's Abbey, and with other regional German priests over their dogged anti-Americanist positions. He had also fiercely resisted the German archdiocese of Milwaukee from extending its jurisdiction out onto the western plains of Minnesota and the Dakotas. It was as if, in Archbishop Ireland's way of reasoning, German Americans' afflictions were somehow well deserved. The former Civil War chaplain and supporter of American imperialism in the wake of the War with Spain came well prepared to lead American Catholics into the Great War with Germany and gleefully pounced on the declaration of war in April 1917. "All citizens of America should have ... confidence in the absolute loyalty to America of others of their fellow citizens," Ireland propounded. After dismissing Irish and Germans as citizens a world away, he trumpeted, "Here we are all Americans ... [and] it is wonderful this homogeneity of the entire people of America in allegiance to the 'Star-Spangled Banner.'" To his own Catholic flock, he demanded that no "reservation of mind, no slackening of earnest act, to be henceforward thought of or allowed."[11]

Whereas little could be done to blunt the impact of anti-German hysteria in the United States, Irish American Catholics, in both word and deed, proved exemplary in their contributions to the war effort. Unlike several Protestant denominations, Catholic moral praxis had long-established "just war" theories to dismiss any pacifistic rigidity.

---

11. John Ireland to C. W. Ames, April 18, 1917, quoted in Wingerd, *Claiming the City,* 132; John Ireland, quoted in O'Connell, *John Ireland and the American Catholic Church,* 517. Wingerd has furnished a telling photo of Archbishop Ireland bearing a "proud military demeanor" while reviewing the St. Thomas University corps of cadets with the Star-Spangled Banner briskly unfurling in the wind behind him. See Wingerd, *Claiming the City,* 131. In May 1917, Ireland gave a thundering exhortation to troops mustering to the colors as reported in the *Southern Messenger,* May 31, 1917. Late in the war, Ireland was still full of gusto for the war effort, telling a group of Minnesota naval recruits that "the man should not live who does not love and cherish his country, and our country is that great assembly of men running from the Atlantic to the Pacific who call themselves Americans." Quoted in *New York Times,* September 28, 1918.

CHAPTER 7

While the hierarchy had clearly set the tone for American Catholic support for the government, the means of implementing it and harnessing the energies of diverse Catholic groups and individuals fell to the Knights of Columbus. Two Paulist priests, John Burke, editor of the *Catholic World*, and Louis O'Hern of St. Paul's College in Washington, organized the drive to provide Catholic chaplains.[12]

Until John Burke successfully engineered the establishment of the NCWC in 1918, the Irish American-dominated Knights of Columbus did yeoman's service in organizing the Catholic contribution to the war effort. Under the Knights' direction, "secretaries" were drafted from volunteers to help run the numerous comfort stations, chapels, and recreation halls in American training camps, and later in Europe. These secretaries organized athletic contests and showed movies to provide "wholesome entertainment," as well as religious training, for soldiers. The Knights were also charged with spearheading Catholic fundraising efforts for the war. In this capacity, they were unequalled among religious organizations, and early in their campaign outdistanced the modest goals established for them. Using local parishes as the basic unit for collection, the Knights, to give one example, more than doubled the goal set for the Archdiocese of New York. In the Archdiocese of Chicago, it was reported than an extraordinarily high percentage of Knights had enlisted in the armed services, and that those who remained were among the greatest contributors to the war effort.[13]

Whereas prelates, such as Gibbons and Ireland, remained largely preoccupied with attending to the "mental and moral preparation of

---

12. John F. Piper, *The American Churches in World War I* (Athens: Ohio University Press, 1985), 96–97; Berard Tierney, "The American Catholic Church's Role in World War I" (M.A. thesis, Niagara University, 1971), 15–16. Of the nearly four thousand conscientious objectors registered during the war, only four were identified as Catholic. See Thomas J. Shelley, "Twentieth-Century American Catholicism and Irish-Americans," in Lee and Casey, eds., *Making the Irish American*, 585, and *New York Times,* "Cardinal Praises Catholics in War," February 20, 1918, p. 20.

13. Maurice Egan Francis and John B. Kennedy, *The Knights of Columbus in Peace and War,* 1: 228, 229, 258–59; Tierney, "The American Catholic Church's Role in World War I," 34; Joseph J. Thompson, *A History of the Knights of Columbus in Illinois* (Chicago: University of Chicago Press, 1922), 342–45.

our people for the war," the practical goal of providing for the spiritual needs of American Catholic servicemen was handed over to Bishop Patrick J. Hayes. In November 1917 Hayes, Auxiliary Bishop of New York, was appointed by Pope Benedict XV as Military Ordinary of the United States. Consequently, when priests joined the service, their obedience to their local bishop was suspended and transferred to Hayes. His mission of providing priests as chaplains was greatly eased by the work of Father John Francis O'Hern, who convinced Secretary of War Newton Baker that earlier-established quotas for Catholic chaplaincies were insufficient for the Catholic contribution to the fighting contingent in Europe. Although Catholics comprised only seventeen percent of the population, Baker authorized an increase in Catholic chaplaincies because he reckoned that the "Catholic denomination ... will constitute perhaps thirty-five percent of the new army." O'Hern turned to the Knights of Columbus to assist in recruiting a cadre of non-commissioned priests to accompany troops embarking for Europe. Predictably, most chaplains were Irish Americans. According to one amicable account, the British, who "held suspect any organization whose membership was largely composed of men of Catholic Irish extraction," soon discovered that whatever the "sympathies of individual members of the Knights of Columbus toward Ireland, there is only one designation to be applied to them, and that is that the Knights are loyal citizens of the country to which they belong."[14]

While cooperating with various wartime conservation measures at home, Irish American Catholics responded generously to the government's call to arms. Urged by their political and ecclesiastical leaders to demonstrate Catholic patriotism, Irish Americans swelled the ranks of regiments serving in the American Expeditionary Force. By most accounts, they acquitted themselves admirably as courageous fighters. Any distinctive military feats accomplished by Irish Americans

14. Circular Letter, James Cardinal Gibbons to the Hierarchy, November 21, 1917, copy in *National Catholic War Council Archives,* Washington, DC; Egan and Kennedy, *Knights of Columbus in Peace and War,* 1: 290; Newton Baker is quoted in Michael Williams, *American Catholics in the War* (New York: Macmillan, 1921), 90; Egan and Kennedy, *Knights of Columbus in Peace and War,* 1:250–51, 285.

CHAPTER 7

during the war were somewhat obscured by their general absorption into the armed services with other Americans in massive divisional formations. The most notable exception to this integration was the 69th Infantry Regiment of New York, familiarly known as the "Fighting 69th." Composed almost entirely of Irish Americans recruited from Catholic athletic clubs and ethnic societies, the "Irish 69th" was in the thick of fighting on the western front in the last year of the war. Memoirs written after the armistice gave insight into the suffering experienced by these soldiers, as well as the camaraderie enjoyed between Catholic soldiers and their chaplains. Catholic chaplains gave witness to their dedication to the men at the front. In a necrology kept by one chaplain, eighteen priests were recorded as killed directly or indirectly throughout the course of the war.[15]

While Americans at large responded to the nation's call to arms in appropriate patriotic terms, Irish Americans responded with a degree of assertive militancy bordering on chauvinism. The most significant impetus in this direction was provided by the community's religious leaders and institutions. Nowhere was this more evident than in the exhortations of the Catholic clergy, which appeared to both completely and conveniently brush aside any Christian imperatives toward nonviolence. Theodore Roosevelt, the aging warrior, and a friend of both Cardinal Gibbons and Archbishop Ireland, was a frequent admirer of the work that the Catholic hierarchy performed in uplifting the martial spirit of the nation. In his second work assaulting the hyphenate problem, *The Foes of Our Own Household*, Roosevelt proudly pointed to the words of Monsignor James Cassidy of St. Mary's Cathedral in Fall River, Massachusetts, as exemplary of Catholic patriotism. What the former president praised was Cassidy's farewell benediction to

---

15. Wittke, *The Irish in America,* 283; Francis P. Duffy, *Father Duffy's Story* (Garden City, NY: Garden City Publishing, 1919); Chaplain George T. McCarthy, *The Greatest Lover* (Chicago: Extension Press, 1920); George Waring, *United States Catholic Chaplains* (New York: Chauncey, Holt, 1924), 319–327. Father Francis Duffy, chaplain to the Fighting 69th regiment produced one of the more memorable memoirs of the Great War in which he extolled the bravery and sacrifice of Irish Catholic soldiers. See Francis Patrick Duffy, *Father Duffy's Story: A Tale of Humor and Heroism, of Life and Death with the Fighting Sixty-Ninth* (New York: George H. Doran Co., 1919).

troops embarking for training camps, in which the venerable cleric declared without apology that "the future would be filled with shame and ignominy if we had been led by those who would have peace at any price."[16]

The ultra-patriotism manifested by the Catholic clergy, the Catholic press, and the Knights of Columbus took its shape from the example provided by the hierarchy. And among the prelates, none had more influence and impact than Cardinal Gibbons. Though generally reserved in his opinions, Gibbons was an avid admirer of the British and worked tirelessly to have American Catholics participate fully in the military effort. At the age of eighty-four, Gibbons maintained a hectic schedule, much of which was dedicated to promoting the work of the National Catholic War Council. Notwithstanding his advancing years and diverse responsibilities, Gibbons did not shirk his duty in supporting the government's war programs. In June 1917, he extended full cooperation to Herbert Hoover's food conservation program and fully supported the Liberty Loan drives, noting that he did not want the Catholic Church to be "weighed in the balance of patriotism and found wanting."[17] The cardinal also lent his energies to buoying the martial vigor of Catholic soldiers. In a sermon during a military Mass at Camp Meade, Maryland, for troops readying to leave for Europe, he counseled:

> Go, then, my friends, unhesitatingly and serene at heart. Whether you come back with wounds or without them, we will be glad to welcome you and accord you the meed that is a hero's due. Remember, such wounds as you may receive will be honorable. You will be proud

---

16. Theodore Roosevelt, *Foes of Our Own Household* (New York: George H. Doran, 1924), 292. This work was first published in 1917.

17. Shortly after the US declaration of war, Gibbons obligingly wrote to the Archbishop of Westminster, "Happy are we to unite with your country ... to ensure the acceptance of those principles of peace and justice which are the guarantees of the permanence of our Christian civilization." See James Cardinal Gibbons to Francis Cardinal Bourne, April 15, 1917, *Gibbons Papers*, Archives of the Archdiocese of Baltimore. His support of the Liberty Loan drives is found in Baltimore *Catholic Review,* June 2, 1917.

CHAPTER 7

of them and will want to show them in years to come. It is with such wounds that you will prove that you possessed the souls and hearts of brave men. Remember what Lord Nelson said on the eve of his great victory. "England expects every man to do his duty." America expects every one of you to do your duty. Go forth to battle and victory, and God be with you.[18]

With such unequivocal encouragement, it was not surprising that Irish American Catholics, anxious to prove their loyalty to the country, contributed significantly to the war effort.

The American Catholic Church, infinitely more interested in demonstrating that American Catholics, particularly those of Irish extraction, were loyal patriotic Americans, had no compunction in deferring issues of Irish freedom to a later date, if at all. This was consistent with its policy leading up to the American entry into the Great War, and when its leading prelate referred to Admiral Lord Nelson's hortative remarks on the eve of the battle of Trafalgar, it merely underscored the reality that any petulant agitation on behalf of a free and totally independent Ireland would not be countenanced. With few exceptions, the American Catholic press followed suit, eschewing any denigration of America's newfound ally Great Britain in favor of crushing the Prussian menace. Middle-class, respectable Irish Americans mirrored the Church's position by evading or subordinating any sympathy for Irish nationalism in deference to the war effort and the crusade to crush the German menace. If not exactly legion, the ranks of these second-generation Irish Americans were nonetheless impressively large.

Perhaps one success story, a person only emerging as a powerful Irish American voice in 1918, would be instructive. Al Smith, the man who a decade later would be the Democratic candidate for president, was a Bowery-born and Lower Manhattan-bred politico, whose persona was that of the quintessential Irish American. Smith

---

18. Manuscript copy of Gibbons's sermon at Camp Meade, June 9, 1918, *Gibbons Papers*, Archives of the Archdiocese of Baltimore. Just what appeal Gibbons's reference to England's Lord Nelson would have for Irish-American Catholic soldiers is difficult to discern.

gloried in his Irish identity and was militantly unapologetic about his Catholicism. At the very moment the Great War was winding down in the blood-soaked fields of northern France, Smith, later dubbed the "Happy Warrior" by Franklin Delano Roosevelt, won the gubernatorial position in the Empire State. Having earlier served several terms as a state assemblyman, Al Smith was serving in the somewhat humdrum position of state sheriff in 1918, largely viewed as a patronage job granted by Tammany Hall and its omnipotent boss Charles Francis Murphy. Once the United States entered the Great War, Smith complied with patriotic expectations by dutifully supporting Liberty Loan drive efforts, encouraging registration and recruitment, and attending farewell ceremonies for troops embarking to Europe.

For all of Smith's Gaelic pride and his self-identification as a son of the Emerald Isle, his ethnic attachment was primarily sentimental and never extended to the politics of Ireland. He attended meetings after the Great War calling for Irish freedom and, as noted earlier, even headed an organization to raise funds for Ireland's destitute women and children. But the emphasis was confined to relief measures, and he assiduously avoided any of the revolutionary rhetoric that marked the debate on Irish nationalism in the immediate postwar era. When Irish political leader Eamon de Valera toured the United States in 1920, Smith met him in Albany, where he cordially hosted a luncheon on his behalf, but the mayor of Albany gave the official public reception and Smith kept all banter with de Valera in a light-hearted vein. Part of his reticence undoubtedly was due to Smith's predilection for not engaging in divisive ethnic tactics (something in which his counterpart in Boston, James Michael Curley, excelled), but much of his hesitation was based on an instinctive understanding that America's interests came well before those of the Irish. On one occasion, Smith had his secretary correct the statement that he planned to speak on behalf of the Irish Republican Army's efforts in their struggle with Great Britain, with the amendment that "the people who gave out this statement to the newspapers ... had no authority from the governor to do so."[19]

19. David Colburn, "Alfred E. Smith: The First Fifty Years, 1873–1924" (PhD dissertation, University of North Carolina, 1971), 197. See also Slayton, *Empire Statesman*, 176–77.

CHAPTER 7

Throughout 1918, virtually all elements of the Irish American Catholic community remained mute on the issue of Ireland's immediate freedom, and conspicuously vocal in their declarations of American patriotism. In the main, the professional Irish remained subdued in their critique of American war policies, even though they refused any effusive praise for Britain. When self-imposed discretion failed to restrain their anti-British invective, government censorship stepped in and resolved the matter. Yet, more than anything, they were fully conscious that they simply did not have the support of moderate and conservative Irish Americans. Moreover, while the United States was at war, they were acutely aware that they held no sway with the influential American Catholic Church. Their best hope was to hitch their wagon to Wilson's vague commitment in January 1918 to the principle of the self-determination of all nations upon the war's conclusion. Even in this hope the radicals were disappointed when, just weeks before the Armistice, the respected Jesuit periodical *America* found itself barred from the mails for printing a series of articles written by an Irish American veteran of the British army, Dr. William Maloney, on Ireland's future in the postwar world.[20]

Epilogue and Conclusions

The Great War ended with the declared Armistice on November 11, 1918. The end of the war created a climate in which, for the first time, nearly all Irish Americans found unanimity in purpose. For a brief period, nearly all Irish American and Catholic factions found themselves on the same page, one that was conveniently, if perhaps inadvertently, provided by President Wilson himself. Little time was squandered. The day following the declaration of the Armistice, November 12, 1918, the Irish Progressive League called for a meeting of the Irish Race Convention. Not to be outdone,

20. Terry Golway, *Irish Rebel*, 249. Most Catholic newspapers refrained from voicing their take on Wilson's commitment until the hierarchy weighed in on the matter. St. Louis's *Western Watchman* was an exception when it took to task the *St. Louis Republic* for dismissing the principle of self-determination as an "impertinent dream" in Ireland's case. See *Western Watchman*, January 18, 1918.

the Clan-na-Gael and FOIF issued an invitation for another Irish rally with an eye towards pressuring the administration to deal squarely with the Irish at the looming peace conference. Greatly attended and highly touted, this convention was held at Madison Square Garden in New York City. Cardinal William O'Connell of the Boston Archdiocese was one of the featured speakers, goading Woodrow Wilson to make good on his pledge of self-determination for all peoples, specifically referring to the Irish people. The aging Fenian, John Devoy, one of the organizers of the spectacle, was nearly beside himself with ecstasy. He had long professed that he would never discuss his radical policies upon bended knee while Church clerics condemned both his beloved cause and its assertive methods. Now, according to his recollections, he tried valiantly to ward off tears as the conservative cleric of Boston clamored for the Wilson administration to attend to the Irish question. For Devoy, this was the first time he could recall that a "Prince of the Church had appeared at such a meeting and given his [approval] to the movement for the complete independence of Ireland."[21]

One of the factors that exhilarated both the Clan-na-Gael and the FOIF was that the mid-November elections held in Ireland had overwhelmingly ushered in Sinn Fein as the majority party, reflecting the fact that Home Rule had been rendered obsolete, and that Ireland, aside from the six counties in Ulster, was inclined to press for complete independence. Despite the exhilaration, both John Devoy and Judge Cohalan were flummoxed by the fact that they had long based their strategy for Irish freedom on the Wilsonian principle of self-determination. Now, the elections in Ireland dangled before them the possibility of achieving their aims by means other than negotiation, a method possibly preferable, given their doubts about

21. Devoy, *Recollections of an Irish Rebel*, 126; Tansill, *America and the Fight*, 280–81. It should be noted that the Carmelite priest Father Peter Magennis was listed on the program as the newly elected president of the FOIF. It would appear that this was an effort by the Clan-na-Gael to lend an aura of respectability to the proceedings. See Alfred Isaacson, *Always Faithful: The New York Carmelites and the Irish People and Their Freedom Movement* (Middletown, NY: Vestigium Press, 2004), 36–37.

CHAPTER 7

Wilson's willingness to intervene in British affairs. Cohalan and Devoy instinctively knew that if they were to have any hope of energizing Irish Americans to support the drive towards a free Ireland, they would have to win the support of the American Catholic Church, most notably its foremost prelate—Cardinal Gibbons. Devoy and Cohalan were committed to engaging Gibbons to speak on behalf of Irish freedom at the next rally of the Irish Race Convention, scheduled for Philadelphia in late February 1919. This was a delicate matter. Cohalan, who knew that Gibbons and the Wilson administration perceived him as a dangerous radical, was compelled to excuse himself from actively influencing the cardinal's presentation. The challenging task of crafting the language of Gibbons's speech was left to John Devoy. For several weeks before the convention, Devoy attempted to reconcile Gibbons's remarks with the more republican aspirations of the Clan-dominated FOIF—the actual host of the Irish Race Convention. Try as he might, Devoy could not prod Gibbons into any full-throated endorsement of outright Irish freedom, and eventually settled on a common ground of holding President Wilson to his commitment to self-determination. "All Americans should stand as one ... for Ireland's inalienable right of self-determination," Gibbons declared, adding that "this great principle should clearly be applied in Ireland's case."[22]

Although clearly shy of what the radicals had hoped, Gibbons's remarks were trumpeted as an indication that the forceful advocacy of Irish freedom was not solely the province of cranky radicalism. Devoy was quite satisfied with the effect, admitting in his recollections that the Irish cause had languished in America for many years until Gibbons, along with nearly thirty other prelates, had endorsed the movement. But this euphoria would prove to be short-lived, and Devoy may have well understood that this highly sensationalized coup was largely chimerical. Events in Ireland were about to take a sharp turn that would divide the agents of Irish freedom in America. Moreover, Wilson's refusal to press self-determination's applicability to Ireland, coupled with the American Catholic Church's reluctance to

---

22. Gibbons quoted in Charles Tansill, *America and the Fight for Irish Freedom*, 300.

hold the president's feet to the fire with respect to Ireland, destroyed whatever momentum the radicals had from the February 1919 Irish Race Convention.[23]

Even before he departed on December 4, 1918 for his junket to France aboard the *S. S. Washington*, preliminary to a later return to the Versailles Conference, Woodrow Wilson was sending signals that he was unlikely to strenuously press for Irish freedom, despite his overall commitment to the self-determination of national aspirants. Clearly, the president believed he had bigger "fish to fry" at Versailles than the matter of Irish freedom. He felt besieged by the petitions that crossed his desk from Irish Americans of nearly all stripes across the political spectrum. He responded respectfully to entreaties from important representatives in the Democratic Party, such as those submitted by Senators Thomas J. Walsh and James D. Phelan, realizing that this kind of importuning was constituent-driven on their part and not imperative or intrusive in nature, and certainly not a threat to the solidarity of the Democratic Party. To Walsh, the president responded that he appreciated the importance of the Irish question and would use his influence "at every opportunity to bring about a just and satisfactory conclusion." He went through the motions of listening solemnly to various Irish American delegations that pressed the case for Irish freedom, making no commitment other than a vague and oblique resolve to consider their case. Days before he was scheduled to return to France for the peace deliberations at Versailles, Tumulty prevailed upon the president to meet with yet another Irish American delegation, decidedly more nationalist in sentiment, that had gathered in New York. Tumulty prefaced his argument with the disclaimer that the president knew that he "was not a professional Irishman," and then cautioned Wilson that a refusal to "see this delegation would simply strengthen the Sinn Fein movement in this country." Glumly, Wilson agreed to a brief meeting with the delegation, but when he learned that Judge Cohalan would most likely be in attendance, he threatened to immediately repair to the docks where his ship was at anchor. Rather than sabotage this important opportunity, Cohalan abstained from attending the meeting, and the

---

23. Golway, *Irish Rebel*, 252.

CHAPTER 7

delegation met with Wilson and implored him to keep the matter of Irish freedom uppermost in his thoughts. Wilson graciously listened, but made no promises. The president confided to Tumulty that he could scarcely "touch this" matter; he was not about to interfere in British internal affairs. Having constructed the ideological bridge spanning the principle of self-determination and the fate of Ireland, Wilson was unlikely to cross it. He was no more likely intrude on British imperial affairs than on French affairs in Indochina. Upon reflection, Wilson found himself annoyed by this most recent delegation's intrusion, indicating that his personal preference was to tell the Irish to "go to hell," but that he refrained from doing so for political reasons. Wilson was tired of the Irish professionals, who had proved to be both an irritant and a disloyal element during the years of American neutrality, and his clear nativist inclinations made him less than sympathetic to Catholic Ireland.[24]

Meanwhile, the American Catholic Church and its press moved forward with cautious and measured steps. Most of the hierarchy and diocesan press during the first half of 1919 placed their confidence in the diplomatic route to Irish freedom. Most of the hierarchy, such as newly installed Dennis Cardinal Dougherty of Philadelphia and the "Prince of Boston," Cardinal O'Connell, were preoccupied by the "brick and mortar" concerns of building the infrastructure of their dioceses. Moreover, O'Connell was consumed with animus toward the National Catholic War Council and was quelling personal scandals raging in his own household. The mainstream diocesan press largely supported the Wilson administration's presumed interest

---

24. John B. Duff, "The Versailles Treaty and the Irish-Americans," *Journal of American History* 55, no. 3 (December 1968): 584–87; Joseph Tumulty to Woodrow Wilson, June 25, 1919, in Link, Wilson, *Papers,* 61:182–83. See also, Jans P. Vought, *The Bully Pulpit and the Melting Pot* (Macon, GA: Mercer University Press, 2004), 144–46. The Progressive Wilson was an enigma on matters of immigration, religion and race. He sanctioned the re-segregation of Federal Department offices, glorified the role of the Ku Klux Klan in his academic works, and hosted and endorsed the White House viewing of the ultimate racist film, the *Birth of a Nation.* On the other hand, while he hammered against the hyphenated American throughout his two terms in office, he vetoed a nativist-inspired Immigration Bill in 1917; a veto that was overridden by Congress.

in self-determination for the Irish people. The few radical Irish American editors, such as O'Mahoney and Father Yorke, extolled and exploited Wilson's supposed commitment to Irish freedom. Yorke, who had earlier castigated Wilson as the great pariah of Irish interests, the "canting hypocrite" and "a degenerate mental hyphenate," did a turnabout, waxing eloquently in his support of Woodrow Wilson, the "champion of democracy ... the advocate of small nations." This wishful thinking continued until June 1919, when it became clear that the aspirations of Irish American champions were relegated to the graveyard by a president who was not going to press the British on the Irish question at Versailles. Between wanting to placate the British in exchange for their support of the League of Nations and not wanting to offend Irish American supporters, Wilson chose the former option. Whatever good intentions Wilson may have had for the Irish paved the road toward the destination good intentions inevitably lead. Fervent Irish nationalists who had rallied around the president in the prelude to Versailles now turned on him by the summer of 1919.[25]

From this point onward, the Irish American case for an independent Ireland began to founder, and in the long run, it was mostly events within Ireland that determined the outcome. On January 21, 1919, Sinn Fein formed a breakaway government (Dail Eireann) and, before the day concluded, members of the Irish Republican Army (IRA) had assassinated two members of the Royal Irish Constabulary, launching what would become known as the Irish War of Independence. For nearly two and a half years, bloody reprisals between revolutionaries

---

25. Yorke's ebullient remarks concerning Wilson can be found in *The Leader*, November 16, 1918. A bevy of Irish American lobbyists traveled to Paris to lend their support to Ireland's case. They included representatives across the spectrum of the Irish American constituency, from the radical to the moderate. Both Senators Phelan and Walsh attempted to pry a commitment out of Wilson during this time, but to no avail. Even Bishop Peter J. Muldoon of Illinois's Rockford Diocese found that his importuning the president to keep Ireland's cause on a par with that of Slavic peoples was rebuked by Wilson's tart reply: "These nations, Bishop, fell into our lap." See Vought, *Bully Pulpit*, 142. On the turnabout of Irish nationalists' support for Wilson, see John French, "Irish-American Identity, Memory, and Americanism During the Eras of the Civil War and First World War" (PhD dissertation, Marquette University, 2009), 258.

CHAPTER 7

and the forces of Great Britain (most notably the infamous British paramilitary police known as the Black and Tans) raged over the breadth of Ireland before a settlement was reached in July 1921. But the proposed treaty, one that granted essential Irish freedom but excluded the six Protestant counties of Ulster, sparked internecine conflict in the form of the Irish Civil War, lasting from June 1922 to May 1923. It divided both the Irish and the Irish Americans, the factions siding with either Eamon de Valera, who rejected the treaty, or Michael Collins, who accepted the treaty as the most viable option. It proved bloodier than the War of Independence, leaving a generation divided and embittered over the course of events. In the end, despite the assassination of Michael Collins, the pro-treaty Nationalists prevailed, and an independent Ireland emerged separate from the six counties of Ulster, which remained part of the United Kingdom.[26]

Professional Irish Americans agonized over the disillusionment in the aftermath of the Versailles settlement. For many of them, it had not come as a total surprise; they instinctively knew that Wilson would not vigorously pressure the British into a settlement of the Irish question. What they had not factored in was the arrival of Eamon de Valera in the United States in June 1919. At the onset of the War of Independence, de Valera, the president of Dail Eireann, decided that a visit to the United States was in the best interests of the Irish cause, leaving Michael Collins behind to prosecute the war. Between June 1919 and December 1920, de Valera roamed the United States to elicit Irish American support for an Irish Republic under his direction, secure financial support for the struggle in Ireland, and gain official governmental recognition of Ireland's independence. The mission would be a mixed success. He was able to raise funds to the tune of $5,500,000, but fell short of attaining his other objectives, particularly any kind of official government endorsement during the waning days of the Wilson administration. But the most significant blow to Irish America came in the power struggle that developed between de Valera and the professional Irish Americans. The Clan-na-Gael would divide over its support of the Irish leader. John Devoy and Judge

---

26. The Irish struggle against the British can be found in Michael Hopkinson, *The Irish War of Independence* (Montreal: McGill-Queen's University Press, 2002).

ONWARD CATHOLIC SOLDIERS

Cohalan became sufficiently disaffected with de Valera, especially over the visitor's insinuation that he was the de facto chief of Irish American nationalists, that they withdrew their general support for his leadership, while Joseph McGarrity of Philadelphia headed a group of professionals throwing their full weight behind de Valera. For much the same reason that Cohalan absented himself when the Irish American delegation met with Wilson dockside before the president's departure to France in 1919, neither he nor Devoy were part of the delegation of Irish Americans sent to Versailles to lobby for Irish interests. The rupture within Irish American professional circles over de Valera rendered both factions largely irrelevant during the remainder of the War of Independence, even though money and arms continued to flow towards revolutionary Ireland. The torch had been passed to a younger generation of Irish American nationalists, and that light flickered rather dimly.[27]

While the theatrics of Irish American professionals played themselves out, there was another chapter in the saga drawing to a close as well. Widespread disappointment among Irish Americans over Wilson's refusal to press for Ireland's liberation caught up with the president during the Senate's debate on the Treaty of Versailles, particularly with respect to his cherished dream—the League of Nations. For many Irish Americans, the vote was a referendum on Wilson's betrayal of Irish aspirations for independence. Many Irish Americans sidled up to Senate Republicans, led by Senator Henry Cabot Lodge, to demand that reservations be added to the treaty,

---

27. Although a Collins proponent, Tim Pat Coogan provides a succinct analysis of de Valera's American mission in *Eamon de Valera: The Man Who Made Ireland* (New York: Barnes & Noble, 1999), 120–35. Devoy's disaffection from de Valera can be traced in successive editions of *Gaelic-American* between the close of 1920 and the end of 1921. Between 1919 and the end of 1921, Irish American nationalists enjoyed their golden age. FOIF saw its membership crest to roughly 300,000, and once the split between the Devoy/Cohalan camp and the McGarrity camps occurred, the latter's pro-de Valera organization (American Association for the Recognition of the Irish Republic) saw its membership peak at nearly 700,000. By the end of 1921, combined efforts had raised nearly $10 million for the Irish War of Independence. See David Brundage, *Irish Nationalists in America: The Politics of Exile, 1798–1998*, 161.

CHAPTER 7

especially those related to the League. Lodge, a first-rate Boston Brahmin, and the professional Irish made for interesting political bedfellows indeed. Despite the fissures forming within the ranks of the professionals, they were able to unite in condemning the treaty's League clauses, both because they had not made provision for a free Ireland and as payback for Wilson's transparent Anglophilic vassalage. Moderate Irish American politicians were divided over the treaty. One, Congressman Bourke Cockran, predicted that the League of Nations would be defeated, "root and branch," as an "abomination that the American people cannot take to their bosom." The treaty came before the Senate on November 19, 1919, and after three votes, two with Lodge's reservations, and one without them, the treaty went down to defeat. Judge Cohalan exultantly cabled his congratulations to Senator William E. Borah, a progressive isolationist from Idaho, and received the complimentary reply: "You have rendered in this fight a service which no other man has rendered or could have rendered." An intransigent and physically disabled Wilson refused to accept any modifications to the treaty and had it sent back to the Senate for another vote in March 1920. The treaty was rejected for a second and final time by a vote of 53 to 38. Both Senators Thomas J. Walsh and James Duval Phelan dutifully, if not enthusiastically, stood with the president, but Irish American Democratic Senator David I. Walsh of Massachusetts joined Lodge as an "irreconcilable," voting against the treaty. In place of the Treaty of Versailles, Congress passed a measure known as the Knox-Porter Resolution that officially ended the war with Germany and her allies. The United States never joined the League of Nations, effectively rendering it an impotent organization. All the same, Irish America largely rejoiced.[28]

---

28. Bourke Cockran's statement is in *The Sunday Morning Star* (Wilmington, DE), October 31, 1919. For the debate in the Senate on March 19, 1920 concerning the Versailles treaty and its League of Nations clause, see Congressional Record, vol, 59, pt. 5 (66th Congress, 2nd Session), 4567–4604), March 19, 1920. The Borah-Cohalan exchange can be found in F. M. Carroll, *American Opinion and the Irish Question,* 147. Additional endorsements of the treaty's defeat can be found in Devoy's *Gaelic-American,* November 29, 1919, and Patrick Ford's *Irish World,* December 6, 1919.

ONWARD CATHOLIC SOLDIERS

Generally, the American Catholic Church maintained a detached posture in the immediate postwar period. As noted earlier, the Church and its press implored the Wilson administration to consider Ireland's position at the peace conference, but once it became clear by the summer of 1919 that support for the Irish cause was not in the offing, Church opinion on the issue settled into a position of relative stasis. Catholic editors grumbled but published few vigorous articles about Ireland's disinheritance, and meekly argued against the treaty and the League of Nations. During the Irish War of Independence, these same Catholic journalists vaguely supported Ireland's revolution but deplored the violence attendant to it. They preferred to join the hierarchy in raising funds for the casualties of Ireland's struggle. Irish American Catholics looked forlornly upon the division that emerged among the ardent nationalists when the split occurred between De Valera and many of the professional Irish. The president of the FOIF, Bishop Michael Gallagher of Detroit, who had replaced Father Magennis as titular head of the organization, sided with Devoy and Cohalan in the struggle against de Valera, preventing any concerted intervention in the raging struggle in Ireland. The only Church figure holding his head above the fray was Cardinal Gibbons, ever the astute diplomat, who maintained his insistence that American matters take precedence over Irish ones. The aged prelate played a deft hand during the crisis over the League of Nations. In a letter sent to President Wilson in July 1919 that subsequently was printed in the *Washington Post*, Gibbons applauded the wisdom of a league of nations, predicting that "when both parties" thoroughly discuss the matter, a salutary agreement will be reached that is "hailed with satisfaction," producing an "intense joy throughout the nation." Wilson, eager to embrace support from any quarter, responded to the cardinal's statement and expressed great pleasure in and sincere appreciation for Gibbon's declaration. Yet in late 1920, when the debate over the League had already reached its climax, Gibbons went out of his way to refute a claim that he had been a firm supporter, by averring that he had stood by "a league of nations with proper reservations and constitutional safeguards." The matter was closed.[29]

29. *Washington Post,* July 19, 1919. On Gibbons's refutation of his unqualified support of the League and his reticence to become directly involved

CHAPTER 7

In his magisterial work *Emigrants and Exiles*, a work that focuses almost entirely on the patterns of Irish emigration from the colonial era to 1921, Kerby A. Miller's final paragraph serves as a fitting conclusion to this study's epilogue. The Irish American nationalists were fortunate that the Easter Rebellion and the Anglo-Irish War occurred "just before the well of Irish-American memories, duty, and guilt ran dry—just before the old Irish worldview became in America nothing more than a shell of largely meaningless clichés." The victory achieved in the Anglo-Irish war, somewhat tempered by the "confusion and embarrassment" over the Irish Civil War that followed, sapped Irish American attention for the homeland. Irish Americans would, in the next decade, struggle with the resurgence of American nativism and the advent of the Great Depression, but these would be exclusively American and Catholic concerns. Ireland would become the stuff of nostalgic and fond rumination.[30]

Much of what has been written in this closing chapter has been epilogue to the study's principal chronological focus—1914 to 1918. It is appropriate at this point to draw conclusions pertinent to the general thesis posited in this study's introduction.

* * * * *

The years between the outbreak of the Great War in Europe and the entry of the United States into that conflict were pivotal ones in the evolution of the Irish American and American Catholic communities. Despite the evident tensions besetting Irish American Catholics from within and without, they emerged triumphantly from the Great War and were transformed in ways that would not have been possible except for the crucible of war. Although American Catholics would have to weather additional storms and trials at the hands of American nativists

---

in Irish matters, see John Tracey Ellis, *The Life of James Cardinal Gibbons*, 2: 288–89. Gibbons would not live to see the emergence of a free Ireland, as he passed from this life on March 24, 1921.

    30. Kerby A. Miller, *Emigrants and Exiles: Ireland and the Irish Exodus to North America* (New York: Oxford University Press, 1985), 555.

over the succeeding four decades, they had gained a substantial measure of acceptance into mainstream American society, something that so many of their political and ecclesiastical leaders had sought for decades. Moreover, American Catholics' loyalty to the country, as well as their conspicuous patriotism and contribution to the war effort, established a bedrock foundation of evidence that established them as loyal and patriotic Americans. And their movement towards the societal mainstream did not come about via capitulation of faith and values; in fact, they did not so much assimilate as they forged inclusion into American society on their own terms. The war served as both a catharsis and a catalyst in allowing this transition to occur.

The transformation that occurred during the years 1914–1918 was not without conflict and division. The catharsis required for such a change had to overcome many obstacles deeply rooted in the Irish Catholic immigrant experience. Decades of rejection and suppression at the hands of nativist forces prevalent in American society had caused many in the Irish American Catholic community to adopt a fortress-like attitude toward Anglo-Saxon Protestant America. Throughout the second half of the nineteenth century, Catholics relied upon their own resources to forge a largely isolated existence within American society. By the turn of the century, this reliance had paid substantial dividends in achieving a modicum of localized political and economic success in many urban centers. The Catholic Church created a nurturing and protective climate in which the immigrant communities could take both solace and pride. And it was this same institution, as most vividly seen in the Americanist controversy, which assumed the lead in prodding these communities toward a more integrative course within American society. The Great War provided the means to hasten this integration towards a successful conclusion.

Despite the apparent divisions that emerged within the community when war broke out in 1914, Irish American Catholics adopted views that were consistent with the expressly stated official American position. They no more wanted a part of the war than American society or the Wilson administration did. Their tenacity in keeping the nation neutral was totally consistent with the president's desires. They adhered to their positions throughout the second year of the war even though

CHAPTER 7

the national sinews of neutrality were increasingly strained by Imperial Germany's employment of unrestricted submarine warfare.

As the Wilson administration labored to weave a truly neutral course of action, it found itself adopting policies that appeared to some in the Irish American community as favoring the Allies. Professional Irish Americans took exception to the mounting pro-Allied movement and established an agenda for Ireland's liberation predicated upon a German victory. They were in many ways not only at variance with mainstream American sentiments regarding the war, but at odds with prevailing attitudes held by most other Irish American Catholics.

In truth, altogether too much has been made of both the representative role and the influence wielded by these ardent nationalists during the years of neutrality. That they were vocal and persistent cannot be denied. But their pronounced German sympathies neither wooed nor captured the imagination and support of the vast majority of Irish American Catholics. By their own admission, they were miniscule in number, considerably disorganized, and noticeably strapped for financial support. Clustered largely in New York and a few other urban centers, their press enjoyed only a limited circulation that paled in comparison to the many Catholic publications readily available throughout the larger Irish American Catholic community. In most of their endeavors, they failed miserably. Their overtures to Irish American labor may have borne occasional success, but fell largely on deaf ears. Despite labor's wariness of Great Britain, it generally backed the government and blunted the larger schemes of radicals and pacifists. And despite several fortuitous opportunities that were presented, the radicals were unable to discredit Irish American support for Home Rule as a viable solution for Irish independence. American entry into the war in 1917 and political instability within Ireland itself would eventually spell doom for Home Rule advocacy.[31]

Privately, Irish American professionals harbored no illusions about their abysmal failure in snaring support within their own community. Throughout the entire period of American neutrality, they were plagued by their own attachment to a German military victory as a means of

---

31. Frank L. Grubbs, *The Struggle for Labor Loyalty: Gompers, the A.F.L. and the Pacifists, 1917–1920* (Durham, NC: Duke University Press, 1968), 149.

freeing Ireland from Britain's grip. This position became steadily more untenable as America drew closer to involvement, and Irish American Catholics never could come around to embracing it. Looking retrospectively from the time Irish Americans rejected the Versailles treaty, much to the professionals' delight, one historian has correctly observed that throughout the years of American neutrality, men like Devoy and Cohalan "did not speak for a majority of the Irish Americans, and the Celtic feeling against Wilson has often been exaggerated."[32]

Occasionally, as in the case of Britain's harsh suppression of the 1916 Dublin uprising, the sentiments of fervent Irish American nationalists dovetailed with those of the greater community. In the view of Irish America, the severe application of British justice was indefensible, and condemnation for it rang loudly from all quarters of the community. However, moderate and conservative Irish American Catholics could not stomach violence as a means of effecting Irish freedom and held the Clan-na-Gael and their confederates responsible for the unfortunate consequences of the feeble attempt to overthrow British rule. Although the Home Rule cause lost measurable support within mainstream Irish American circles, the Clan benefitted little as a result. One scholar may well have "hit the nail on the head" when he suggested that the Ireland created by the Easter uprising, the "terrible beauty" of which Yeats wrote, precipitated an identity crisis for the American Irish. The shape of Irish history from the Rising until liberation in 1923 was "too much for most Americans and many Irish Americans to absorb. Somehow, a real Ireland had emerged, exciting, bloody, and confusing, which had virtually nothing to do with Irish American identity. Independent Ireland and Irish America would go their own separate way."[33]

The professionals suffered their most significant setbacks during the campaign and election of 1916. Wed to the Hughes candidacy merely to repudiate the Wilson administration's pro-British policies, ardent Irish American nationalists failed to wean the greater community from supporting the Democratic ticket. Exasperated with its inability

32. John B. Duff, "The Versailles Treaty and the Irish-Americans," *Journal of American History* 55 (December 1968): 583.
33. Williams, *'Twas Only an Irishman's Dream*, 187.

CHAPTER 7

to influence the direction of American foreign policy, the *Irish World* glumly observed during the campaign that only two of ninety Irish American congressmen fulfilled their constituents' expectations. It referred to the remaining legislators with the derisive quip, "[They] outrageously misrepresent us."[34] Irish American politicians may well have possessed a better grasp of reality, however, for Irish Americans voted for Wilson in substantial numbers, and they did so in their best interests as Americans.

John Devoy's *Gaelic-American* may well be a case study when it comes to assessing the fundamental flaw in the professional's strategic approach. Arguably the most prominent figure in the professional camp, his *Gaelic-American* rolled out its first edition in September 1903. The most popular of Irish American newspapers, it boasted at one time a national circulation of nearly 30,000 subscribers. While the paper had some characteristics of the many other ethnic weeklies circulating in the early twentieth century, its fundamental goal differed from the rest. From start to finish, the *Gaelic-American* (despite its name) would not be an Irish immigrant's guide to assimilation in America. It did not catalogue the difficulties, triumphs, tragedies and struggles of a mostly working-class Irish American community here in the United States. It did not address the immigrants' concerns about employment, better housing, safer working conditions, and an end to child labor, issues so vital to Irish Americans in the Progressive era.

"Instead of trying to turn the Irish into better Americans," one observer has noted, "the paper existed to propagate the gospel according to the Clan-na-Gael." It did not actually target the great mass of Irish America and Catholic America. Despite its tendency toward hyperbole and sarcasm, the sophisticated journalistic quality of Devoy's writing catered to a highly literate and educated audience within Irish America. It was not intended for mass consumption, a somewhat flawed strategy in and of itself, as the targeted audience had a stake in succeeding in the United States. Few Irish immigrants (poor, working, or established) gave much serious thought to returning to their native land; they were here in the United States to stay. Under certain circumstances, Devoy, singularly devoted to the cause of Irish

---

34. *Irish World*, October 21, 1916.

freedom, was able to attract a degree of interest from the larger Irish American and Catholic community, but he rarely won over dedicated converts to his cause. In this respect, the Catholic press may well have been more successful in its appeal to Irish American sensitivities.[35]

Irish American Catholics continued to keep pace with the national sentiment about the war by falling squarely behind the administration when relations with Germany soured to the point that diplomatic ties were severed in 1917. Irish American support for the administration was virtually uniform during the diplomatic crises of February 1917, and presaged the undisguised endorsement given to the president's declaration of war in April of that year. This largely unqualified approbation merely capped a process that was long in the making. The Irish American Catholic community had been conditioned to respond obediently and loyally to the government and saw the war as an opportunity to prove their worthiness as American citizens.

The opportunities presented by America's entry into the war were not lost on Irish American Catholics. Long denigrated as potential subversives by nativists, they were anxious to demonstrate their patriotism with a fervor that would silence their critics forever. This desire animated their herculean contributions to the war effort. The Church manifestly understood the unique moment provided by the war for American Catholics to become incorporated into the national fabric. Cardinal Gibbons, long a leader in efforts to Americanize the Catholic Church, was in the vanguard of this inclusive process. Along with Archbishop Ireland, Gibbons was singularly focused on presenting American Catholics as patriots of the highest order. When Ireland congratulated him for "holding the Church in the foreground" in this mission, Gibbons replied:

> I am trying to do all that I can that the Church may be of full service to the country during these trying days, and no ground will be left after the ordeal is over upon which the enemies of the Church might endeavor to raise up unfair charges against her.[36]

35. Terry Golway, *Irish Rebel*, 233.
36. Archbishop John Ireland to James Cardinal Gibbons, December 28, 1917,

CHAPTER 7

Gibbons's dexterity in promoting the war effort at all costs was most keenly revealed in his adroit handling of Benedict XV's peace initiative in August 1917. Realizing that Wilson could not possibly embrace the pontiff's proposal, Gibbons never pressed the president on the matter and allowed him to gently decline the papal overture. Later, when Benedict asked Gibbons to personally intervene with Wilson to pursue a separate Austrian armistice in October 1918, Gibbons elected to write a vaguely benign letter in response. Though supportive of Benedict's desire for peace, Gibbons, pragmatic prelate that he was, knew papal intervention would not work.

Whereas Gibbons was chiefly responsible for establishing the tone of the American Catholic response to the declaration of war, the institutional Church added its considerable energies to the war effort. The Catholic press, predominantly administered by Irish American Catholics, rallied to the government's standard from the moment of America's declaration of war, and summoned the faithful to respond with patriotic brio and to eschew any dissenting opinions. Through the vast organizational network of institutional Catholicism, Irish American Catholics generously collaborated with the various domestic wartime measures and entered the armed services in prodigious numbers. With unparalleled success, the Knights of Columbus, a largely Irish American Catholic fraternal organization, were primarily responsible for implementing the American Catholic response to the war. Some in the Knights' leadership expressed concern over the inordinate attention paid to the few Irish American extremists who opposed the government. To counter this negative publicity, the Knights ensured that the Catholic contribution to the war effort was above reproach. America's entry into the war furnished the Knights with an occasion to defend Catholic loyalty from the assaults of nativists. Referring to the commendable Catholic response to the nation's need, the final report of the Knights of Columbus Commission on Religious Prejudice of August 1917 proudly refuted nativist claims of Catholic disloyalty as baseless and ludicrous. Based on their contributions, Cardinal Farley, in a speech titled "Catholics and the War" delivered on March 2, 1918,

---

and James Cardinal Gibbons to Archbishop John Ireland, December 31, 1917, *Gibbons Papers*, Archives of the Archdiocese of Baltimore.

rhetorically asked: "Is there a single thing that Catholics could do for their country which they have not done?"[37]

Gibbons's and Farley's emphatic defense of Catholic loyalty and patriotism during the war was aided by a precipitous decline in nativist anti-Catholic invective by the year 1914. During the years of American neutrality, nativist publications feebly tried to disprove Catholic loyalty to the nation by spinning the most incredible tales of Catholic duplicity, including claims that Romanists were involved in domestic terrorism and were providing intelligence to the Germans. Once the United States entered the war, nativists continued to allege that Catholics were untrustworthy when it came to their willingness to uphold the nation's values and that, as a potential "fifth column," they should be scrupulously monitored in the interests of public welfare. During these years, fewer readers were believing nativist tropes, and fewer still maintained their subscriptions. It seemed that Protestant subscribers could not make the imaginative leap to believe that Benedict XV should supplant the Kaiser as America's principal bogeyman. All the significant nativist newspapers and magazines experienced sharp declines in readership. Financially strapped, several were compelled to close shop. Even *The Menace* struggled to remain a viable outfit. After undergoing several name changes and relocations, this most popular of all nativist news organs ceased publication in 1942.[38]

Defending the Church against nativist attacks frequently took an aggressive and militant tone during the war years, and usually crowded out news of the European conflict and Ireland's struggle for liberation from the headlines of the Catholic press. Irish American Catholics seized opportunities to compare themselves favorably to American Protestants, particularly in matters of patriotism. The establishment of the Committee of Historical Records reflected a desire by the National Catholic War Council to flaunt American Catholic participation in the war effort. The armed services did not record the religious affiliation of men in the field, so this committee undertook the arduous task of searching parish files and Catholic societies' memberships to compile

37. Farley quoted in Dohen, *Nationalism and American Catholicism,* 160, n.58.
38. Nordstrom, *Danger on the Doorstep,* 194–95.

CHAPTER 7

evidence of Catholic participation. Efforts such as these furnished additional support for the contention that the Church was still laboring to prove Catholic patriotism. Daniel J. Ryan, the director of the Bureau of Historical Records for the National Catholic War Council, made special reference to supporting Catholic contributions:

> Records of War are forceful proofs of devotion to country. As Catholics, we are aware, and, like all good citizens, are fully appreciative of the role that our co-religionists played in America's part in the world conflict ... We should, however, have the tested record to show.[39]

Unlike their Protestant countrymen, American Catholics enjoyed a unity of purpose conditioned by years of obedience to authority and institutional discipline. Only two or three Catholics opposed entry into the armed services on religious grounds, and while there were nearly seventy pacifist clergymen from other denominations, none were reported from Catholic clerical ranks. When Baltimore's *Catholic Review* heard that three Protestant ministers had petitioned for exemption from military service, the editor gloated that Catholic priests would never shirk their patriotic duty and promised to "keep count of all Ministers whose patriotism is all in words."[40]

American Catholics had resented nativist Protestant attacks that far predated the outbreak of the Great War in 1914. During the period of American neutrality, this resentment found expression in Irish American Catholic denigration of Britain's purported altruism in the war. Given the length and breadth of British oppression in Catholic Ireland, it was virtually impossible for most Irish Americans to applaud British victories or endorse their motives in the war. It is revealing, however, that Irish American Catholics maintained a remarkable degree of balance in their assessments of the various European belligerents and adhered to strict neutrality. Moreover, they exercised great restraint in

---

39. Daniel J. Ryan, "American Catholic War Records," *American Ecclesiastical Review* 82 (June 1930): 592.

40. Abrams, *Preachers Present Arms,* 135, 197; *Baltimore Catholic Review,* April 14, 1917.

advancing the cause of a free Ireland by means of physical force. The majority of Irish Americans were shedding their attachment to their former homeland in an open, complete, and irrevocable embrace of their adopted home. For most Irish Americans, the chant of "perfidious Albion," and their sporting interest in "twisting the Lion's tail" at every opportunity, had lost their former luster. Francis Hackett may well have spoken of his fellow Irish Americans when he suggested, towards the end of the Great War, that greater America "may like their Irishman, they may want to be hospitable to his emotions, but they cannot belie the admiration and respect they have long given England."[41]

Creative tension was at the root of the Irish American Catholic experience during the war. It found expression in ambivalence towards both the British government and their own Protestant countrymen. Their desire to be accepted on an equal footing with Anglo-Saxon Protestants frequently clashed with their inclination to distrust them and wall themselves off within the safe havens of fortress Catholicism. The defensive quality of Irish American Catholicism before and during the war reflected these ambivalent feelings. While belting out the full-throated patriotic verses of George M. Cohan's songs, Irish Americans undoubtedly were voicing their genuine love for their adopted homeland. But they also betrayed significant anxieties about feeling at home in this land. When Daniel F. Cohalan boldly claimed that Irish Americans had always been "present in the defense of the flag and support of American institutions," he revealed an anxiety that America doubted this loyalty. These dynamic tensions, only inchoate at the turn of the century, were immensely magnified once the war began and ultimately forced the Irish American Catholic community to resolve them.[42]

Irish American Catholics resolved their uncertain position in American society by fully emerging during the war as militant Catholic Americans. Moreover, they did not entirely assimilate into American society, as the term itself infers an act of submission on their part; instead, they proved themselves worthy of American citizenship and

---

41. Francis Hackett, *Ireland: A Study in Nationalism* (New York: B. W. Huebsch, 1918), 16.

42. Brooklyn *Tablet*, April 21, 1917.

CHAPTER 7

did so largely on their own terms. In this respect they hoped to model for other Catholic ethnics what it meant to be good American Catholics. Along the way, they never completely abandoned their ethnic Irish identity, as it lived on in myriad cultural ways that were rooted in this unique identity.[43] Their adoption of American and Catholic positions made a casualty out of their exclusively Irish identification and outlook. Nowhere was this more evident than in their attraction to the Knights of Columbus, an organization that gloried in two fundamental principles—defense of the faith and love of country. As the Knights enjoyed unprecedented growth in membership, purely Irish ethnic organizations waned. The war merely accelerated a process that was already in process and helped Irish American Catholics make the transition to a new era. Cecil Spring Rice, Britain's uncertain and flawed observer of the American scene in Washington, was finally on the mark when he informed Sir Arthur Balfour that Britain need not be concerned about Irish American agitation once the United States had entered the war:

> Irishmen here who are anxious to be accepted on the footing of loyal American citizens will leave the Irish organizations ... When they are faced with the question of whether they wish to be branded as openly disloyal, they will, I think, refuse to accept the consequences.[44]

Spring Rice was correct. Irish American Catholics could not accept the consequences of disloyalty to the nation. In fact, it was the furthest thing from their minds.

43. The term "militant American Catholics" has been appropriated from Timothy J. Meagher's study of the Worcester Irish-American community. See Meagher's article in *From Paddy to Studs,* 86. What was apparent in Massachusetts was true in virtually all urban areas of the country: Catholicism was the central integrating force among different classes and ethnic groups. See Paula M. Kane, *Separatism and Subculture: Boston Catholicism, 1900–1920* (Chapel Hill: University of North Carolina Press, 1994), 314–25. Identity issues are discussed in Meagher, *Columbia Guide to Irish American History,* 119.

44. Sir Cecil Spring Rice to Arthur Balfour, November 30, 1917, in Stephen A. Gwynn, ed., *The Letters and Friendships of Sir Cecil Spring Rice,* 1:408.

BIBLIOGRAPHY

Primary Sources

Manuscript Collections

    Archives of the Archdiocese of Baltimore
        James Cardinal Gibbons Papers
    Library of Congress
        Robert Lansing Papers
        Joseph P. Tumulty Papers
        T. J. Walsh Papers
    Archives of the National Catholic War Council, Washington, DC
    New York Public Library
        Roger Casement Papers
        William Bourke Cockran Papers
        Joseph McGarrity Papers
        John Quinn Papers

Published Documents and Papers, Collected Letters

    Baker, Ray S. and William E. Dodd, eds. *The Public Papers of Woodrow Wilson*. 6 vols. New York: Harper and Brothers, 1925–1927.
    Documents Relative to the Sinn Fein Movement. London: His Majesty's Stationery Office, 1921.
    Gwynn, Stephen A., ed. *The Letters and Friendships of Sir Cecil Spring-Rice*. 2 vols. London: Macmillan, 1929.
    Himber, Alan, ed. *The Letters of John Quinn to William Butler Yeats*. Ann Arbor: University of Michigan Research Press, 1983.
    Isaacson, Alfred, ed. *Irish Letters in the New York Carmelites' Archives*. Boca Raton, FL: Vestigium Press, 1988.
    Link, Arthur S., ed. *The Papers of Woodrow Wilson, 1856–1919*. 69 vols. Princeton, NJ: Princeton University Press, 1966–1989.

BIBLIOGRAPHY

Shaw, Albert, ed. *The Messages and Papers of Woodrow Wilson.* 2 vols. New York: Review of Reviews Corp., 1924.

U.S. Congress. *Congressional Record.* 63rd–65th Congresses, 1914–1918.

Newspapers

Catholic Citizen (Milwaukee)
Catholic Messenger (Davenport, IA)
Catholic News (New York)
Catholic Register (Denver)
Catholic Register (Kansas City)
Catholic Review (Baltimore)
Catholic Standard and Times (Philadelphia)
Catholic Telegraph (Cincinnati)
Catholic Transcript (Hartford)
Catholic Universe (Cleveland)
Freeman's Journal (Dublin)
Gaelic-American (New York)
Indiana Catholic (Indianapolis)
Irish World (New York)
Michigan Catholic (Detroit)
New York Times (New York)
New York World (New York)
New World (Chicago)
Our Sunday Visitor (Huntington, IN)
Southern Messenger (San Antonio/Galveston)
The Leader (San Francisco)
The Monitor (San Francisco)
The Pilot (Boston)
The Tablet Brooklyn)
True Voice (Omaha)
Washington Post (Washington, DC)
Western Watchman (St. Louis)
A sampling of other national newspapers

BIBLIOGRAPHY

Periodicals

America
American Catholic Quarterly
American Ecclesiastical Review
Ave Maria
Catholic Fortnightly Review
Catholic World
Columbiad
Literary Digest
Mid-America
New Republic
Sacred Heart Review

Contemporary Works, Memoirs, Autobiographies

Beer, Thomas. *The Mauve Decade.* New York: Alfred A. Knopf, 1926.
Curley, James Michael. *I'd Do It Again: A Record of All My Uproarious Years.* New York: Arno Press, 1957.
Devoy, John. *Recollections of an Irish Rebel.* New York: Charles D. Young Company, 1929.
Duffy, Francis P. *Father Duffy's Story.* Garden City, NY: Garden City Publishing, 1919.
Gibbons, James Cardinal. *A Retrospect of Fifty Years.* New York: John Murphy, 1916.
Kelley, Francis C. *The Bishop Jots It Down.* Boston: Little, Brown, 1939.
Lansing, Robert. *War Memoirs of Robert Lansing.* Indianapolis: Bobbs-Merrill, 1935.
Leslie, Shane. *The Irish Issue in Its American Aspect.* New York: Scribner's, 1917.
McCartan, Patrick, FRCS,I. *With De Valera in America.* New York: Brentano, 1932.
McGuire, James K. *The King, The Kaiser and Irish Freedom.* New York: Devin-Adair, 1915.
―――. *What Germany Could Do for Ireland.* New York: Devin-Adair, 1916.

BIBLIOGRAPHY

O'Brien, William, and Desmond, Ryan, eds. *Devoy's Post Bag.* New York: C. J. Fallon, n.d.
O'Connell, William Cardinal. *Recollections of Seventy Years.* Boston: Little, Brown, 1934.
O'Leary, Jeremiah. *My Political Trial and Experiences.* New York: Jefferson Publishing, 1919.
Roosevelt, Theodore. *Fear God and Take Your Own Part.* New York: George H. Doran, 1916.
———. *Foes of Our Own Household.* New York: George H. Doran, 1916.
Tumulty, Joseph P. *Woodrow Wilson as I Know Him.* New York: George H. Doran, 1921.
Von Bernstorff, Johann. *My Three Years in America.* London: Skeffington & Son, 1922.

Pamphlets

A Statement of the American Truth Society in Defense of Its President Against an Unjust Attack upon Him by the President of the United States. New York: 1916.
Strong Words from Mr. Redmond. Treason to the Home Rule Cause. London: Sir Joseph Causton & Sons, 1916.

Secondary Sources

Abrams, Ray H. *Preachers Present Arms: The Role of the American Churches in World Wars I & II, with Some Observations on the War in Vietnam.* Scottsdale, AZ: Heald Press, 1969.
Allswang, John. *A House for All Peoples.* Lexington: University of Kentucky Press, 1971.
Anbinder, Tyler. *Five Points.* New York: Free Press, 2001.
Barrett, James R. *The Irish Way: Becoming American in the Multiethnic City.* New York: The Penguin Press, 2012.
Barry, Colman J., OSB, *The Catholic Church and German Americans.* Milwaukee: Bruce Publishing, 1953.
Beadles, John A. "The Syracuse Irish, 1812–1928: Immigration, Catholics, Socioeconomic Status, Politics and Nationalism." PhD dissertation, Syracuse University, 1974.

BIBLIOGRAPHY

Blum, John Morton. *Joe Tumulty and the Wilson Era*. Boston: Houghton-Mifflin, 1951.

Bonadio, Felice A. "The Failure of German Propaganda in the United States, 1914–1917." *Mid-America* 41 (January 1959): 40–57.

Brown, Thomas. *Irish-American Nationalism*. Philadelphia: Lippincott, 1966.

Brundage, David. *Irish Nationalists in America: The Politics of Exile, 1798–1998*. New York: Oxford University Press, 2016.

Brusher, Joseph, SJ. *Consecrated Thunderbolt: A Life of Father Peter Yorke of San Francisco*. San Francisco: Joseph F. Wagner, Inc., 1973.

Buckley, John Patrick. "The New York Irish: Their View of American Foreign Policy, 1914–1921." PhD dissertation, New York University, 1974.

Burchell, R. A. *The San Francisco Irish, 1848–1880*. Berkeley: University of California Press, 1980.

Carroll, F. M. *American Opinion and the Irish Question, 1910–1923*. New York: St. Martin's Press, 1978.

Clark, Dennis J. *The Irish in Philadelphia: Ten Generations of Urban Experience*. Philadelphia: Temple University Press, 1973.

Connable, Alfred, and Edward Silberfarb. *Tigers of Tammany*. New York: Holt, Rinehart, and Winston, 1967.

Connolly, Sean. *On Every Tide: The Making and Remaking of The Irish World*. New York: Basic Books, 2022.

Crighton, John C. *Missouri and the World War, 1914–1917*. Columbia: University of Missouri Press, 1947.

Cronin, Mike. *A History of Ireland*. New York: St. Martin's Press, 2002.

Cross, Robert D. *The Emergence of Catholic Liberalism in America*. Chicago: Quadrangle Press, 1967.

Cuddy, Edward. *Irish-Americans and National Isolationism, 1914–1917*. New York: Arno Press, 1967.

Curran, Robert Emmett, *Papist Devils in British America, 1574-1783*. Washington, DC: The Catholic University of America Press, 2014.

BIBLIOGRAPHY

D'Agostino, Peter R. *Rome in America: Transnational Catholic Ideology from the Risorgimento to Fascism.* Chapel Hill: The University of North Carolina Press, 2004.

DiGiovanni, Stephen Michael. *Archbishop Corrigan and the Italian Immigrants.* Huntington, IN: Our Sunday Visitor Publishing, 1994.

Dolan, Jay P. *American Catholic Experience: A History from Colonial Times to the Present.* Notre Dame, IN: University of Notre Dame Press, 1992.

———. *The Irish Americans: A History.* New York: Bloomsbury Press, 2008.

Doyle, David N. *Irish Americans: Native Rights and National Empires.* New York: Arno Press, 1976.

Doyle, David N., and Owen Dudley Edwards, eds. *America and Ireland, 1776–1976: The American Identity and the Irish Connection.* Westport, CT: Greenwood Press, 1976.

Egan, Maurice Francis, and John B. Kennedy. *The Knights of Columbus in Peace and War.* 2 vols. New Haven, CT: Knights of Columbus Press, 1920.

Ellis, John Tracy. *The Life of James Cardinal Gibbons.* 2 vols. Milwaukee: Bruce Publishing, 1952.

Ellis, John Tracy, ed. *Documents of American Catholic History.* Milwaukee: Bruce Publishing, 1956.

Emmons, David M. *The Butte Irish: Class and Ethnicity in an American Mining Town.* Urbana and Chicago: University of Illinois Press, 1989.

Esslinger, Dean R. "American Catholicism and Irish Attitudes toward Neutrality, 1914–1917: A Study of Catholic Minorities." *Catholic Historical Review* 57 (June 1967): 194–216.

Formisano, Ronald, and Constance K. Burns, eds. *Boston, 1700–1980: The Evolution of Urban Politics.* Westport, CT: Greenwood Press, 1984.

Gerson, Louis. *The Hyphenate in Recent American Politics and Diplomacy.* Lawrence: University of Kansas Press, 1964.

BIBLIOGRAPHY

Glazer, Nathan and Daniel P. Moynihan. *Beyond the Melting Pot.* Cambridge, MA: MIT Press, 1963.

Golway, Terry. *Irish Rebel: John Devoy and America's Fight for Irish Freedom.* New York: St. Martin's Press, 1998.

Grayson, Richard. *Belfast Boys: How Unionists and Nationalists Fought and Died Together in the First World War.* London: Continuum Books, 2009.

Grey, Miriam Nyhan, ed. *Ireland's Allies: America and the 1916 Easter Rising.* Dublin: University College Dublin Press, 2016.

Gwynn, Denis. *The Life of John Redmond.* London: Burns, Oates & Washburn, 1932.

Hammack, David C. *Power and Society: Greater New York at the Turn of the Century.* New York: Russell Sage Foundation, 1982.

Handlin, Oscar. *Boston's Immigrants: A Study in Acculturation.* Boston: Belknap Press, 1982.

Higham, John. *Strangers in the Land: Patterns of American Nativism, 1860–1925.* New York: Atheneum Press, 1963.

Jones, Maldwyn. *American Immigration.* Chicago: University of Chicago Press, 1960.

Karson, Marc. *American Labor Unions and Politics, 1900–1918.* Carbondale: Southern Illinois University Press, 1958.

Kaufmann, Christopher. *Faith and Fraternalism: The History of the Knights of Columbus, 1882–1982.* New York: Scribner's, 1982.

Kazin, Michael. *War Against War: The American Fight for Peace, 1914–1918.* New York: Simon & Schuster, 2017.

Kelly, Mary C. *The Shamrock and the Lily: The New York Irish and the Creation of a Transatlantic Identity, 1845–1921.* New York: Peter Lang, 2013.

Kenny, Kevin. *The American Irish: A History.* New York: Pearson Education, 2000.

Kibler, M. Alison. *Censoring Racial Ridicule: Irish, Jewish, and African American Struggles over Race and Representation.* Chapel Hill: University of North Carolina Press, 2015.

Krickus, Richard. *Pursuing the American Dream: White Ethnics and the New Populism.* Bloomington: Indiana University Press, 1976.

BIBLIOGRAPHY

Leary, William M. "Woodrow Wilson, Irish-Americans, and the Election of 1916." *Journal of American History* 54 (June 1967): 57–72.

Lee, J. J., and Marion Casey, eds. *Making the Irish American: History and Heritage of the Irish in the United States.* New York: New York University Press, 2006.

Levine, Edward. *The Irish and Irish Politicians.* Notre Dame, IN: Notre Dame University Press, 2016.

Link, Arthur S. *Wilson: Campaigns for Progressivism and Peace, 1916–1917.* Princeton, NJ: Princeton University Press, 1965.

———. *Wilson: Confusions and Crises, 1915–1916.* Princeton, NJ: Princeton University Press, 1964.

———. *Wilson: The Struggle for Neutrality, 1914–1915.* Princeton, NJ: Princeton University Press, 1960.

Lovell, S. D. *The Presidential Election of 1916.* Carbondale: Southern Illinois University Press, 1980.

Luebke, Frederick C. *Bonds of Loyalty: German Americans and World War I.* DeKalb: Northern Illinois University Press, 1974.

McAvoy, Thomas T. *The Americanist Heresy in Roman Catholicism, 1895–1900.* New York: Baracaldo Press, reprint 2020.

———. *The Great Crisis in American Catholic History, 1895–1900.* Chicago: Quadrangle Press, 1957.

McCaffrey, Lawrence. *The Irish Diaspora in America.* Bloomington: Indiana University Press, 1976.

———. *Irish Nationalism and the American Contribution.* New York: Arno Press, 1976.

McGurrin, James. *Bourke Cockran: A Free Lance in American Politics.* New York: Charles Scribner's Sons, 1948.

May, Henry F. *The End of American Innocence: A Study of the First Years of Our Own Time, 1912–1917.* Chicago: Quadrangle Press, 1964.

Meagher, Timothy J. *The Columbia Guide to Irish American History.* (New York: Columbia University Press, 2005.

BIBLIOGRAPHY

———, ed. *From Paddy to Studs: Irish-American Communities in the Turn of the Century Era, 1880–1929.* New York: Greenwood Press, 1986.

———. *Inventing Irish America: Generation, Class, and Ethnic Identity in a New England City, 1880–1928.* Notre Dame, IN: Notre Dame University, 2001.

Merwick, Donna. *Boston Priests: A Study of Social and Intellectual Change.* Cambridge, MA: Harvard University Press, 1973.

Miller, Kerby A. *Emigrants and Exiles: Ireland and the Irish Exodus to North America.* New York: Oxford University Press, 1985.

Morris, Charles R. *American Catholic: The Saints and Sinners Who Built America's Most Powerful Church.* New York: Crown Publishing Group, 1997.

Moynihan, James. *The Life of Archbishop Ireland.* New York: Macmillan, 1953.

Murray, Damien. *Irish Nationalists in Boston: Catholicism and Conflict, 1900–1928.* Washington, DC: The Catholic University of America Press, 2018.

Nelson, Bruce. *Irish Nationalists and the Making of the Irish Race.* Princeton, NJ: Princeton University Press, 2012.

Nordstrom, Justin. *Danger on the Doorstep: Anti-Catholicism and American Print Culture in the Progressive Era.* Notre Dame, IN: Notre Dame University, 2006.

O'Connell, Marvin Richard. *John Ireland and the American Catholic Church.* St. Paul: Minnesota Historical Society Press, 1988.

O'Dea, John. *History of the Ancient Order of Hibernians and the Ladies' Auxiliary.* 3 vols. Philadelphia: National Board of the A.O.H., 1923.

O'Halpin, Eunan. *The Decline of the Union: British Government in Ireland, 1892–1920.* Syracuse, NY: Syracuse University Press, 1987.

O'Toole, James M. *Militant and Triumphant: William Henry O'Connell and the Catholic Church in Boston, 1859–1944.* Notre Dame, IN: Notre Dame University Press, 1992.

BIBLIOGRAPHY

Pusey, Merlo J. *Charles Evan Hughes.* 2 vols. New York: Columbia University Press, 1963.

Reid, B. L. *The Lives of Roger Casement.* New Haven, CT: Yale University Press, 1976.

Rodechko, James Paul. *Patrick Ford and His Search for America: A Case Study of Irish-American Journalism, 1870–1913.* New York: Arno Press, 1976.

Rogers, James Silas. *Irish-American Autobiography: Athletes, Priests, Pilgrims, and More.* Washington, DC: The Catholic University of America Press, 2017.

Rosenzweig, Roy. *Eight Hours for What We Will: Workers and Leisure in an Industrial City, 1870–1920.* New York: Cambridge University Press, 1983.

Ryan, Daniel J. *American Catholic War Records.* Washington, DC: Catholic University of America Press, 1941.

Ryan, Dennis P. *Beyond the Ballot Box: A Social History of the Boston Irish, 1845–1917.* Rutherford, NJ: Associated University Presses, 1983.

Shannon, William. *The American Irish: A Political and Social Portrait.* New York: Macmillan, 1963.

Slawson, Douglas J. *Ambition and Arrogance: Cardinal William O'Connell of Boston and the American Catholic Church.* Cobalt Productions, 2007.

Smith, Daniel. *American Intervention, 1917: Sentiment, Self-Interest, or Ideals?* Boston: Houghton-Mifflin, 1966.

———. *Robert Lansing and American Neutrality, 1914–1917.* New York: De Capo Press, 1972.

Strout, Cushing. *The American Image of the Old World.* New York: Harper and Row, 1963.

Tansill, Charles C. *America and the Fight for Irish Freedom, 1866–1922.* New York: Devin Adair, 1957.

Tarpey, Marie Veronica. *The Role of Joseph McGarrity in the Struggle for Irish Independence.* New York: Arno Press, 1976.

Tentler, Leslie Woodcock. *American Catholics: A History.* New Haven, CT: Yale University Press, 2020.

BIBLIOGRAPHY

Viereck, George Sylvester. *Spreading Germs of Hate.* New York: Scribner's, 1930.

Ward, Alan J. *Ireland and Anglo-American Relations, 1899–1921.* Montreal: McGill University Press, 1969.

Will, Allen Sinclair. *The Life of Cardinal Gibbons, Archbishop of Baltimore.* Baltimore: E. P. Dutton, 1922.

Wingerd, Mary Lethert. *Claiming the City: Politics, Faith, and the Power of Place in St. Paul.* Ithaca, NY: Cornell University Press, 2001.

Witcover, Jules. S*abotage at Black Tom: Imperial Germany's Secret War in America, 19141917.* Chapel Hill, NC: Algonquin Books, 1989.

Wittke, Carl. *The Irish in America.* Baton Rouge: Louisiana State University Press, 1956.

INDEX

Abbelen, Peter, 101–2
Adams, John Quincy, 22
Addams, Jane, 31
Abrams, Ray, 155
Alemany, Joseph, 41
America (journal), 131, 159, 172, 184, 193, 203, 209, 212, 218, 227, 235, 242, 272, 279, 296, 310. *See also* Richard Tierney (editor)
American Catholic Church, 1, 74, 124, 141, 245–46; clerical domination of Irish, 85–95; centrality of parish, 87–89; effusion of loyalty and patriotism when war declared, 285– position on Mexico, 171–72; subordination of clergy to hierarchy, 154; staying neutral course, 180. *See also* Irish American Caholics
American Irish Historical Society, 204
Americanists, 99–104
Americanist Controversy 98–104
Americanization, 12, 118–19, 244, 252, 283
American Protective Association (APA), 8, 115
American Truth Society, 144, 149, 181, 190, 198, 250, 296
Anaconda Mines, 38
Ancient Order of Hibernians 7, 57, 64, 90, 97, 120, 144, 162, 181, 197, 209, 234, 241, 262, 269, 276, 285; cancel 1918 convention, 296
Anti-British foreign policy, 62–63, 148
Anti-Chinese bigotry, 62–63, 174
Anti-Catholicism, 5, 16, 252. *See also* nativism
Anti-German hysteria, 300–303
Arabic, 190–93, 199
Armed Neutrality League, 182
Asquith, H.H., 69–70
Aud, 224
Austria, 158

Bachelor's Walk, 136–37
Bagley, A.G., 291–92
Baker, Newton, 305
Balfour, Arthur, 284, 330
Baltimore Sun, 192
Barry, Commodore Jack, 134–35, 201
Barry, J.T., 234
Baseball, 61
Bay of Tralee, 223
Beer, Thomas, 92
Belgium, 126, 144, 163–65, 271; her neutrality violated, 163; German plundering of, 163, 208
Benedict XV, 167, 190, 214–15, 216n10, 247, 263, 294n1, 305, 326–27

INDEX

Berlin, 214
Birth of a Nation, 174
Black and Tans, 316
Black Tom Island, 216–19
Blaine, James G., 24
Boer War, 63
Boxing, 60–61
Bogus Oath, 115
Bonanzo, Monsignor Giovanni, 263
Borah, William F., 318
Boston, 27–28
Boston Transcript, 236
Bowers, Henry F., 80–81
Boxing, 60–61
Boy–Ed, Karl, 200, 217
British Parliament (London), 68–70, 136–38
Brown, Thomas, 117, 120
Broderick, David C., 42
Bryan, William Jennings, 31, 170, 180, 188, 190, 261
Bryce Report, 132, 178
Buckley, Christopher A., 42
Buckley, John P., 153, 265
Buffalo Catholic Union and Times, 206
Burke, Rev. John, 158–59, 165, 186, 193, 236, 299, 300, 304
Burleson, Albert S., 295–96
Butler, Col. Edward, 33
Butte Miners Union (BMU), 38, 197–98

Cahensly, Peter, 100
Callahan, Patrick, 278–80
Campbell, William, 226, 237
Campbell-Bannerman, Sir Henry, 67
Carnegie Hall, 133, 231–32, 243, 281, 290

Carranza, Venustiano, 128–29, 170–73, 212, 256
Carson, Sir Edward, 135–37, 186, 222
Carter-Harrisons, 31–32
Casement, Sir Roger, 131, 146, 185–86, 223, 229, 244, 249, 251; incredulous of Gibbons, 151–52; his part in the Easter rising, 223; schemes to aid Germany, 146–48; his trial and execution, 238–42
Casserly, Eugene, 42
Cassidy, Harvey, 140
Cassidy, Rev. James, 306–7
Catholic Citizen (Milwaukee), 141, 196. See also Humphrey Desmond (editor)
Catholic Messenger (Iowa), 137, 142, 186, 204, 228, 237, 275. *See also* Fred Sharon (editor)
Catholic News (Chicago)) 166, 207, 219, 234, 277. See also Thomas V. Shannon (editor)
Catholic Press, 93, 117–18, 135, 141, 146, 149–50; 155–56, 163, 211, 214, 218, 234–39, 247–48, 264, 274–75, 299–300, 319, 325–26; effusion of loyalty and patriotism when war declared, 285–88; circulation, popularity, and Irish American imprint, 95–98; campaigns to uplift Irish American virtue, 203–7; quiet on *Birth of a Nation,* 175; visceral reaction to Easter rising executions, 234–37; wages war with anti-Catholic bigots
Catholic Register (Kansas City), 195–96

INDEX

Catholic Review (Baltimore), 140, 274–75, 328. *See also* Rev. C.P. Thomas (editor)
Catholic Standard and Times (Philadelphia), 172, 236. *See also* John J. O'Shea (editor) and Edward P. Spillane (editors)
Catholic Total Abstinence Union, 119
Catholic Telegraph (Cincinnati), 228, 237, 265. *See also* Dr. Thomas Hart (editor)
Catholic Transcript, (Hartford), 192–94, 228–29, 271. *See also* Rev. Thomas O' Flanagan (editor)
Catholic Universe (Cleveland), 214, 226, 256. *See also* William McKearney (editor)
Catholic World, 158–59, 186, 193, 236, 289, 299. *See also* Rev. John Burke (editor)
Central Powers, 156, 163, 166, 281
Chicago, 28, 31
Cincinnati, 301
Clancy, Charles J., 225
Church Peace Union, 278
Clan na Gael, 7, 66–68, 117, 137, 141, 144–46, 167–68, 186, 204, 210, 213, 219–20, 222–23, 229, 247–48, 279, 296, 311, 316, 323–24; failure to court Irish American Catholics, 150, 168; financial woes, 144, 168, 244; hopes for German victory, 144–45; pressure Wilson on self-determination, 311; sustaining the neutral course, 145
Clark, James T., 189
Clarke, William J., 257
Clay, Henry, 22
Cleveland, Grover, 24, 63, 106

Cockran, Bourke, 135, 160, 196, 209, 231–32, 261, 266, 269, 278, 283, 297, 318
Cohalan, Daniel F., 67–68, 146, 183, 222, 232, 239, 243, 279, 296, 311, 313, 317–19, 323, 229, 329; excuses himself with meeting with Wilson, 313; nearly convicted of pro-German conspiracy, 296; split with de Valera, 316–17
Colby, Bainbridge, 261
Collins, Michael, 316
Columbiad, 291–92
Conness, John, 41
Connolly, James, 42, 225
Conrad, Joseph, 225
Cooper Union, 132
Corbett, Jim, 59–60
Corrigan, Bishop Michael, 2–3, 101, 107–8
Cotter, Rev. James H., 206
Coughlin, John, 32
Crimmins, John B., 225
Croker, Richard, 30
Croly, Herbert, 260
Cuddy, Edward, 137, 265
Cunningham, William D., 204
Curley, James Michael, 28, 160, 175, 244, 309
Cushing, 187, 192

Dail Eireann, 316
Daly, Marcus, 37–38
Daughters of the American Revolution, 202
Debs, Eugene, 111
Democratic party, 30; 250, 252, 262, 268–69; Irish American attachment to, 23, 266, 260

345

INDEX

Democratic Convention 1916, 252–55
Dempsey, Rev. Timothy, 154
Denver, 37
Denver Catholic Register, 290
Dernberg, Dr. Bernhard, 182, 187–89
Desmond, Humphrey, 141, 157–58, 186, 196, 221, 229, 248, 275, 289
De Valera, Eamonn, 309, 316
Devoy, John, 10, 57, 132, 135, 138, 144–45, 148, 164, 182, 186, 189, 198, 208, 214, 222, 229, 232, 241, 244, 249, 259, 266, 273, 281–82, 294, 311–12, 319, 323; accuses Wilson of delaying House resolution on Casement's behalf, 241; admits *Lusitania* sets back cause, 208–9; antipathy for Wilson, 134–35, 253; blames Wilson for apprising British of Rising, 232; chides Gibbons for his support of Redmond, 198; counters British censorship, 148–49; crafts speech for Gibbons, 312; critical of Knights of Columbus, 204, 244; disputes with Catholic church, 151; leader of Clan-na-Gael, 66–68; urges strict neutrality in 1916, 251; splits with de Valera, 316–17; von Igel Raid, 217–18
Diaz, Porfirio, 128
Dillon, John, 224–25
Dolan, Jay P., 1
Donohoe, Michael, 209
Dooley, Martin, 56
Dougherty, Cardinal Dennis James, 314
Dowling, Victor, 261
Doyle, Michael F., 239, 244, 251–52
Dublin, 136, 211, 224–25

Dublin Castle, 224
Dunne, Edward F., 261
Dunne, Finley Peter, 55–56
Dunne, William Fitzgibbons, 51
Egan, Patrick, 142, 162, 227
Easter Rising, 38, 42, 174, 211, 230–38, 249, 320, 323; American Catholic relief efforts, 245–47
Election of 1916, 250–64, 323
Elliott, Walter, and *The Life of Father Hecker,* 103–4
Emmons, David, 39n26, 285
Extension Magazine, 262

Falaba, 187–88, 192
Famine Immigrants, 61–62, 75
Farley, Cardinal John, 86, 153–54, 190, 196, 227, 246–47, 287, 326–27; eager to squash Irish American Catholic dissent, 298–99
Farrell, James T., 45; author of *Studs Lonigan Trilogy,* 55
Farrelly, Bishop John P., 286–87
Feehan, Bishop Patrick, 101, 104
Father Mathew Society, 119
Fenians, 65; attack British Canada, 65–66
Fillmore, Millard, 22, 75
Finlander Hall, 38
Fitzgerald, John J., 28, 271, 284
Five Points, 105
Flag Day 1916, 254
Flaherty, John, 291
Flannery, Rev. Edward, 262
Flynn, Ed, 30
Foley, Reverend M.J., 172
Ford, A. Brendan, 148, 189, 193, 214, 221, 271, 281–83
Ford, Patrick, 115
Fox, Elmer, 290

INDEX

France, 164–65
Franklin Park, 134–35, 201
Freeman's Journal, 141, 156–57, 185, 193, 248, 271, 273, 282–83; 295
Friends of Irish Freedom (FOIF), 210, 220, 227, 246–47, 249, 275, 298, 319; pressure Wilson on self-determination, 311; suspends activities in 1917, 296
Friends of Irish Liberty, 232
Friendly Sons of St. Patrick, 162, 185, 205, 256, 285
Friends of Peace, 190

Gaelic-American, 132, 136, 138, 145, 160, 190, 198, 204, 244, 279, 294, 324; banned from mail, 296. *See also* John Devoy (editor)
Gaelic football, 58, 67
Gainer, Joseph H., 29
Gallagher, Bishop Michael, 279, 319
Gannon, Rev. Peter, 192, 228, 236
Garrison, Lindley, 277
Gavegan, Edward J., 232
George, Henry, 106–7; and *Poverty and Progress,* 106
Germania statues, 301
German Americans, 15, 214
German Central Alliance, 144, 182
German-Irish Central Legislative Committee, 181, 190
German military, 144, 207, 271; and use of submarines, 177, 199, 208, 322; resumption of unrestricted submarine policy, 213–16, 271, 273; relax unrestricted submarine warfare in 1916, 220; sabotage, 215–20

Gibbons, Cardinal James 3, 10, 86, 141, 151–53, 165, 192, 198–99, 247, 274, 277, 304, 306, 319, 325–26; and condemnation of Easter rising, 226–27; Americanist controversy, 100–104, 108–10; Anglophilic leanings, 151–52, 168; on Catholic loyalty and patriotism, 257–58; endorses self-determination, 312; on *Lusitania,* 190, 194; on Mexican Revolution, 129–30, 171, 173; eager to squash Catholic dissent, 298; promotes Catholic patriotism in war with Spain, 113; urges strict neutrality, 154; supports declaration of war, 286; support for Home Rule, 140–41; supports Preparedness campaign, 277–78; tentative endorsement of League, 319; throws his support to war effort, 307–8
Gladstone, William, 66, 69
Glennon, Bishop John, 301
Glynn, Martin, 261, 269; and "He Kept Us Out of War."
Goethe, 301
Goff, John, W., 209
Gompers, Samuel, 190
Gore, Thomas P., 199, 261
Grace, William R., 41
Great Anthracite Coal Strike (1902), 50
Great Britain, 141, 144, 178, 316, 322
Great War, 1, 14, 38–39, 61, 86, 106, 153, 169, 196, 214, 258, 293, 308–10, 321. *See also* World War I
Gregory, Thomas, 217
Grey, Sir Edward, 139, 210, 239–41
Griffin, Jerome, 162

347

INDEX

Griffith, D.H., 174–75
Grimes, Bishop John, 140, 247
Gulflight, 187, 192

Hackett, Francis, 209, 225–26, 234, 242–43, 260, 329
Hague, Frank 29
Hanna, Bishop Edward, 246
Harding, Richard, 164–65
Harper's Weekly, 77
Harrigan, Edward, 53–55
Harris, Frank, 185
Hart, Dr. Thomas, 141–42, 182, 194, 237, 264, 275, 289
Hart, Tony, 53–54
Hartley, Bishop James J., 96
Hayes, Bishop Patrick, 305
Hay-Pauncefote Treaty, 133
Hearst, William Randolph, 149
Herbert, Victor, 210
Hobson, Bulmer, 223
Holy Name Society, 5, 97
Home Rule, 9, 67–72, 136, 139–42, 144, 159, 162, 168, 185–87, 222, 225, 227, 229, 233, 243, 247, 311, 322–23
Hoover, Herbert, 307
Hopkins, John Patrick, 31
House, Col. Edward M., 180, 214
House of Lords, 68–70
Howard, Sir Henry, 166
Howells, William Dean, 53–54, 230
Hudson, Rev. D.E., 289
Huerta, Victoriano, 128–29, 170
Hughes, Bishop John, 8, 21,
Hughes, Charles Evan, 251, 256, 258–62, 265–69, 277, 323
Hughes, William, 141, 236, 242, 248, 264
Husting, Paul O., 252

Indiana Catholic, 136, 141, 157, 159, 182; 206, 235, 248, 283. *See also* Joseph P. O'Mahoney (editor)
Intemperance, 118–19
Ireland, 140, 225
Ireland, 293, 312–13, 315, 323 325
Ireland, Bishop John 3, 122–23, 175, 303, 304, 306; in Americanist controversy, 101–3, 106; little sympathy for German Americans, 302–3; promote Catholic patriotism in war with Spain, 113; and *Church in Modern Society*, 113–14; proponent of Preparedness campaign, 278
Irish American Catholics 4, 10–12, 15, 131, 150, 162, 200–207, 229, 249; as Americans, 9; in presidential elections, 22, 265; antipathy towards blacks, 176; among labor leaders,48–52; attraction to political power, 25–26; Catholic chaplains, 306; centrality of parish, 84–90; emphasizing loyalty to U.S. government, 251, 257; explosion of patriotism, 293–94; political machines and their dynamics, 26–43; pre-famine church, 84; immigrants planting roots, 52; indignation over Casement execution, 238–42; Irish nationalism secondary to interests as Americans, 293; socio-economic mobility 44–51; pre-famine church, 84; toward cultural inclusion, 52–61; pursuing neutral course, 144; swell ranks of AEF; visceral reaction to Easter rising

INDEX

executions, 233–38; vote in their own interests, 267–68
Irish American Nationalism; its collapse in 1917, 297; turn on Wilson, 315
Irish Civil War, 316, 320
Irish Immigration 20, 22; in Jacksonian era, 22; Famine immigrants, 23; in 1910 census, 23
Irish Fellowship Club, 189
Irish Nationalism, 221. *See also* Irish American Nationalism, 221
Irish Parliamentary (IPP), 137–38, 249
Irish Progressive League, 310
Irish Race Conventions 10, 31, 66, 208, 243, 310, 312–13; Irish societies denounce Devoy's convocation of convention in 1916, 220
Irish Republican Army, 309, 315
Irish Republican Brotherhood (IRB), 65, 72, 222–23
Irish 69th Regiment, 203
Irish Relief Funds, 245–46
Irish Volunteers, 72, 160, 222–24
Irish War of Independence, 315, 317, 320
Irish World, 115, 148, 159, 189–90, 214, 219–21, 266, 271, 273–74, 279, 281, 294–95, 324; banned from mail, 295
Italian American Catholics 60, 105

Jackson, Andrew, 22
Jeffries, Jim, 60
Jennings, Michael J., 244
Jersey City, 216–19
"Jiggs", 56–57
Johnson, Hiram, 266

Johnson, Jack, 60, 105
Joint American and Mexican Peace Commission, 213
Jones, Mary Harris, 51–52

Kaiser Wilhelm, 147, 158, 184–85, 272–73, 327
Keane, Bishop John, 102
Kelly, "Honest John", 30
Kelley, Rev. Francis C., 131, 170; 173, 212, 262
Kenna, Michael 32
Kensington Riots 21
King's Own Scottish Borderers, 136–37
Knights of Columbus, 2, 5, 7, 64, 90, 94–95, 97, 119, 244, 269, 291–92, 304–5, 326, 330; Commission on Religious Prejudice, 278–79, 326; combat APA's Bogus Oath, 115; contribute to war effort, 304; in Mexico, 212–13; loyalty to government, 203–4; perceived as loyal Americans, 305; support for neutrality, 163, 197; support Preparedness campaign, 278; to contribute to volunteer army, 291; to expunge any Catholic disloyalty, 291–92
Knights of Labor, 49, 51, 108–10
Knights of St. Patrick, 205, 240
Know Nothings, 30, 75
Knox-Porter Resolution, 318
Ku Klux Klan (KKK), 13, 174

Lackaye, Wilton, 205
Land League, 69
Lansing, Robert, 180, 200, 202, 214, 237–38
Larkin, James, 38–39

349

INDEX

Lattimer, PA, 50
League of Nations, 67, 315, 317–18
Leary, William M., 265–67
Leay, F.P., 269
Leo XIII, 2, 81, 102–5, 109
Leslie, Shane, 136, 140, 162, 209, 234, 239
Link, Arthur S., 169, 269
Lippmann, Walter, 230
Literary Digest, 230
Lodge, Henry Cabot, 317–18
Logue, Cardinal Michael, 151, 247
Lomasney, Martin 28, 252
Lonigan, Patrick, 55–57
Lord Castlereagh, 236
Louvain, 165
Lowell, MA, 89
Loyola, Ignatius, SJ, 81
Lusitania, 180, 187–208, 214, 261, 277–79, 284
Lynch, Rev. Frederick, 278

Mac Neill, Eoin, 224, 233
McCarthy, Patrick J., 29
McCumber, Porter, Jr., 297
McCormack, Vance, 261, 266
Mc Faul, Bishop James A., 257–58
McGarrity, Joseph, 67, 138, 145, 147, 160, 186, 222, 239, 243, 282; continues support of de Valera, 317
McGivney, Rev. Michael, 5, 94
McGlynn, Rev. Edward, 107–9
McGooey, John, 30
McGuiness, Edwin D., 29
McGuire, James J., 173
McGuire, James K., 140, 183, 240, 282
McKearney, William A., 214, 226, 289–90

McLaughlin, James, 181, 209, 241, 275
McLemore, Jeff A., 199, 261, 283–84
McManus, George, 56–57
McQuaid, Bishop Bernard, 2–3, 101, 104, 106
Madero, Francisco, 128
Madison Square Garden, 151, 190, 311
Magennis, Rev. Peter, 210, 298, 319; chastised by Cardinal Farley, 298–99
Malone, Dudley Field, 170
Manners, J. Hartley, 121
Martine, James E., 239, 250
Maxwell, Sir John, 224–25, 229, 233
May, Henry F., 179–80
Mayo, Rear Admiral Henry T., 129
Mercier, Cardinal Desire Joseph, 140, 165
Messmer, Bishop Sebastian, 301
Meunter, Erich, 216n11
Mexican Revolution, 127–31, 211, 261
Meyer, Kuno, 183–85
Michigan Catholic, 141, 236, 242, 248, 264. *See also* William Hughes (editor)
Miller, Kirby A., 320; *Emigrants and Exiles,* 320
Milwaukee, 35–36, 301
Mitchell, John, 49–50
Mitchell, John Purroy, 185, 205, 284
Molly McGuires, 48
Monk, Mary, 21
Mott, John, M., 213, 262
Monitor (San Francisco), 282
Morgan, J.P., 199, 273
Mount St. Mary's College, 87

INDEX

Mundelein, Cardinal George, 203, 262
Munsterberg, Hugo, 183
Murphy, Charles F., 30, 160, 244, 261, 308

Nast, Thomas, 63, 77
National Americanization Day, 201, 204
National Catholic War Council (NCWC), 300, 306 314, 327; Committee of Historical Records, 327–28
Nativism, 72, 74–75, 80, 88, 326–28; and APA, 80–82; and Secret Oath, 82; precipitous decline by 1914, 327
New Republic, 209, 225, 230, 242, 260
New World, 156, 159, 185, 193, 234, 242, 264, 274. *See also* Thomas V. Shannon (editor)
New York Evening Sun, 182, 277
New York Times, 129, 173, 190, 192, 219, 250n1, 257–58
New York Times Magazine, 241–42
New York World, 263
Noll, Rev, John P., 153, 156
Nordstrom, Justin, 7
Notre Dame Academy, 87

Oates, Mary, 1,
O'Brien, Morgan J., 285
O'Connell, Cardinal William 2, 47, 86, 93, 103, 123, 151, 153, 174–75, 190, 235–36, 263, 280, 288, 300–301, 311, 314
O'Connell, Daniel (Albany), 29–30
O'Connell, Daniel, 65
O'Connell, Bishop Denis, 102

O'Donnell, Patrick, H., 189
O'Donnell, Rev. Patrick, 244
O'Donnell, Patrick H., 209
Donohoe, Michael, 209
O'Gorman, James A., 133, 197, 209, 285
O'Flanagan, Thomas, 157, 192–94, 228–29, 237, 265, 271, 289
O'Hern, Rev. Louis, 304–5
O'Leary, Jeremiah, 145, 149, 181, 198, 202, 255–56, 259, 267, 276, 282; his publication *Bull* banned from mail, 296; obstructs draft and is arrested, 296
O'Leary, Joshua, 198, 250–51
O'Mahoney, Joseph P., 136, 141, 146, 157, 159, 164, 166, 182, 185, 193, 235, 272, 277, 283, 314
O'Neil, Eugene, 55
O'Shea, John, J., 172
O'Sheel, Shaemus, 199
O'Sullivan, John L., 58–59
Orange Riots, 19
Our Sunday Visitor, 115, 153, 156

Paddy, 54
Panama Tolls Controversy, 133–34, 136
Parker, Sir Gilbert, 153, 178
Parnell, Charles, 66
Pascendi Dominici Gregis, 105
Peg O' My Heart, 121
Pendergast, "Big Jim", 34
Pendergast, Tom, 34–35
Pershing, John, 211–12
Phelan, James D., 42–43, 197, 204, 240, 257, 283, 313, 318
Phelan, Rev. D.S., 155
Pilot, (Boston), 158, 174–75, 235–36, 242, 248

351

INDEX

Pittsburgh Catholic, 137, 157, 173, 192, 264, 279. *See also* Francis P. Smith (editor)
Pius X, 157, 166, 214
Playboy of the Western World, 94, 120
Polk, Frank L., 240
Polk, James K, 22
Powderly, Terence, 109
Power, Monsignor James, 299
Powers, Johnny, 32
Praeger, Robert, 301
Presbyterians, 16–18
Progressive Era, 1, 5–6, 126, 293, 324
Providence, R.I. 29
Puck, 63

Quigley, Eugene, 256
Quinn, John, 93, 136, 161–62, 185, 196–97, 209, 225, 233–34, 239–43, 260, 280–81, 284–85, 297

Rankin, Jeannette, 283, 289
Ratchford, Michael, 49
Redmond, John, 9, 67–70, 136–38, 141, 144, 154, 158, 186–87, 224–25, 227, 233–34, 237, 249
Rerum Novarum, 2
Retrospect of Fifty Years, 257
Riordan, Bishop Patrick W., 41
Rome, 126; as head of transnational church, 126; urging neutrality in 1914, 126–27
Roosevelt, Theodore, 50, 56, 72, 106, 186, 258, 266–67, 278, 284, 306; anti-hyphen, 258–59; *Foes of Our Own Household,* 306
Root-Bryce Arbitration Treaty, 132
Russell, AE, 161
Russell Brothers, 58

Russell, Bishop William T., 286
Ryan, Daniel J., 328
Ryan, John T., 296
Ryan, Michael J., 136, 138–39, 145, 160, 233, 237

San Francisco, 40–41
Satolli, Cardinal Francesco, 103
Schweiger, Capt. Walter, 196
Scots-Irish, 16–17; as immigrants 17–18
Self-determination for Ireland, 272, 294
Shannon, Thomas V., 156, 159, 234, 242, 264, 273, 283
Sharon, Fred, 137, 142, 186, 204, 237
Simmons, William J., 176
Sinn Fein, 139, 154, 208, 222, 224, 248, 298–99, 311, 315
Skeffington, Francis, 234
Smith, Al, 297, 308–9
Smith, Francis, 137, 157,186, 192, 194, 264, 290
Socialism, 38, 109–10
Southern Messenger (San Antonio/ Galveston), 226, 237
Spanish American War, 113
Spaulding, Bishop John, 114–15
Spillane, Edward P., 236
Spring Rice, Sir Cecil, 139, 149, 210, 226–27, 230, 233, 238, 240, 298, 330
SS Dolphin, 129
SS Washington, 313
St. Louis, 89
St. Paul, MN, 301
Sullivan Roger Charles, 67
Sussex, 199, 214, 218, 278; German response to Sussex Notes, 220
Synge, John M., 57, 94, 120

INDEX

Taft, William Howard, 72, 106, 132, 206
Tammany Hall 27, 30, 260–61
Testem benevolente, 102–4
The Book of the Red and Yellow, 170
The Church and Modern Society, 113–14
The Life of Father Hecker, 104
The Leader, 227, 248, 202. *See also* Rev. Peter Yorke (editor)
The Menace 8, 195, 327 and Bogus Oath, 115
The Monitor (San Francisco), 227, 264
The Tablet (Brooklyn), 97, 166, 182, 203n69, 204, 212, 219, 235, 256, 299. *See also* Rev. John L. Whelan (editor)
There's a Typical Tipperary Over Here, 14
Third Plenary Council of Baltimore, 100
Thomas, Rev. C.P., 274–75
Thompson, William, 31
Tierney, Rev. Richard, 131, 156, 159, 172, 184, 203, 209, 212, 218, 235, 242, 272, 279, 282, 296
Towne, Charles, 257
Traynor, William J.H., 81
Trinity College, 87
True Voice (Omaha), 192, 227, 236. *See also* Rev. Peter Gannon (editor)
Truman, Harry S., 35
Tumulty, Joseph, 173, 179, 212, 241, 251–53, 258, 262–63, 313
Turkey, 185
Tweed, William M., 76, 79

Ulster 16, 18, 136, 316
Ulster Volunteers, 71–72, 136

United Irish League of America (UILA), 72, 138, 225, 227, 231, 233
United Irish Society of Philadelphia, 189
United Mine Workers of America (UMWA), 48–50
Urban II, 283
Ursulines, 21
U.S. Civil War Draft Riots, 78

Vaughan, Cardinal Herbert, 151
Venezuela Border Dispute, 62
Vera Cruz, 129
Versailles Treaty, 311, 315, 317, 323; Senate debate over and its defeat, 317–18
Viereck, George Sylvester, 145, 150, 199, 259
Villa, Pancho, 170, 174, 211–12
von Bernstorff, Johann, 145, 149, 189, 214, 230, 273
von Igel, Wolf, 217, 296
von Papen, Franz, 200, 217
von Rintelen, Franz, 199
Vorbeck, J.C., 258–59
Vorhees, Daniel, 63

Walsh, David I., 159–60, 252, 318
Walsh, Joseph C., 162, 225, 283
Walsh, Thomas J., 39, 42, 133, 197, 260, 262, 266, 269, 313, 318
Washington Post, 230, 319
Watson, Tom, 8; and *Tom Watson's Magazine,* 8
Welland Canal, 217
Western Federation of Miners, 39, 42
Western Watchman (St. Louis), 155, 172, 290
Whelan, Rev. John L., 166, 182, 194, 212, 220, 235, 256, 275, 290

INDEX

White Anglo-Saxon Protestants (WASP) 10, 16, 25, 48
Wilson, Woodrow 31–32, 43, 131, 133–34, 169, 172, 179–80, 196, 198–99, 218, 238, 240–41, 250–51, 264–65, 268, 276, 281; and anti-hyphen campaign, 134–35, 201–3, 252, 254–55, 259; contending with German use of U-Boats, 179; delights over Cohalan's difficulties, 296; expresses gratitude to Irish Americans and Catholics on eve of war, 276, 288; hesitant to press British on Ireland, 313–15; ignores British maritime interference, 179–81; Mexican policy, 170–71, 174, 211–13; "Peace without Victory" speech, 272; rumors of insulting Gibbons and Ireland, 262–63; self-determination of nations, 272, 294; urging strict neutrality, 153
Wisconsin Legion of Loyalty, 301
Wittke, Carl, 162
World War I, 95, 124. *See also* Great War

Yeats, William Butler, 185, 196, 323
Young Men's Christian Association (YMCA), 212–13, 262–63
Yorke, Rev. Peter, 154, 227, 232, 244, 264, 268, 292, 314

Zapata, Emiliano, 128, 131
Zimmerman, Arthur, 147, 280–81
Zimmerman Telegram, 280–81

www.ingramcontent.com/pod-product-compliance
Lightning Source LLC
Chambersburg PA
CBHW030251010526
44107CB00053B/1662